GRE
高频真词表

北京新东方研发中心 编著
韩 冰 潘晨光

浙江教育出版社·杭州

图书在版编目(CIP)数据

GRE高频真词表 / 北京新东方研发中心，韩冰，潘晨
光编著. -- 杭州：浙江教育出版社，2018.1（2018.5重印）
ISBN 978-7-5536-6268-8

Ⅰ.①G… Ⅱ.①北… ②韩… ③潘… Ⅲ.①GRE一词
汇－自学参考资料 Ⅳ.①H313

中国版本图书馆CIP数据核字(2017)第216198号

GRE高频真词表
GRE GAOPIN ZHEN CI BIAO
北京新东方研发中心　韩　冰　潘晨光　编著

责任编辑	马立改
美术编辑	韩　波
封面设计	大愚设计
责任校对	罗　曼
责任印务	时小娟
出版发行	浙江教育出版社
	地址：杭州市天目山路40号
	邮编：310013
	电话：（0571）85170300－80928
	邮箱：dywh@xdf.cn
	网址：www.zjeph.com
印　　刷	三河市良远印务有限公司
开　　本	710mm×1000mm　1/16
成品尺寸	168mm×230mm
印　　张	22.75
字　　数	426 000
版　　次	2018年1月第1版
印　　次	2018年5月第2次印刷
标准书号	ISBN 978-7-5536-6268-8
定　　价	50.00元

序一

很多同学在备考 GRE 期间，最头疼的问题往往就是复杂繁多的词汇。2013 年，韩老师和我在实际教学过程中发现，同学们经常反映手里词汇资料词条多则七千有余，记忆负担沉重；少则在实际考试中复现率低，背诵性价比不高。我们在想，为何不基于每场考试的真实考情，整理一份真正针对现行 GRE 考试的词汇书呢？于是《GRE 高频真词表》（以下简称"佛脚词汇"）计划应运而生。

相信刚走出考场的同学，对于本次考试里那些晦涩难懂的词汇一定记忆犹新，佛脚词汇表希望能够展示那些真正在考试中有价值的词汇。经过 2013~2014 年的积累，佛脚词汇初版词表共整理全年难词 1163 个，并有针对性地给出了同义词词对 274 对，让大家在解答相关题目时更加游刃有余。我们将初版词汇表汇总成 PDF，于网上免费公开，当时的定位是同学们考前两个月必备的高性价比词汇材料。与此同时，恰逢北京新东方学校的圣诞班与寒假班，经过线下与线上成百上千名同学的集体试用，大家在肯定之余，也给出了诸多宝贵的改进意见，这坚定了我们打磨完善佛脚词汇表的信心。

2013~2017 年收集记录难词从未间断，我们免费制作了 2.0~6.0 版本，并于每个季度推出，词汇数目增加 1700 个，同义词词对增加至 550 对。此时，我们已经发现，每次有效收集整理的难词数明显减少，从同学们的实际反馈也看出，佛脚词汇相较于手中其他资料，词汇复现率更高。为了使词汇书针对性更强，我们决定在原有的佛脚词库基础上，整理加入常考短语与阅读题目中的难词，最终收录主词 2400 余个，同义词词对 850 余对。

这是一本经历了多个网络公开版才得以浓缩出来的词汇材料。至此，我们不妨总结一下本书都有哪些优势：

- 从 GRE 改革以来积累至今，选择真正意义上可能的 GRE 重点词汇，剔除无意义的词汇，切实反映词汇考点动向。
- 特别添加常考"六选二"同义词词对、美国当代英语语料库（Corpus of Contemporary American English）注词词频、常考反义词、派生词、外教原创例句，多维度诠释词汇。
- 英文释义参考韦氏词典与美国传统词典，中文释义力图忠实于语境。

佛脚词汇蕴含着一种和 GRE 战斗的精神，代表着我们竭尽全力减轻大家考试负担的同时，又保证和考试高度统一的不懈追求，也是我们六年多来教学与实战经验的浓缩。我们当然不会就此满足，GRE 佛脚词汇将继续不断地迭代更新下去。在此，诚挚感谢读者们的积极反馈，以及北京新东方程黛苑老师与武汉新东方冷楠老师的诸多宝贵意见与建议。

语言是活的，由于每个人对于词汇的理解仁者见仁，又限于实际教学与考试经验，所以在实际使用过程中难免会遇到中文翻译上的一些分歧。如果读者朋友有更好的理解方式，望不吝赐教，共同进步。《GRE 高频真词表》读者意见反馈邮箱：fojiaocihui@163.com。

潘晨光
于北京新东方大厦

这一次，在乐词
GRE 佛脚词汇表独家登陆乐词 APP

尘埃落定！我一直期待 GRE 佛脚词汇表能以一种让我满意的姿态展现在你的屏幕上，现在终于等到了这一刻。

在我刚刚准备 GRE 考试的时候，还没有铺天盖地的 APP。每日只能拿着厚重的红宝书，看到不认识的单词就重重地画一个圈，对自己表现不满意的一页就使劲地折上页脚，但我很怀念那本被我摸得脏兮兮的词汇书，它有一种厚重的历史感和温馨的仪式感。现在一看到它，我还是会回想起昏暗的灯光下在北五环伏案备课的自己，今天的我再也无法企及那时候努力的自己。

2016 年 3 月我们第一次与乐词团队碰撞。那天，我们都觉得佛脚词汇表马上就要与大家见面了，没想到一张词表做了一年。我和乐词团队说，乐词 APP 上的这个版面要我来做主。我想他们当年应该是恨我恨到骨子里的，因为佛脚词汇表里很多的词条释义和其他词汇书格格不入，我曾经花了一个下午的时间跟乐词团队解释"六选二"到底是什么。他们瞪着大眼睛问我："这个很有必要么？为什么就不能一个单词干干净净地放在那里？"我说："六选二这个词条是 GRE 佛脚词汇表的核心。"在不能妥协的地方我绝不退让，因为 GRE 佛脚词汇表与生俱来就不是给所有人读的，也不会成为"烂大街"的词汇书。于是，他们为我开辟了一个在任何其他上线的词汇书上都没有的条目，叫做"六"。哈哈，我也希望，你的 GRE 能够这样就"六"起来。在此衷心感谢乐词团队包容我的"任性"。

乐词有着强大的技术支撑，让每一个单词都能真正地"跃然屏上"。单词自动匹配了乐词的词根词缀库，使用时能在单词上方看到这个单词的来历。这也给一些需要通过词根词缀拆解来背单词的同学们带来了福音。"六"和"反"这两个词条会在单词下方呈现，让你们背到爽翻天。

在乐词 APP 中，我们也附上了 GRE 佛脚词汇完整版的 3167 个例句。为了让这些例句在句子复杂度和话题度上最大限度地逼近填空题，我们经过了多轮修订，请大家千万不要错过这些精挑细选的例句。当然如果你还有更好的例句，请千万做一个热心的读者，告诉我。

乐词 APP 是一个有着自己哲学的 APP。它不仅仅能呈现单词，还可以制订学习计划，帮助你克服懒惰。在开启 GRE 佛脚词汇表的学习前，一定要制订一个任务计划，具体到每天背诵多少个单词，分成多少组，之后系统会自动提醒你背诵单词。每组单词背诵结束后，还会有丰富的小练习，帮助你巩固记忆，遇到不认识的单词也可以添加到自己的单词本中反复查看。扫描封底的乐词优惠码可立即优惠购买 GRE 佛脚词汇乐词版。

贴心的乐词，还为大家提供了原版词书排序、正序以及逆序三种选择。很多同学都知道 GRE 佛脚词汇表是一个纯手工乱序的词汇书。如果你希望正序、逆序背诵佛脚词汇表，那么乐词就是你唯一的选择喽！购买乐词版的 GRE 佛脚词汇表将会得到持续的更新服务，后续有新词上线，我们将会第一时间免费更新给同学们！

这一次，在乐词！我们又一次相聚。欢迎你把 GRE 佛脚词汇表装进你的口袋。我期待着有一天能在地铁上、公交站台，看到你打开乐词 GRE 佛脚词汇表努力的样子！

韩　冰
于北京新东方大厦

各版本说明

目前《GRE 高频真词表》一共有纸质书完整版，纸质书便携版，乐词APP版三大版本。为了方便大家选择，这里解释一下各版本区别：

《GRE高频真词表》（GRE佛脚词汇表）各版本说明

各版本	中文释义	英文释义	例句	词频	六选二	派生词	反义词	助记	短语表
完整版	√	√	√	√	√	√	√		√
便携版	√	√		√					
乐词版	√	√	√		√	√	√	√	√

其中纸质书完整版与便携版在主词条上保持一致。我们还会定期根据考试情况更新词表，由于电子版更新起来方便快捷，所以乐词 APP 版本在词序上会与纸质书略有不同。

参考同学们的记忆特点，我们给出了如下记忆方案：

	当日背诵	当日复习 1	当日复习 2	当日复习 3	当日复习 4
DAY-1	List 1~2	List 1~2			
DAY-2	List 3~4	List 1~2	List 3~4		
DAY-3	List 5~6	List 3~4	List 5~6		
DAY-4	List 7~8	List 1~2	List 5~6	List 7~8	
DAY-5	List 9~10	List 3~4	List 7~8	List 9~10	
DAY-6	List 11~12	List 5~6	List 9~10	List 11~12	
DAY-7	List 13~14	List 7~8	List 11~12	List 13~14	
DAY-8	List 15~16	List 1~2	List 9~10	List 13~14	List 15~16
DAY-9	List 17~18	List 3~4	List 11~12	List 15~16	List 17~18
DAY-10	List 19~20	List 5~6	List 13~14	List 17~18	List 19~20
DAY-11	List 21~22	List 7~8	List 15~16	List 19~20	List 21~22
DAY-12	List 23~24	List 9~10	List 17~18	List 21~22	List 23~24

（注：List 25 作为新增 List，暂不计入背诵计划。）

使用说明

本书主要分为两大部分：主词表部分与短语表部分

在主词表部分中，每个标签的意义为下：

本书所收录的所有词汇都属于近些年考过的高频单词。为了让读者更加深刻地理解词汇在实际中的运用，我们参考了美国当代英语语料库（Corpus of Contemporary American English）中主词条出现的频率，由低到高将词频分为 1~5 五个等级，供读者参考。

单词的中英文释义。每个词的释义，并不是机械地搬运词典释义，而是结合具体考点语境做出对应的解释。英文释义从《韦氏大学词典》（Merriam-Webster's Collegiate Dictionary）simple definition 或 full definition 当中选择性摘录，同时也参考了美国传统词典 (American Heritage Dictionary) 的释义。

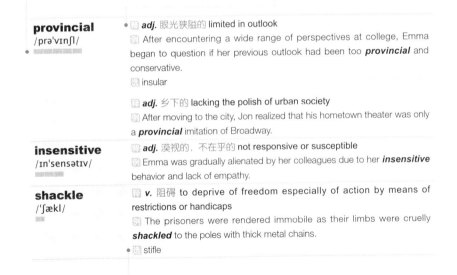

provincial
/prəˈvɪnʃl/

- *adj.* 眼光狭隘的 limited in outlook
  After encountering a wide range of perspectives at college, Emma began to question if her previous outlook had been too *provincial* and conservative.
  insular

  adj. 乡下的 lacking the polish of urban society
  After moving to the city, Jon realized that his hometown theater was only a *provincial* imitation of Broadway.

insensitive
/ɪnˈsensətɪv/

- *adj.* 漠视的，不在乎的 not responsive or susceptible
  Emma was gradually alienated by her colleagues due to her *insensitive* behavior and lack of empathy.

shackle
/ˈʃækl/

- *v.* 阻碍 to deprive of freedom especially of action by means of restrictions or handicaps
  The prisoners were rendered immobile as their limbs were cruelly *shackled* to the poles with thick metal chains.
  stifle

在 GRE 考试中，有一种题型叫做句子等价（sentence equivalence），俗称"六选二"。其中绝大多数情况下是要求考生选择一对同义词，使句子的逻辑变得通顺。基于实际考试，我们将考过的六选二词对予以标明，使所背即考点，性价比更高。

注意：(1) 有的时候两个词在原考题语境中是一对正确选项（比如说 inferable from 与 entailed by）抛离了语境可能不是一对同义词，会使读者产生困惑，不用纠结，做到面熟即可。

(2) 有的时候"选"标签下给出的词汇的词性可能与主词词性不一致，不用在意。比如说 precocious 这个词给出的"选"为 maturity，是因为在考试中考的是 precocious 的名词词性，而陪考的同义词也为名词词性。此类现象，并非笔误，请读者理解。

由资深外教逐条编写的原创例句，从英语母语者角度诠释一个词在语境中的具体运用。

我们希望考生能够做到举一反三，记忆一个词的同时能够将一系列的词都记住，所以也罗列了部分词汇的常考派生词，旨在提高背诵记忆的性价比。

cumbersome /ˈkʌmbərsəm/	**adj.** 笨拙的 unwieldy because of heaviness and bulk • The train journey was uncomfortable because the lady seated next to me was carrying some **cumbersome** baggage that she refused to store away in the roof rack. unwieldy • cumber（v. 阻碍，挡路）
encomium /enˈkoʊmiəm/	**n.** 赞美 glowing and warmly enthusiastic praise Sir John Rose, the former boss of Rolls-Royce, deserves the **encomium** he receives from the public as he is a truly tremendous business leader. tribute invective
decelerate /ˌdiːˈseləreɪt/	**v.** 减缓 to decrease the rate of progress of The software company decided to **decelerate** their pace of introducing new products, and focus on improving existing ones.
revitalize /ˌriːˈvaɪtəlaɪz/	**v.** 使…复活 to make active, healthy, or energetic again The shampoo commercial dishonestly claimed that the product could **revitalize** tired hair and cure split ends.
indisputable /ˌɪndɪˈspjuːtəbl/	**adj.** 不容置疑的 impossible to question or doubt Given the **indisputable** video-replay evidence, the referee had no choice but to overturn the touchdown. • refutable
roost /ruːst/	**v.** 栖息 to settle down for rest or sleep Some species of birds prefer to **roost** in the shady woods during the day as they are kept safe from predators due to the use of camouflage.

☐ provincial ☐ insensitive ☐ shackle ☐ cumbersome ☐ encomium
☐ decelerate ☐ revitalize ☐ indisputable ☐ roost

在 2011 年之前，老 GRE 时代考过一种题型叫做"类比反义"，我们摘取了此类题目中常考的反义词选项。经过对实际考试的分析发现，在老 GRE 时代考过的反义关系也会在新 GRE 填空题目中体现，比如说空格对应某个元素取其反义词，所以这个部分很有记忆的价值。

致谢

佛脚，感恩有你

终于，我将这本佛脚词汇表呈现于你面前。从 2013 年来到北美项目部开始教授 GRE 课程到今天，已有四年时间。日子过得真快，无论我今天在北京学校做什么工作，教什么课程，教 GRE 的这段日子都是让我最为难忘和感谢的。写佛脚词汇表的这几年，它伴随着我从一名新教师成长为一名成熟教师，用它作为纪念我青春的礼物，足矣。

佛脚词汇表从来不是我一个人的作品，想要感谢的人太多！

感谢北京新东方学校的领导，特别要感谢吴强老师、谢强老师和史岜老师对青年教师的支持和认可。北京学校提供了一片广阔的天地给我们，让我们能接触到更多的学生，接受更为专业的培训。每一个想法在这里都会得到尊重，人生的第一份工作就在新东方，我很幸福。

感谢我的同事潘晨光老师和二次元美少女程黛苑老师。和晨光、黛苑老师在 2013 年相识，一致的工作理念让我们很快成为了工作中的好伙伴，我们一起开启了 GRE 教学的新篇章。虽然我现在调入了 SAT 项目，但是每次看到他们穿梭在各大校区，战斗在 GRE 一线，感觉我们仍然像以前一样，为了学生、课堂奋不顾身。

感谢北美项目部的同事们，你们是佛脚词汇表的第一批读者。看到你们因为佛脚词汇表而在 GRE 考试中又有了可喜的进步，并夸奖佛脚词汇表的"神奇"，我心里会高兴得飞起来。尤其要感谢我的搭档万炜老师和高宇琪老师，我的 GRE 课堂因为你们才变得完整。

感谢新东方大愚的编辑老师们，这本佛脚词汇表是在编辑老师一遍一遍的"催促"下完稿的。没有他们的保驾护航，佛脚词汇表不可能这么顺利地上架和你见面。

最后，感谢这几年来一直在使用佛脚词，义务"宣传"佛脚词汇表的同学们。我知道或许我们不再见面，但希望当你拿到这本 GRE 佛脚词汇表时，还能想起曾经你我一同在水清、魏公村、国贸以及任何角落奋斗的日子。

哦，对了，还有正在使用佛脚词汇表的你，我相信奇迹即将来临……

韩 冰

于北京新东方大厦

目　录

《GRE 高频真词表》就是风靡网络的

"GRE 佛脚词汇表"正式版

扫码关注 GRE 佛脚词汇官方平台，获取最新资料

读者意见与建议反馈：fojiaocihui@163.com

音频

divulge
/dɪ'vʌldʒ/
释 *v.* 泄露 to make known something private or secret
例 Despite pressure from reporters to discuss the scandal in which Senator Scottsdale was embroiled, the press secretary would not **divulge** the details of the senator's upcoming public address.
反 keep secret

inadvertent
/ˌɪnəd'vɜːrtənt/
释 *adj.* 粗心的，不留意的 marked by or resulting from carelessness; negligent
例 Online shopping increases the chances of **inadvertent** ordering due to its increased convenience and accessibility.
反 careful, intentional
派 advertent（adj. 注意的，小心的）

释 *adj.* 不是故意的 not deliberate or considered; unintentional
例 The student made an **inadvertent** call to her parents when the cell phone in her back pocket pressed against the wall.

panegyric
/ˌpænə'dʒɪrɪk/
释 *n.* 赞文，赞美 a formal eulogistic composition intended as a public compliment
例 The president delivers a **panegyric** at the Tomb of the Unknown Soldiers every year on Veteran's Day.
派 panegyrical（adj. 赞美的）

draconian
/drə'koʊniən/
释 *adj.* 极其严苛的 exceedingly harsh or very severe
例 The unusually severe ordinances banning all rehearsals in private venues were denounced by musicians as **draconian**.
近 stringent, rigorous

hodgepodge
/'hɑːdʒpɑːdʒ/
释 *n.* 混杂，混合物 a mixture of different things
例 The Senator tried to increase his chances of winning by proposing a **hodgepodge** of measures appealing to different interests in the Democratic Party rather than enforcing a singular message.
近 patchwork, welter, pastiche

incontrovertible
/ˌɪnkɑːntrə'vɜːrtəbl/
释 *adj.* 不容置疑的 impossible to dispute
例 Age may be an **incontrovertible** number, but "old" is just a state of mind to me.
派 controvert（v. 反驳，争论）

---

 divulge   inadvertent   panegyric   draconian   ☑hodgepodge
☑ incontrovertible

impartial
/ɪmˈpɑːrʃl/

释 *adj.* 公正的，不偏不倚的 not partial or biased
例 Judges play an important role in a country's system of justice as *impartial* decision-makers who are not swayed by emotions, relations or selfish gains.
选 disinterested, fair, detachment
派 partial（adj. 有偏见的，偏袒的）

endemic
/enˈdemɪk/

释 *adj.* 地方性的，流行的 prevalent in or limited to a particular locality, region, or people
例 Almost all the organisms in the Western Ghats are *endemic* to India and need to be conserved to ensure their continued survival for future generations.
选 native, domestic, indigenous
反 exotic, imported, introduced

释 *adj.* （问题、情形）常见的 common in or inherent to an enterprise or situation
例 The *endemic* corruption that had long crippled Nigeria was clamped down when Muhammadu Buhari took the office in 2015 and prosecuted hundreds of people.

minuscule
/ˈmɪnəskjuːl/

释 *adj.* 微小的 very small and tiny
例 Singapore may be a *minuscule* country, but it sure is a crowded one with almost 8,000 people per square kilometer!
选 diminutive

lucrative
/ˈluːkrətɪv/

释 *adj.* 盈利的，赚钱的 producing wealth
例 Although many novelists write for artistic reasons, others are lured by the money as popular success in writing can also be extremely *lucrative*.

compensate
/ˈkɑːmpenseɪt/

释 *v.* 弥补 to offset an error, defect, or undesired effect
例 In order to *compensate* for the loss of natural wetlands used by migrating snow geese, conservationists in the 1960s and 1970s established wetland refuges in the northern prairies.

释 *v.* 抵消 to serve as or provide a substitute or counter balance
例 The baker intelligently *compensated* for the lack of baking powder by using carbonated water in the pancake recipe.
选 offset

discursive
/dɪsˈkɜːrsɪv/

释 *adj.* 杂乱无章的 moving from topic to topic without order; rambling
例 This biography of Charles Dickens is not a succinct portrait of the writer as it is padded with many undigested and *discursive* excerpts from his personal writings and letters.
选 aimless, digressional, rambling

释 *adj.* 推论的 marked by analytical reasoning
例 The mathematician excelled professionally due to his *discursive* mind, but his lack of empathy made him a loner in his personal life.

☑ impartial   ☑ endemic   ☑ minuscule   ☑ lucrative   ☑ compensate
☑ discursive

presuppose
/ˌpriːsəˈpouz/
釋 *v.* 假定 to require as an antecedent in logic or fact
例 The burnt timbers and broken pottery found by the archaeologists *presupposed* the destruction of a previous settlement.

intermediary
/ˌɪntərˈmiːdieri/
釋 *adj.*（作为）中间人（的）acting as a mediator
例 Many Hong Kong banks make use of their extensive customer networks and familiarity with conditions in China to serve as *intermediary* organizations between Chinese and overseas businessmen.

derogate
/ˈderəgeɪt/
釋 *v.* 贬低 to cause to seem inferior
例 It was not right of the construction supervisor to *derogate* the foreign workers in such a demeaning manner for a trivial mistake that could have been made by anyone.
派 derogatory（adj. 贬低的）

overbearing
/ˌouvərˈberɪŋ/
釋 *adj.* 专横的，压倒性的 often trying to control the behavior of other people in an annoying or unwanted way
例 My sister eventually moved out of the house as her mother-in-law was too *overbearing* and always restricted her choices and decisions.
选 dominant

zealous
/ˈzeləs/
釋 *adj.* 对（某人或偶像）狂热的 marked by fervent partisanship for a person, a cause, or an ideal
例 The politician was too *zealous* in his push for implementing large-scale social initiatives and ended up losing votes from other minority populations.
选 impassioned, fervent, fiery, passionate
派 zealotry（n. 狂热的态度或行为）

extraneous
/ɪkˈstreɪniəs/
釋 *adj.* 不重要的，不相关的 not important
例 Deleting my social media accounts has allowed me to cut out *extraneous* activities so I can focus on what really matters.
选 irrelevant

釋 *adj.* 外部的 coming from the outside
例 The attendants were on the lookout for people attempting to smuggle *extraneous* food and drinks into the stadium.

rehash
/ˈriːhæʃ/
釋 *v.*（没有实质改变地）重提 to bring forth again in another form without significant alteration
例 As Jerry had to deliver a speech this morning on a very short notice, he decided to *rehash* a talk that he had already given last week at the University of Cambridge.
选 recycle

perfunctory
/pərˈfʌŋktəri/
釋 *adj.* 敷衍的，草率的 acting with indifference, showing little interest or care
例 Manuel was so solitary and aloof that he would gladly spend months with just *perfunctory* contact with other people.
选 cursory, casual

presuppose intermediary derogate overbearing zealous
extraneous rehash perfunctory

(3)

compound /ˈkɑːmpaʊnd/	**v.** 混合，合成 to form by combining separate things
	例 Many words in Creole languages are formed by *compounding* different parts of words from various native dialects.
	v. 使…变糟糕 to make worse
	例 The instability of the regime, *compounded* by global economic woes, unfortunately led to a national debacle.
envy /ˈenvi/	**v.** 嫉妒 to feel a desire to have what someone else has
	例 The girl *envied* her best friend for having received the most expensive Barbie doll for Christmas.
	选 covet
	派 enviable（adj. 令人嫉妒的）
defensive /dɪˈfensɪv/	**adj.** 被动防守的，防御的 in a situation which you are forced to defend or protect someone or something
	例 Xin grew very *defensive* of her younger brother and vehemently maintained his innocence when the crowd started accusing him of being a thief.
unbounded /ʌnˈbaʊndɪd/	**adj.** 不受限制的，无限的 not limited in any way
	例 Many parents are reluctant to expose their children to the internet too early as they fear that the *unbounded* space of online culture would lead them astray.
	选 immoderate, expansive
specious /ˈspiːʃəs/	**adj.** 似是而非的，假的 falsely appearing to be right
	例 The senator's claim that he is not interested in running for a second term is *specious* given the extremely visible fund-raising activities of his campaign committee.
	选 artificial, forged, fabricated, spurious
	反 valid, veritable, impeccable
aimless /ˈeɪmləs/	**adj.** 漫无目的的 not having a goal or purpose
	例 The college sophomore sampled different courses and activities in an *aimless* fashion as he had not decided on his future career path.
	选 discursive
ingenuous /ɪnˈdʒenjuəs/	**adj.** 纯朴的，真诚的 having or showing the innocence, trust, and honesty characteristic of young people
	例 She was too *ingenuous* to have wholeheartedly believed every single word that the salesman said in his sales pitch.
	选 simple
	反 guileful
intrinsic /ɪnˈtrɪnsɪk/	**adj.** 固有的，本质的，内在的 belonging to the essential nature of a thing
	例 Some people argue that greed is such an *intrinsic* part of being human that it is the basis of all evil acts and can never be eradicated from any society.
	选 inherent

☑compound ☑envy ☑defensive ☑unbounded ☑specious
☑aimless ☑ingenuous ☑intrinsic

inevitable /ɪnˈevɪtəbl/	釋 *adj.* 不可避免的，必然的 sure to happen 例 When a witness describes a crime scene, it is ***inevitable*** that some details will be forgotten or misremembered. 近 unavoidable, preordained, ineluctable
intransigent /ɪnˈtrænzɪdʒənt/	釋 *adj.* 不妥协的，固执的 completely unwilling to change 例 The company was so ***intransigent*** with its "no social media" policy that it gradually lost its competitive edge in the market and was trampled over by the new startups. 近 resolute, obduracy
detached /dɪˈtætʃt/	釋 *adj.* 不受感情影响的，公正的 not influenced by emotions or personal interest 例 Unlike coworkers who delighted in office gossip, Felicia remained ***detached*** and appeared completely indifferent to these matters. 釋 *adj.* 脱离的 not joined or connected 例 Some of the housemates ended up burning themselves while cooking as the skillet had long been ***detached*** from its handle but no one had bothered informing the housekeeper.
inveterate /ɪnˈvetərət/	釋 *adj.* 根深蒂固的 firmly and long established; deep-rooted 例 Kenji was an ***inveterate*** procrastinator who put off doing his work until the last minute for nearly every task. 反 casual 釋 *adj.* 习惯性的 persisting in an ingrained habit; habitual 例 The stray cat became an ***inveterate*** beggar in the restaurant and could be seen pestering customers for food every night.
backhanded /ˌbækˈhændɪd/	釋 *adj.* 不直接的 oblique or indirect 例 Even though Agee's letters seemed harsh and critical, they actually provided ***backhanded*** encouragement to the young writer. 釋 *adj.* 含沙射影的，讽刺挖苦的 having derogatory or insulting implications 例 Although the woman thought she was praising the man's weight loss, he interpreted her comments as a ***backhanded*** compliment and stormed off.
affable /ˈæfəbl/	釋 *adj.* 和蔼可亲的 easy and pleasant to speak to 例 Jaelyn and Sean are temperamental opposites as Jaelyn is outgoing and ***affable***, while Sean is reserved and aloof. 近 easygoing, cordial, genteel 反 irascible
whimsy /ˈwɪmzi/	釋 *n.* 突发奇想 an unusual, unexpected, or fanciful idea 例 Her paintings of bullfights are so successful as they convey both a sense of ***whimsy*** and a deep respect for the long-held tradition. 近 capriciousness 派 whimsical（adj. 突发奇想的，多变的）

☑ inevitable ☐ intransigent ☑ detached ☑ inveterate ☑ backhanded
☐ affable ☑ whimsy

tenacious
/tə'neɪʃəs/

释 *adj.* 坚定的 very determined to do something
例 His peers respected him as a *tenacious* and diplomatic man who could remain steadfast in his beliefs yet tactful in his negotiations.
选 resolve, endurance
派 tenacity（n. 坚定）

释 *adj.* 持续的 continuing for a long time
例 Evolution is a *tenacious* process that began with appearance of life on Earth.

sardonic
/saːr'dɑːnɪk/

释 *adj.* 嘲讽的，讥笑的 scornfully or cynically mocking
例 The comedian's *sardonic* wit is hilarious as long as one is not the object of his rant.

skullduggery
/skʌl'dʌgəri/

释 *n.* 欺骗，作假 secret or dishonest behavior or activity
例 For all its corporate *skullduggery*, it's hard to deny that Uber has some clever promotions at times.

legitimate
/lɪ'dʒɪtɪmət/

释 *adj.* 合法的 being in compliance with the law
例 The birth of his only son by his wife left King Henry with a *legitimate* heir.

释 *adj.* 合理的 valid or justifiable
例 African Americans' discontent during the civil rights movement was *legitimate* because they suffered from a lack of freedom and equality.

释 *v.* 使…合理，合法 to make (something) real, accepted, or official or to show that (something) is fair or reasonable
例 A scientist should not automatically reject folkways that might at first seem silly or superstitious; scientific qualifications are not a license for smugness nor do they *legitimate* prejudice or bias.

plagiarize
/'pleɪdʒəraɪz/

释 *v.* 抄袭 to reproduce or otherwise illegitimately use as one's own
例 Despite accusations to the contrary, it is unlikely that he intended to *plagiarize* the articles since he had cited them in his bibliography.

disavow
/,dɪsə'vaʊ/

释 *v.* 否认 to say that one is not responsible for or does not support something
例 It is common for politicians to *disavow* their earlier promises to suit the current political atmosphere in the country.

deplete
/dɪ'pliːt/

释 *v.* 耗尽 to use most or all of
例 The battery life on the new phone is excellent and is never *depleted* even after a full day's use.
派 depletion（n. 耗尽）

ridicule
/'rɪdɪkjuːl/

释 *v.* 嘲笑，耻笑 to laugh at and make jokes about
例 The unusual designs of John Harrison were always *ridiculed* by his peers until they were finally recognized as some of the best in the history of clock making.
选 deride
派 ridiculous（adj. 荒谬的）

☑ tenacious ☑ sardonic ☑ skullduggery ☑ legitimate ☐ plagiarize
☐ disavow ☐ deplete ☐ ridicule

undermine
/ˌʌndərˈmaɪn/

释 *v.* 削弱 to make (someone or something) weaker or less effective
例 The tumbling of equity markets around the world has erased wealth and ***undermined*** confidence.
选 subvert, impair, undercut, weaken

self-serving
/ˌselfˈsɜːrvɪŋ/

释 *adj.* 自私的 having or showing concern only about one's own needs and interests
例 Professor Fernandez was dubious about the so-called humanitarian aspects of the colonial government and insisted that their actions were actually ***self-serving***.

perishable
/ˈperɪʃəbl/

释 *adj.* 易消亡的，短暂的 likely to spoil or decay quickly
例 This kind of wood is very ***perishable*** when exposed to weather, but keeps extremely well in dry conditions.
派 perish（v. 消亡）

capricious
/kəˈprɪʃəs/

释 *adj.* 变化多端的 changing often and quickly
例 Kate's impulsive nature and sudden whims led her friends to label her ***capricious***.
选 impulsive, cavalier, fickle, versatile, volatile, flighty, erratic
反 resolute, steadfast
派 caprice（n. 突发奇想，怪念头）

egotism
/ˈiːɡoʊɪzəm/

释 *n.* 自大 an inflated sense of one's own importance
例 His character, notwithstanding the ***egotism*** which often made him act selfishly, had an amiable and engaging side.

unqualified
/ˌʌnˈkwɑːlɪfaɪd/

释 *adj.* 完全的 complete or total
例 The launch of the iPad was an ***unqualified*** success for Apple.
选 unalloyed

释 *adj.* 不合格的 not having the skills, knowledge, or experience needed to do a particular job or activity
例 Apple labeled the prospective employee as ***unqualified*** for the position after noticing a lack of technical experience on his resume.

magisterial
/ˌmædʒɪˈstɪriəl/

释 *adj.* 权威的 authoritative
例 Wanting desperately to be perceived as learned and authoritative despite his young age, Johnson adopted a ***magisterial*** tone when speaking in public.

chauvinistic
/ˌʃoʊvɪˈnɪstɪk/

释 *adj.* 极端爱国的 believing that one's country, gender or other group is better than any other
例 Many right-wing Americans hate cosmopolitanism and hold a ***chauvinistic*** belief in their country's superiority.

 undermine self-serving perishable capricious ☑ egotism
☑ unqualified ☐ magisterial ☐ chauvinistic

sleek
/sliːk/

adj. 光滑的，线条流畅的 straight and smooth in design or shape
Despite the convertible's *sleek* appearance, the car was slower than an 18-wheeler truck.

adj. 时髦的，吸引人的 stylish and attractive
Alfred has created a reputation among his fellow lawyers for his choice of *sleek* suits whenever he has to make an appearance at the Supreme Court.

astringent
/əˈstrɪndʒənt/

adj. 严厉的，尖刻的 very critical in a sharp and often clever way
The professor's *astringent* insight into the debate on global warming influenced his students to support alternative energy.

ambivalent
/æmˈbɪvələnt/

adj. （情感、态度）矛盾的 having simultaneous and contradictory attitudes or feelings toward an object, person, or action
After having a big fight with his girlfriend, Richard was *ambivalent* about going through with his plans to propose to her.

ameliorate
/əˈmiːliəreɪt/

v. 改善，提升 to make better or more tolerable
Ameliorating the effects of climate change only creates temporary solutions against the more deep-rooted problems that continue to pervade the environment.
improve

exemplar
/ɪgˈzemplɑːr/

n. 典型 a typical example
The Notre Dame cathedral in Paris is an *exemplar* of French Gothic architecture with its use of pointed arches and flying buttresses.
model

grudge
/grʌdʒ/

v. 不愿给予或承认 to be unwilling to give or admit
He *grudged* the time and energy needed to deliver the boring, mandatory weekly reports to his boss.

n. 怨恨 a deep-seated feeling of resentment or rancor
Despite their handshakes at the end of the match, the hockey players on opposing teams bore harsh *grudges* against each other and fought shortly after.

sweeping
/ˈswiːpɪŋ/

adj. 广泛的 extensive
From the top of the hill, Brandon could see a *sweeping* view of the lake and a nearby village.

adj. 全面的 marked by wholesale and indiscriminate inclusion
The mayor's *sweeping* generalizations about the rival community bred anger among the citizens of both towns.

extirpate
/ˈekstərpeɪt/

v. 根除 to destroy or remove completely
While some locals think that the squirrels are cute, environmentalists say they are an invasive species and should be *extirpated*.
eliminate
propagate
extirpation（n. 消灭，根除）

☐ sleek   ☐ astringent   ☐ ambivalent   ☐ ameliorate   ☐ exemplar
☐ grudge   ☐ sweeping   ☐ extirpate

parity /ˈpærəti/	🔲 *n.* 平等 equality 🔲 Achieving gender **parity** is important for workplaces because it fosters a positive outlook for its employees and sends the right message to the larger community. 🔲 equality
utilitarian /juːtɪlɪˈteriən/	🔲 *adj.* 实用的 made to be useful rather than to be decorative or comfortable 🔲 Some people place emphasis on the looks of a car, but others only see it as a **utilitarian** asset to help them commute. 🔲 functional 🔲 decorative, embellishing 🔲 *adj.* 功利的，实用主义的 of or relating to utilitarianism 🔲 The politician advocated **utilitarian** ideals of increasing the overall good and reducing the amount of suffering across the entire population.
elicit /iˈlɪsɪt/	🔲 *v.* 引起 to call forth or draw out 🔲 The article that criticized millennials as stupid and foolhardy **elicited** hundreds of angry responses when it first appeared in the newspaper. 🔲 draw
intoxicate /ɪnˈtɑːksɪkeɪt/	🔲 *v.* 使…陶醉，沉醉 to excite or elate to the point of enthusiasm or frenzy 🔲 The young king was **intoxicated** by the huge extent of power and control he possessed upon his sudden reign.
inchoate /ɪnˈkoʊət/	🔲 *adj.* 早期的 being in a beginning or early stage 🔲 The **inchoate** design of the research project will be refined and improved as researchers narrow down their goals. 🔲 completely formed 🔲 *adj.* （在早期）混乱的 imperfectly informed or developed 🔲 The egg contained the **inchoate** embryo of a chick that would never survive hatching. 🔲 explicit
rebuff /rɪˈbʌf/	🔲 *n.* （粗鲁的）回复 a blunt or abrupt repulse or refusal 🔲 His request for the director's meeting to be rescheduled was met by a stark **rebuff** from the secretary who refused to assist him. 🔲 *v.* （粗鲁地）拒绝 to reject bluntly, often disdainfully 🔲 Rose **rebuffed** her boyfriend's proposal and refused to accept the ring.
construe /kənˈstruː/	🔲 *v.* 理解 to understand the meaning of 🔲 Amber could not **construe** the meaning of the difficult SAT word even after the professor's multiple explanations. 🔲 interpret 🔲 construction（n. 理解）

 parity utilitarian elicit intoxicate ☐ inchoate
☐ rebuff ☐ construe

fallacy
/'fæləsi/

释 *n.* 错误，谬论 a false or mistaken idea
例 The *fallacy* in this argument lies in the author's deep-seated bias in his choices of evidence.
反 validity
派 fallacious（adj. 错误的）

increment
/'ɪŋkrəmənt/

释 *n.* 增长，递增 the action or process of increasing especially in quantity or value
例 The annual *increment* in study loan interests means that students are faced with insurmountable debts at the end of their studies.
派 incremental（adj. 增加的）

deteriorate
/dɪ'tɪriəreɪt/

释 *v.* 恶化 to make (something) worse
例 When the brilliant writer Oliver Sacks was diagnosed with cancer, his condition *deteriorated* very quickly and the doctors could not help him.
选 worsen, decline
反 improve
派 deterioration（n. 恶化）

grandiose
/'grændioʊs/

释 *adj.* 宏伟壮观的 impressive because of uncommon largeness, scope, effect, or grandeur
例 Beyoncé's birthday party was *grandiose* and extravagant, with white swans and a chocolate fountain made of solid gold.

释 *adj.* 妄自尊大的 characterized by excessive self-importance or affected grandeur
例 Kanye West has a *grandiose* sense of importance which he unabashedly announces to the world.

truncate
/'trʌŋkeɪt/

释 *v.* 缩短 to make shorter
例 The resourceful teacher *truncated* her usual lectures into snippets that her busy students could study while riding the bus or waiting in line.
选 shorten, foreshorten

haphazard
/hæp'hæzərd/

释 *adj.* 无序的，凌乱的 having no plan, order, or direction
例 The shooting victim felt so disoriented after the attack that he started moving in a *haphazard* fashion and was unable to walk in a straight line.
选 helter-skelter, random

quizzical
/'kwɪzɪkl/

释 *adj.* 好奇而疑惑的 expressive of puzzlement, curiosity, or disbelief
例 When the statistics teacher introduced the idea of standard deviation, a few of the students nodded in comprehension while others gave her *quizzical* looks.

fallacy　increment　deteriorate　grandiose　truncate
haphazard　quizzical

provincial
/prəˈvɪnʃl/

adj. 眼光狭隘的 limited in outlook

After encountering a wide range of perspectives at college, Emma began to question if her previous outlook had been too ***provincial*** and conservative.

insular

adj. 乡下的 lacking the polish of urban society

After moving to the city, Jon realized that his hometown theater was only a ***provincial*** imitation of Broadway.

insensitive
/ɪnˈsensətɪv/

adj. 漠视的，不在乎的 not responsive or susceptible

Emma was gradually alienated by her colleagues due to her ***insensitive*** behavior and lack of empathy.

shackle
/ˈʃækl/

v. 阻碍 to deprive of freedom especially of action by means of restrictions or handicaps

The prisoners were rendered immobile as their limbs were cruelly ***shackled*** to the poles with thick metal chains.

stifle

cumbersome
/ˈkʌmbərsəm/

adj. 笨拙的 unwieldy because of heaviness and bulk

The train journey was uncomfortable because the lady seated next to me was carrying some ***cumbersome*** baggage that she refused to store away in the roof rack.

unwieldy

cumber（v. 阻碍，挡路）

encomium
/enˈkoʊmiəm/

n. 赞美 glowing and warmly enthusiastic praise

Sir John Rose, the former boss of Rolls-Royce, deserves the ***encomium*** he receives from the public as he is a truly tremendous business leader.

tribute

invective

decelerate
/ˌdiːˈseləreɪt/

v. 减缓 to decrease the rate of progress of

The software company decided to ***decelerate*** their pace of introducing new products, and focus on improving existing ones.

revitalize
/ˌriːˈvaɪtəlaɪz/

v. 使…复活 to make active, healthy, or energetic again

The shampoo commercial dishonestly claimed that the product could ***revitalize*** tired hair and cure split ends.

indisputable
/ˌɪndɪˈspjuːtəbl/

adj. 不容置疑的 impossible to question or doubt

Given the ***indisputable*** video-replay evidence, the referee had no choice but to overturn the touchdown.

refutable

roost
/ruːst/

v. 栖息 to settle down for rest or sleep

Some species of birds prefer to ***roost*** in the shady woods during the day as they are kept safe from predators due to the use of camouflage.

 provincial insensitive shackle cumbersome encomium
decelerate revitalize indisputable roost

corroborate /kəˈrɑːbəreɪt/	释 *v.* 佐证，提供证据证明 to support with evidence or authority 例 Scientists' theories about the origin of the universe were later *corroborated* by solid evidence. 反 controvert, deny
proclivity /prəˈklɪvəti/	释 *n.* 倾向，偏好 a strong natural liking for something 例 William's only weakness lies in his overly trusting nature and *proclivity* to see everyone as a friend. 近 predilection, penchant, preference
hysteria /hɪˈstɪriə/	释 *n.* 歇斯底里，情绪失控 excessive or uncontrollable emotion, such as fear or panic 例 A journalist should not contribute to mass *hysteria* by reporting rumors or sensationalist stories.
speculate /ˈspekjuleɪt/	释 *v.* 推测，猜测 to think about something and make guesses about it 例 At this point, we can only *speculate* about the election results as a portion of the votes remain uncounted. 近 conjecture
conducive /kənˈduːsɪv/	释 *adj.* 有益的，有帮助的 tending to promote or assist 例 The loud and hectic atmosphere of the coffee shop was not *conducive* to studying for the exam.
vexation /vekˈseɪʃn/	释 *n.* 烦恼 something that worries or annoys a person 例 Commuting to work through the heavy morning traffic has proven to be a source of daily *vexation* for many Londoners. 近 chagrin 派 vexatious（adj. 令人烦恼的），vex（v. 使烦恼）
disdain /dɪsˈdeɪn/	释 *v.* 蔑视，鄙视 to strongly dislike or disapprove of (someone or something) 例 People who were born and raised in Brooklyn typically *disdain* the expensive new lofts and fancy stores that are being built. 近 opprobrium, contempt
caterwaul /ˈkætərwɔːl/	释 *v.* 发出难听的声音 to make a very loud and unpleasant sound 例 I was able to fall asleep even though the neighbor's cats were *caterwauling* through the night. 近 shriek 释 *v.* 严厉抗议 to protest or complain noisily 例 The hungry preschoolers *caterwauled* for lunch to be served.
efficacious /ˌefɪˈkeɪʃəs/	释 *adj.* 有效果的 having the power to produce a desired result or effect 例 Copying your notes by hand may seem tedious, but it is an *efficacious* way of revising for the exam.

 corroborate
 proclivity
 hysteria
 speculate
 conducive
□ vexation □ disdain □ caterwaul □ efficacious

alienate
/ˈeɪliəneɪt/

v. 疏远 to cause (someone) to feel that she or he no longer belongs in a particular group, society, etc.

Being rude **alienates** people who might otherwise be open to dialogue with the opposing side.

反 reunite

派 alien（adj. 陌生的）

v. 使…变得不友好 to cause (someone) to stop being friendly, helpful, etc., towards one

Having **alienated** his former friends, the recluse relied only on his books for company.

analgesic
/ˌænəlˈdʒiːzɪk/

n. 止痛药 a drug that relieves pain

Many use aspirin as an **analgesic** for daily aches and pains.

adj. 止痛的 capable of relieving pain

Time is nature's best **analgesic** drug to help us relieve the pain from losing loved ones.

anatomize
/əˈnætəˌmaɪz/

v. 解剖 to cut in pieces in order to display or examine the structure and use of the parts

The Body Worlds exhibitions present human bodies that are preserved and **anatomized** for various purposes.

v. 分析 to analyze

After **anatomizing** the structural framework of the bridge on the digital model, the engineer discovered the flaws in the original design.

embargo
/ɪmˈbɑːrgoʊ/

n. 贸易禁令 a government order that limits trade in some way

Because of the long-standing US-Cuba trade **embargo**, most Cubans are forced to maintain their original 1950s automobiles.

contemplate
/ˈkɑːntəmpleɪt/

v. 深入思考 to think deeply or carefully about

Lina Wertmuller's film _Love and Anarchy_ **contemplates** the two concepts in its title without taking a position on them.

近 ponder

dogmatic
/dɔːgˈmætɪk/

adj. 教条的 expressing personal opinions or beliefs as if they are certainly correct and cannot be doubted

The young religious believer was too **dogmatic** in his views and ended up alienating many of his old friends.

近 doctrinaire, rigid

 alienate □ analgesic anatomize embargo contemplate
□ dogmatic

concrete /ˈkɑːŋkriːt/	释 *adj.* 真实的 existing in reality or in real experience; perceptible by the senses; real 例 The use of the CERN lab led to a number of **concrete** discoveries that revealed the nature of sub-atomic particles. 释 *adj.* 具体的 of or relating to an actual, specific thing or instance; particular 例 The **concrete** details of the new agricultural law give large corporations more power than the local farmers had originally believed.
equitable /ˈekwɪtəbl/	释 *adj.* 平等的，公平的 just or fair 例 The brothers wanted to reach an **equitable** agreement on how to divide the inheritance from their parents.
fervent /ˈfɜːrvənt/	释 *adj.* 情感强烈的，热烈的 exhibiting or marked by great intensity of feeling 例 The presidential candidate won over voters by showing a **fervent** desire to change existing housing policies.
alleviate /əˈliːvieɪt/	释 *v.* 减轻 to reduce the pain or trouble of 例 Some environmentalists fear that the practices contributing to global warming are so established in industrialized nations that there are no simple ways to **alleviate** their effects. 选 mitigate 反 aggravate, exacerbate
contagious /kənˈteɪdʒəs/	释 *adj.* 传染的，有感染力的 communicable by contact 例 Wang had to stay at home for two weeks while he had chicken pox as it is a **contagious** illness and can be easily passed to others by physical contact.
pedantic /pɪˈdæntɪk/	释 *adj.* 卖弄知识的，迂腐的 narrowly, stodgily, and often ostentatiously learned 例 The host of the new science TV show has become so popular because he explains complex ideas without being **pedantic** or boring.
unwieldy /ʌnˈwiːldi/	释 *adj.* 体积庞大而笨重的 difficult to handle, control, or deal with because of being large, heavy, or complex 例 I bought my grandmother an electric hand-held blender after she complained that using the heavy mortar has proven to be too **unwieldy** for her in recent years. 选 cumbersome
vociferous /voʊˈsɪfərəs/	释 *adj.* 吵吵嚷嚷的 expressing feelings or opinions in a very loud or forceful way 例 Even students who were usually quiet and obedient were **vociferous** in their opposition to the dress code.

 concrete
 equitable
 fervent
 alleviate
 contagious
□ pedantic
□ unwieldy
□ vociferous

profess
/prəˈfes/

释 *v.* 宣称 to say or declare (something) openly
例 Some business owners continue to *profess* their interests in finding foreign expertise for well-paying positions despite massive unemployment in the country.
选 proclaim

obeisance
/oʊˈbiːsns/

释 *n.* 尊敬，敬意 respect for someone or something
例 The new employee paid *obeisance* to all his superiors and older coworkers by bowing to each of them.

diffuse
/dɪˈfjuːs/

释 *v.* 扩散 to spread about or scatter; disseminate
例 It was hard to contain the biological attack as the poisonous gas *diffused* quickly around the city due to high temperatures.
选 disperse, spread

释 *adj.* 啰嗦的 characterized by verbosity; wordy
例 The journal reviewers rejected her article as they found the overall argumentative framework too *diffuse* and unclear.
选 wordy

fulminate
/ˈfʌlmɪneɪt/

释 *v.* 抨击，辱骂，愤怒，谴责 to utter or send out with denunciation
例 The politicians *fulminate* about defeating the terrorists, but they don't talk much about the costs or sacrifices that will be required.
反 praise
派 fulmination（n. 严厉谴责）

voluble
/ˈvɑːljəbl/

释 *adj.* 健谈的，话多的 talking a lot in an energetic and rapid way
例 The normally *voluble* Mr. Bell was uncharacteristically cryptic in discussing the film in an interview last week.

sterling
/ˈstɜːrlɪŋ/

释 *adj.* 符合最高标准的，优秀的 conforming to the highest standard
例 The board of directors assert that their priority is hiring someone with a *sterling* reputation for honesty.

surmount
/sərˈmaʊnt/

释 *v.* 克服，战胜 to prevail over
例 Negotiations were suspended indefinitely as all parties could not find solutions to *surmount* the impasse.
派 insurmountable（adj. 无法战胜的）

释 *v.* 站在…的顶峰 to stand or lie at the top of
例 In order to *surmount* Mount Everest, the hiker had to spend weeks training and getting used to the elevation.

Word List 02

音 频

prying /ˈpraɪɪŋ/	释 *adj.* 窥视的 trying to find out about other people's private lives 例 The maid was fired as she was caught snooping around the master bedroom and **prying** into the personal lives of her clients.
inhibit /ɪnˈhɪbɪt/	释 *v.* 抑制，限制 to hold in check 例 Laws **inhibit** citizens from doing whatever they please. 选 hinder, bridle, suppress 反 catalyze 派 inhibitor（n. 抑制物）
censure /ˈsenʃər/	释 *v.* 指责 to criticize severely; to blame 例 Book reviewers who are reluctant to openly **censure** a book may imply their criticism by avoiding enthusiastic praise. 选 reprehend 派 censorious（adj. 苛求的）
peripatetic /ˌperɪpəˈtetɪk/	释 *adj.* 巡游的 itinerant; traveling from place to place 例 The **peripatetic** monk roamed from monastery to monastery on Mt. Athos. 选 itinerant 反 stationary
stringent /ˈstrɪndʒənt/	释 *adj.* 非常严格的 very strict or severe 例 With age, Mary started to appreciate that the **stringent** upbringing she used to despise had actually inculcated in her a sense of discipline and humility.
dwindle /ˈdwɪndl/	释 *v.* 减少，下降 to gradually become smaller 例 After months of unemployment, the man's bank account **dwindled** to nothing. 选 contract 反 increase
underrate /ˌʌndəˈreɪt/	释 *v.* 低估 to rate or value（someone or something）too low 例 The fact that the world is round is so much taken for granted today that there is a tendency to **underrate** its significance when it was first proven.

16

prying ☑ inhibit ☑ censure ☐ peripatetic ☑ stringent ☑
dwindle ☑ underrate ☑

incursion
/ɪnˈkɜːrʒn/

n. 侵入，侵犯 a hostile entrance into a territory

The Huns made **incursions** into central Europe and defeated many standing armies.

retreat

incur（v. 获得，招惹）

n. 进入 an entering in or into

Every October, Canadian Geese make a loud **incursion** into New England.

pastiche
/pæˈstiːʃ/

n. 【贬】模仿作品 a work that imitates the style of previous works

The critic described the work as **pastiche** and lacking its own sense of originality.

n. 混合物 a mixture of different things

The columnist commented that New York is a **pastiche** of cursing and kvetching and laughing too loud, unlike Boston which is less cacophonous.

hodgepodge

dishearten
/dɪsˈhɑːrtn/

v. 使⋯士气低落 to cause (a person or group of people) to lose hope, enthusiasm, or courage

It is unavoidable for physicians to be **disheartened** when they see their patients dying from preventable causes.

depress, dismay

hearten（v. 鼓舞）

emulate
/ˈemjuleɪt/

v. 模仿，通过模仿而超越 to strive to equal or excel

The feminist poet's witty diatribes against social convention were so often **emulated** by other writers that her style became conventional.

imitate

innovate, originality

adduce
/əˈduːs/

v. 引用⋯证明 to mention or provide (something, such as a fact or example) as evidence or proof to support an argument

Not studying, skipping class, being lazy, and never doing homework were all reasons **adduced** to explain why Zhangjie failed his important test.

emblematic
/ˌembləˈmætɪk/

adj. 象征的，代表的 representing something (such as an idea, state, or emotion) that cannot be seen by itself

Folk painter Grandma Moses has become such an enduring icon that many consider her **emblematic** of America.

totemic

indict
/ɪnˈdaɪt/

v. 指控 to charge with a fault or offense

A biography must fairly depict both the strengths and the weaknesses of the subject, and avoid overly praising or **indicting** parties concerned.

excoriate

indictment（n. 控诉）

discontinue /ˌdɪskən'tɪnjuː/	释 *v.* 终止 to end (something) 例 Germany announced that it would ***discontinue*** all nuclear power generation by 2022.
wary /'weri/	释 *adj.* 谨慎小心的 marked by keen caution, cunning, and watchfulness, especially in detecting and escaping danger 例 Not wishing to shock her conservative teachers, Helen was ***wary*** of attempting radical new artistic styles in her paintings.
opprobrium /ə'proʊbriəm/	释 *n.* 辱骂 very strong disapproval or criticism of a person or thing especially by a large number of people 例 Politicians choose to be public figures who expose themselves to the possibility of public criticism and ***opprobrium***. 近 vitriol, disdain 反 irreproachable 派 opprobrious（adj. 骂人的，侮辱的）
aesthetic /es'θetɪk/	释 *adj.* 美学的 of or relating to art or beauty 例 I bought the paintings not because they were famous, but because they were bold and gave great ***aesthetic*** pleasure. 释 *adj.* 吸引人的 pleasing in appearance 例 The architect was lauded for constructing an ***aesthetic*** rather than a utilitarian building as it perfectly merged form and function.
expedite /'ekspədaɪt/	释 *v.* 加速，加快 to cause (something) to happen faster 例 Since regular shipping would take weeks, the student had no choice but to pay extra fees to ***expedite*** the shipping of his textbooks. 近 facilitate, accelerate 派 expedient（adj. 有利的，出于私利的）
captivate /'kæptɪveɪt/	释 *v.* 吸引 to attract and hold the attention of (someone) by being interesting, pretty, etc. 例 Steve was ***captivated*** by the intricacy of the ice crystals forming on his windowpane and couldn't take his eyes off them. 近 enamored
irreversible /ˌɪrɪ'vɜːrsəbl/	释 *adj.* 不可逆的 impossible to change back to a previous condition or state 例 Global warming will have severe, pervasive and ***irreversible*** effects if we do not act fast enough now.
emotive /i'moʊtɪv/	释 *adj.* 引起情绪的 causing strong emotions for or against something 例 During an ***emotive*** outburst, Alex Rodriguez kicked dirt over the home plate and yelled at the umpire.

☐ discontinue   ☐ wary   ☐ opprobrium   ☑ aesthetic   ☐ expedite
☐ captivate   ☐ irreversible   ☑ emotive

refine /rɪˈfaɪn/	释 *v.* 提纯 to remove the unwanted substances in (something)
	例 After gold is mined, it must be ***refined*** to remove dirt and base metals.
	释 *v.* 提升，提高 to improve (something) by making small changes
	例 The techniques now available to livestock breeders will be ***refined*** to increase the chances of breeding top-quality animals.
exhilarate /ɪgˈzɪləreɪt/	释 *v.* 使…喜悦或兴奋 to cause (someone) to feel very happy and excited
	例 The car ride ***exhilarated*** the children, who loved speeding up and down the mountain curves.
solitary /ˈsɑːləteri/	释 *adj.* 单独的 not involving or including anyone or anything else
	例 Thomas Edison found collaboration essential and debunked the popular stereotype of the ***solitary*** inventor who struggled alone in a garret.
jar /dʒɑːr/	释 *v.* 使…不安 to make (someone) feel uneasy
	例 The loud music and chaotic lighting of the dance club ***jarred*** her senses so much that she had to leave after a few minutes.
	释 *v.* 抵触，冲突 to clash or conflict
	例 I found the play very unsettling as its realistic plot and characters ***jarred*** with the dystopian themes and setting.
	派 jarring（adj. 相冲突的）
unfettered /ʌnˈfetərd/	释 *adj.* 不受限制的，自由的 not controlled or restricted
	例 Twitter makes ***unfettered*** communication possible, which allows ideas to spread but creates the possibility for abuse.
flummery /ˈflʌməri/	释 *n.* 假恭维 meaningless or deceptive language
	例 The actor is seen as unpretentious because he tries to avoid the flattery and ***flummery*** that his celebrity brings.
implacable /ɪmˈplækəbl/	释 *adj.* 不能安抚的，毫不妥协的 opposed to someone or something in a very angry or determined way that cannot be changed
	例 The manager refused to lay off any of his employees and remained ***implacable*** even when the board pressured him.
	选 unyielding, inexorable
arduous /ˈɑːrdʒuəs/	释 *adj.* 困难的 demanding great effort or labor; difficult
	例 Although many of the students found the assignment ***arduous***, Harrison completed it with ease.
	释 *adj.* 艰难的 testing severely the powers of endurance; strenuous
	例 After encountering many dangers, Bilbo Baggins finally completed his ***arduous*** trek across Middle Earth.
	选 taxing, laborious

conciliatory
/kənˈsɪliətɔːri/

圈 *adj.* 安抚的，调和的 having the intention or effect of making angry people calm

例 Superintendent Reynolds is predicted to have a less confrontational term of office than her predecessor as she is more **conciliatory** and would be able to appease disgruntled citizens.

近 placatory

optimism
/ˈɑːptɪmɪzəm/

圈 *n.* 乐观 a feeling or belief that good things will happen in the future

例 Although numerous setbacks and surprises await them in the weeks of negotiations ahead, leaders of both parties are full of **optimism** that their differences can be resolved.

派 optimistic（adj. 乐观的）

vindicate
/ˈvɪndɪkeɪt/

圈 *v.* 证明…的清白 to show that (someone) should not be blamed for a crime, mistake, etc.

例 After the real murderer confessed, the accused man was quickly **vindicated** and freed from jail.

近 defense, exonerate, exculpate

反 calumniate

malady
/ˈmælədi/

圈 *n.* 疾病 a disease or illness

例 The villagers believed that some evil spell had settled on their community after a mysterious **malady** swept through the flocks of chickens and resulted in gruesome deaths.

warrant
/ˈwɔːrənt/

圈 *v.* 保证 to give assurance

例 The king **warranted** that all his knights had behaved honorably while on their quest.

圈 *v.* 为…提供依据 to serve as or give adequate ground or reason for

例 The students felt that Prof. Nardin's meticulous teaching **warranted** the university's recognition so they wrote a letter of nomination for her to be awarded the next teaching prize.

派 unwarranted（adj. 毫无依据的）

puncture
/ˈpʌŋktʃər/

圈 *v.* 刺穿 to make a hole (in something) with a sharp point

例 Sunfish have sharp spines that will **puncture** the skin if not handled with care.

圈 *v.* 削弱，使…无效 to make useless or ineffective as if by a puncture

例 Her sense of jubilation at receiving an award was instantly **punctured** by the delivery of very tragic news.

ascribe
/əˈskraɪb/

圈 *v.* 归因于 to think of as coming from a specified cause, source, or author

例 It's absurd to **ascribe** personality traits to an entire generation.

clandestine
/klænˈdestɪn/

圈 *adj.* 秘密的，隐蔽的 done secretly

例 To keep their negotiations secret, the leaders of rival groups in the country arranged **clandestine** meetings.

近 covert, surreptitious

□ conciliatory   □ optimism   □ vindicate   □ malady   □ warrant
□ puncture   □ ascribe   □ clandestine

equivocal /ɪ'kwɪvəkl/	*adj.* 模棱两可的，有歧义的 having two or more possible meanings Because the columnist's published opinions were undeniably *equivocal*, we were left wondering what her true intentions were. ambiguous
elucidate /i'luːsɪdeɪt/	*v.* 阐释，阐明 to make something (typically hard to understand) clear or easy to understand The professor tried to *elucidate* the essential concepts of thermodynamics to the confused students.
propaganda /ˌprɑːpə'gændə/	*n.* 政治宣传 ideas or statements that are often false or exaggerated and that are spread in order to help a cause, a political leader, a government, etc. During World War I, the use of posters quickly helped the US to spread their *propaganda* of Germans as bloodthirsty Huns.
putative /'pjuːtətɪv/	*adj.* 公认的，假定的 generally believed or assumed to be something The *putative* effects of not having a college diploma are typically true, but a few individuals, such as Mark Zuckerberg, are exceptions.
conjecture /kən'dʒektʃər/	*v.* 猜测 to form an opinion or idea without proof or sufficient evidence Scientists require observable data, not *conjecture*, to support a hypothesis. speculate, uncertain
coalesce /ˌkoʊə'les/	*v.* 聚合，团结 to come together to form one group or mass The smartphone proved to be a great technological leap as it *coalesced* information into a single, personal object. coalition (n. 合并)
tractable /'træktəbl/	*adj.* 易管理的，易控制的 easily managed or controlled Many users find Mac OS more *tractable* and easier to navigate than the Windows interface. compliant incorrigible, headstrong, insoluble intractability (n. 桀骜不驯，难以管理)
warble /'wɔːrbl/	*v.* 低吟浅唱 to sing a melody of low pleasing sounds Contestants in the talent show primped in the green room mirrors and *warbled* harmonies while waiting for their turn to impress the judges. croon
knotty /'nɑːti/	*adj.* 复杂的 difficult or complicated The film *Sullivan's Travels* is a lighthearted comedy that also deals with *knotty* social and political issues. complicated

equivocal elucidate propaganda ☐ putative conjecture

☐coalesce ☐tractable ☐warble ☐knotty

dichotomy
/daɪˈkɑːtəmi/

释 *n.* 矛盾的事物 something with seemingly contradictory qualities
例 Tourism presents a ***dichotomy*** for nature conservation as tourists may play a big part in funding efforts but they also destroy habitats and ecosystems.
选 contradictory

释 *n.* 一分为二 bifurcation
例 A ***dichotomy*** of two lizard populations resulted when one section of the species was cut off from the rest by a mountain range.

restive
/ˈrestɪv/

释 *adj.* 不服管理的 stubbornly resisting control
例 The ***restive*** heir to the throne was assassinated by his rivals as he refused to submit to the king.
选 intractable

释 *adj.* 不安的，没有耐心的 marked by impatience or uneasiness
例 The mother tried to silence the ***restive*** child by offering sweets.
选 skittish, fractious

courteous
/ˈkɜːrtiəs/

释 *adj.* 有礼貌的 very polite in a way that shows respect
例 Drivers here have never been ***courteous*** to cyclists, but the new traffic regulations and fines may persuade them to drive more considerately now.
派 courtesy（n. 彬彬有礼）

invigorate
/ɪnˈvɪɡəreɪt/

释 *v.* 使…有活力 to give life and energy to
例 The crisp mountain air of the Alps ***invigorated*** David's zest for life after months of boring and grueling office work.
选 refreshing
反 emaciate
派 vigorous[adj. 精力充沛的（与spirited考同义词）]

truculent
/ˈtrʌkjələnt/

释 *adj.* 好争斗的 easily annoyed or angered and likely to argue
例 Germany is in a ***truculent*** mood after years of footing the bills for successive Euro-crises.
选 bellicose, combative, aggressive, pugnacious
反 benevolent, gentle

释 *adj.* 言语刻薄的 scathingly harsh
例 Newspaper op-eds frequently offer ***truculent*** criticism of existing policies, rather than suggest improvements or new ideas.

congenial
/kən'dʒiːniəl/

adj. 友善的 very friendly
例 The new employee was unsure what to think of the CEO after colleagues described him alternately as **congenial** and tyrannical, generous and merciless.
派 congeniality（n. 情投意合）

adj. 适宜的，令人愉悦的 pleasant and harmonious
例 To relax, I often listen to the **congenial** music of Bach and Mozart.

adj. 意气相投的 having the same nature, disposition, or tastes
例 I love hosting wine tastings and enjoying fine vintages with a **congenial** group of wine lovers.

insouciance
/ɪn'suːsiəns/

n. 无忧无虑，不操心 a feeling or appearance of not worrying about anything
例 No one would have guessed that Blake was broke as he wore an expression of **insouciance** on his face every day.
近 nonchalance
派 insouciant（adj. 漫不经心的）

devastate
/'devəsteɪt/

v. 严重破坏 to destroy much or most of (something)
例 Studies have shown that pollutants that enter bodies of water through the sewage system can **devastate** fish populations.
近 ruinous

v. 使…痛苦 to cause (someone) to feel extreme emotional pain
例 Her mother's passing **devastated** her so much that she could barely eat or sleep for weeks.

keen
/kiːn/

adj. 对…感兴趣的 very excited about and interested in something
例 While some are **keen** to begin driving, I am terrified of getting behind the wheel.
近 eager

adj. 强烈的，浓烈的 pungent; acrid
例 The **keen** smell of blue cheese made Tania feel sick in the stomach.

adj. 聪明的，敏锐的 having or marked by intellectual quickness and acuity
例 Given her **keen** intellect and creativity, it comes as no surprise that Sally has risen the ranks of her company in such a short time.

ethos
/'iːθɑːs/

n. （团体的）气质，氛围，信仰等 the distinguishing character, sentiment, moral nature, or guiding beliefs of a person, group, or organization
例 A libertine's general **ethos** is the shameless pursuit of all pleasures.

flagrant
/'fleɪɡrənt/

adj. 臭名昭著的 so bad as to be impossible to overlook
例 The coach was furious that the referee did not issue a penalty despite the **flagrant** foul committed by the striker.
近 egregious

☑ congenial ☑ insouciance ☑ devastate ☐ keen ☑ ethos
☐ flagrant

solitude
/ˈsɑːlətuːd/

摹 *n.* 孤独 a state or situation in which one is alone, often by choice

例 It is perfectly healthy for one to enjoy *solitude* without feeling lonely or in need of company.

anachronism
/əˈnækrənɪzəm/

摹 *n.* 时代错乱 something (such as a word, an object, or an event) that is mistakenly placed in a time where it does not belong in a story, movie, etc.

例 The presence of a ticking clock on a mantelpiece in *Julius Caesar* is a famous example of *anachronism* in literature.

摹 *n.* 不合时宜，过时 one that is out of its proper or chronological order, especially a person or practice that belongs to an earlier time

例 The use of the abacus for calculations in Chinese medicine shops is an *anachronism* that has survived the ages.

turbid
/ˈtɜːrbɪd/

摹 *adj.* 浑浊的 having sediment or foreign particles stirred up or suspended

例 The river was *turbid* after several days of rain and stormy weather.

反 limpid

摹 *adj.* 混乱的 in a state of turmoil

例 The *turbid* frenzy of the crowd reached a hysterical note when the rock star finally appeared after a two-hour delay.

confine
/kənˈfaɪn/

摹 *v.* 限制 to keep within limits

例 Many animal rights advocates have protested to having large animals *confined* to cages and limited spaces in zoos.

选 limit, circumscribe

venerate
/ˈvenəreɪt/

摹 *v.* 尊敬 to feel or show deep respect for

例 Martha Graham was *venerated* by her students and colleagues for her inventive and brilliant choreography.

选 respect

反 deride

派 venerable（adj. 令人尊敬的），veneration（n. 尊敬）

premeditate
/ˌpriːˈmedɪteɪt/

摹 *v.* 预谋，提前谋划 to think, consider, or deliberate beforehand

例 The bank robbery was clearly *premeditated* as the burglars had foreseen all possible obstacles to their escape.

反 impulse

insular
/ˈɪnsələr/

摹 *adj.* 孤立的 separated from other people or cultures

例 Honeybees tend to be less *insular* than earth bees as they search for food together and signal their individual findings to one another.

摹 *adj.* 思想狭隘的，守旧的 not knowing about or being interested in new or different ideas

例 Amazonian tribes have been the subject of intense research as their *insular* nature has preserved a number of social habits that are long lost in the industrial world.

选 provincial

派 insularity（n. 狭隘）

consolidate /kən'sɑːlɪdeɪt/	📖 *v.* 巩固 to make (something, such as a position of power or control) stronger or more secure 📝 After **consolidating** all rival companies under his control, the business tycoon finally held a monopoly over the fossil fuel industry. 🔄 consolidation（n. 巩固）
upheaval /ʌp'hiːvl/	📖 *n.* （引起混乱的）巨变 a major change or period of change that causes a lot of conflict, confusion, anger, etc. 📝 Although other European states broke apart under the stress of political **upheaval**, the seventeenth-century Dutch republic proved remarkably resilient. 🔄 convulsion
unyielding /ʌn'jiːldɪŋ/	📖 *adj.* 不妥协的，固执的 not changing or stopping 📝 Besides being smart and passionate, an innovator must also have an **unyielding** desire to succeed. 🔄 implacable
mendacious /men'deɪʃəs/	📖 *adj.* 欺骗的，不诚实的 not honest 📝 Isn't it obvious that Hitler's propaganda was not only **mendacious** but downright evil? 🔄 prevarication, disingenuous 🔀 veracious 🔄 mendacity（n. 欺骗）
sonorous /'sɑːnərəs/	📖 *adj.* 声音洪亮的 having a sound that is deep, loud, and pleasant 📝 The **sonorous** call of the French horn creates a stark contrast to the breathy notes of the piccolo.
fertile /'fɜːrtl/	📖 *adj.* 多产的（既可以指农作物，也可以指思想、想法等）able to reproduce or to produce a large amount of something 📝 The odyssey, or a hero's journey, has been a **fertile** idea for all kinds of writers throughout history. 🔄 bountiful 🔀 impoverished 🔄 fertility（n. 肥沃）
decadent /'dekədənt/	📖 *adj.* （思想）堕落的，颓废的 having low morals and a great love of pleasure, money, fame, etc. 📝 The reality star gave in to the **decadent** lifestyle of Hollywood with her growing fame and wealth. 🔄 disreputable 📖 *adj.* 庸俗的、低俗的、媚俗的 attractive to people of low morals who are only interested in pleasure 📝 The formerly straight-A student became a **decadent** outcast when he became addicted to drugs.

☐ consolidate upheaval unyielding  mendacious sonorous
☑ fertile ☐ decadent

indispensable /ˌɪndɪˈspensəbl/	释 *adj.* 不可缺少的 extremely important and necessary 例 Because howler monkeys rarely leave the trees in their arboreal habitat, the continued well-being of the rain forest is ***indispensable*** to their survival. 选 essential, crucial
covert /ˈkoʊvɜːrt/	释 *adj.* 秘密的，隐蔽的 secret or hidden 例 President Reagan's national security adviser said that ***covert*** action in such regions as Central America was necessary to protect the United States' allies. 选 clandestine 反 open
instinct /ˈɪnstɪŋkt/	释 *n.* 本能 a natural or inherent aptitude, impulse, or capacity 例 The natural ***instincts*** of the lioness are to protect her cub at all costs. 派 instinctive（adj. 本能的）
discern /dɪˈsɜːrn/	释 *v.* 识别，察觉 to detect or recognize 例 Because elephants can hear sounds at frequencies too low for human ears, they can communicate in ways that humans cannot directly ***discern***. 选 detect, discover 派 discernible（adj. 可察觉的），discerning（adj. 有洞察力的），discernment（n. 敏锐，精明）
orientation /ˌɔːriənˈteɪʃn/	释 *n.* 取向，态度 a usually general or lasting direction of thought, inclination, or interest 例 She should not have felt offended by the speech just because its political ***orientation*** was markedly different from hers. 选 bias 反 decline 释 *n.* 方向 the relative position or direction of something 例 The ***orientation*** of the Egyptian pyramids demonstrates a deep understanding of astronomy by the ancient people.
riddle /ˈrɪdl/	释 *n.* 难题，谜题 a mystifying, misleading, or puzzling question posed as a problem to be solved or guessed 例 Many fairy tales feature a main character who tries to answer a difficult ***riddle*** in the quest of attaining some reward. 选 enigma, puzzle, conundrum
jejune /dʒɪˈdʒuːn/	释 *adj.* 无聊的 immature and unsophisticated 例 Many people claim to find celebrity gossip ***jejune***, but most continue to read tabloid newspapers and magazines in their free time out of pure boredom. 选 vapid
clownish /ˈklaʊnɪʃ/	释 *adj.* 小丑般的，滑稽的 acting in a silly or funny way 例 Even though the class trickster meant no harm by flooding the school canteen, the principal still decided to suspend him for his ***clownish*** antics.

☑ indispensable ☑ covert ☑ instinct ☑ discern ☑ orientation
☐ riddle ☑ jejune ☐ clownish

indifferent
/ɪnˈdɪfrənt/

释 *adj.* 冷漠的，不感兴趣的 not interested in or concerned about something

例 I was *indifferent* to buying the couch until the clerk pointed out that it was 80% off the listed price.

选 apathy

释 *adj.* 客观公正的 characterized by a lack of partiality; unbiased

例 Even though the examiners knew the student quite well, they still gave a fair and *indifferent* assessment of the candidate's capability in their report.

lethargic
/ləˈθɑːrdʒɪk/

释 *adj.* 无精打采的 feeling a lack of energy or a lack of interest in doing things

例 She decided to visit the doctor after having felt listless and *lethargic* for months on end.

选 somnolent, indolent

clique
/kliːk/

释 *n.* 小团体 a small exclusive group of friends or associates

例 She felt miserable after her usual *clique* in school decided to alienate her for no discernible reason.

派 cliquish（adj. 小团体的，分帮结派的）

fungible
/ˈfʌndʒəbl/

释 *adj.* 可替代的 interchangeable or replaceable

例 If you want to keep your employees happy, you should make them feel individually valued and less *fungible.*

选 interchangeable

complimentary
/ˌkɑːmplɪˈmentri/

释 *adj.* 赞美的 expressing praise or admiration for someone or something

例 The student theater production received *complimentary* reviews, much to the delight of the director and her team.

派 compliment（n. 赞美）

empirical
/ɪmˈpɪrɪkl/

释 *adj.* 根据观察或经验的（表客观）originating in or based on observation or experience

例 Greek philosophers used *empirical* evidence from nature to understand the fundamental laws of nature.

反 speculation, conjecture

conform
/kənˈfɔːrm/

释 *v.* 符合，遵守 to obey or agree with something

例 Most human behavior is conventional and tends to *conform* to a norm.

选 square with

派 conformity（n. 一致）

释 *v.* 随大流，从众 to do what other people do

例 The school required that all students *conform* to the rigid dress code.

solicitous
/səˈlɪsɪtəs/

释 *adj.* 关心的，殷切的 showing great attention or concern to another

例 Her *solicitous* demeanor was deceptive as she was ultimately acting for her own selfish gains.

派 solicitude[n. 关心（与concern考同义词）]

音频

insult /ɪnˈsʌlt/	*v.* 侮辱，辱骂 to do or say something that is offensive to (someone) ***Insulting*** a colleague's appearance is inappropriate in the setting of an academic conference.
acrimony /ˈækrɪmoʊni/	*n.* 尖刻，犀利 harsh or biting sharpness especially of words, manner, or disposition The ***acrimony*** between the divorcing couple was clear in how they wrestled over every asset in court. bitterness, rancor acrimonious（adj. 尖酸刻薄的）
misconception /ˌmɪskənˈsepʃn/	*n.* 误解，错觉 a false idea or belief The depiction of the lone wolf is largely a ***misconception*** as wolves are social creatures that prefer to run in packs.
mundane /mʌnˈdeɪn/	*adj.* 平凡的，无聊的 dull and ordinary Doing the dishes may be a ***mundane*** chore but it helps to keep pests out of the house. exotic, unearthly
ambiguous /æmˈbɪɡjuəs/	*adj.* 有歧义的，模糊不清的 able to be understood in more than one way Bob was unable to interpret the ***ambiguous*** trail markers as they seemed to point in both directions of the path. equivocal ambiguity（n. 含糊不清）
allure /əˈlʊr/	*v.* 引诱 to entice by charm or attraction Many wealthy men have found themselves quickly ***allured*** to the sultry appearance and biting wit of the femme fatale. charm
cagey /ˈkeɪdʒi/	*adj.* 小心的；谨慎的 wary; careful The bear was ***cagey*** about the free food and walked around many times before finally approaching it. *adj.* 狡猾的；机敏的 crafty; shrewd The chimpanzee is a ***cagey*** primate that uses primitive stone tools to hunt for food and protect themselves.

heresy
/ˈherəsi/

n. 与主流观点相悖的观点 a belief or opinion that does not agree with the official belief or opinion of a particular religion or belief system

例 After years of building up his case with strong evidence, his findings went from controversial **heresy** to established wisdom.

parsimony
/ˈpɑːrsəmoʊni/

n. 吝啬 the quality of being very unwilling to spend money

例 It is surprising that the old man is now known for his **parsimony** as he used to spend lavishly on his friends and family in his younger days.

近 stingy, illiberal

反 munificent

派 parsimonious（adj. 吝啬的）

cunning
/ˈkʌnɪŋ/

adj. 狡猾机智的 clever and deceptive

例 In the film *Zootopia*, Nick is a **cunning** fox who tricks his fellow animals with fake and sad stories.

反 naive

adj. 技艺高超的 dexterous or crafty in the use of special resources

例 With only his teeth and wood, the **cunning** beaver can make large dams that divert the flow of a river.

近 craft

highlight
/ˈhaɪlaɪt/

v. 使…突出 to make or try to make others notice or be aware of

例 Hurricane Katrina **highlighted** the dire need for infrastructure improvements in New Orleans.

近 accentuate

judicious
/dʒuˈdɪʃəs/

adj. 有正确判断力的 having or showing good judgment

例 Because of his broad-ranging knowledge of the 19th century, Foner is able to provide the most thorough and **judicious** account of Lincoln's attitudes toward slavery.

反 unwise

disguise
/dɪsˈgaɪz/

v. 隐藏，伪装 to obscure the existence or true state or character of

例 **Disguised** by the night, the ninja slipped into the house unnoticed.

far-fetched
/ˌfɑːrˈfetʃt/

adj. 不切实际的 not likely to happen or be true

例 The lawyer presented a very **far-fetched** story that made it hard to believe that her client was truly innocent.

eclipse
/ɪˈklɪps/

v. 使…不重要 to make (something) less important or popular

例 The use of bulky television sets has been **eclipsed** by the invention of sleek plasma screens.

v. 超出 to surpass

例 Arctic animals may have adapted to the cold climate in exceptional ways, but humans have **eclipsed** them with their ability to use fire.

近 outdo

n. 日食，月食 the total or partial obscuring of one celestial body by an

例 The ancient Maya predicted solar **eclipses** with great accu watching the movements of the planets.

☑ heresy ☑ parsimony ☑ cunning ☑ highlight ☐ jud
☑ disguise ☐ far-fetched ☐ eclipse

impulsive
/ɪmˈpʌlsɪv/

释 *adj.* 冲动的，不加思索的 doing things or tending to do things suddenly and without careful thought

例 Her *impulsive* spending habits could not be tamed even with careful financial planning and a structured allowance.

选 capricious, hasty

---

exculpate
/ˈekskʌlpeɪt/

释 *v.* 开脱罪责 to prove that someone is not guilty of doing something wrong

例 People can be especially skilled at coming up with ways to *exculpate* themselves while reproaching others.

选 vindicate

派 exculpation（n. 脱罪）

---

overblow
/ˌoʊvərˈbloʊ/

释 *v.* 夸大 to exaggerate

例 We have no real reason to fear artificial intelligence as its dangers are usually *overblown*.

---

obfuscate
/ˈɑːbfʌskeɪt/

释 *v.* 使…困惑，混淆 to make (something) more difficult to understand

例 The professor's rambling lecture only *obfuscated* the differences between Plato and Aristotle.

选 obscure, mystify

释 *v.* 使…昏暗 to darken

例 The shadows *obfuscated* the already dim street and made it easier for criminals to strike.

---

droll
/droʊl/

释 *adj.* 古怪的，搞笑的 having an odd and amusing quality

例 The cartoonist was known for his *droll* and charming depiction of family life.

派 drollness（n. 诙谐，幽默）

---

inconclusive
/ˌɪnkənˈkluːsɪv/

释 *adj.* 无结果的，不确定的 leading to no conclusion or definite result

例 Despite the *inconclusive* results of the allergy test, Nora was certain that she was allergic to guava.

---

disperse
/dɪˈspɜːrs/

释 *v.* 使…分散，散发 to go or move in different directions

例 The fragrance of lavender was *dispersed* in the air the moment Lisa opened the bottle of perfume.

选 dissipate

反 focus

ᵗⁱfy

释 *v.* 详细阐述 to increase the volume of a sound or make an idea more well known

例 The journalist indirectly *amplified* criticism of government corruption in ˈbing attack on the city hall in the newspapers today.

ɹke larger or greater

st, the policy officer *amplified* his voice with a bullhorn so that his orders.

.tion（n. 大量），ample（adj. 大量的）

□ overblow　　□ obfuscate　　□ droll
□ amplify

exaggerate /ɪg'zædʒəreɪt/	释 *v.* 夸大 to make (something) larger or greater than normal 例 The story had become so ***exaggerated*** that the Chihuahua that bit Jon became a 6-foot Great Dane by the fifth telling. 选 overrate 反 minimize 派 exaggeration（n. 夸大）
unwitting /ʌn'wɪtɪŋ/	释 *adj.* 不知情的 not aware of what is really happening 例 Despite consumer protections, some companies still manage to drop in extra charges on ***unwitting*** consumers. 释 *adj.* 无意的 not intended or planned; unintentional 例 Scientists argue that the dense smog covering Los Angeles is an ***unwitting*** consequence of America's car culture.
inclusive /ɪn'kluːsɪv/	释 *adj.* 包罗万象的、全面的 taking a great deal or everything within its scope; comprehensive 例 The ***inclusive*** coverage of the introductory science course spans all branches of science, including physics, chemistry and biology. 选 generic
diatribe /'daɪətraɪb/	释 *n.* 谩骂 a bitter, abusive denunciation 例 The manager's ***diatribe*** shocked her employees, who neither expected nor deserved such bitter, abusive language. 选 rant 反 encomium, eulogy
promulgate /'prɑːmlgeɪt/	释 *v.* 宣布、宣传 to make known (a decree, for example) by public declaration; announce officially 例 The religious government spent a lot of effort in ***promulgating*** the new set of religious laws. 选 disseminate
consilience /kən'sɪlɪəns/	释 *n.* 一致、符合 the linking together of principles from different disciplines especially when forming a comprehensive theory 例 By linking ancient philosophy, empirical research and modern technology, nineteenth century thinkers devised a new ***consilience*** of thought, which we now know as science.
ebullient /ɪ'bʌlɪənt/	释 *adj.* 热情洋溢的 lively and enthusiastic 例 It would be a stretch to say that Lauren is ***ebullient*** as she is merely warm and cordial around her friends. 反 impassive, restraint
bolster /'boʊlstər/	释 *v.* 支持 to give support to 例 The testimony of the witness inadvertently strengthened the case of Wang's accusers even though it was intended to ***bolster*** his defense. 选 buttress, prop up 反 undermine

dispute /dɪ'spjuːt/	释 **v.** 争辩，反对 to engage in argument or oppose 例 Mary told her friends that she was **disputing** with her ex-husband over custody.
exposition /ˌekspə'zɪʃn/	释 **n.** 阐释，解释 clear explanation 例 The man's **exposition** of his actions did not persuade his girlfriend to stay with him as she remained convinced that he had cheated on her. 释 **n.** 展览会 a public show or exhibition 例 All of Matisse's paintings were displayed at the free **exposition** in the Metropolitan Museum of Art.
coddle /'kɑːdl/	释 **v.** 溺爱 to treat (someone) with too much care or kindness 例 Compassion does not necessarily mean **coddling** and comforting your children under all circumstances.
nuance /'nuːɑːns/	释 **n.** 小差异 a very small difference in color, tone, meaning, etc. 例 The singer's recording sold so well because it displayed sensitive **nuances** of musical taste and expression. 选 subtlety
peculiar /pɪ'kjuːliər/	释 **adj.** 不寻常的 not usual or normal 例 When the housemates noticed a **peculiar** odor coming from the fridge, they immediately cleaned it out and disposed of all expired food.
egalitarian /iˌgælɪ'teriən/	释 **adj.** 平等的 aiming for equal wealth, status, or other qualities for all people 例 It is hard for a completely **egalitarian** society to exist because there will always be small differences between people, such as intelligence and leadership abilities.
propitiate /prə'pɪʃieɪt/	释 **v.** 安抚 to make (someone) pleased or less angry by giving or saying something desired 例 The Vikings **propitiated** the gods by offering mead and meat at the temple altar. 反 arouse hostility
futile /'fjuːtl/	释 **adj.** 无用的 pointless or useless 例 The fact that most hypotheses turn out to be wrong does not mean that hypothesizing is **futile**, since disproving wrong ideas is part of science. 选 fruitless, pointless, vain 派 futility（**n.** 无效）
unassuming /ˌʌnə'suːmɪŋ/	释 **adj.** 谦虚的，低调的 not having or showing a desire to be noticed, praised 例 What made Doug stand out in this sea of brilliant scholars is his humility and **unassuming** nature. 选 modest, humble 反 presumptuous

amicable
/ˈæmɪkəbl/

adj. 和善的 showing a polite and friendly desire to avoid disagreement and argument

Amicable disputes among friends are typically brought to an end with a round of drinks at the pub.

agreeable

unfounded
/ʌnˈfaʊndɪd/

adj. 毫无根据的 lacking a sound basis

The rumors of layoffs were shown to be *unfounded* when the company hired ten new people.

groundless, unwarranted, baseless

plastic
/ˈplæstɪk/

adj. 能适应的，灵活的 capable of adapting to varying conditions

This species exhibited *plastic* traits that were utilized differently according to the changes in the environment.

malleable

adj. 易受影响的，敏感的 easily influenced; impressionable

The *plastic* minds of youths are easily swayed and fooled by all sorts of external threats and stimuli.

apocalypse
/əˈpaːkəlɪps/

n. 大灾难 a great disaster

The aboriginal tribe prophesized that the end of the world would be brought about by an *apocalypse* from the heavens.

apocalyptic（adj. 灾难性的）

authoritative
/əˈθɔːrəteɪtɪv/

adj. 权威的，可信的 clearly accurate or knowledgeable

The claim that fluoride is a mind controlling drug does not have *authoritative* support from the scientific community.

definitive, cogent

clamorous
/ˈklæmərəs/

adj. （为提要求而）吵吵闹闹的 noisily insistent

In order to have the final say on the matter, the teacher lifted his voice above the *clamorous* protests of the teenagers.

placate
/ˈpleɪkeɪt/

v. 安抚 to cause (someone) to feel less angry about something

It is not wise to *placate* aggressive groups by making more concessions as they will simply demand more.

appease, conciliatory

antagonize

implacable（adj. 难以平息的）

far-reaching
/ˌfaːrˈriːtʃɪŋ/

adj. 影响广泛的 having a wide range or effect

The detonation of the nuclear bomb on Bikini Island had *far-reaching* environmental effects that left the island barren.

disinterested
/dɪsˈɪntrɛstəd/

adj. 客观公正的 not influenced by personal feelings, opinions, or concerns

All information in a history textbook should be presented in a *disinterested* rather than biased tone.

fair, impartial

prejudiced

disinterestedness（n. 客观公正，冷漠）

---

embolden /ɪmˈboʊldən/	释 **v.** 鼓舞，鼓励 to make (someone) more confident 例 Liam's recent series of business accomplishments **emboldened** him to start his own company. 选 encourage
incompatible /ˌɪnkəmˈpætəbl/	释 **adj.** 无法共存的，不可兼容的 not able to exist together without trouble or conflict; not able to be used together 例 We had to buy a travel adaptor in the UK as our electric plugs were **incompatible** with the British outlets. 反 harmonious
stale /steɪl/	释 **adj.** 不新鲜的 not fresh; old or unpleasant (as in food) 例 The bread went **stale** after being left out overnight and could only be used as croutons. 释 **adj.** 缺乏新鲜感的 boring or unoriginal 例 In the comments of the term paper, the professor remarked that the student's **stale** arguments lacked creativity or innovation. 选 banal
lionize /ˈlaɪənaɪz/	释 **v.** 重视，尊敬 to treat (someone) as a very important and famous person 例 After being **lionized** as a celebrity by his congregation for years, the pastor signed a contract to pursue a career as a televangelist. 选 eulogize
preachy /ˈpriːtʃi/	释 **adj.** 说教的，好为人师的 trying to teach something (such as proper or moral behavior) in a way that is annoying or unwanted 例 The speaker attempted to warn the students about the dangers of cigarettes, but his condescending tone was interpreted as **preachy** rather than informative. 选 sanctimonious 派 preach（v. 布道，说教）
illusory /ɪˈluːsəri/	释 **adj.** 虚假的 based on something that is not true or real 例 Her dreams of an Olympic career became an **illusory** dream after she was tragically paralyzed in a car accident.
profit-monger /ˈprɑːfɪtˌmʌŋgər/	释 **n.** 贪婪的人 a person, business or profession marked by avarice and greed 例 Despite the record success of the company, the CEO proved to be a **profit-monger** and refused to issue a single holiday bonus.
felicitous /fəˈlɪsɪtəs/	释 **adj.** 合适 very well suited for some purpose or situation 例 I made the **felicitous** discovery of an umbrella by the side of the road just as the weather turned stormy. 释 **adj.** 喜悦的，令人愉悦的 pleasant or delightful 例 Fred's **felicitous** lottery win allowed him to quit his job and pursue his passion in music.

□ embolden □ incompatible □ stale □ lionize □ preachy
□ illusory □ profit-monger □ felicitous

averse
/əˈvɜːrs/
釋 *adj.* 反感的 having an active feeling of repugnance or distaste
例 As Juan does not believe in introspection, he is *averse* to examining his own feelings and motives.
派 aversion（n. 反感）

trigger
/ˈtrɪgər/
釋 *v.* 触发 to cause (something) to start or happen
例 The assassinations of Archduke Franz Ferdinand of Austria and his wife *triggered* the First World War in 1914.

integrity
/ɪnˈtegrəti/
釋 *n.* 正直 the quality of being honest and fair
例 As one of its measures to demonstrate *integrity*, Amazon allows a complete money-back guarantee on all its products.

conservation
/ˌkɑːnsərˈveɪʃn/
釋 *n.* 保护 a careful preservation and protection of something
例 *Conservation* efforts to save the cheetahs have been met by resistance from local bush poachers who rely on illegal hunting for their livelihood.

釋 *n.* 环保 the controlled use and systematic protection of natural resources, such as forests, soil, and water systems
例 Water *conservation* is crucial to countries that have huge populations and scarce rainfall or natural water sources.

spontaneous
/spɑːnˈteɪniəs/
釋 *adj.* 自主的，自发的 controlled and directed internally
例 Many of the physical changes that come with child birth are *spontaneous* and occur as a result of internal hormonal changes in the mother.
选 intuitive

釋 *adj.* 自然的，不刻意的 not apparently contrived or manipulated
例 The restaurant critic's *spontaneous* expression of admiration for the food took the waiter by surprise.

pushover
/ˈpʊʃoʊvər/
釋 *n.* 易被打败的人 an opponent that is easy to defeat
例 Because everyone was certain that the Democratic candidate would win, the Republicans supported a *pushover* in order to conserve resources for the following election.

釋 *n.* 容易的事 something that is easy to do
例 The GRE exam has a deserved reputation for its difficulty, but the SAT is a *pushover*.

comprehensive
/ˌkɑːmprɪˈhensɪv/
釋 *adj.* 全面的 covering completely or broadly
例 Her political success came from her *comprehensive* vision for the nation that included every social constituency.
选 generic, inclusive, exhaustive, thorough
派 comprehend（v. 理解，包含）

insufferable
/ɪnˈsʌfrəbl/
釋 *adj.* 无法忍受的 too unpleasant to deal with or accept
例 Mother-in-laws have a reputation as *insufferable* busybodies who make newlyweds miserable.

☐ averse   ☐ trigger   ☐ integrity   ☐ conservation   ☐ spontaneous
☐ pushover   ☐ comprehensive   ☐ insufferable

sequential
/sɪˈkwenʃl/

adj. 有序的 happening in a series or sequence

Following the recipe directions in a **sequential** way is essential to thickening mayonnaise.

successively

surreptitious
/ˌsɜːrəpˈtɪʃəs/

adj. 秘密的，鬼鬼祟祟的 done in a secret way

She knew that anything done in a **surreptitious** manner was likely to arouse the suspicions of her superiors.

clandestine, covert

dispassionate
/dɪsˈpæʃənət/

adj. 客观的 not influenced or affected by emotions

He sought to provide a **dispassionate** analysis of political and economic issues by consulting a steady stream of books, articles and speeches.

transient
/ˈtrænʃnt/

adj. 短暂的 not lasting long

The Aurora Borealis is a **transient** phenomenon that is only visible on the clearest of nights.

transience（n. 短暂）

vacant
/ˈveɪkənt/

adj. 空的 not filled, used, or lived in

When the throne stands **vacant**, the prime minister holds power until the new king can be identified.

adj. 面无表情的，茫然的 devoid of thought, reflection, or expression

Although the prisoner feigned stupidity with the **vacant** expression on his face, he was constantly plotting his great escape.

canned
/kænd/

adj. 千篇一律的 lacking originality or individuality as if massproduced

Many of the customer relations officers are incompetent and only capable of delivering **canned** responses promising follow-ups.

formulaic

adj. 预先录制的 prepared or recorded in advance

Sitcoms typically have **canned** applause tracks that are played at funny moments in each episode.

soft-pedal
/ˌsɔːftˈpedl/

v. 弱化，减弱…的影响 to treat or describe (something) as less important than it really is

Seeing the wretched emotional state she was in, I had no choice but to **soft-pedal** the huge consequences of her actions.

feign
/feɪn/

v. 假装 to give a false appearance of

As the man kept staring at Barbara, she picked up a magazine and **feigned** interest in one of its articles.

false

daunting

/ˈdɔːntɪŋ/

释 *adj.* 令人畏惧的，望而生畏的 very difficult to do or deal with

例 Although visitors may initially find touring the city by subway to be *daunting*, they will soon realize that it is an easy way to get around.

选 formidable, sensational, forbidding

反 resolute

downright

/ˈdaʊnraɪt/

释 *adv.* 完全地 completely

例 When our pet cat died, the entire family felt *downright* awful.

autonomous

/ɔːˈtɑːnəməs/

释 *adj.* 自治的 having the power or right to govern itself

例 The Roomba is an *autonomous* vacuum cleaner that can clean floors with no person present.

释 *adj.* 独立自主的 responding, reacting, or developing independently of the whole

例 Psychology has slowly evolved into an *autonomous* scientific discipline that now develops independently from other sciences.

indeterminate

/ˌɪndɪˈtɜːrmɪnət/

释 *adj.* 不确定的 not able to be stated or described in an exact way

例 I decided to buy an extra bottle of wine because the clerk said it would be an *indeterminate* amount of time before more is shipped.

opulent

/ˈɑːpjələnt/

释 *adj.* 豪华的，昂贵的 very comfortable and expensive

例 The millionaire squandered his wealth to fund his *opulent* lifestyle of acquiring branded goods and eating at Michelin starred restaurants.

释 *adj.* 富裕的 very wealthy

例 The diamond-encrusted watch was only a minor trinket for the *opulent* oil tycoon.

选 affluent

派 opulence（n. 富裕，丰富）

pervasive

/pərˈveɪsɪv/

释 *adj.* 普遍的 existing in or spreading through every part of something

例 Recent empirical studies have found no basis for the *pervasive* idea that women are more emotional than men.

选 rife

offset

/ˈɔːfset/

释 *v.* 抵消 to cancel or reduce the effect of (something)

例 For Nike, the financial damage caused by the stock market crash was *offset* by the sale of undeveloped real estate.

选 compensate

omnipresent

/ˌɑːmnɪˈpreznt/

释 *adj.* 处处都有的 present everywhere simultaneously

例 In seventeenth-century New England, religious leaders constantly warned people about the *omnipresent* Devil who would lure them into sin.

选 ubiquitous, universal

□ daunting   □ downright   □ autonomous   ■ indeterminate   □ opulent
□ pervasive   □ offset   □ omnipresent

entangle
/ɪnˈtæŋgl/

释 *v.* 纠缠 to cause (something) to get caught in or twisted with something else

例 The fisherman pulled his haul from the sea and removed the fish that were *entangled* in the net.

派 entanglement（n. 纠缠）

释 *v.* 使…卷入困境 to get (someone) involved in a confusing or difficult situation

例 Not wanting to become *entangled* in crime, the young man stayed inside every afternoon to do his homework and read.

dilatory
/ˈdɪlətɔːri/

释 *adj.* 拖延的 tending or intended to cause delay

例 The senator never formally declared her opposition to the proposed legislation; instead, she engineered a series of *dilatory* actions to slow its progress.

选 laggard

派 dilate（v. 拖延）

generic
/dʒəˈnerɪk/

释 *adj.* 一般的，通用的 relating to or descriptive of an entire group or class; general

例 Siri will default to a *generic* web search for the vast multitude of requests or queries.

选 inclusive

sensational
/senˈseɪʃənl/

释 *adj.* 极好的 exceedingly or unexpectedly excellent or great

例 I found the scientific report rather unprofessional as it described the benefits of the drug in an exaggerated and *sensational* manner.

释 *adj.* （通过可怕的细节）令人兴奋的，耸人听闻的 causing very great excitement or interest with shocking details

例 Although the website purports to be a legitimate news source, it really only covers *sensational* celebrity gossip.

选 daunting, lurid

explicable
/ˈeksplɪkəbl/

释 *adj.* 可以解释的 possible to explain

例 Scientists claimed that the UFO sighting was, in fact, an *explicable* phenomenon caused by solar flares.

反 mysterious

派 explicate（v. 解释）

pernicious
/pərˈnɪʃəs/

释 *adj.* 有害的，致命的 causing great harm or damage often in a way that is not easily seen or noticed

例 The deterioration of the ozone layer is *pernicious*, with the loss of penguin habitats being just one of the tragic results.

□ entangle □ dilatory □ generic □ sensational □ explicable
□ pernicious

convoluted
/ˈkɑːnvəluːtɪd/

▷ *adj.* 难懂的，复杂的 very complicated and difficult to understand

▷ 例 The author produced a lucid and succinct argument by avoiding *convoluted* sentence structures and writing in a straightforward style.

▷ 近 intricate, tortuous

bureaucracy
/bjʊˈrɑːkrəsi/

▷ *n.* 官僚机构 a system of government or business that has many complicated rules and ways of doing things

▷ 例 I advise you to file in your appeal early as the university's *bureaucracy* is known to be opaque and obscure in handling such cases speedily.

widespread
/ˈwaɪdspred/

▷ *adj.* 广泛的 common over a wide area or among many people

▷ 例 The *widespread* shock at the eventual guilty verdict was mostly caused by biased news stories that had predicted acquittal.

▷ 近 extensive, prevalent

compliant
/kəmˈplaɪənt/

▷ *adj.* 顺从的，迎合的 ready and willing to comply

▷ 例 As a result of decades of oppression, the people became *compliant* and yielded readily to the government's demands.

▷ 近 tractable

▷ 派 comply（v. 顺从，遵守）

trifling
/ˈtraɪflɪŋ/

▷ *adj.* 不重要的 having little value or importance

▷ 例 Despite the *trifling* appearance of the plastic bracelet, it holds great sentimental value as a gift from my childhood friend.

▷ 近 minimal

compunction
/kəmˈpʌŋkʃn/

▷ *n.* 后悔感，犯罪感 a feeling of guilt or regret

▷ 例 Sally often acts without *compunction* and feels no remorse from harming or inconveniencing her friends.

cynical
/ˈsɪnɪkl/

▷ *adj.* 认为人性自私的，愤世嫉俗的 believing or showing the belief that people are motivated chiefly by base or selfish concerns

▷ 例 Sam is widely regarded as a *cynical* man because his actions and speech reveal a deep distrust of human nature and motives.

pretentious
/prɪˈtenʃəs/

▷ *adj.* 炫耀的 having the quality wanting to be regarded as more impressive, successful, or important than one really is

▷ 例 The *pretentious* candidate thought he would win by accusing his opponent of committing logical fallacies in the debate.

customary
/ˈkʌstəmeri/

▷ *adj.* 惯常的，（某人）特有的 usual or typical of a particular person

▷ 例 It is *customary* for guests to remove their shoes when entering our home.

vilify
/ˈvɪlɪfaɪ/

▷ *v.* 诽谤，辱骂 to utter slanderous and abusive statements against

▷ 例 The CEO of this pioneering company may be *vilified* by his competitors, but he remains loved by the consumers for his charismatic persona and brilliant products.

☐ convoluted   ☐ bureaucracy   ☑ widespread   ☐ compliant   ☐ trifling
☐ compunction   ☐ cynical   ☐ pretentious   ☐ customary   ☐ vilify

tantamount
/ˈtæntəmaʊnt/

adj. （数量、效果等）相同的 equal to something in value, meaning, or effect

While a few thousand voters in Iowa may not be **tantamount** to the will of the American people, they should not be seen as immaterial to it as well.

synonymous with

unflinching
/ʌnˈflɪntʃɪŋ/

adj. 坚定的，不退缩的 staying strong and determined even when things are difficult

He was **unflinching** in the face of his enemies and retook power shortly after being exiled on the island.

adj. （表达）直白的 looking at or describing something or someone in a very direct way

This TV series was **unflinching** in its portrayal of domestic violence and did not shy away from showing its brutal and oppressive sides.

prototype
/ˈproʊtətaɪp/

n. 原型 an original model on which something is patterned

Upon seeing the excellent quality of the **prototype**, the company president decided to expedite the mass production of the new phone model.

n. 典型 a standard or typical example

Becoming a reality star before entering Hollywood is a common **prototype** that many B-listers pursue to gain fame.

□ tantamount　　□ unflinching　　□ prototype

音频

equanimity
/,ekwə'nɪməti/

n. 平静，镇定 calm emotions when dealing with problems or pressure

Everyone adored Tom as he was always able to restore his co-workers' **equanimity** with charm and good humor whenever the work pressure became unbearable on the set.

excitability

espouse
/ɪ'spaʊz/

v. 支持 to express support for (a cause, belief, etc.)

Unlike previous candidates, Megan **espoused** gender equality and pushed forth more benevolent political reforms.

advocate, defend, champion

abjure

inattention
/,ɪnə'tenʃn/

n. 不留心，不注意 failure to carefully think about, listen to, or watch someone or something

The thief's successful escape was due to the **inattention** of the security team who were staring at their cell phones during the crime.

fractious
/'frækʃəs/

· skittish

adj. 愤怒的 full of anger and disagreement

As the debate grew increasingly **fractious**, friendships among the co-workers fell apart.

skittish

· restive

adj. 爱惹事的，不服管的 inclined to make trouble

The **fractious** observers in the courtroom were finally removed by the bailiff after many unheeded warnings to maintain their composure.

restive

disorganize
/dɪs'ɔːrgənaɪz/

v. 打乱，破坏 to destroy or interrupt the orderly structure or function of

A primary goal of the hacker group "Anonymous" is to **disorganize** corrupt and oppressive global organizations.

figurative
/'fɪgjərətɪv/

symbolic

adj. （形象化）比喻的 based on or making use of figures of speech; metaphorical

You should not take every word that she says literally as she likes to speak in a **figurative** manner.

symbolic

entail /ɪnˈteɪl/	释 **v.** 包括，包含，使⋯必然，牵涉 to have (something) as a part, step, or result 例 China's membership in the WTO **entails** a commitment to participating in international conferences.
impeccable /ɪmˈpekəbl/	释 **adj.** 完美无瑕的 having no flaws 例 The paper used **impeccable** logic, but the journal rejected it anyway. 选 flawless
stifle /ˈstaɪfl/	释 **v.** 抑制 to not allow oneself to do or express (something) 例 Francis learned that by **stifling** his anger and resentment, he could avoid conflicts and overcome opponents. 选 shackle 释 **v.** 使⋯窒息 to kill by depriving of oxygen 例 Without their spacesuits, the astronauts would be **stifled** in space due to the lack of oxygen. 选 smother
pragmatic /præɡˈmætɪk/ *realistic*	释 **adj.** 实际的 practical 例 Mary's **pragmatic** attitude was appreciated by her colleagues because it ensured work productivity and efficiency. 选 realistic
didactic /daɪˈdæktɪk/	释 **adj.**（过分的道德层面的）说教的 excessively moralizing 例 Although some young readers may enjoy this entertaining fable, I find it pious and overly **didactic**. 选 preachy
dazzle /ˈdæzl/	释 **v.** 使⋯目眩，使⋯惊叹 to greatly impress or surprise (someone) by being very attractive or exciting 例 The guests at the lavish Cinco de Mayo party were **dazzled** by the mariachi bands and colorful piñatas.
stalwart /ˈstɔːlwərt/	释 **adj.** 坚定的，忠诚的 loyal and resolute 例 Wuyong remained a **stalwart** employee in the company even though he had been headhunted several times in the past years. 释 **adj.** 结实的，强壮的 strong and imposing 例 Brutus was a **stalwart** opponent to Julius Caesar and died at the hands of Caesar's supporters.
archaic /ɑːrˈkeɪɪk/	释 **adj.** 过时的 old and no longer used 例 In a world where we can easily reach one another through texts, emails and social media messages, leaving a voicemail can seem **archaic** and unnecessary. 选 antediluvian, outdated

☐ entail ☐ impeccable ☐ stifle ☐ pragmatic ☐ didactic
☐ dazzle ☐ stalwart ☐ archaic

palliate /'pælieɪt/	释 *v.* 减缓 to make the effects of (something, such as an illness) less painful, harmful, or harsh 例 Morphine is sometimes used to **palliate** the suffering of terminally ill patients. 派 palliative（adj. 治标而不治本的）
accede /ək'siːd/	释 *v.* 同意 to agree to a request or a demand 例 We were forced to **accede** to the kidnapper's demands after all negotiations failed. 释 *v.* 加入 to become a party (as to an agreement) 例 After World War II, Germany **acceded** to the demands of the Allied forces and surrendered control to the USA, Britain, and the USSR.
consort /'kaːnsɔːrt/	释 *v.* 陪伴 to keep company 例 She came under the police's radar after having been observed **consorting** with the triad leaders every night.
hostile /'haːstl/	释 *adj.* 不友好的，敌对的 not friendly 例 It is best to avoid rabid mammals because they are **hostile** to anything that comes near them.
ubiquitous /juː'bɪkwɪtəs/	释 *adj.* 到处存在的，广泛的 seeming to be seen everywhere 例 Apple ranks fifth worldwide in the number of computers sold in 2016, and was thus far less **ubiquitous** than you might think. 选 omnipresent, universal 反 unique
authenticate /ɔː'θentɪkeɪt/	释 *v.* 验证，证明…是真实的 to prove that something is real, true, or genuine 例 The sellers had to get their famous paintings **authenticated** by art specialists before they were put up for sale at the auction. 反 apocryphal, bogus 派 authentic（adj. 真实的）
condescend /ˌkaːndɪ'send/	释 *v.* 带着优越感对待人 to deal with people in a patronizingly superior manner 例 The way she **condescends** to her employees is disrespectful and downright disgusting. 释 *v.* 屈尊 to descend to the level of one considered inferior; to lower oneself 例 Despite their years of education and high salaries, the doctors **condescended** to clean the hospital bathrooms when the workers went on strike.
predilection /ˌpredl'ekʃn/	释 *n.* 倾向，偏好 a natural liking for something 例 Given that most seabirds nest on ocean cliffs and islands, the marbled murrelet's **predilection** for nesting in forests many miles from the sea is unusual. 选 proclivity, preference

diminutive
/dɪˈmɪnjətɪv/

adj. 极小的 extremely or extraordinarily small

The bee hummingbird has an average length of only two inches, making it the most **diminutive** of all hummingbird species.

minuscule

illustrious
/ɪˈlʌstrɪəs/

adj. 杰出的 admired and respected very much because a lot was achieved

George Washington was an **illustrious** general and statesman who successfully steered the USA during the country's infancy.

distinguished, prominent

unconscionable
/ʌnˈkɑːnʃənəbl/

adj. 丧心病狂的，违背良心的 not guided or controlled by conscience

Robots are **unconscionable** automatons that are controlled by algorithms and strict rules of performance.

adj. 过分的，不合理的 beyond prudence or reason; excessive

The terrorist attack in France was an **unconscionable** assault on the world's freedoms.

trivial
/ˈtrɪvɪəl/

adj. 不重要的 not important

Readers of history often marvel that momentous events were triggered by actions that seemed **trivial** at the time.

inconsequential, immaterial

momentous

callow
/ˈkælou/

adj. 幼稚的，稚嫩的 lacking adult sophistication

Mr. Jackson was too shallow, **callow** and inexperienced for a position demanding maturity.

sketchy
/ˈsketʃi/

adj. 粗略的 done quickly without many details

It is better to be prepared for the meeting with a fully-formed plan than a **sketchy** outline.

superficial, undeveloped, rudimentary

sketch (n. 草图)

bemuse
/bɪˈmjuːz/

v. 使…困惑 to cause (someone) to be confused and often also somewhat amused

The teacher was **bemused** by the class troublemaker's sudden obedient behavior, and wondered what had triggered the change.

v. 吸引 to occupy the attention of

The Cirque du Soleil has **bemused** audiences young and old throughout the world for their awe-inspiring performances.

exotic
/ɪgˈzɑːtɪk/

adj. 外来的 introduced from another country

The new trade agreement permitted the import of unpasteurized, **exotic** cheeses that had previously been banned for purported health reasons.

adj. 奇异的，异域风情的 strikingly, excitingly, or mysteriously different or unusual

In the classroom filled with blonde-haired students, Bill stood out with his **exotic** red hair.

☐ diminutive　　☐ illustrious　　☐ unconscionable　　☐ trivial　　☐ callow
☐ sketchy　　☐ bemuse　　☐ exotic

intuition
/ˌɪntuˈɪʃn/

n. 直觉 a feeling that guides a person to act a certain way without fully understanding why

Many believe that ghost hunters are phony because they are guided solely by *intuition* rather than empirical evidence.

episodic
/ˌepɪˈsɑːdɪk/

adj. 暂时的 limited to the duration of an episode

Cable television saw a proliferation of *episodic* crime dramas after the success of *Law and Order*.

adj. 不连续的，（时间上）分散的 happening or appearing at different times

Despite a few *episodic* instances of flirtation, Max did not seem seriously interested in Sharon.

dovish
/ˈdʌvɪʃ/

adj. 爱好和平的 advocating peace, conciliation or negotiation in preference to confrontation or armed conflict

Hippies were *dovish* in their attitude to the Vietnam War and protested it nonviolently.

pacific

dove（adj. 爱好和平的人）

realm
/relm/

n. 领域 an area of activity, interest, or knowledge

The anthropology professor hoped that his latest book would appeal to popular as well as to scholarly readers, thereby earning him acclaim in both *realms*.

n. 国度 a country that is ruled by a king or queen

The smallest *realm* in the entire world, the Kingdom of Tavolara, is a five-square kilometer island near Italy.

presage
/ˈpresɪdʒ/

v. 预测，预言 to give or be a sign of (something that will happen or develop in the future)

For many natives, the arrival of the Spanish conquistadors *presaged* the return of their indigenous sun god.

portend

distinctive
/dɪˈstɪŋktɪv/

adj. 独特的，有显著区别的 different in a way that is easy to notice

Although Eudora Welty and William Faulkner wrote in *distinctive* styles, comparison between the two is inevitable because they both lived in and wrote about Mississippi.

concomitant
/kənˈkɑːmɪtənt/

adj. 相伴随的，与…同时发生的 accompanying especially in a subordinate or incidental way

Lead is a *concomitant* by-product of silver production.

abstemious
/əbˈstiːmiəs/

adj. 有节制的（尤指在饮食方面） not eating and drinking too much

Bearing in mind that she had an early morning the next day, Hilary was very *abstemious* at the dinner party and only drank half a glass of wine.

austere, moderate

versatile
/'vɜːrsətl/
■■■■■

釋 *adj.* 多变的 changing or fluctuating readily
例 The Pittsburgh Steelers prefer **versatile** defensive players who can play safety, cornerback, or linebacker.
选 fickle, volatile, flighty, erratic, capricious
反 unchangeable

釋 *adj.* 多功能的 having many uses or applications
例 The new antifungal agent has **versatile** uses, from treating Dutch elm disease to rescuing water-damaged works of art from mold.

vacillate
/'væsəleɪt/
■■■■■■■■

釋 *v.* 犹豫不决 to swing indecisively from one course of action or opinion to another
例 The doctor **vacillated** so frequently on disease-prevention techniques that his colleagues accused him of inconsistency.
选 fluctuate, irresolution
反 resolve

釋 *v.* 摇摆 to fluctuate or oscillate
例 The metronome made regularly clicking noises as it **vacillated** back and forth.

devious
/'diːviəs/
■■■

釋 *adj.* 欺骗的 willing to lie and trick people in order to get what is wanted
例 Some people thought Carly was a **devious** politician who gained votes through dishonest means.

釋 *adj.* 弯曲的，蜿蜒的 not straight or direct
例 After cutting a **devious** path through the Rocky Mountains, the highway finally straightens upon reaching the plains of eastern Colorado.
选 indirect

suffice
/sə'faɪs/
■■■■■■■

釋 *v.* 足够 to be or provide as much as is needed
例 Sometimes the illusion of facts will **suffice** to convince people that something is true.
派 sufficient（adj. 充足的）

astute
/ə'stuːt/
■■■■

釋 *adj.* 敏锐的 having or showing an ability to notice and understand things clearly
例 Sherlock Holmes is an **astute** detective who can judge situations correctly and use what he discovers, even small details, to solve crime.
选 shrewd

outrage
/'aʊtreɪdʒ/
■■■■■

釋 *v.* 使…生气 to make (someone) very angry
例 Protesters were **outraged** by the closure of the local park and picketed in front of the city hall.

consensus
/kən'sensəs/
■■■■■■

釋 *n.* 意见一致 a general agreement about something
例 The recent poll shows that there is **consensus** among citizens that the plan to increase military spending is foolish.
选 accord
反 divergence, dissent
派 consent（v. 同意）

□ versatile □ vacillate □ devious □ suffice □ astute
□ outrage □ consensus

metaphor
/ˈmetəfər/

释 *n.* 比喻 a word or phrase for one thing that is used to refer to another thing in order to show or suggest that they are similar

例 Virgil uses the image of bees as a ***metaphor*** to describe the hard-working inhabitants of Carthage.

释 *n.* 象征 an object, activity, or idea that is used as a symbol of something else

例 The moment at which Tommie Smith and John Carlos raised their fists during the 1968 Summer Olympics has become a ***metaphor*** of human rights in the USA.

outstrip
/ˌaʊtˈstrɪp/

释 *v.* 胜出，超出 to be or become better, greater, or larger than (someone or something)

例 Human abilities still far ***outstrip*** even the most powerful computers.

querulous
/ˈkwerələs/

释 *adj.* 抱怨的 complaining in an annoyed way

例 She was looking forward to working at home quietly, but the ***querulous*** child disrupted her plans by constantly making a racket.

salient
/ˈseɪliənt/

释 *adj.* 明显的，显眼的 very important or noticeable

例 The Panama Canal is the most ***salient*** economic symbol of Central America.

选 prominent, obtrusive, conspicuous, visible

culmination
/ˌkʌlmɪˈneɪʃn/

释 *n.* 最终，结果 the end or final result of something

例 The US Civil War was the ***culmination*** of decades of debate about the morality and constitutionality of slavery in the nation.

camaraderie
/ˌkɑːməˈrɑːdəri/

释 *n.* 志同道合之情谊 a feeling of good friendship among the people in a group

例 The good-natured ***camaraderie*** among baseball players is visible when they play pranks in the dugout.

选 solidarity

cordial
/ˈkɔːrdʒəl/

释 *adj.* 热情友好的 politely pleasant and friendly

例 The ***cordial*** and unpretentious talk of her friendly co-workers made Amanda feel comfortable.

选 easygoing, affable, conviviality

tribute
/ˈtrɪbjuːt/

释 *n.* 赞美，致敬 something done, said, or given to show respect, gratitude, or affection

例 When George Harrison died, Ringo Starr and Paul McCartney played several Beatles songs together as a ***tribute*** to their former band mate.

选 encomium

反 denunciation

observant
/əbˈzɜːrvənt/

释 *adj.* 观察仔细的，善于观察的 paying strict attention or good at noticing what is going on around you

例 As an ***observant*** vegetarian, Willow would not use a spoon that had touched meat.

□ metaphor　　□ outstrip　　□ querulous　　□ salient　　□ culmination
□ camaraderie　　□ cordial　　□ tribute　　□ observant

collegiality
/kəˌlidʒiˈæləti/

釋 *n.* 同事关系，同僚身份 the cooperative relationship of colleagues
例 The warm *collegiality* among members of the IT department often led to several rounds of drinks at the local pub.

pensive
/ˈpensɪv/

釋 *adj.* （悲伤地）思考的，沉思的 lost in serious or sad thought
例 Luke is in a *pensive* mood and has been sitting in the corner quietly for quite some time.

penance
/ˈpenəns/

釋 *n.* 忏悔；（表示悔罪或赎罪的）自我惩罚，苦行 something that you do or are given to do in order to show that you are sad or sorry about doing something wrong
例 The judge ordered the juvenile to fulfill 100 hours of community service as *penance* for stealing a video game from Walmart.

rile
/raɪl/

釋 *v.* 使…生气 to make agitated and angry
例 His blunt speech has *riled* voters throughout the campaign and resulted in consequences that no amount of apology could make up for.
反 calm

lambaste
/læmˈbeɪst/

釋 *v.* 严厉批评 to criticize (someone or something) very harshly
例 In Schaller's contradictory introduction to the book, she alternately applauds and *lambastes* humankind's role in animal conservation.
近 denounce
反 extol

undercut
/ˌʌndərˈkʌt/

釋 *v.* 削弱 to make (something) weaker or less effective
例 Years of constant water erosion have *undercut* the foundation to the old bridge and caused it to collapse.
近 subvert, impair, undermine

harrow
/ˈhærou/

釋 *v.* 折磨，使…痛苦 to torment or vex
例 The campers were completely *harrowed* by their encounter with the large beast in the middle of the night.
反 assuage

paradigm
/ˈpærədaɪm/

釋 *n.* 典范 a model or pattern for something that may be copied
例 Upon reaching the rank of Eagle Scout, the young man was praised by his community as a *paradigm* of virtue and civic duty.
近 model

dissent
/dɪˈsent/

釋 *v.* 持不同意见 to publicly disagree with an official opinion, decision, or set of beliefs
例 Scholars and experts *dissented* so much from the decision of the committee that the award was eventually revoked.

initiate
/ɪˈnɪʃieɪt/

釋 *v.* 开始，启动 to begin
例 At the beginning of each school year, the administration office conducts a ceremony to help *initiate* the freshman class.

釋 *v.* 介绍入门知识 to teach (someone) the basic facts or ideas about something
例 The fraternity *initiated* the college student into their ranks with an elaborate hazing ritual.

☐ collegiality   ☐ pensive   ☐ penance   ☐ rile   ☐ lambaste
☐ undercut   ☐ harrow   ☐ paradigm   ☐ dissent   ☐ initiate

mutual
/ˈmjuːtʃuəl/

adj. 相互的，共同的 shared between two or more people or groups

With the ***mutual*** distrust between Democrats and Republicans, Congress was at a standstill and neither party offered to work with the other.

robust
/roʊˈbʌst/

adj. 强壮的 strong and healthy

It was no surprise to the horse trainer that the ***robust*** thoroughbred outpaced the competition and won the Kentucky Derby.

strong

adj. 稳定无误的 capable of performing without failure under a wide range of conditions

How can we be sure that Windows 10 is ***robust*** enough for a commercial launch, if we don't test its performance with a variety of different computers and processors?

betoken
/bɪˈtoʊkən/

v. 预示 to be a sign of (something)

According to the Roman augur, the flight of birds ***betokened*** the future success of King Tarquinius.

signify

conceal
/kənˈsiːl/

v. 隐藏 to hide (something or someone) from sight

John asked us to ***conceal*** ourselves in the closet before his unsuspecting wife arrived for her surprise birthday party.

veil, hide

outnumber
/ˌaʊtˈnʌmbər/

v. （数量上）超过 to be more than (someone or something) in number

Although the Persians ***outnumbered*** the Athenians at Marathon, the Greeks won a resounding victory and repelled the enemy from their shores.

itinerant
/aɪˈtɪnərənt/

adj. 巡游的 traveling from place to place especially covering a circuit

Nineteenth-century portrait painter Deborah Goldsmith lived as an ***itinerant*** artist, which was unusual for respectable women of her social class then.

peripatetic

demonize
/ˈdiːmənaɪz/

v. 妖魔化 to represent as diabolically evil

Like many antagonists of genetic engineering, Honeycutt attempted to ***demonize*** glyphosate, claiming that his son's autism symptoms were caused by it.

sober
/ˈsoʊbər/

adj. 严肃认真的 having or showing a very serious attitude or quality

After planning to buy all sorts of extravagant items, Chip was forced to make ***sober*** and rational decisions about what he could really afford.

level-headed

sobriety（n. 严肃）

incendiary /ɪnˈsendieri/	释 *adj.* 纵火的，能引起燃烧的 tending to inflame 例 Far from healing the wound, the salve was an *incendiary* agent that brought more swelling and pain. 派 incense（v. 点燃，激怒） 释 *adj.* 煽动性的，引起愤怒的 causing strong emotion or conflict 例 The *incendiary* rhetoric of the presidential candidate encouraged his supporters to attack his opponent. 释 *n.* 煽动者 a person who excites factions, quarrels, or sedition : agitator 例 To the British, Patrick Henry is an *incendiary* who incited the American Revolution, but to the Americans, he remains a national hero.
salutary /ˈsæljəteri/	释 *adj.* 有益的，有益健康的 producing a beneficial effect 例 Studies suggest that deep relaxation, if practiced regularly, can strengthen the immune system and produce many other equally *salutary* physiological changes.
replete /rɪˈpliːt/	释 *adj.* 充满的 having much or plenty of something 例 After trick or treating for four full hours, Bobby and Susie had Halloween bags *replete* with candy.
snobbish /ˈsnɑːbɪʃ/	释 *adj.* 自命不凡的 having or showing the attitude of one who thinks one is better than other people 例 We were taken aback by the *snobbish* attitude of the waiter when we asked for the cheapest bottle of wine on the menu.
seditious /sɪˈdɪʃəs/	释 *adj.* 煽动叛乱的 disposed to arouse or take part in rebellion or treason 例 John Brown hoped to spark revolution in the South with his *seditious* attack on the government arms depot at Harpers Ferry.
expatriate /ˌeksˈpeɪtriət/	释 *v.* 驱逐 to banish 例 The man was *expatriated* for speaking out against his government at a public event.
synopsis /sɪˈnɑːpsɪs/	释 *n.* 概要 a short description of the most important information about something 例 Rather than reading *The Great Gatsby* in full, the student read a short *synopsis* of the book online to help her write the book report.
affirmative /əˈfɜːrmətɪv/	释 *adj.* 积极的 positive 例 The award from the governor thanking him for his work at the soup kitchen was an *affirmative* sign that his efforts had helped many poor people in the state. 选 positive 释 *adj.* 肯定的 asserting that something is true or correct 例 When asked by the fierce Mrs. Gatsby if he had done his homework, the student gave an *affirmative* nod even though he had clearly not completed it.

emendation
/ˌiːmenˈdeɪʃn/

釋 *n.* 校订 the act or practice of emending
例 Some amount of ***emendation*** is necessary when publishing a diary to remove errors and clarify the writing.
选 revision
派 emend（v. 修订）

collective
/kəˈlektɪv/

釋 *adj.* 集体的 shared or done by a group of people
例 The ***collective*** efforts of the humanitarian team in Nicaragua resulted in new houses for the village within a few weeks.

synonymous
/sɪˈnɑːnɪməs/

釋 *adj.* 意思相同的 having the same meaning
例 The famous Jolly Roger flag became ***synonymous*** with pirates everywhere after being flown by many English buccaneers in the eighteenth century.
派 synonym（n. 同义词）

釋 *adj.* 与…意义相当的 having the same connotations, implications, or reference
例 Ever since that first ball-lowering in 1907, Times Square has become ***synonymous*** with New Year's Eve.
选 tantamount

modicum
/ˈmɑːdɪkəm/

釋 *n.* 少量 a small amount
例 Ellis frequently describes his father as being more concerned about his business and showing only a ***modicum*** of affection to his children.

retrenchment
/rɪˈtrentʃmənt/

釋 *n.* 削减（尤指经费） reduction or curtailment
例 When the business was hit by the financial crisis, the CEO had no choice but to consider a large-scale ***retrenchment*** of his staff.
选 curtailment

magnify
/ˈmæɡnɪfaɪ/

釋 *v.* 放大 to make greater
例 High speeds may increase the excitement of driving, but they also ***magnify*** its dangers and risks.

釋 *v.* 夸大 to exaggerate
例 The size of the aggressive cat was ***magnified*** with each telling of the story until it was eventually described as a ferocious lion.

obligatory
/əˈblɪɡətɔːri/

釋 *adj.* 强制的，必须的 compulsory
例 When you hear the sirens of an ambulance, it is ***obligatory*** that you pull over to the side of the road.
派 obligation（n. 义务）

commensurate
/kəˈmenʃərət/

釋 *adj.* 相等的，相似的 equal or similar to something in size, amount, or degree
例 David's salary was not ***commensurate*** with his enormous responsibilities.
选 proportionate

long-winded
/ˌlɔːŋˈwɪndɪd/

adj. 冗长无聊的 tediously long in speaking or writing

Instead of offering a concise account of the robbery, the witness gave a *long-winded* description filled with useless details.

verbose, prolix

slippery
/ˈslɪpəri/

adj. 滑的 difficult to stand on because of being smooth, wet, icy, etc.

It is a common comedic trope to place a *slippery* banana peel on the ground and make the unsuspecting pedestrian fall.

adj. 难懂的 not easy to understand or identify in an exact way

The child offered a *slippery* excuse to his parents concerning his whereabouts that morning.

elusive

adj. 不可靠的 not able to be trusted

You can avoid being tricked by the *slippery* salesman by doing proper research prior to your trip to the car dealership.

hefty
/ˈhefti/

adj. 又大又重的 large and heavy

I was unable to get a decent hold on the *hefty* television while moving, and ended up dropping it down the stairs.

forbidding
/fərˈbɪdɪŋ/

adj. 令人畏惧的，可怕的 not friendly or appealing

There were very few applicants for this job as its *forbidding* job scope was not commensurate with the pay offered.

daunting

wide-ranging
/ˌwaɪdˈreɪndʒɪŋ/

adj. 广泛的 extensive in scope

This website has *wide-ranging* sports coverage, spanning reports of the latest games to descriptive write-ups of sportsmen.

diligent
/ˈdɪlɪdʒənt/

adj. 努力的，刻苦的 characterized by steady, earnest, and energetic effort

Having personally experienced the reward of being *diligent*, NASA astronaut Ellen Ochoa encouraged college students to consistently study hard if they wished to pursue careers in science and engineering.

industrious

punctilious
/pʌŋkˈtɪliəs/

adj. 谨慎小心的 very careful about behaving properly and doing things in a correct and accurate way

Patricia is so *punctilious* that she cannot tolerate others deviating in the least from rules and conventions.

engaging
/ɪnˈɡeɪdʒɪŋ/

adj. 吸引人的 very attractive or pleasing in a way that holds your attention

Nick was utterly monotonous in his speech, unlike Colin who spoke in a captivating and *engaging* way.

winning

□ long-winded □ slippery □ hefty □ forbidding □ wide-ranging
□ diligent □ punctilious □ engaging

evanescent
/ˌevəˈnesnt/

adj. 短暂的 lasting a very short time

The painter attempted to capture the ***evanescent*** beauty of the Virginia spiderwort flower that remains in bloom for only a single day.

momentary

lasting, perpetual, durable

free-for-all
/ˈfriːfərɔːl/

n. 混战，多人为所欲为的失控场面 an uncontrolled fight or competition that involves many people

By 5 AM on Black Friday, Walmart was a ***free-for-all*** for hundreds of shoppers fighting over the hottest holiday deals.

rudimentary
/ˌruːdɪˈmentri/

adj. 基本的 basic or simple

All science majors were required to take a ***rudimentary*** chemistry class during their first term at the university.

elementary, sketchy, embryonic

bustling
/ˈbʌslɪŋ/

adj. 忙乱的，繁忙的 full of energetic and noisy activity

In the movie *Home Alone*, the McCallister family forgot about their son, Kevin, as they dashed through the ***bustling*** airport in a frenzy.

prioritize /praɪˈɔːrətaɪz/	释 *v.* 使…优先 to organize (things) so that the most important thing is done or dealt with first 例 In order to complete the tasks on the list, we need to **prioritize** the items so that the most important jobs are finished first.
envision /ɪnˈvɪʒn/	释 *v.* 想象 to think of (something that you believe might exist or happen in the future) 例 Feminist welfare research **envisions** a more equitable world in which states, markets, and families run in a fairer manner.
circumscribe /ˈsɜːrkəmskraɪb/	释 *v.* 限制 to limit the size or amount of (something) 例 Rules about search warrants exist to **circumscribe** police intrusions. 选 confine, limit
reminiscent /ˌremɪˈnɪsnt/	释 *adj.* 引起回忆的 reminding one of, or being reminded of, past events 例 The old photo of Jane's wedding day thirty years ago was **reminiscent** of her days of youth and bliss. 释 *adj.* 缅怀往事的，怀旧的 having many thoughts of the past 例 Jane grew quietly **reminiscent** when she discovered an old family photo album in the cabinet.
symmetrical /sɪˈmetrɪkl/	释 *adj.* 对称的 having sides or halves that are the same 例 Although the flower appeared **symmetrical**, it actually had an uneven number of petals. 派 asymmetrical（adj. 不对称的）
overthrow /ˌoʊvərˈθroʊ/	释 *v.* 推翻 to remove (someone or something) from power especially by force 例 During the non-violent Velvet Revolution, Czechoslovakian students and demonstrators **overthrew** the communist party and established a parliamentary republic.
juvenile /ˈdʒuːvənl/	释 *adj.* 幼稚的，不成熟的 reflecting psychological or intellectual immaturity 例 Having committed the crime when he was under 18, the burglar was a **juvenile** delinquent and received a minimal sentence.

elude
/ɪˈluːd/

释 **v.** 逃跑，逃避 to avoid or escape (someone or something) by being quick, skillful, or clever

例 Treating people with respect and dignity is the one habit that seems to *elude* people the most.

释 **v.** 使…无法理解 to fail to be understood or remembered by (someone)

例 If I do not use a grocery list, one ingredient or another would always *elude* my memory by the time I get to the grocery store.

选 puzzle

派 elusive（adj. 难懂的）

释 **v.** 使…无法得到 to fail to be achieved by (someone)

例 In winning the Man Booker Prize, novelist Kiran Desai achieved an honor that had *eluded* her mother, who had been a thrice runner-up in the past.

jettison
/ˈdʒetɪsn/

释 **v.** 拒绝，放弃 to throw overboard; to reject (something, such as a plan or idea)

例 The playwright's approach is startling as it *jettisons* conventional theatrical devices and provokes the notion of normalcy.

detriment
/ˈdetrɪmənt/

释 **n.** 损坏，破坏 something that will cause damage or injury to something or someone

例 Although the compound is abundantly present in the air, it is not a *detriment* to our health unless it becomes an underwater sediment.

选 deleterious

派 detrimental（adj. 有害的）

baroque
/bəˈroʊk/

释 **adj.** 奢华的，复杂的 characterized by grotesqueness, extravagance, complexity, or flamboyance

例 The cathedral was covered in *baroque* carvings of gremlins, devils, and stylized flora.

quixotic
/kwɪkˈsaːtɪk/

释 **adj.** 不切实际的 foolishly impractical, especially in the pursuit of ideals

例 There is nothing *quixotic* about the manager's ambition to improve employment opportunities for women at the executive level as she has a concrete plan to achieve these goals.

选 idealistic

释 **adj.** 变化多端的，变幻莫测的 capricious or unpredictable

例 It is easy to spot Snuggles amongst the brood of kitten as he is the most *quixotic* of the lot, and would come up with all sorts of unimaginable antics.

mockery
/ˈmaːkəri/

释 **n.** 嘲笑 insulting or contemptuous action or speech

例 During the eighteenth century, the colonists tarred and feathered effigies of royal officials, thus constituting an act of *mockery* of British rule.

选 derision

tactful
/ˈtæktfl/

adj. 为他人着想的，圆滑的 careful not to offend or upset other people

With the great cultural differences between the countries, the diplomat made sure to be as *tactful* as possible when visiting the house of the Indian prime minister.

trendy
/ˈtrendi/

adj. 时髦的 very fashionable

Whereas big hair was a *trendy* fashion in the 1980s, it is considered a faux pas today.

subsidize
/ˈsʌbsɪdaɪz/

v. 资助，赞助 to help someone or something pay for the costs of (something)

Unlike in the US and most other developed markets, mobile operators in India do not *subsidize* smartphones.

subsidization（n. 补助）

numinous
/ˈnuːmɪnəs/

adj. 超自然的 supernatural, mysterious

Because they believed trees and nature had *numinous* qualities, the druids revered the local flora.

occult

anomalous
/əˈnɑːmələs/

adj. 不寻常的，异常的 not expected or usual

Because these speeding particles' compositions were quite different from those of other low-energy cosmic rays, scientists dubbed them *anomalous* cosmic rays.

aberrant

anomaly（n. 反常）

mawkish
/ˈmɔːkɪʃ/

adj. 恶心做作的 sad or romantic in a foolish or exaggerated way

The sentimentality of Tom's screenplay was so extreme that it bordered on being *mawkish*.

invidious
/ɪnˈvɪdiəs/

adj. 令人反感的 unpleasant and likely to cause bad feelings in other people

It is *invidious* and unprofessional to embarrass one's co-workers in front of the boss.

austere
/ɔːˈstɪr/

adj. 朴素的，没有装饰的 simple or unadorned

Ancient Greek statues look plain and *austere* to us now, but evidence shows that they were originally painted with bright colors.

反 ornate

adj. 严肃的 having a serious and unfriendly quality

At the funeral, the congregation sat *austere* and silent while grieving the loss of their close friend.

adj. 生活简朴的 relating to or having a strict and simple way of living that avoids physical pleasure

The hermit committed to living an *austere* lifestyle and gave away all his possessions except for a single wooden cross.

abstemious

impede /ɪmˈpiːd/	*v.* 阻碍 to slow the movement, progress, or action of (someone or something) Gwen's ambitious desert hike was ***impeded*** by the heat that sapped her energy and eventually forced her to turn around early. assist impediment（n. 阻碍）
frank /fræŋk/	*adj.* 真诚的 marked by free, forthright, and sincere expression The compassionate principal sat the student down to have a ***frank*** discussion about ending his misbehavior. forthright, candor
disjunction /dɪsˈdʒʌŋkʃn/	*n.* 分离，分裂 a lack of connection between things that are related or should be connected There was a clear ***disjunction*** in the demonstration at City Hall as protestors received separate instructions and refused to cooperate.
finicky /ˈfɪnɪki/	*adj.* 挑剔的 very hard to please Sarah is very hard to please as she is such a ***finicky*** manager who demands every little detail to be perfect.
hazardous /ˈhæzərdəs/	*adj.* 危险的 involving risk or danger The catastrophe at the Three Mile Island nuclear facility resulted in the spillage of ***hazardous*** materials and the abandonment of the island.
chicanery /ʃɪˈkeɪnəri/	*n.* 欺骗，诡计 deception by artful subterfuge or sophistry Some skeptics consider the Search for Extraterrestrial Intelligence (SETI) to be wrongheaded, while others go so far as to accuse SETI scientists of outright ***chicanery***. subterfuge
verifiable /ˈverɪfaɪəbl/	*adj.* 可验证的 capable of being verified With the rise of the internet, any fact cited, such as celebrity trivia, is immediately ***verifiable*** within seconds. testable
demonstrable /ˈdemənstrəbl/	*adj.* 可证明的 able to be proven or shown When the astronauts returned to Earth with rocks from the Moon, they had ***demonstrable*** proof that it was not made from cheese. *adj.* 明显的 apparent, evident There was ***demonstrable*** wear and tear on the bike, despite the vendor's claims that it was brand new.
pertinacious /ˌpɜːrtnˈeɪʃəs/	*adj.* 坚持的，固执的 holding tenaciously to a purpose, belief, opinion, or course of action Michael Jordan's ***pertinacious*** desire to excel was evident in his competitive behavior in both sports and life.

scarce
/skers/

［释］ *adj.* 缺乏的 not plentiful or abundant
［例］ With the current drought in California, water is **scarce** and must be conserved as much as possible.
［选］ deficient
［派］ scarcity（n. 不足，缺乏）

lavish
/'lævɪʃ/

［释］ *adj.* 奢华的 having a very rich and expensive quality
［例］ The mansions in Newport, RI are **lavish** testaments to the wealth and power of the oligarchs of the Gilded Age.
［选］ sumptuous

［释］ *adj.* 大量使用的，浪费的 giving or using a large amount of something
［例］ My estranged cousin left me a **lavish** sum of money in his will that allowed me to quit my job and travel the world.

［释］ *v.* 挥霍，浪费 to expend or bestow with profusion
［例］ The low-rung employee always **lavished** praise on his boss with the hopes that it would help him rise through the ranks.

sanguine
/'sæŋgwɪn/

［释］ *adj.* 乐观的 confident and hopeful
［例］ The report was **sanguine** about the future of the ailing economy, and predicted that conditions would improve within months.
［选］ optimistic

waver
/'weɪvər/

［释］ *v.* 摇摆不定 to become unsteady because of weakness, emotion, tiredness, etc.
［例］ It is bewildering why Martha's kindness never **wavered** despite Chip's coldness toward her.
［选］ oscillate
［反］ steady
［派］ unwavering（adj. 坚定的）

engender
/ɪn'dʒendər/

［释］ *v.* 产生 to cause to exist or to develop
［例］ Low levels of taxation and inflation coupled with economic growth **engendered** a society with high amounts of disposable income.
［选］ yield, inaugurate, induce
［反］ eradicate

elusive
/i'luːsɪv/

［释］ *adj.* 难懂的 hard to understand, define, or remember
［例］ Despite hours of careful reading, the author's highly convoluted argument remains **elusive** and obscure to me.
［选］ cryptic

［释］ *adj.* 难以捕捉的 hard to find or capture
［例］ Many subatomic nuclear particles are **elusive** and nearly imperceptible: they are hard to track as well as to detect.
［选］ evasive, slippery

□ scarce □ lavish □ sanguine □ waver □ engender □ elusive

ponder /ˈpɑːndər/	🔲 **v.** 沉思，仔细思考 to think about or consider (something) carefully 🔲 Sir Isaac Newton discovered gravity when he was **pondering** the cause of an apple's fall from a tree. 🔲 contemplate
proliferate /prəˈlɪfəreɪt/	🔲 **v.** 快速增长 to increase in number or amount quickly 🔲 University courses in postcolonial studies **proliferated** in the late twentieth century in response to new studies being conducted on colonial languages and identities. 🔲 abound
paucity /ˈpɔːsəti/	🔲 **n.** 少量 a small amount of something 🔲 The **paucity** of impact craters on Venus suggests that erosion may have smoothed the planet's surface over the past billion years. 🔲 vacuousness, dearth
univocal /juˈnɪvoʊkl/	🔲 **adj.** （意思）唯一的 having one meaning only 🔲 Because the terms "mechanism" and "vitalism" had various meanings in nineteenth-century biological thought, they should not be mistakenly regarded as **univocal** terms. 🔲 **adj.** 明确的，不模糊的 unambiguous 🔲 In the first US election, George Washington was the **univocal** victor as he had received all the elector college votes.
dejected /dɪˈdʒektɪd/	🔲 **adj.** 沮丧的 sad because of failure, loss, etc. 🔲 After the Eagles lost the Super Bowl, Philadelphians were collectively **dejected** by their city's championship drought.
surplus /ˈsɜːrpləs/	🔲 **n.** 多余，过量 an amount (such as an amount of money) that is more than the amount that is needed 🔲 Having a **surplus** of cheap labor is becoming less of a lure to manufacturers given the rise and improvement of technology and machines.
impertinent /ɪmˈpɜːrtnənt/	🔲 **adj.** 粗鲁的 rude and showing a lack of respect 🔲 The **impertinent** child spoke back aggressively to his parents in the departmental store, much to the astonishment of on-lookers. 🔲 presumptuous 🔲 **adj.** 不相关的 not pertinent 🔲 The judge was frustrated by the defendant's **Impertinent** responses to the lawyer's questions, and eventually held him in contempt of court for such deliberately elusive behavior.
one-of-a-kind /wʌnˈəvəˈkaɪnd/	🔲 **n.** 独一无二 a person or thing that is not like any other person or thing 🔲 The Parthenon marbles are **one-of-a-kind** in Classical art that are the pride of the British Museum.

apropos
/ˌæprə'poʊ/

adj. 合适的 being both relevant and opportune

It was *apropos* that it was *Shark Week* on television at the same time that we were studying the creature in our biology course.

prep. 至于… with regard to

Because nothing that Vinnie said was *apropos* to the conversation, we treated him like an annoyance and ignored him.

ingratiate
/ɪn'ɡreɪʃieɪt/

v. 讨好 to gain favor or approval for (yourself) by doing or saying things that people like

The expert saleswoman knew how to *ingratiate* the buyers and convince them of buying products they did not truly need.

concoct
/kən'kɑːkt/

v. 编造，捏造 to invent or develop (a plan, story, etc.) often in order to trick or deceive someone

The CEO *concocts* these extreme ideas to business partners without a single clue of the actual practicalities involved in executing them.

disgorge
/dɪs'ɡɔːrdʒ/

v. 吐 to empty whatever is in the stomach through the mouth

By *disgorging* partially digested food into the chick's mouth, the mother sparrow ensures the survival of her brood for another day.

v. 喷吐，吐露 to discharge the contents of

In a video recording of the most recent eruption, Mount St. Helens was seen *disgorging* lava and ash high into the sky for a prolonged period of time.

baseless
/'beɪsləs/

adj. 毫无根据的 groundless or unwarranted

She responded to the new lawsuit by debunking it a total fiction and a *baseless* attack on her prestige.

momentary
/'moʊmənteri/

adj. 短暂的 lasting a very short time

Luanne's sense of victory upon completing the essay assignment was only *momentary* because she had to start on the second one immediately.

evanescent, fleeting

acute
/ə'kjuːt/

adj. 严重的，关键的 of critical importance or consequence

Greece defaulted on many of its loans when the economic crisis was at its most *acute*.

adj. 敏锐的 keenly perceptive or discerning; penetrating

Psychics cannot tell the future, but they have an *acute* intuition about what their clients are thinking and feeling.

incisive

acuity（n. 敏锐）

adj. 剧烈的，强烈的 extremely sharp or severe; intense

Jack experienced a sudden, *acute* pain when the tennis ball hit him hard on his forehead.

severe

☐ apropos ☐ ingratiate ☐ concoct ☐ disgorge ☐ baseless
☐ momentary ☐ acute

debilitate /dɪˈbɪlɪteɪt/	释 *v.* 使…衰弱，使…虚弱 to impair the strength of 例 During the siege of Leningrad, famine swept through villages and *debilitated* entire populations.
resent /rɪˈzent/	释 *v.* 憎恨，生气 to be angry or upset about (someone or something that you think is unfair) 例 In Dorothy West's novel *The Living is Easy*, the main character *resents* her father's authority over her independence. 派 resentful（adj. 充满愤恨的）
delightful /dɪˈlaɪtfl/	释 *adj.*（形容事物）令人愉悦的，令人高兴的 highly pleasing 例 Readers who find rare words *delightful* cannot help but love the novel *The Maytrees*.
decisive /dɪˈsaɪsɪv/	释 *adj.* 果决的，坚定的 resolute or determined 例 The senator was highly respected as a *decisive* and impartial figure of authority. 释 *adj.* 决定性的 determining what the result of something will be 例 The fate of the team was sealed after the manager made the *decisive* step of withdrawing them from the competition. 释 *adj.* 明显的 very clear and obvious 例 By defeating Bayern Munich by ten goals, Real Madrid made a *decisive* statement on its status as the best team in the world. 近 unmistakable
testimony /ˈtestɪmoʊni/	释 *n.* 证词，证据 proof or evidence that something exists or is true 例 The security camera footage provided the most damning *testimony* of the crime.
nominal /ˈnɑːmɪnl/	释 *adj.* 名义上的 existing as something in name only 例 Car buyers should ignore the *nominal* price of a car, since dealers will always give a discount. 释 *adj.* 微不足道的 very small in amount 例 Despite having to drive three hours for the work conference, I was only reimbursed a *nominal* amount for gas.
simultaneous /ˌsaɪmlˈteɪniəs/	释 *adj.* 同时的 happening at the same time 例 The panel on Biotechnology is *simultaneous* with another on Cryptography, so you will have to choose which you prefer to go to.
monotonous /məˈnɑːtənəs/	释 *adj.* 单调的 tediously uniform or unvarying 例 The candidate responded to the *monotonous* campaign by making jokes and trying to entertain her staffers. 近 repetitive
divination /ˌdɪvɪˈneɪʃn/	释 *n.* 预言，占卜 a prediction uttered under divine inspiration 例 Croesus misinterpreted the oracle at Delphi's *divination*, and attacked the Persians thinking he would win.

□ debilitate   □ resent   □ delightful   □ decisive   □ testimony
□ nominal   □ simultaneous   □ monotonous   □ divination

virtuosity /ˌvɜːrtʃuˈɑːsəti/	*n.* 精湛的技艺 great ability or skill shown by a musician, performer, etc. 例 By the age of 12, the young pianist had the **virtuosity** to play Chopin perfectly.
manifest /ˈmænɪfest/	*adj.* 显然的，明显的 easy to understand or recognize 例 At the Battle of Milvian Bridge, a burning cross was made **manifest** in the sky and the Emperor Constantine immediately converted to Christianity following his victory. 近 obvious, self-evident
	v. 清晰地展示，显露出 to show (something) clearly 例 Brianna's vague answers **manifested** her lack of knowledge about the project. 近 reveal 派 manifestation（n. 显然）
purview /ˈpɜːrvjuː/	*n.* 视野，范围，权限 an area within which someone or something has authority, influence, or knowledge 例 The new ban on gum chewing only applies to the **purview** of this school and is invalid outside its grounds.
annex /əˈneks/	*v.* 附加 to add to something earlier, larger, or more important 例 After **annexing** the shed to our home, we added insulation and electricity to turn it into a livable bedroom.
	v. 吞并 to incorporate (a country or other territory) within the domain of a state 例 The territory of Alaska was **annexed** to the USA following its purchase from Russia in 1867.
shriek /ʃriːk/	*v.* 叫喊，尖叫 to make a loud, high-pitched cry 例 Janice **shrieked** when the mouse ran over her feet unabashedly. 近 caterwaul
ephemeral /ɪˈfemərəl/	*adj.* 短暂的 lasting for a markedly brief time 例 Any problems in their friendship are **ephemeral** and unlikely to leave a dent on their long-lasting relationship. 近 short-lived, transitory 反 enduring 派 ephemeron（n. 生命极短暂之物）
erudite /ˈerudaɪt/	*adj.* 博学的 having or showing knowledge that is learned by studying 例 Because Russell was such a good public speaker, many people assumed he was an **erudite** scholar without bothering to check up on his credentials. 近 learned 反 unlettered

□ virtuosity　　□ manifest　　□ purview　　□ annex　　□ shriek
□ ephemeral　　□ erudite

plague /pleɪɡ/	**v.** 困扰 to cause worry or distress to

plague
/pleɪɡ/

v. 困扰 to cause worry or distress to
Despite his brilliant career, Gerald was **plagued** by doubts and could not dispel his feeling of inferiority.

n. 瘟疫，灾害 a disease that causes death and that spreads quickly to a large number of people
Scientists now know that the deadly Black Death **plague** can be cured with simple antibiotics.

counterintuitive
/ˌkaʊntərɪnˈtuːɪtɪv/

adj. 违反常理的，与直觉相反的 not agreeing with what seems right or natural
Although it may seem **counterintuitive** to conduct strength training while injured, experts say it's the best way to heal.

intriguing
/ɪnˈtriːɡɪŋ/

adj. 非常有趣的 extremely interesting
It's **intriguing** to scholars that this whole line of research is so full of paradoxes.
fascinating

magnanimous
/mæɡˈnænɪməs/

adj. 大度的，慷慨的 having or showing a generous and kind nature
It is difficult to reconcile the publicly **magnanimous** side of the congresswoman with her private pettiness.
generous, benevolent

untether
/ʌnˈteðər/

v. 释放，脱离 to free from or as if from a tether
Colin **untethered** the horse and let it go free into the wild highlands.
divorce

formulaic
/ˌfɔːrmjuˈleɪɪk/

adj. 刻板的，俗套的 containing or made from ideas or expressions that have been used many times before and are therefore not very new or interesting
The movie was criticized for employing stock characterizations that perpetuated **formulaic** depictions of stereotypes.
canned

gambit
/ˈɡæmbɪt/

n. 计谋，策略 a calculated move
Realizing that he was behind by just 1% in the polls, the incumbent Senator made a final **gambit** by attacking his opponent's credibility in a series of television ads.

vivacious
/vɪˈveɪʃəs/

adj. 活力四射的 happy and lively in a way that is attractive
In this film, the dull rhetoric and plodding behavior of the hero make him a splendid foil to the witty and **vivacious** heroine.
phlegmatic
vivacity（n. 活力）

stratify
/ˈstrætɪfaɪ/

v. 分层级 to divide or arrange into classes, castes, or social strata
Many cities in this country were **stratified** into economic bands following the war, which resulted in a long-term segregation of the different populations.
hierarchical
stratification（n. 分层）

☐ plague ☐ counterintuitive ☐ intriguing ☐ magnanimous ☐ untether
☐ formulaic ☐ gambit ☐ vivacious ☐ stratify

exceptional
/ɪk'sepʃənl/

- *adj.* 不寻常的 not usual
- AC/DC's surprise performance at Bonnaroo Festival capped the *exceptional* weekend of music and fun.
- 选 preternatural

- *adj.* 杰出的，超常的 better than average
- The valedictorian was an *exceptional* student with a record high GPA and a passion to serve the community.

slump
/slʌmp/

- *v.* 急速下跌 to decrease suddenly and by a large amount
- During the recent drought in California, housing prices *slumped* in certain parts of the state.

pessimistic
/ˌpesɪ'mɪstɪk/

- *adj.* 悲观的 having or showing a lack of hope for the future
- Even the team's most *pessimistic* moments prior to the biopsy didn't envisage a disease so aggressive.

dilute
/daɪ'luːt/

- *v.* 削弱，减轻 to lessen the strength of (something)
- The board proposed that Shah *dilute* the political message in his film so as to make it acceptable to a larger audience.

- *v.* 稀释 to make thinner or less strong by adding water or another liquid
- The instructions on the bottle were clear: the medicine needed to be *diluted* in water before consumption.

palatable
/'pælətəbl/

- *adj.* 美味的 having a pleasant or agreeable taste
- Jim did not find sushi *palatable* because he hated the taste of fish, both cooked and raw.
- 选 appetizing

- *adj.* 称心如意的，可接受的 pleasant or acceptable to someone
- A good physician tries to prepare patients psychologically for news that might not be immediately *palatable*.

stagnate
/'stægneɪt/

- *v.* 停滞 to stop developing, progressing, moving, etc.
- Wage growth has *stagnated* since the 1990s for workers of all education levels.
- 派 stagnant（adj. 停滞的）

esoteric
/ˌesə'terɪk/

- *adj.* 难懂的 difficult to understand
- Johnson's writing is considered *esoteric* and arcane because it is filled with obscure references and baffling digressions.
- 选 arcane, recondite, abstruse

befuddle
/bɪ'fʌdl/

- *v.* 使…困惑 to confuse
- Sherlock solves mysteries that *befuddle* the detectives of Scotland Yard, while Watson writes about their adventures in *The Strand*.
- 选 perplex

deliberate
/dɪˈlɪbərət/

v. 深思熟虑 to think about or discuss something very carefully in order to make a decision

Writing letters by hand requires the author to *deliberate* over his words more carefully than firing off an angry e-mail would.

calculation

adj. 故意的 done or said in a way that is planned or intended

Despite appearing to speak off the top of his head, Prof. Kim actually plans all his lectures in a very thorough and *deliberate* manner.

antithesis
/ænˈtɪθəsɪs/

n. 相反，对立 the exact opposite of something or someone

Scientific discoveries frequently defy common sense, but this does not entail that one is the *antithesis* of the other.

antithetical (adj. 对立的)

valediction
/ˌvælɪˈdɪkʃn/

n. 告别 an act of bidding farewell

While *valedictions* were logical and necessary in the age of handwritten letters, the sheer volume of modern e-mails makes formal signoffs unnecessary.

valedictory (adj. 告别的)

hamstring
/ˈhæmstrɪŋ/

v. 损坏 to damage or ruin the force or effectiveness of (something or someone)

The drone industry largely sees itself as *hamstrung* by an overreaching Federal Aviation Administration.

impair

complacent
/kəmˈpleɪsnt/

adj. 自我感觉良好的，自满的 marked by self-satisfaction especially when accompanied by unawareness of actual dangers or deficiencies

Although Lamar was 40 years old, unmarried, unemployed, and living with his mom, he felt *complacent* about his life.

hinder
/ˈhɪndər/

v. 阻碍 to make (something, such as a task or action) slow or difficult

Even overt deficiencies in the author's work have not *hindered* its respectful reception by most modern critics.

inhibit, block

formidable
/ˈfɔːrmɪdəbl/

adj. 可怕的 causing fear, dread or apprehension

The difficulties we will encounter in the year ahead may be even more challenging and *formidable* than those of last year.

daunting

adj. 令人惊叹的，令人敬畏的 tending to inspire awe or wonder

Volkswagen has long been a symbol of the efficiency and engineering skills that made Germany one of the most *formidable* economies in the world.

adj. 艰巨的，难对付的 very difficult to deal with

The giant Goliath was a *formidable* opponent, but David managed to slay him with a single slingshot.

☐ deliberate ☐ antithesis ☐ valediction ☐ hamstring ☐ complacent
☐ hinder ☐ formidable

impenetrable
/ɪmˈpenɪtrəbl/

adj. 难懂的 impossible to understand

Because postmodernist critics often rely on difficult language, their prose frequently seems ***impenetrable*** to non-specialists.

adj. 无法穿透的，无法进入的 incapable of being penetrated or pierced

Fort Knox is an ***impenetrable*** fortress that houses the remaining US federal gold.

obtrude
/əbˈtruːd/

v. 强迫，强加于 to force or impose (as oneself or one's ideas) without warrant or request

I never should have been so rude as to ***obtrude*** my opinions upon other people.

v. 闯入（流行的说法是乱入）to become involved with something or to become noticeable in an unpleasant or annoying way

I hate to speak ill of Tom but will be forced to do so if he continues to ***obtrude*** into this discussion.

debunk
/ˌdiːˈbʌŋk/

v. 拆穿，揭露…的错误 to show that something (such as a belief or theory) is not true

A few years ago, popular TV shows started ***debunking*** famous myths, such as the belief in the yeti.

umbrage
/ˈʌmbrɪdʒ/

n. 生气，不悦 a feeling of being offended by what someone has said or done

Some of the most popular musicians working today have taken ***umbrage*** with Spotify's insistence on an equal, free subscription tier.

affinity
/əˈfɪnəti/

n. 倾向，偏好 a liking for or an attraction to something

I have a natural ***affinity*** for the coast as I grew up on the island-city, Singapore.

n. 密切联系 likeness based on relationship or causal connection

Affinities between the intricate design of high gothic architecture and the polyphonic art of Bach do exist.

ramification
/ˌræmɪfɪˈkeɪʃn/

n. 结果，后果 something that is the result of something else

Gender inequality is a pressing human issue that also has huge ***ramifications*** for jobs, productivity, and GDP growth.

n. 分支 branch

Humans represent only a single ***ramification*** of the primate family tree.

immerse
/ɪˈmɜːrs/

v. 浸润，浸泡 to put (something) in a liquid so that all parts are completely covered

The weather was so warm that he could not wait to ***immerse*** himself into the ice cold pool.

v. 全心沉浸在…中 to make (yourself) fully involved in some activity or interest

The concept of virtual reality, a technology that ***immerses*** people in an artificial world, has been around for years but has never taken off.

☐ impenetrable   ☐ obtrude   ☐ debunk   ☐ umbrage   ☐ affinity
☐ ramification   ☐ immerse

demise
/dɪˈmaɪz/

释 *n.* 死亡，灭亡 death
例 The cause of Mozart's *demise* is a long-standing medical enigma: over the years, physicians have suggested more than 100 possibilities, including poisoning, malnutrition, kidney disease, and heart failure.

释 *v.* 让位 to transmit by succession or inheritance
例 Upon the death of Queen, the throne will *demise* to her daughter, who will become the second Queen of this country.

compassionate
/kəmˈpæʃənət/

释 *adj.* 同情的 feeling or showing concern for someone who is sick, hurt, poor, etc.
例 As a *compassionate* nun, Mother Theresa devoted her life to helping poor people throughout the world.
近 warmhearted
反 indifferent

音频

---

ignorant
/ˈɪɡnərənt/

▶ *adj.* 无知的 destitute of knowledge or education
▶ Some clients talk about sports so much that it pays to read up on it frequently and not remain *ignorant* about the field.
▶ unfamiliarity

▶ *adj.* 不知情的，无意识的 unaware or uninformed
▶ The police officer let him off with a warning as he had just arrived in the country and was *ignorant* of the precise traffic rules in this area.

---

immortal
/ɪˈmɔːrtl/

▶ *adj.* 不朽的，永存的 marked by the quality or state of someone or something that will never die or be forgotten
▶ Apocalypse is the *immortal* character in the movie *X-Men* who had been asleep for a few thousand years.
▶ immortality（n. 不朽）

---

assuage
/əˈsweɪdʒ/

▶ *v.* 安抚，缓和 to make (something, such as an unpleasant feeling) less painful, severe, etc.
▶ Selling homemade potholders on Etsy will not *assuage* Jeff's economic problems.
▶ intensify

---

expiation
/ˌekspiˈeɪʃn/

▶ *n.* 赎罪 the act of making atonement
▶ Some people will no doubt insist that Tokyo hasn't done enough in its *expiation* of war memories.
▶ expiate（v. 赎罪）

---

loquacious
/ləˈkweɪʃəs/

▶ *adj.* 话多的 liking to talk and talking smoothly and easily
▶ Dan is a *loquacious* boy whose verbal charm is quite simply unsurpassed.
▶ garrulous
▶ taciturn
▶ loquacity（n. 啰嗦）

---

marginal
/ˈmɑːrdʒɪnl/

▶ *adj.* 边缘的，不重要的 not very important
▶ An effective member of a debating team must focus clearly on the principal issue and avoid *marginal* argument.
▶ peripheral, fringe

☐ ignorant ☐ immortal ☐ assuage ☐ expiation ☐ loquacious
☐ marginal

adjuration /ˌædʒʊˈreɪʃən/	**n.** 恳求 an earnest, solemn appeal
	The lawyer made an **adjuration** for his client to accept the plea from the prosecutors as it would be in his best interests to do so.
dreary /ˈdrɪri/	**adj.** 令人悲伤的 causing unhappiness or sad feelings
	Although the weather was particularly **dreary**, we stood outside all day at the race track.
callous /ˈkæləs/	**adj.** 冷漠的 not feeling or showing any concern about the problems or suffering of other people
	The miser was uncompassionate to the end and showed a **callous** disregard for the poor and homeless.
	heartless
discount /ˈdɪskaʊnt/	**v.** 低估，轻视 to minimize the importance of
	It was no surprise that Jim became sunburned after **discounting** the importance of sunscreen when he traveled to Australia.
	undervalue
ostentatious /ˌɑːstenˈteɪʃəs/	**adj.** 炫耀的 marked by or fond of conspicuous or vainglorious and sometimes pretentious display
	Christina is a very **ostentatious** celebrity who wears luxurious dresses covered with gold and diamonds.
	反 modest
thwart /θwɔːrt/	**v.** 破坏，阻止 to prevent (someone) from doing something or to stop (something) from happening
	Youku is taking steps to **thwart** users who fake their location in order to get access to shows and movies.
	frustrate
distress /dɪˈstres/	**v.** 使…紧张，使…忧虑，使…不适 to worry or upset (someone)
	The university launched a campaign aimed at increasing awareness of mental health and supporting students who are **distressed**.
raillery /ˈreɪləri/	**n.** 打趣 friendly joking about or with somebody
	We may enjoy the occasional **raillery** and pranks in the office, but are absolutely serious when dealing with clients.
	banter
exasperate /ɪgˈzæspəreɪt/	**v.** 使…生气 to make (someone) very angry or annoyed
	The tedious application process **exasperated** the student, who had to spend long hours filling out a 30-page form.
	irascibility
feckless /ˈfekləs/	**adj.** 虚弱的，无能的 weak or ineffective
	Gwen was wrong to suggest that Carson was a **feckless** supervisor just because he had made a mistake in his proposal recently.
	adj. 粗心的，不负责任的 careless and irresponsible
	If animal parents were judged by human standards, the cuckoo would be one of nature's more **feckless** creatures as it lays her eggs in others' nests and leaves the nurturing to them.

stigma
/ˈstɪɡmə/

n. 污点 a set of negative and often unfair beliefs that a society or group of people have about something

Linda was determined to undermine the **stigma** that her male colleagues had of female executives.

stigmatize（v. 玷污，抹黑）

attenuate
/əˈtenjueɪt/

v. 使减弱 to make (something) weaker or less in amount, effect, or force

Chomsky's belief that speech is not an evolutionary adaptation has been **attenuated** over time.

adj. 变弱的 reduced especially in thickness, density, or force

The path became overgrown and **attenuate** after authorities closed off pedestrian access to it.

enigmatic
/ˌenɪɡˈmætɪk/

adj. 难懂的 full of mystery and difficult to understand

The artist Eugene Delacroix remains an **enigma** shrouded in mystery.

perplexing, puzzle, riddle, conundrum

unambiguous

condemn
/kənˈdem/

v. 谴责 to say in a strong and definite way that someone or something is bad or wrong

Because all members of this organization are idealists, they **condemn** the idea of compromising their core beliefs.

impugn
/ɪmˈpjuːn/

v. （因人不诚实而）批评，抨击 to criticize (a person's character, intentions, etc.) by suggesting that someone is not honest and should not to be trusted

The mayoral candidate was quick to issue counterattacks when his integrity was **impugned** by unknown sources.

champion

elaborate
/ɪˈlæbərət/

adj. 精心制作的，精细的 planned or carried out with great care

As a party planner, Nora was accustomed to organizing **elaborate** weddings with no expense spared for hundreds of guests.

v. 详细阐述 to expand something in detail

The police chief declined to **elaborate** on the decision to fire the misbehaving officer or to release the officer's name.

simplify

pejorative
/pɪˈdʒɔːrətɪv/

adj. （话语）轻蔑的 having negative connotations, tending to disparage or belittle

People who use the word "meritocracy" as a positive description are probably unaware of its original satirical and **pejorative** connotations.

□ stigma   □ attenuate   □ enigmatic   □ condemn   □ impugn
□ elaborate   □ pejorative

blithe
/blaɪð/

[词] *adj.* 无忧无虑的，轻松的 of a happy lighthearted character or disposition

[例] Emma has a very *blithe* attitude when she is traveling as she is freed from her troubles at work and home.

[反] grave

[词] *adj.* 轻率的 lacking due thought or consideration

[例] Little did Kyle know that the *blithe* decision he made to act in the local play would result in hundreds of hours spent on tiring rehearsals.

refute
/rɪˈfjuːt/

[词] *v.* 驳倒，否认 to prove that (something) is not true

[例] This paper was so controversial as it *refuted* all prior theories on the genotypic evolution of the gorilla species.

[派] irrefutable[adj. 无可辩驳的（与conclusive考同义词）]

vacuous
/ˈvækjuəs/

[词] *adj.* 空的，空洞的 emptied of or lacking content

[例] The house looked barren and *vacuous* after all the furniture and carpeting were removed.

[反] plentiful

[派] vacuity（n. 空白，空虚）

[词] *adj.* 愚蠢的 marked by lack of ideas or intelligence

[例] Despite their *vacuous* expressions, pigs are rather intelligent creatures capable of thought and emotion.

enervate
/ˈenərveɪt/

[词] *v.* 使…衰弱 to make (someone or something) very weak or tired

[例] Long hours and the constant stress *enervated* David, who in the end, had no choice but to resign from his work and take a long vacation.

[近] debilitate

[反] strengthen

[词] *adj.* 虚弱的 lacking physical, mental, or moral vigor

[例] His current frail and *enervate* frame is a far cry from what it used to be in his days as a top sportsman.

honorific
/ˌɑːnəˈrɪfɪk/

[词] *adj.* 尊敬的 giving or expressing honor or respect

[例] An *honorific* doctorate does not require the recipient to write a dissertation; he or she is simply recognized for his or her achievements.

disprove
/ˌdɪsˈpruːv/

[词] *v.* 驳斥 to show that (something) is false or wrong

[例] Galileo *disproved* the idea that the Sun revolves around the Earth.

[派] disproof（n. 反驳）

extinguish
/ɪkˈstɪŋgwɪʃ/

[词] *v.* 熄灭 to cause (something) to stop burning

[例] Firefighters were able to *extinguish* the flames in less than 15 minutes.

[近] douse

[反] ignite

[词] *v.* 使…灭绝 to cause the end or death of (something)

[例] Widespread use of the pesticide DDT *extinguished* America's peregrine falcon everywhere but the East Coast.

□ blithe □ refute □ vacuous □ enervate □ honorific
□ disprove □ extinguish

excoriate /ˌeksˈkɔːrieɪt/	释 **v.** 强烈斥责，严厉指责 to censure scathingly 例 The old staff **excoriated** their new CEO for creating confusing and inconvenient new policies. 近 crab, indict
immutable /ɪˈmjuːtəbl/ ▢▢▢▢▢▢	释 **adj.** 不变的 not subject or susceptible to change 例 An animal's instinctive responses need not be **immutable** as they sometimes adjust over time due to natural selection. 近 determinate 派 mutate（v. 变异，变化）
hypercritical /ˌhaɪpərˈkrɪtɪkl/ ▢	释 **adj.** 吹毛求疵的 criticizing other people or things too strongly or too often 例 The athletes in this league had to adopt relaxation techniques as it had a **hypercritical** and stressful culture.
momentous /moʊˈmentəs/ ▢▢▢▢	释 **adj.** 重要的 very important 例 Serkin said that this **momentous** performance took him 50 years to prepare. 反 trivial
esteem /ɪˈstiːm/ ▢▢▢	释 **n.** 尊敬 respect and affection 例 The cash prize that accompanies a Nobel Prize is only secondary to the international **esteem** that the winner receives.
traumatic /traʊˈmætɪk/ ▢▢▢▢▢▢	释 **adj.** 心灵受创伤的 emotionally upset 例 Experiencing **traumatic** incidents during childhood is associated with an increased risk of psychopathology and violent criminality.
secretive /ˈsiːkrətɪv/ ▢▢ ▢▢	释 **adj.** 鬼鬼祟祟的，秘密的 not letting people see or know what you are doing or thinking 例 Many people are skeptical of Area 51's **secretive** function and claim that it is a cover for the existence of aliens. 近 furtive
delegate /ˈdelɪɡət/ ▢▢▢▢▢ ▢▢▢▢▢	释 **n.** 代表 a person who is chosen or elected to vote or act for others 例 The candidate received the Democratic Party nomination after the majority of the state **delegates** voted for her. 释 **v.** 委托 to give (control, responsibility, authority, etc.) to someone 例 The housewife **delegated** individual house chores to each member of the family so that she could get a break.
abeyance /əˈbeɪəns/ ▢▢▢▢▢▢▢▢	释 **n.** 中止，暂停 temporary inactivity 例 Until it is shown that the service is legal, the launch of the service shall be put in **abeyance**. 反 fulfillment

▢ excoriate ▢ immutable ▢ hypercritical ▢ momentous ▢ esteem
▢ traumatic ▢ secretive ▢ delegate ▢ abeyance

blatant
/ˈbleɪtnt/

　adj. 吵吵闹闹的 noisy especially in a vulgar or offensive manner
　The sound of the trombone may seem ***blatant*** and rough to some, but it is highly melodious and expressive to me.

　adj. 明目张胆的 completely obvious, conspicuous, or obtrusive especially in a crass or offensive manner
　Buddy's ***blatant*** disregard for the speed limit incurred a hefty fine and a suspension of his license for six months.
　conspicuous

flamboyant
/flæmˈbɔɪənt/

　adj. 引人注意的，酷炫的 having a very noticeable quality that attracts a lot of attention
　Art historian Kate Duncan lavishly praised the contemporary beadwork of Native American people in the high-plateau region for their outstanding and ***flamboyant*** forms.
　showy

lucid
/ˈluːsɪd/

　adj. 清晰的 very clear and easy to understand
　In stark contrast to the vague and often rambling comments of other students, Jessica's remarks were refreshingly ***lucid***.
　clarity
　vague, murky

opaque
/oʊˈpeɪk/

　adj. 难懂的 difficult to understand or explain
　That critic's writing is so obscure and dense that all the students found it too ***opaque*** to comprehend.
　inaccessible
　transparent, understandable

　adj. 不透明的 not letting light through
　Breweries know that colored glass is best for beer because the ***opaque*** bottles allow less light to reach the liquid, which could potentially spoil the product.

alarmism
/əˈlɑːrmɪzəm/

　n. （毫无根据的）担忧，危言耸听 the often unwarranted exciting of fears or warning of danger
　The ***alarmism*** around the potential of artificial intelligence to exceed general human intelligence strikes me as premature.
　alarm[v. 使惊恐（和unsettle考同义词）]

divisive
/dɪˈvaɪsɪv/

　adj. 引起争议的，引起分裂的 causing a lot of disagreement between people and causing them to separate into different groups
　This bill incited such vigorous debate and partisanship that it was dubbed the most ***divisive*** bill in history.
　controversial
　unifying

torpor
/ˈtɔːrpər/

　n. 麻木，迟钝，懒散 a state of not being active and having very little energy
　As Billy had only slept for three hours, his ***torpor*** was visible at the stand-up comedy performance and resulted in him being booed off stage.
　exciting, celerity

indolent /ˈɪndələnt/	释 *adj.* 懒惰的 not liking to work or be active 例 Parents always struggle with ***indolent*** teenagers sleeping for 12 hours every day and feeling extreme fatigue after 2 hours of work.
compulsory /kəmˈpʌlsəri/	释 *adj.* 强制的 having the power of forcing someone to do something 例 It is ***compulsory*** for anyone who wishes to drive to pass the driver's exam.
revelation /ˌrevəˈleɪʃn/	释 *n.* 揭露 an act of revealing to view or making known 例 The meal at El Bulli was such a ***revelation*** to the chef that he immediately incorporated molecular gastronomy to his repertoire of cooking techniques.
contingency /kənˈtɪndʒənsi/	释 *n.* 可能事件 something (such as an emergency) that might happen 例 Both business parties wanted to make sure they were prepared for all possible ***contingencies***, so they had their best lawyers work on a detailed contract.
prolific /prəˈlɪfɪk/	释 *adj.* 多产的 producing a large amount of something 例 Gwendolyn Brooks was a ***prolific*** writer who wrote more than twenty books of poetry as well as numerous essays and reviews.
alacrity /əˈlækrəti/	释 *n.* 欣然同意 a quick and cheerful readiness to do something 例 When Beth received an acceptance letter from Harvard University, she immediately accepted it with ***alacrity***. 反 reluctance, hesitance
transcend /trænˈsend/	释 *v.* 超越 to rise above or go beyond the limits of 例 Data privacy is a concern that ***transcends*** national borders. 释 *v.* 胜出，超出 to outstrip or outdo in some attribute, quality, or power 例 The beauty of Yeats' poetry seemed to ***transcend*** the limits of the English language. 派 transcendent（adj. 超凡的，卓越的） 释 *v.* 克服，战胜 to triumph over the negative or restrictive aspects of 例 The famous photo of the young Afghan Girl ***transcended*** the impersonal reporting of the war and added a human element to the coverage of the conflict. 近 overcome
resonate /ˈrezəneɪt/	释 *v.* 回响 to produce or exhibit resonance 例 The tuning fork always ***resonates*** at a specific pitch upon being struck. 释 *v.* 引起共鸣 to evoke a feeling of shared emotion or belief 例 His patriotic message not only ***resonated*** in the towns of rural America but also far beyond the country's shores. 近 ring true
uncharacteristic /ˌʌnˌkærəktəˈrɪstɪk/	释 *adj.* 不典型的，不寻常的 not typical or distinctive 例 The sudden outburst of anger was ***uncharacteristic*** of the typically docile priest.

☐ indolent ☐ compulsory ☐ revelation ☐ contingency ☐ prolific
☐ alacrity ☐ transcend ☐ resonate ☐ uncharacteristic

impetuous
/ɪmˈpetʃuəs/

释 *adj.* 鲁莽的，仓促的 acting or done quickly and without thought
例 Stacy tends to make decisions with little thought and thus suffers constantly from her *impetuous* nature.
近 precipitate
反 deliberate

disparate
/ˈdɪspərət/

释 *adj.* 不同的 different from each other
例 Pardis Sabeti is known for her talents in *disparate* fields: she not only developed a means of tracing natural selection in the genome but also sings in a successful rock band.
近 heterogeneous, dissimilar, variant, diverse
反 homogeneous

respite
/ˈrespɪt/

释 *n.* 暂歇，休息 an interval of rest or relief
例 A smoking break gives a much needed *respite* from the exhausting toil of office work.
近 lull, relief, break

rankle
/ˈræŋkl/

释 *v.* 使…生气，愤怒 to cause (someone) to feel angry or irritated especially for a long time
例 Delivery charges can sometimes *rankle* customers and discourage them from going through with the online transactions.
近 gall

acquiesce
/ˌækwiˈes/

释 *v.* 默许，默认 to accept, agree, or allow something to happen by staying silent or by not arguing
例 He refuses to *acquiesce* to the boss's demand that he attend a corporate retreat.
近 accession

remedy
/ˈremədi/

释 *v.* 补救，完善 to solve, correct, or improve (something)
例 The large bed invited the weary traveler to *remedy* his jet lag.

释 *n.* 治疗的方法，治疗的药物 a medicine or treatment that relieves pain or cures a usually minor illness
例 Although aspirin can be an effective *remedy* for aches and pains, it can also produce unwanted side effects such as stomach aches.
近 recipe

congruous
/ˈkɑŋgruəs/

释 *adj.* 一致的，适合的 being in agreement, harmony, or correspondence
例 The candidate's claim that he would not add to the national debt was not *congruous* with his other promises about ending poverty.

gadfly
/ˈgædflaɪ/

释 *n.* 讨人厌的人 someone who annoys people by being very critical
例 The ancient Athenians described Socrates as a *gadfly* whose constant questioning annoyed many citizens in the city.

shrink
/ʃrɪŋk/

v. 缩小 to become smaller in amount, size, or value

Due to inflation, the value of the South African Rand has **shrunk** in recent years.

v. 畏缩 to quickly move away from something shocking, frightening, or disgusting

When the spider appeared beside Pablo, he **shrunk** away in fear.

recoil

overwrought
/ˌoʊvərˈrɔːt/

adj. 情绪激动的，过于忧虑的 very excited or upset

Laura was too **overwrought** to stay at the party after seeing her ex-boyfriend kiss another girl.

impassive

purposeful
/ˈpɜːrpəsfl/

adj. 有目的的，故意的 having a clear aim or purpose

Bobby Fisher's **purposeful** move to sacrifice his pawn so as to move his rook resulted in a checkmate for his opponent.

designed

prognosis
/prɑːɡˈnoʊsɪs/

n. 诊断 a medical opinion about how an illness will progress

After Tabatha was diagnosed with breast cancer, the doctor gave her a detailed **prognosis** of how the disease would pan out.

n. 预言 a judgment about what is going to happen in the future

Even though many of Nostradamus's **prognoses** have come true, skeptics still continue to argue that the vague language of his poems does not refer to specific events.

malleable
/ˈmæliəbl/

adj. 易适应的，能适应的 able to adjust to changing circumstances; adaptable

Long appreciated for its **malleable** qualities, aluminum can be formed to fit over any container.

plastic

forgo
/fɔːrˈɡoʊ/

v. 放弃（优势）to give up the enjoyment or advantage of : do without

To end his lecture on time, Professor Bruke decided to **forgo** his final point and address it instead at the next class meeting.

encumber
/ɪnˈkʌmbər/

v. 阻碍 to cause problems or difficulties for

Women who work in offices are often **encumbered** by their male colleagues' expectations that they will be polite and nonthreatening.

barbarity
/bɑːrˈbærəti/

n. 野蛮，残忍 extreme cruelty

Philosopher Cornel West argues that both European and African civilizations have uneven histories, with notable instances of **barbarism** during some eras and humanism during others.

cruelty, crudity

□ shrink □ overwrought □ purposeful □ prognosis □ malleable
□ forgo □ encumber □ barbarity

sanctimonious /ˌsæŋktɪˈmoʊniəs/	■ *adj.* 假装道德高尚的，假正经的 pretending to be morally better than other people ■ The priest's ***sanctimonious*** talk about the value of family angered the diverse community. ■ preachy, didactic
repugnant /rɪˈpʌgnənt/	■ *adj.* 令人厌恶的 causing a strong feeling of dislike or disgust ■ Most of us feel naturally ***repugnant*** about questioning our core beliefs and principles. ■ repugnance（n. 深恶痛绝）
pseudonym /ˈsuːdənɪm/	■ *n.* 假名 a name that someone (such as a writer) uses instead of his or her real name ■ Many people are reluctant to reveal any ***pseudonyms*** that they might use on social media as they do not want their identities to be uncovered.
explicit /ɪkˈsplɪsɪt/	■ *adj.* 明白的，清楚的 very clear and complete and leaving no doubt about the meaning ■ Though the conferees did not voice their ***explicit*** support for the resolution, they conveyed approval by applauding.
inexorable /ɪnˈeksərəbl/	■ *adj.* 无动于衷的，无情的 not capable of being persuaded by entreaty; relentless ■ A new research shows that aging is not an ***inexorable*** process, but rather the outcome of a genetic program that can be manipulated. ■ implacable
dissemble /dɪˈsembl/	■ *v.* 隐藏（感情、意见等），伪装 to hide your true feelings, opinions, etc. ■ Katie ***dissembled*** her true feelings of disappointment with a big smile. ■ behave honestly
scintillating /ˈsɪntɪleɪtɪŋ/	■ *adj.* 生动有趣的，机智幽默的 very clever, amusing, and interesting ■ Many readers do not expect science books to be ***scintillating***, but Mary Roach's works are just that: brilliant, lively and entertaining.
luminary /ˈluːmɪneri/	■ *n.* 杰出人物 a very famous or successful person ■ The numerous honors that writer Kenzaburo Oe has received, including the Nobel Prize, testify to his status as a ***luminary***.
empower /ɪmˈpaʊər/	■ *v.* 授权 to give power to (someone) ■ ***Empowered*** by the new title, the CEO fired all his rivals and solidified his control in the company. ■ *v.* 提升…的影响力 to promote the self-actualization or influence of ■ In the 1970s, the Women's Rights Movement worked to ***empower*** millions to achieve a successful professional career.

□ sanctimonious   □ repugnant   □ pseudonym   □ explicit   □ inexorable
□ dissemble   □ scintillating   □ luminary   □ empower

deference
/ˈdefərəns/

释 *n.* （因地位高或年长而）尊敬 respect and esteem due a superior or an elder

例 It is customary to show **deference** to the Pope by kneeling in front of him and kissing his ring.

近 respectful

反 contempt

lugubrious
/ləˈguːbriəs/

释 *adj.* 悲伤的 full of sadness or sorrow

例 The director complained that the sitcom's theme song was downright **lugubrious** and resembled funereal music.

近 gloomy

反 facetious, sprightly

denounce
/dɪˈnaʊns/

释 *v.* 批评 to criticize (someone or something) harshly and publicly

例 The scientific organization **denounced** the journal for showing bias in selecting their articles for publication.

近 lambaste

反 advocate, praise

parochial
/pəˈroʊkiəl/

释 *adj.* 地方性的 limited to only the things that affect your local area

例 The speaker announced that her primary focus would be on broad global concerns rather than on **parochial** issues.

近 provincial

释 *adj.* 狭隘的，范围有限的 limited in range or scope

例 According to critics, the scholar's paper on recycling was a **parochial** attempt that failed to consider the efforts made by corporations.

lament
/ləˈment/

释 *v.* 哀叹，哀悼 to express sorrow, regret, or unhappiness about something

例 Bill **lamented** his tragic loss following the earthquake that wiped out his family and home.

primitive
/ˈprɪmətɪv/

释 *adj.* 原始的 of, belonging to, or seeming to come from an early time in the very ancient past

例 The Neanderthals used to be seen as **primitive** cave-dwellers, but recent evidence suggests they had elaborate social rituals and complex technology.

近 ancient

释 *adj.* 简单的，基本的 very simple and basic

例 Instead of buying a new hammer, Butch made a **primitive** object that barely resembled the store-bought version.

近 rudimentary

hamper
/ˈhæmpər/

释 *v.* 阻碍 to slow the movement, progress, or action of (someone or something)

例 Studies of longevity among turtles are sometimes **hampered** by the fact that the subjects live so long that researchers retire before the studies can be completed.

distill
/dɪ'stɪl/

v. 蒸馏 to let fall, exude, or precipitate in drops or in a wet mist

Shortly after the mixture is boiled, the alcohol cools in the copper pipe and is *distilled* as pure alcohol.

v. 提炼 to extract the essence of

Despite the extreme length of the article, Lisa could *distill* the main argument to one sentence.

imitate
/'ɪmɪteɪt/

v. 模仿 to do the same thing as

It was hilarious to observe the little girl *imitating* her father's every word and act.

inimitable（adj. 无可比拟的，独特的）

encyclopedic
/ɪn,saɪklə'piːdɪk/

adj.（如大百科全书般）全面的 dealing with or knowing a subject thoroughly or completely

Despite never having attended a single baseball game, George had an *encyclopedic* knowledge of the sport from reading statistics in the newspaper.

exhaustive

euphemism
/'juːfəmɪzəm/

n. 委婉语 a mild or pleasant word or phrase that is used instead of one that is unpleasant or offensive

Although many people in today's world choose to speak explicitly, the tradition of *euphemism* is still very much alive.

unpolished

nondescript
/'naːndɪskrɪpt/

adj. 平庸的 lacking distinctive qualities; having no individual character or form

The new office buildings appeared drab and *nondescript* as they lacked any distinctive architectural features.

unexceptional

adverse
/'ædvɜːrs/

adj. 不利的，有害的 bad or unfavorable

You should take some preventive measures on your summer beach trip as being out in the sun for a long time can have *adverse* effects on your skin.

unfavorable

allied

adversity（n. 逆境），adversary（n. 对手）

enduring
/ɪn'dʊrɪŋ/

adj. 长期的 lasting, continuing

Jane Eyre is among the most *enduring* of feminist novels and is still widely read more than 150 years after its publication.

enliven
/ɪn'laɪvn/

v. 使活跃 to give life, action, or spirit to

Enlivened by the arrival of the main act, the crowd cheered loudly and filled the concert venue with their excited screams.

half-formulated
/ˌhæfˈfɔːrmjuleɪtɪd/

- *adj.* 新出现的 coming into view, existence, or notice
- The **half-formulated** plan of going camping never took off as no one was willing to make the effort to do some research.

dubious
/ˈduːbiəs/

- *adj.* 可疑的，不确定的 causing doubt, uncertainty, or suspicion
- The accuracy of astrological predictions may be **dubious**, but the basis of astronomy is thoroughly provable.
- suspect
- indubitable（*adj.* 不容置疑的）

churlish
/ˈtʃɜːrlɪʃ/

- *adj.* 不礼貌的 not polite
- It may seem **churlish** to speak ill of strangers, but I had to do so as my reputation was at stake.
- complaisant

outlandish
/aʊtˈlændɪʃ/

- *adj.* 奇异的 very strange or unusual
- Anna was dressed in such an **outlandish** shade of neon green that the whole crowd turned to look at her the moment she entered the room.
- conventional

- *adj.* 外来的，异国的 of or relating to another country
- Kilts are an **outlandish** custom to anyone not living in Scotland.

serendipitous
/ˌserənˈdɪpətəs/

- *adj.* 偶然的 happening by luck
- The biologist's amazing discovery was the result of a series of largely **serendipitous** events.
- fortuitous

☐ half-formulated   ☐ dubious   ☐ churlish   ☐ outlandish   ☐ serendipitous

Word List 07

音 频

---

mercurial
/mɜːrˈkjʊriəl/

- *adj.* 性格多变的 changing moods quickly and often
- The mayor is renowned for her **mercurial** temperament of being warm and talkative at one moment, and utterly aloof the next.
- volatile, inconstant
- persistent

---

deceive
/dɪˈsiːv/

- *v.* 欺骗 to make (someone) believe something that is not true
- The investors whom Bernie Madoff **deceived** never got back the money that they lost in his scams.
- deceitful（adj. 骗人的）

---

fortuitous
/fɔːrˈtuːɪtəs/

- *adj.* 偶然的 happening by chance
- Zoologists hope to learn whether minor variations in the migration routes of certain animals are intentional or merely **fortuitous**.
- accidental, serendipitous

- *adj.* 幸运的 having or showing good luck
- It certainly was **fortuitous** that I found a $20 bill on the ground!

---

fathom
/ˈfæðəm/

- *v.* 理解 to understand the reason for (something)
- In an attempt to **fathom** why Hawaii's fish population has been declining, scientists started monitoring numerous species closely and tracking their movements.
- unfathomable（adj. 无法理解的）

---

remuneration
/rɪˌmjuːnəˈreɪʃn/

- *n.* 酬金 an amount of money paid to someone for the work that person has done
- You will be offered no **remuneration** for the extra number of hours put in unless otherwise arranged with the manager.

---

sparkling
/ˈspɑːrklɪŋ/

- *adj.* 闪闪发光的 shining with brilliant points of light like stars
- Her **sparkling**, blue eyes left many men completely infatuated and enraptured.

---

luxuriant
/lʌɡˈʒʊriənt/

- *adj.* 繁茂的 having heavy and thick growth
- Tom Selleck is easily recognized by his thick, **luxuriant** moustache, which generally serves to enhance his portrayal of macho characters onscreen.
- rampant

- *adj.* 奢华的 having an appealingly rich quality
- The **luxuriant** bubble bath completely relaxed me after a long day at work.

☐ mercurial ☐ deceive ☐ fortuitous ☐ fathom ☐ remuneration
☐ sparkling ☐ luxuriant

credential
/krə'denʃl/

▪ *n.* 证明 something that gives a title to credit or confidence

▪ The various medical diplomas in the doctor's office served as visible *credentials* to reassure patients of his professional expertise.

recoil
/rɪ'kɔɪl/

▪ *v.* 畏缩 to quickly move away from something that is shocking, frightening, or disgusting; to react to something with shock or fear

▪ When the snake slithered across the driveway, the pit bull *recoiled* in fear and dashed inside the house.

▪ shrink

scandalous
/'skændələs/

▪ *adj.* 令人震惊的，反感的 shocking or offensive, damaging to the reputation

▪ The website posted *scandalous* photos of the singer kissing a woman who was clearly not his wife.

erode
/ɪ'roʊd/

▪ *v.* 削弱，逐渐毁坏 to diminish or destroy by degrees

▪ When we learned that the lawyer had lied about his law degree, our faith in his ability to try the case completely *eroded*.

tenuous
/'tenjuəs/

▪ *adj.* 站不住脚的，脆弱的 not certain, definite, or strong: flimsy, weak, or uncertain

▪ The temporary shelter that Nora had built was extremely strong and showed no signs of *tenuous* groundwork.

▪ *adj.* 纤细的 very thin and slender

▪ Despite the *tenuous* appearance of silk, it remains as one of the strongest fabrics in the world.

▪ substantial

fluctuate
/'flʌktʃueɪt/

▪ *v.* 波动，起伏，上上下下 to change level, strength, or value frequently

▪ The intensity of the waves *fluctuated* throughout the day and left us unsure about the safety of the tides.

▪ vacillate, vary

▪ stabilize

contentious
/kən'tenʃəs/

▪ *adj.* 引起争议的 likely to cause people to argue or disagree

▪ The intensity of the scientist's language was startling even in the notoriously *contentious* world of nineteenth-century geology.

▪ controversial, fraught, polemical

▪ *adj.* 爱争论的 likely or willing to argue

▪ Because Beth had a *contentious* personality, her teachers constantly encouraged her to join the debate team.

patchwork
/'pætʃwɜːrk/

▪ *n.* 混合物 something made of miscellaneous or incongruous parts or elements

▪ Lee's narrative remains a *patchwork* of lies, excuses and conflicting stories.

▪ hodgepodge, welter

flabbergast /ˈflæbərˌɡæst/	**v.** 使…惊讶 to shock or surprise (someone) very much The students' public demonstration in the main square completely ***flabbergasted*** the dean who had been unaware of their complaints and dissatisfaction.
temperate /ˈtempərət/	**adj.** （气温）温和的 having temperatures that are not too hot or too cold The basil plant thrives in ***temperate*** climates and will not survive through the four seasons in your garden. **adj.** 自我克制的，脾气温和的 emotionally calm and controlled Despite having received a call about the passing of his mother, Will remained ***temperate*** at work until he could get home and cry. **adj.** 适度的 keeping or held within limits As a known shopaholic, Mary asked her husband to take her credit cards so that she could remain ***temperate*** in her spending.
benighted /bɪˈnaɪtɪd/	**adj.** 无知的，愚昧的 having no knowledge or education At first, Elon Musk was a ***benighted*** failure in the car industry, but now his company, Tesla, is a success.
undiscriminating /ˌʌndɪˈskrɪmɪneɪtɪŋ/	**adj.** 不加区分的 indiscriminate The ***undiscriminating*** use of fertilizers for all crops and plants will prove to be disastrous for our environment in the long run. **adj.** 没有鉴别力的 lacking sensitivity, taste, or judgment It would be difficult for you to become a chef if you have an ***undiscriminating*** palate that cannot notice subtle differences in the combinations of taste.
palpable /ˈpælpəbl/	**adj.** （通过触摸）可感知的 capable of being touched or felt I urged Tania to seek medical advice when the spot in her arm grew into a ***palpable*** lump. perceptible, material, tangible intangible **adj.** 明显的 easily perceptible The tension in the room was ***palpable*** as the two parties were both displaying openly hostile attitudes.
effusive /ɪˈfjuːsɪv/	**adj.** 感情过分流露的 expressing a lot of emotion Children are usually very ***effusive*** as they do not understand the interpersonal boundaries of sharing feelings and affections. emotional, lyrical
habitable /ˈhæbɪtəbl/	**adj.** 宜居的 suitable or fit to live in NASA plans to transport housing pods to Mars so as to make the planet ***habitable*** for humans.
codify /ˈkɑːdɪfaɪ/	**v.** 整理 to put (things) in an orderly form The Mesopotamian king Hammurabi ***codified*** his kingdom's laws and had them placed on tablets throughout the kingdom. catalog

duplicate
/ˈduːplɪkeɪt/

释 *v.* 复制 to make an exact copy of (something)

例 The law office could now ***duplicate*** legal briefs speedily with the purchase of a new copier.

sluggish
/ˈslʌɡɪʃ/

释 *adj.* 迟钝的 moving slowly or lazily

例 The children were ***sluggish*** after a long day at school and could hardly drag their feet out of the school gate.

选 listless

反 dynamic

sway
/sweɪ/

释 *v.* 影响，控制 to exert a guiding or controlling influence on

例 In the *Game of Thrones*, the king is easily ***swayed*** by the whims and wishes of her manipulative mother, Cersei Lannister.

释 *v.* 摇摆 to cause to sway: set to swinging, rocking, or oscillating

例 During the hurricane, the satellite dish ***swayed*** in the wind until it finally fell over.

ornamental
/ˌɔːrnəˈmentl/

释 *adj.* 装饰性的，美观的 used to make something more attractive

例 The ***ornamental*** sculpture was always an issue of contention for the couple they could not agree on where to place it in the house.

选 decorative

convivial
/kənˈvɪviəl/

释 *adj.* 好交际的，欢聚的 of or relating to social events where people can eat, drink, and talk in a friendly way with others

例 The new friends all had a great time at the ***convivial*** party as the ambience was warm and unpretentious.

multifarious
/ˌmʌltɪˈferiəs/

释 *adj.* 各种各样的 of many and various kinds

例 More than 30,000 species of brachiopods have been identified, making them one of the most ***multifarious*** forms of life on Earth.

panacea
/ˌpænəˈsiːə/

释 *n.* 万能灵药 a remedy for all ills or difficulties

例 Despite its far-reaching impact, the Civil Rights Act of 1964 was not a ***panacea*** for all racism in the country.

选 cure-all

countenance
/ˈkaʊntənəns/

释 *v.* 赞同 to accept, support, or approve of (something)

例 The mayor was reluctant to ***countenance*** the use of force to stop the riots.

inflammatory
/ɪnˈflæmətɔːri/

释 *adj.* 煽动性的 tending to excite anger, disorder, or tumult; seditious

例 Every time an ***inflammatory*** e-mail came from Zieve, he got angry and found it difficult to focus on work.

选 provocative

taint
/teɪnt/

释 *v.* 玷污，破坏 to hurt or damage the good condition of (something)

例 Darrel's DUI ***tainted*** his permanent record and prevented him from getting a proper job.

☐ duplicate ☐ sluggish ☐ sway ☐ ornamental ☐ convivial
☐ multifarious ☐ panacea ☐ countenance ☐ inflammatory ☐ taint

rigorous /ˈrɪɡərəs/	📖 *adj.* 严格的 very strict and demanding 📝 I was initially excited to enroll in the CrossFit course, but the workouts were too ***rigorous*** for me to keep up. 📖 *adj.* 细致的，准确的 done carefully and with a lot of attention to detail 📝 After ***rigorous*** analyses of the results, the chemist believed he had discovered a new element.
delude /dɪˈluːd/	📖 *v.* 迷惑，欺骗 to cause (someone) to believe something that is not true 📝 Jason's gullibility is remarkable as he is ***deluded*** by even the most outrageous assertions.
ill-advised /ˈɪləd'vaɪzd/	📖 *adj.* 不明智的，不合理的 not wise or sensible 📝 The teenager made an ***ill-advised*** move to invest all his hard-earned salary into aggressive investment schemes and ended up losing all of it. 🔁 misguided
prosaic /prəˈzeɪɪk/	📖 *adj.* 普通的，寻常的 everyday or ordinary 📝 The table may appear to be a ***prosaic*** example of American craftsmanship, but its true value lies beneath its apparent simplicity. 📖 *adj.* 散文（体）的 characteristic of prose as distinguished from poetry 📝 Herodotus eschewed poetry and used the ***prosaic*** language of everyday speech in his *Histories* to retell the events of the Persian Wars. 📖 *adj.* 缺乏创意的 dull or unimaginative 📝 The reviewer criticized the artist for being an unimaginative imitator of Pollock after seeing his ***prosaic*** attempt at modernism.
malfeasance /mælˈfizns/	📖 *n.* 违法行为 wrongdoing or misconduct especially by a public official 📝 The mayor's past ***malfeasances*** prevented him from being elected again because the citizens had not forgiven him. 🔁 fraudulence
egregious /ɪˈgriːdʒəs/	📖 *adj.* 极坏的 conspicuously bad or offensive 📝 I advise you to clean up these ***egregious*** errors in translation as they would leave a bad impression on your readers. 🔁 flagrant
counterfeit /ˈkaʊntərfɪt/	📖 *adj.* 伪造的 made in imitation of what is genuine with the intent to defraud 📝 The cashier called the customer back after noticing that the notes she had received were actually ***counterfeit***. 🔁 misrepresent
volatile /ˈvɑːlətl/	📖 *adj.* 性格多变的 having or showing extreme or sudden changes of emotion 📝 After Henry's most recent outburst at the Dairy Queen, his wife demanded that he seek counseling for his ***volatile*** temper. 🔁 fickle, versatile, flighty, erratic, capricious

conundrum
/kə'nʌndrəm/

译 *n.* 难题 a confusing or difficult problem

例 The Red Sea town of Aydhab presents scholars with a **conundrum**: medieval records describe it as a major port for ships engaged in trade, yet today there is no trace of a harbor at the site.

近 enigma, puzzle, riddle

contrive
/kən'traɪv/

译 *v.* 设计 to plan with cleverness or ingenuity; to devise

例 It is difficult to distinguish between the things that charismatic people do spontaneously and those that are carefully **contrived** for effect.

gratify
/'grætɪfaɪ/

译 *v.* 使…满意 to make (someone) happy or satisfied

例 Despite not wanting a beach vacation, Pete **gratified** his fiancé by booking a trip to Cancun.

近 please

deflate
/dɪ'fleɪt/

译 *v.* 使…泄气，使…挫败 to make (someone) lose confidence or pride

例 When the straight-A student received a "C" on his book report, his confidence was **deflated** and he thought he would never gain admittance to Harvard.

译 *v.* 使…漏气 to lose air or gas from inside

例 Tom Brady received a four-game suspension for **deflating** footballs to make them easier to throw.

译 *v.* 缩小，减轻 to reduce in size, importance, or effectiveness

例 The hype over manuka honey was much **deflated** by scientific reports of its exaggerated efficacy.

近 soothe

anthropogenic
/ˌænθrəpə'dʒɛnɪk/

译 *adj.* 人为的 caused by humans

例 **Anthropogenic** emissions of CO_2 and other hydrocarbons, such as methane, are key contributors to global climate change.

conflate
/kən'fleɪt/

译 *v.* 合并 to combine (as two readings of a text) into a composite whole

例 The world financial crisis **conflated** many political, social, and cultural issues.

animate
/'ænɪmeɪt/

译 *adj.* 活着的，有生命的 having life

例 It is such a sight to see millions of **animate** creatures scurry about the forest floor in the middle of the night.

译 *v.* 鼓励，使…有活力 to give spirit and support to

例 Kristen was **animated** by her family's cheering near the finish line and managed to complete the last half mile of the marathon.

近 rouse, inspire, galvanize

contemporary
/kən'tempəreri/

译 *adj.* 当代的，现代的 happening or beginning now or in recent times

例 **Contemporary** gender norms associate the caregiver role with feminine identity and the breadwinner role with masculine identity.

近 topical

译 *adj.* 同时代的 from the same time period

例 Although Monet and Courbet were **contemporary** artists of the 1860s, their paintings are vastly different.

□ conundrum □ contrive □ gratify □ deflate □ anthropogenic
□ conflate □ animate □ contemporary

underlie
/ˌʌndərˈlaɪ/

释 *v.* 成为…的根据，构成…的基础 to form the basis or foundation of (an idea, a process, etc.)

例 It is hard to fathom that atoms *underlie* all objects, diverse and similar, in the universe.

释 *v.* 位于…之下 to lie or be located under (something)

例 Nashville is actually supported by a massive cave that *underlies* the city.

anecdote
/ˈænɪkdoʊt/

释 *n.* 趣闻，轶事 a short account of an interesting or humorous incident

例 Jules got Jane's attention with an *anecdote* about meeting Kim Kardashian.

ministration
/ˌmɪnɪˈstreɪʃən/

释 *n.* （牧师的）职务 the act or process of ministering

例 The congregation grew increasingly disillusioned by the pastor because his *ministrations* began to focus on paranoia about the Rapture.

banal
/bəˈnɑːl/

释 *adj.* 无聊的 boring or ordinary

例 Dorothy criticized the movie for being *banal*, uncreative, and a rip-off of an earlier film.

近 stale

反 arresting

flippant
/ˈflɪpənt/

释 *adj.* 轻率无礼的，不严肃的 lacking proper respect or seriousness

例 This new book traces the cultural history of bubble gum in an understandably *flippant* tone.

反 earnest

派 flip（v. 翻转，adj. 鲁莽的）

invective
/ɪnˈvektɪv/

释 *n.* 辱骂，侮辱 harsh or insulting words

例 The debaters became increasingly strident and antagonistic, with each of them ultimately resorting to *invective*.

反 laud, encomium

paltry
/ˈpɔːltri/

释 *adj.* 少量的 very small or too small in amount

例 Having received only a *paltry* amount of pocket change, the beggar spat at the feet of the passerby.

近 insufficient, meager

miserly
/ˈmaɪzərli/

释 *adj.* 吝啬的 hating to spend money

例 Typically, people who are *miserly* with money are *miserly* with emotions.

近 stingy, parsimonious

renowned
/rɪˈnaʊnd/

释 *adj.* 出名的 known and admired by many people for some special quality or achievement

例 The architect was *renowned* for his controversial and daring buildings which frequently worn awards.

近 celebrated

派 renown（n. 名气，名声）

exhaustive
/ɪgˈzɔːstɪv/

adj. 全面的 including all possibilities

例 The archaeologist's examination of the evidence was complimented for being remarkably careful and thoroughly *exhaustive*.

近 encyclopedic

反 incomplete

polemical
/pəˈlemɪkl/

adj. （爱）争辩的 of or involving strongly critical or disputatious writing or speech

例 He earns our respect for consistently giving honest and constructive feedback without being *polemical*.

近 contentious

反 conciliatory

facile
/ˈfæsl/

adj. 轻率的，肤浅的 too simple and not showing enough thought or effort

例 Since your doctorate thesis must offer a completely original reading, you must avoid making *facile* and obvious claims.

adj.【贬】轻而易举的 done or achieved in a way that is too easy

例 The weightlifter achieved a *facile* victory as there were no other competitors in her age category.

transparent
/trænsˈpærənt/

adj. 透明的 able to be seen through

例 By placing *transparent* plastic wrap over the bread dough, one can witness the effects of the yeast on the gluten.

adj. 易懂的 easy to notice or understand

例 How was it possible for you to miss his gestures of affection when they were so overbearingly *transparent*?

adj. 坦诚的 honest and open

例 Although the committee promised a *transparent* investigation into the official's e-mails, certain members of the public believe backroom deals prevented her from being charged.

unimpeachable
/ˌʌnɪmˈpiːtʃəbl/

adj. 毋庸置疑的 not able to be doubted or questioned

例 Since everyone makes mistakes, even the best of scholars fail to be completely *unimpeachable*.

近 blameless

派 impeach(v. 控告)

tortuous
/ˈtɔːrtʃuəs/

adj. 复杂难懂的，曲折的 complicated, long, and confusing

例 Obtaining a working visa in a foreign country frequently entails a convoluted and *tortuous* application process.

近 convoluted

perturb
/pərˈtɜːrb/

v. 使…不安 to cause (someone) to be worried or upset

例 The release of the tell-all memoir clearly *perturbed* all the parties named and implicated in the author's allegations.

☐ exhaustive   ☐ polemical   ☐ facile   ☐ transparent   ☐ unimpeachable
☐ tortuous   ☐ perturb

flighty
/'flaɪti/

adj. 多变的 given to capricious or unstable behavior

Berger's writing style is **flighty** and tends to shift from one subject to another without any warning.

fickle, versatile, volatile, erratic, capricious

adj. 易激动的 easily excited

The family dog was a **flighty** creature who barked whenever someone approached.

infectious
/ɪn'fekʃəs/

adj. 传染的 spreading or capable of spreading rapidly to others

Lupus is a serious disease but it is not **infectious** so you cannot catch it from your friend.

gall
/gɔːl/

v. 使…生气 to make (someone) feel annoyed or angry

The school bribery charges **galled** the entire population as they have had long-standing faith in the school officials.

rankle

n. 愤怒 a state of exasperation

Taken aback by the **gall** of the interviewee, the recruiting officer naturally did not extend him the job offer.

compelling
/kəm'pelɪŋ/

adj. 有趣的 very interesting

Even if this tale is not altogether factual, I find it nonetheless highly captivating and **compelling**.

interesting

adj. 有说服力的 capable of causing someone to believe or agree

Factual and forensic evidence makes a suicide verdict the most **compelling** answer to the mystery of his death.

overt
/oʊ'vɜːrt/

adj. 明显的 open to view

Tammy's **overt** rudeness in snapping at her manager during the meeting got her into serious trouble.

fraudulent
/'frɔːdʒələnt/

adj. 欺诈的 done to trick someone for the purpose of getting something valuable

The company met its financial obligations by engaging in **fraudulent** activities and was eventually charged and declared bankrupt.

malfeasance

perilous
/'perələs/

adj. 危险的 full of danger

Thousands of migrants try to reach Spain each year by attempting **perilous** sea journeys from western Africa or across the Mediterranean Sea.

precarious, dangerous

cataclysm
/'kætəklɪzəm/

n. 灾难 something that causes great destruction, violence, etc.

The volcanic eruption of Mount Vesuvius was a violent **cataclysm** that buried the city of Pompeii.

cataclysmic（adj. 巨变的）

☐ flighty   ☐ infectious   ☐ gall   ☐ compelling   ☐ overt
☐ fraudulent   ☐ perilous   ☐ cataclysm

concede
/kənˈsiːd/

释 *v.* 承认 to admit (something) usually in an unwilling way

例 After over an hour of restless discussion, the husband finally ***conceded*** that he had overreacted and admitted he was wrong.

近 acknowledge

horrific
/həˈrɪfɪk/

释 *adj.* 可怕的 causing horror or shock

例 To this day, the Holocaust remains a ***horrific*** symbol of the terrors of World War II.

multitudinous
/ˌmʌltɪˈtuːdɪnəs/

释 *adj.* 很多的 very many

例 There were months of terrible weather as ***multitudinous*** tornadoes barraged the Midwest.

downplay
/ˌdaʊnˈpleɪ/

释 *v.* 轻描淡写 to make (something) seem smaller or less important

例 The shrewd dictator publicized the prosperity of one small village in order to ***downplay*** the economic hardships that plagued most of his country.

purport
/pərˈpɔːrt/

释 *n.* 中心思想 meaning conveyed, professed, or implied

例 He did not understand the ***purport*** of her remarks and needed his colleagues to clarify the matter.

释 *v.* (虚假地)声称 to claim to be or do a particular thing when this claim may not be true

例 Although Chris ***purported*** not to know who broke the microwave, his parents continued to accuse him for trying to cover up for his brother.

mediocre
/ˌmiːdiˈoʊkər/

释 *adj.* 平庸的，平凡的 of moderate or low quality, value, ability, or performance

例 Although Schoenberg's compositions were seen as groundbreaking in his time, they are today frequently perceived in a rather ***mediocre*** light.

irritate
/ˈɪrɪteɪt/

释 *v.* 使…不高兴 to provoke impatience, anger, or displeasure in

例 Angela Merkel's decision to pursue a more open policy regarding Syrian immigrants has ***irritated*** the conservatives in the parliament.

stilted
/ˈstɪltɪd/

释 *adj.* 不自然的，僵硬的 awkward especially because of being too formal

例 Conversations that take place in elevators are often ***stilted***.

placid
/ˈplæsɪd/

释 *adj.* 平静的 not easily upset or excited

例 Far from being aggressive, bears in some national parks are surprisingly ***placid*** when approached by humans.

近 gentle

erratic
/ɪˈrætɪk/

释 *adj.* 飘忽不定的，没规律的 acting, moving, or changing in ways that are not expected or usual

例 The art market is so ***erratic*** that stock-market prices seem to be predictable in comparison.

近 fickle, versatile, volatile, flighty, capricious

释 *adj.* 古怪的 deviating from what is ordinary or standard

例 Mark Zuckerberg and Bill Gates are both college dropouts who took ***erratic*** paths to wealth and success.

ingenious

/ɪnˈdʒiːniəs/

adj. 天才的，聪明的 very smart or clever

The "like" button on Facebook is an *ingenious* feature that lets the site predict the posts a user hopes to see in the future.

clever

awkward

renaissance

/ˈrenəsɑːns/

n. 复苏 revival

Bike riding is enjoying a *renaissance* in a nearby city thanks to the new bike lanes.

revival

n. [首字母大写时，特指]文艺复兴时期 the humanistic revival of classical art, architecture, literature, and learning that originated in Italy in the 14th century and later spread throughout Europe

The art *Renaissance* began in the fifteenth century when many people in Europe rediscovered the Classical tradition.

endorse

/ɪnˈdɔːrs/

v. 公开支持 to publicly or officially say that on supports or approves of (someone or something)

Katy Perry, an American pop star, *endorsed* Hillary Clinton for President and sang at a Clinton rally.

sanction, commend, authorize, support

oppose

v. 代言…产品 to publicly say that you like or use (a product or service) in exchange for money

In the 1960s, this company famously got Whitey Ford to *endorse* its products and appear in a short film.

harbinger

/ˈhɑːrbɪndʒər/

n. 前兆 something that shows what is coming

Some scientists believe that Adelie penguins are *harbingers* of global warming, and that their population decline may presage climatic changes throughout the Antarctic.

herald

v. 预兆 to be a harbinger of

The sight of the black sails *harbingered* the arrival of Captain Cook from his round-the-world voyage.

malign

/məˈlaɪn/

adj. 邪恶的，恶毒的 having or showing intense often vicious ill will

The United Nations Army did not have *malign* intentions when they approached the local civilians, but instead wanted to help them.

v. 贬损，诋毁 to say bad things about (someone or something) publicly

Maligned by bullies on social media for several months, Kim grew depressed and dropped out of school from embarrassment.

imperative
/ɪmˈperətɪv/

释 *adj.* 重要的 very important
例 It is *imperative* that you fill in this claim form clearly if not your travel expenses will not be reimbursed.

释 *n.* 命令，要求 a command, rule, duty, etc., that is very important or necessary
例 The general gave an *imperative* to his troops to seize the bridge from the hands of the enemies.

ethical
/ˈeθɪkl/

释 *adj.* 道德的 morally right and good
例 Regardless of the legality, it is not *ethical* to do harm to one's neighbors.

consequential
/ˌkɑːnsəˈkwenʃl/

释 *adj.* 重要的 having significant consequences
例 Since Watson has limited time, he had to prioritize *consequential* problems over minor ones.
反 nugatory

释 *adj.* 自以为是的 self-important
例 After winning the lottery, John acted like an old-money aristocrat and saw himself as more *consequential* than he really was.

释 *adj.* 结果的 happening as a result
例 The continuous downpour over the week resulted in a *consequential* overgrowth of everyone's lawns.
派 consequence（n. 重要性，结果）

perpetuate
/pərˈpetʃueɪt/

释 *v.* 持续，使…继续 to cause (something that should be stopped, such as a mistaken idea or a bad situation) to continue
例 Having junk food within easy reach will only *perpetuate* your binge-eating problem.

anathema
/əˈnæθəmə/

释 *n.* 极其讨厌的人或事 someone or something that is very strongly disliked
例 Having an office job is *anathema* to Nancy as she absolutely detests following a routine.

释 *n.* 诅咒，强烈的谴责 a vehement denunciation; a curse
例 The witch looked into her crystal ball and uttered an *anathema* under her breath.

illuminate
/ɪˈluːmɪneɪt/

释 *v.* 阐述清楚 to make (something) clear and easier to understand
例 The book by Richard Dawkins *illuminated* the complexity of life on earth.
选 clarify

enchanting
/ɪnˈtʃæntɪŋ/

释 *adj.* 迷人的 charming
例 The full moon and soft music had an *enchanting* effect on the young lovers who could not pull their eyes away from each other.

☐ imperative ☐ ethical ☐ consequential ☐ perpetuate ☐ anathema
☐ illuminate ☐ enchanting

mishandle
/ˌmɪsˈhændl/

🈁 *v.* 虐待，粗暴对待 to treat roughly
🈂 It was clear that the package was ***mishandled*** by the deliveryman as there were dents all over the box.

🈁 *v.* 错误地处理，处理不当 to deal with or manage wrongly or ignorantly
🈂 The security officer at the banquet completely ***mishandled*** the situation by confusing the identities of all the guests.

fickle
/ˈfɪkl/

🈁 *adj.* 多变的 changing opinions often
🈂 Ryan's ***fickle*** attitude in choosing the restaurant for dinner left Lucy fuming in hunger.
🈯 versatile, volatile, flighty, erratic, capricious

countermand
/ˈkaʊntərmænd/

🈁 *v.* 撤销（命令） to cancel (an order) especially by giving a new order
🈂 The president ***countermanded*** the orders of his generals and told the troops not to attack the enemy's bridge.

mollify
/ˈmɑːlɪfaɪ/

🈁 *v.* 安抚 to make (someone) less angry ; to calm (someone) down
🈂 Although easily angered by our mischievous behavior, our mother could also be immediately ***mollified*** by our expressions of remorse.
🈯 inflame

gloomy
/ˈɡluːmi/

🈁 *adj.* 悲伤的 causing feelings of sadness
🈂 I would rather not watch this ***gloomy*** film now as it is supposed to be a celebratory evening.
🈯 lugubrious, cheerless

音频

| **methodical** /məˈθɑːdɪkl/ | ▦ *adj.* 有条理的 arranged, characterized by, or performed with method or order |
| | 例 Employing a *methodical* assembly-line production will ensure a consistent output of the same end-product. |

| **hortatory** /ˈhɔːrtəˌtɔri/ | ▦ *adj.* 劝告的，激励的 marked by exhortation or strong urging |
| | 例 The weather channel issued a *hortatory* warning about the impending blizzard that will cause severe delays. |

innate /ɪˈneɪt/	▦ *adj.* 天生的 existing from the time a person or animal is born
	例 Many linguists believe that the human ability to learn language is *innate* and forms an essential part of our nature.
	近 inborn

displace /dɪsˈpleɪs/	▦ *v.* 驱逐 to force (people or animals) to leave the area where they live
	例 Many animals in the rainforest were *displaced* from their homes due to extensive logging.
	▦ *v.* 取代，代替 to take the job or position of (someone or something)
	例 Many fear that robots will *displace* blue collar workers in factories and leave them without reliable careers.

apprehend /ˌæprɪˈhend/	▦ *v.* 逮捕 to arrest or seize
	例 The police said that the three thieves had not been identified or *apprehended* but that they probably lived nearby.
	派 apprehension（n. 逮捕，了解）
	▦ *v.* 理解 to notice and understand (something)
	例 The unfortunate racoon *apprehended* the danger too late and could no longer avoid the giant bear trap.
	▦ *v.* 害怕，恐惧 to anticipate especially with anxiety, dread, or fear
	例 Brianna nervously *apprehended* the results of the test for which she had not studied.
	近 trepidation
	反 intrepid

disarray
/ˌdɪsəˈreɪ/

n. 杂乱，混乱 a lack of order

During the military coup in Thailand, social order was thrown into *disarray* as people took to the streets.

v. 使混乱 to throw into disorder

My house was completely *disarrayed* by the preparations for the move and was too messy for guests to see.

---

tedious
/ˈtiːdiəs/

adj. 冗长无聊的 boring and too slow or long

Nancy decided to quit her office job as she found it too banal and *tedious*.

boring, dreary

---

irascible
/ɪˈræsəbl/

adj. 易怒的，坏脾气 becoming angry very easily

I advise you to stay away from Liam as the long working hours have made him highly *irascible* lately.

exasperation

---

fastidious
/fæˈstɪdiəs/

adj. 小心谨慎的，挑剔的 very careful about how you do something

Mr. Duhigg is a *fastidious* reporter who always makes sure that all his figures are accurate before sending them in to his superiors.

indiscriminate

---

occlude
/əˈkluːd/

v. 阻塞 to close up or block off

Pouring grease down the sink can *occlude* the pipes.

---

impair
/ɪmˈper/

v. 损害 to make (something) weaker or worse

Some scientists claim that repeated exposure to sustained noise *impairs* blood-pressure regulation and might even make people prone to hypertension.

subvert, undercut, undermine, compromise, vitiate

---

laudatory
/ˈlɔːdətɔːri/

adj. 赞美的 expressing or containing praise

O'Reilly insisted that his book is generally *laudatory* of Reagan despite reviews claiming otherwise.

laud（v. 赞美）

---

prevalent
/ˈprevələnt/

adj. 流行的，普遍的 common or widespread

Many of us have no clue that mental illness is so *prevalent* that it touches almost every family.

extensive, widespread

---

deprecate
/ˈdeprəkeɪt/

v. 贬损，诋毁 to criticize or express disapproval of (someone or something)

Dr. Abraham not only understated his accomplishments but *deprecated* his laudable rise to recognition.

detract

deprecatory（adj. 指责的，贬低的）

☐ disarray   ☐ tedious   ☐ irascible   ☐ fastidious   ☐ occlude
☐ impair   ☐ laudatory   ☐ prevalent   ☐ deprecate

portend
/pɔːrˈtend/

🔈 **v.** 预示，预兆 to be a sign or warning that something usually bad or unpleasant is going to happen

📝 Some conservative economists claim that the high numbers of people on social security **portend** budget problems for the program.

🔁 predict, presage

🔀 portent（n. 预兆，凶兆）

self-defeating
/ˌselfdɪˈfiːtɪŋ/

🔈 **adj.** 违背自己利益的，弄巧成拙的 injurious to one's or its own purposes or welfare

📝 Willie thought that cheating on the math exam would help him achieve high marks, but it proved to be **self-defeating** when he was caught by the teacher.

proclaim
/prəˈkleɪm/

🔈 **v.** 宣布 to say or state (something) in a public, official, or definite way

📝 Brett Favre solemnly **proclaimed** his retirement at a press conference after the Super Bowl.

🔁 profess

meddle
/ˈmedl/

🔈 **v.** 干涉 to interest oneself in what is not one's concern

📝 Some people think that children should not **meddle** in the affairs of their parents as they do not have adult maturity.

overshadow
/ˌoʊvərˈʃædoʊ/

🔈 **v.** 超出，超过 to exceed in importance

📝 Ryan's speech was so impressive that it completely **overshadowed** those of his competitors.

🔁 outlast

🔈 **v.** 遮盖 to cast a shadow over

📝 Lunar eclipses occur when the moon **overshadows** the sun and the light on earth diminishes.

🔁 obscure

somnolent
/ˈsɑːmnələnt/

🔈 **adj.** 无聊的，令人昏昏欲睡的 very boring or causing a person to fall asleep

📝 The workers all became sleepy and **somnolent** around 2:30 in the afternoon.

🔁 lethargic

precipitate
/prɪˈsɪpɪteɪt/

🔈 **v.** 加速 to cause (something) to happen quickly or suddenly

📝 It may not be clear from the footage that it was indeed Ryan's rude comments that **precipitated** the fight in the restaurant.

🔈 **adj.** 鲁莽的 happening very quickly or too quickly without enough thought or planning

📝 The executive was criticized for his **precipitate** move of implementing sweeping changes without fully considering the consequences.

🔀 deliberate

onerous
/ˈɑːnərəs/

囊 *adj.* 繁重的，费力的 difficult and unpleasant to do or deal with
例 Elena was dismayed at how *onerous* the course requirements were and wondered how she would ever be able to finish all those assignments.
近 burdensome

comity
/ˈkɑːməti/

囊 *n.* 友好，和谐 friendly social atmosphere
例 The diplomat tried to create *comity* by showing respect for the foreign officials.
近 civility

douse
/daʊs/

囊 *v.* 熄灭 to extinguish
例 Firefighters were wary of *dousing* the fire with too much water for fear of contaminating underground aquifers.
近 extinguish

asseverate
/əˈsevəˌreɪt/

囊 *v.* 郑重声明 to affirm or declare positively or earnestly
例 At the conclusion of her speech, she *asseverated* her commitment to workers' rights.

arbitrary
/ˈɑːrbətreri/

囊 *adj.* 武断的，任性的 not planned or chosen for a particular reason
例 His response was filled with *arbitrary* statements that seemed directed to nothing or no one in particular.

囊 *adj.* 随意的 existing or coming about seemingly at random or by chance or as a capricious and unreasonable act of will
例 The order of the interviewees is completely *arbitrary* and does not show our preferences at all.
近 capricious

discretion
/dɪˈskreʃn/

囊 *n.* 自由决定 power of free decision or latitude of choice within certain legal bounds
例 Regaining mayoral control of schools was Michael Bloomberg's greatest legislative achievements as it enabled the City Hall to gain *discretion* over education policy for the first time.

囊 *n.* 谨慎 the quality of having or showing discernment or good judgment; the quality of being discreet; circumspection
例 Because he showed financial *discretion* with the first month's allowance, Ari received a "raise" from his parents.
近 judicious

sacrosanct
/ˈsækroʊsæŋkt/

囊 *adj.* 神圣而不可侵犯的 most sacred or holy
例 Professions once seemingly free from litigation are no longer *sacrosanct*.

quiescent
/kwiˈesnt/

囊 *adj.* 静止的，不活跃的 not active
例 Some geysers discharge continuously, whereas others erupt briefly and then remain *quiescent* for hours or days.
近 calm
反 restless
派 quiescence（n. 静止）

evasive
/ɪ'veɪsɪv/

adj. 回避的，闪烁其词的 not honest or direct

The prose of Richard Wright's autobiographical "Black Boy" is straightforward and not **evasive**.

elusive, equivocal

defer
/dɪ'fɜːr/

v. 推迟 to put off; to delay

Ken asked if he could **defer** starting his car payments by a year since he was short of money.

v. 顺从 to submit to another's wishes, opinion, or governance usually through deference or respect

The prime minister **deferred** to the Attorney General for the precise wording of the new bill as he was not a legal expert.

innocuous
/ɪ'nɑːkjuəs/

adj. 无害的 having no adverse effect; harmless

Although many swimmers fear encountering jellyfish in the ocean, most species are actually **innocuous** and do no harm to humans.

harmless, benign, inoffensive

caustic

adj. 平淡乏味的，无恶意的 not likely to offend or provoke to strong emotion; insipid

As Anna had intended her joke to be **innocuous**, she was genuinely shocked when her best friend became offended.

arcane
/ɑːr'keɪn/

adj. 难懂的，鲜为人知的 known or understood by only a few people

The National Museum has a huge collection of **arcane** artifacts that seem curiously out of place in our contemporary world.

esoteric, recondite, abstruse

permanent
/'pɜːrmənənt/

adj. 长期稳定的 continuing or enduring without fundamental or marked change; stable

Julia was offered a **permanent** position at her firm, but was not sure if she wanted to settle in there.

entice
/ɪn'taɪs/

v. 诱惑 to attract artfully or adroitly or by arousing hope or desire

Companies eager to expand abroad have offered bonuses to employees to **entice** them to move overseas.

unmistakable
/ˌʌnmɪ'steɪkəbl/

adj. 清晰的，一目了然的 not capable of being mistaken or misunderstood

When the death ray emanated from the box, it was an **unmistakable** sign that Indiana Jones had found the real Ark of the Covenant.

decisive

antecedent
/ˌæntɪ'siːdnt/

n. 前事 something that came before something else and may have influenced or caused it

The portable CD player is the bulkier **antecedent** to the modern MP3 player.

precursor

overstate
/ˌoʊvərˈsteɪt/

v. 夸大 to say that (something) is larger or greater than it really is

Some people tend to **overstate** their experience on their resume, but these falsehoods are typically detected by a quick internet search.

understate

relish
/ˈrelɪʃ/

v. 喜爱 to enjoy or take pleasure in (something)

Jennifer Lawrence **relished** her moment of glory when she won her first Oscar for Best Actress.

delight

trepidation
/ˌtrepɪˈdeɪʃn/

n. 恐惧，害怕 a nervous or fearful feeling of uncertain agitation

Having a strong fear of heights, Bill entered the elevator with **trepidation**.

apprehension

intrepid（adj. 无畏的，勇敢的）

synergy
/ˈsɪnərdʒi/

n. 协同作用 the increased effectiveness that results when two or more people or entities work together

The **synergy** between Disney and Pixar resulted in spectacular CGI films such as *Toy Story*.

universal
/ˌjuːnɪˈvɜːrsl/

adj. 普世的 existing or true at all times or in all places

The **universal** laws of physics are equally applicable on Earth and on Alpha Centauri.

omnipresent, ubiquitous

adj. 普遍的 present or occurring everywhere

Although fossil fuels are a **universal** source of energy, many developed countries are looking to alternative energy sources such as wind.

dampen
/ˈdæmpən/

v. 抑制，削弱 to check or diminish the activity or vigor of

Dampened by the oppressive humidity, we decided to end our bike ride early and have a drink at a local café.

deaden

predate
/ˌpriːˈdeɪt/

v. 先于 to exist or happen at an earlier time than (something or someone)

Though feminist in its implications, Yvonne Rainer's 1974 film **predated** the filmmaker's active involvement in feminist politics.

antedate, precede

premise
/ˈpremɪs/

n. 前提 a proposition antecedently supposed or proved as a basis of argument or inference

The paper was completely debunked as it took blatant falsehoods for its **premises**.

motivate
/ˈmoʊtɪveɪt/

v. 激励 to provide with a motive

Motivated by the prospect of a large bonus, the architect completed the plans for the new skyscraper in half the time allotted to him.

□ overstate □ relish □ trepidation □ synergy □ universal
□ dampen □ predate □ premise □ motivate

linkage
/ˈlɪŋkɪdʒ/

释 *n.* 连接，联结 a connection or relationship between two or more things

例 In New York City, the NYDOT planned the subway system to be the most effective *linkage* between the city's major monuments.

hypocrisy
/hɪˈpɑːkrəsi/

释 *n.* 虚伪，伪善 the false assumption of an appearance of virtue or religion

例 The *hypocrisy* of the "no cellphone" rule was evident when the students walked in on the teacher texting her friends.

选 insincerity

redundant
/rɪˈdʌndənt/

释 *adj.* 重复的，冗余的，赘述的 needlessly wordy or repetitive in expression

例 Fannie Lou Hamer's statement "I'm sick and tired of being sick and tired" was made intentionally *redundant* with the purpose of raising awareness of civil rights.

反 economical

mitigate
/ˈmɪtɪgeɪt/

释 *v.* 减缓 to make less severe or intense

例 Many animals are able to *mitigate* the harmful effects of cold weather by means of feathers, fur or blubber.

选 abate, ameliorate, temper

wane
/weɪn/

释 *v.* 减少，衰退 to decrease gradually in size, amount, intensity, or degree; decline

例 Since many dance companies rely on government subsidies, *waning* government support for the arts has reduced opportunities for dancers.

选 ebb, decline

释 *v.* 结束 to approach an end

例 We grew nostalgic about our four years in high school as our teenage years *waned* and adulthood beckoned.

释 *v.* （月亮）亏 to show a progressively smaller illuminated area, as the moon does in passing from full to new

例 With each passing moment, the light from the dying light bulb *waned* until the room became entirely dark.

accountable
/əˈkaʊntəbl/

释 *adj.* （对某事）负责任的 required to be responsible for something

例 Multinational corporations generally exploit workers around the world and avoid being *accountable* for their actions.

派 accountability（n. 责任）

释 *adj.* 可以解释的 capable of being explained

例 For tax purposes, it is required that all of the bakery's purchases be *accountable*.

□ linkage　　　□ hypocrisy　　　□ redundant　　　□ mitigate　　　□ wane
□ accountable

fecund
/ˈfiːkənd/

释 *adj.* 多产的 fruitful in offspring or vegetation
例 Cottontail rabbits are known for being remarkably **fecund**, with some individual females producing up to 35 offspring a year.
派 fecundity（n. 繁殖力，创造力）

释 *adj.* 有创造力的，硕果颇丰的 intellectually productive or inventive
例 The mystery author is remarkably **fecund** and publishes up to two books a year.

reflective
/rɪˈflektɪv/

释 *adj.* 反思的，沉思的 characterized by or given to serious thinking or contemplation
例 Confronted with the death of several close friends, Craig sat in silence and became **reflective** about human mortality.
近 pensive

precedent
/ˈpresɪdənt/

释 *n.* 先例 an easier occurrence of something similar
例 Michelangelo was one of the most adventurous designers whose creations never copied their **precedents.**
派 unprecedented（adj. 史无前例的）

recant
/rɪˈkænt/

释 *v.* （公开正式地）否认 to withdraw or repudiate (a statement or belief) formally and publicly
例 Even though Galileo was correct in his belief that the Earth revolved around the Sun, he was forced by the church to **recant**.
近 repudiate
反 affirm

rambling
/ˈræmblɪŋ/

释 *adj.* 跑题的，冗长的 lengthy and digressive
例 Unlike her predecessor's **rambling** prose, Susan Hubel's reports were both succinct and comprehensive.

释 *adj.* 闲逛的 habitually roaming
例 **Rambling** around the country by riding the rails is not as glamorous as generally portrayed in the movies.

inure
/ɪˈnjʊr/

释 *v.* 习惯于（不好的事物）to habituate to something undesirable
例 During the Medieval age, peasants were **inured** to dirty conditions and coarse clothing.

eccentric
/ɪkˈsentrɪk/

释 *adj.* 古怪的 strange or unusual
例 Oscar Wilde was an **eccentric** writer who wore unusual clothes and shocked people with his ideas.

mercenary
/ˈmɜːrsəneri/

释 *adj.* 唯利是图的 serving merely for pay or sordid advantage
例 Selling a kidney is illegalized as the process of organ donation should have no **mercenary** aspect.
近 exploitative

negligible
/ˈneglɪdʒəbl/

释 *adj.* 可忽略的，不重要的 not significant or important enough to be worth considering; trifling

例 Oil companies seeking permission to drill in the Alaskan wild argue that the effect on wildlife is *negligible*.

近 insignificant, inconsequential, trifling

puerile
/ˈpjʊrəl/

释 *adj.* 稚嫩的，幼稚的 silly or childish especially in a way that shows a lack of seriousness or good judgment

例 Rick's *puerile* love of dirty jokes annoyed his colleagues during a recent work trip in Orlando.

plausible
/ˈplɔːzəbl/

释 *adj.* 看起来合理的 appearing to be true, fair or reasonable

例 Although the bystander's account of the car accident seemed *plausible*, the police officer eventually found many loopholes in it.

反 unbelievable

派 implausible（adj. 难以置信的）

释 *adj.* 表面上可行的 appearing worthy of belief

例 Despite the lack of concrete proof, the sheer scale of the universe makes it *plausible* that life exists on other planets.

baffle
/ˈbæfl/

释 *v.* 使…困惑 to confuse (someone) completely

例 Twitter completely *baffles* my grandparents as they are not used to social media.

simplistic
/sɪmˈplɪstɪk/

释 *adj.* 过于简化的 too simple

例 Attributing all homelessness to a lack of motivation is a *simplistic* explanation that does not account for the many complex factors involved.

chivalrous
/ˈʃɪvəlrəs/

释 *adj.* 勇敢的 valiant

例 The character Don Juan is a dark, adventurous soul with a *chivalrous* spirit.

释 *adj.* 绅士风度的，礼貌的 showing respect and politeness especially toward women

例 Holding doors open for women is a *chivalrous* act that does not make up for underpaying them.

反 boorish

apathetic
/ˌæpəˈθetɪk/

释 *adj.* 漠不关心的 not having or showing much emotion or interest

例 She grew increasingly *apathetic* about all aspects of life after her soul mate died.

近 passivity

派 apathy（n. 冷漠，无情）

dedicate
/ˈdedɪkeɪt/

释 *v.* 致力于，奉献于 to commit to a goal or way of life

例 Michael Phelps *dedicated* his teen years to the pool with the sole aim of making it to the Olympics.

□ negligible □ puerile □ plausible □ baffle □ simplistic
□ chivalrous □ apathetic □ dedicate

blemish
/ˈblemɪʃ/

v. 玷污，破坏 to hurt or damage the good condition of (something)
The phone was slightly ***blemished*** when Lucy accidentally dropped it on the floor.
defect

n. 污点 a mark that makes something imperfect or less beautiful
The only ***blemish*** on Djokovic's otherwise perfect record was when he dropped out of a quarter-final with an eye infection.

inertia
/ɪˈnɜːrʃə/

n. 不动，不活跃 lack of movement or activity especially when movement or activity is wanted or needed
The home office's ***inertia*** in dealing with this application resulted in massive delays and dire consequences.
inactive
inert（adj. 迟缓的）

n.（思想上的）惰性 a feeling of not having the energy or desire that is needed to move, change, etc.
Do not count on him to come in to work on weekends as his ***inertia*** would most likely keep him in bed.

intelligible
/ɪnˈtelɪdʒəbl/

adj. 可以理解的，清楚的 able to be understood
The announcement that came over the loudspeaker was barely ***intelligible*** due to disruptions in sound frequencies.
readable

primacy
/ˈpraɪməsi/

n. 首要，首位 the state of being most important or strongest
The ***primacy*** of compromise to a long-lasting relationship should not be underrated.

untenable
/ʌnˈtenəbl/

adj.（论点）经不起反驳的，站不住脚的 not capable of being defended against attack or criticism
One objection to the argument is that it rests on an ***untenable*** theory.
baseless

incivility
/ˌɪnsəˈvɪləti/

n. 不礼貌 a rude or impolite attitude or behavior
People could abide politicians' ***incivility*** but not their corruption.

laconic
/ləˈkɑːnɪk/

adj. 简洁的，用词少的 using few words in speech or writing
Through his term, Governor was considered ***laconic*** and inactive: he said little and did even less.
terse, curt, taciturn
garrulous, voluble

confess
/kənˈfes/

v. 坦白，承认 to admit that you did something wrong or illegal
I had to ***confess*** to breaking the thermometer when my chemistry teacher angrily threatened to punish the whole class unless the culprit owned up.

demoralize
/dɪ'mɔːrəlaɪz/

閥 *v.* 使…泄气 to weaken the morale of (a person or group)

例 Jay was so **demoralized** after losing his first job that he sunk into depression.

paragon
/'pærəgaːn/

閥 *n.* 典范，模范 a model of excellence or perfection

例 Roderick is respected because he devotes himself to charity and remains a **paragon** of frugality despite his immense wealth.

近 model

反 travesty

outmoded
/ˌaʊt'moʊdɪd/

閥 *adj.* 过时的 no longer useful or acceptable

例 The use of cassette players is **outmoded** in this age of cell phones and digital music.

近 obsolete, fusty, unfashionable

fleeting
/'fliːtɪŋ/

閥 *adj.* 短暂的 passing swiftly

例 Rosemary seems to fear that her husband's interest in her is only **fleeting** and dependent on her looks.

近 momentary

反 perennial

scrutinize
/'skruːtənaɪz/

閥 *v.* 仔细检查 to examine something carefully especially in a critical way

例 Although the archaeologist **scrutinized** the symbols on the cave wall, she was unable to read them because they were too faint.

incentive
/ɪn'sentɪv/

閥 *n.* 激励 something that encourages a person to do something or to work harder

例 A passenger has less **incentive** to pay more to travel faster if the seat is comfortable.

反 deterrent

contradictory
/ˌkaːntrə'dɪktəri/

閥 *adj.* 对立的 involving, causing, or constituting a contradiction

例 When the second witness came forward and offered a **contradictory** statement, the detective was certain that one was lying.

sectarian
/sek'teriən/

閥 *adj.* 狭隘的 limited in character or scope

例 The presented laws were considered **sectarian** by many because they represented the extreme views of the recently created party.

閥 *adj.* 教派的，派系的 relating to religious or political sects and the differences between them

例 **Sectarian** violence between Israelis and Palestinians often erupts in the Levant.

moribund
/'mɔːrɪbʌnd/

閥 *adj.* 濒临死亡的 approaching death

例 The company, considered **moribund** in recent years, now attracts millions of consumers worldwide.

□ demoralize   □ paragon   □ outmoded   □ fleeting   □ scrutinize
□ incentive   □ contradictory   □ sectarian   □ moribund

galvanize /ˈgælvənaɪz/	释 *v.* 刺激 to stimulate or shock with an electric current 例 Mary Shelley's *Frankenstein* portrays a scientist who uses electricity to *galvanize* his creation to life. 选 animate, rouse 释 *v.* 激起…意识，激发…行动 to arouse to awareness or action 例 With the impassioned halftime speech, the coach *galvanized* his players to overcome the 1-0 deficit and win the soccer match.
interchangeable /ˌɪntərˈtʃeɪndʒəbl/	释 *adj.* 可交换的，相似的 capable of being used in place of each other 例 There are many different brands of paper clips, but they seem *interchangeable* to customers. 选 fungible
exiguous /egˈzɪgjuəs/	释 *adj.* 极其缺乏的 excessively scanty 例 Some entrepreneurs have made large fortunes in a year or two of trade despite starting out with *exiguous* capital. 选 scanty
truism /ˈtruːɪzəm/	释 *n.* 真理 an undoubted or self-evident truth 例 "All men are created equal" is a famous *truism* first offered in the opening statement of the Declaration of Independence.
valorize /ˈvæləraɪz/	释 *v.* 规定价格（引申为赞美） to give or assign a value to, especially a higher value 例 The feminist speaker argued that we should not *valorize* men simply for their restraint in harassing women. 选 exalt
meticulous /məˈtɪkjələs/	释 *adj.* 谨慎的 very careful about doing something in an extremely accurate and exact way 例 Woodrow Wilson was *meticulous* in all aspects of his life and would even arrange the office furniture personally. 选 painstaking, exactitude, thorough, exacting
satire /ˈsætaɪər/	释 *n.* 讽刺，嘲讽 humor that shows the weaknesses or bad qualities of a person, government, society, etc. 例 Even though South Park seems like a cartoon on first glance, it actually offers biting *satire* on all topics of popular culture. 选 mockery
proprietary /prəˈpraɪəteri/	释 *adj.* 业主所持有的，私有的 kept private by an owner 例 *Proprietary* data should be stored securely so that employees cannot access it after they leave the company.
evenhanded /ˈiːvnˌhændɪd/	释 *adj.* 公平的 not favoring one side or group over another 例 The guidance counselor claimed that he was being *evenhanded* in giving each of the fighting students a hearing.

amorphous
/əˈmɔːrfəs/

释 *adj.* 无固定形状的 having no definite or clear shape or form
例 Nancy shrieked when a dark and strangely *amorphous* shadow filled the room.

释 *adj.* 难以归类的 of no particular type; anomalous
例 Braxton is not a member of a single clique, his friend group is too *amorphous* and spread out among different circles.

apolitical
/ˌeɪpəˈlɪtɪkl/

释 *adj.* 对政治不感兴趣的 not interested or involved in politics
例 Although the magazine claimed to be *apolitical*, its commentary on the war on drugs demonstrated a liberal bent.

obviate
/ˈɑːbvieɪt/

释 *v.* 免除 to make (something) no longer necessary
例 Now that everyone has a cell phone, they have *obviated* the need for wristwatches and alarm clocks.
近 displace

释 *v.* 避免 to prevent or avoid
例 Eating a large breakfast before the road trip *obviates* the need to make a lunch stop.
近 avert, preclude

prescience
/ˈpresiəns/

释 *n.* 先知 the ability to know what will or might happen in the future
例 Kundera's previous books tellingly predicted our Instagram era with uncanny *prescience*.
派 prescient（adj. 有先见之明的，预知的）

audacious
/ɔːˈdeɪʃəs/

释 *adj.* 大胆的，无畏的 intrepidly daring
例 The *audacious* student brazenly asked the teacher why she had stopped wearing her wedding ring.
反 timid
派 audacity（n. 大胆）

释 *adj.* 无礼的 contemptuous of law, religion, or decorum
例 In an *audacious* challenge to the Catholic church, Martin Luther posted 95 "theses" on the door of All Saints Church in Wittenburg to call for reform.
近 brazen

释 *adj.* 大胆创新的 marked by originality and verve
例 Mae West's disregard for popular conventions and norms during her film career earned her a reputation for being an *audacious* actress.

animadversion
/ˌænɪmədˈvɜːrʒən/

释 *n.* 批判，责骂 a critical and usually censorious remark
例 The alimony negotiations between the former spouses collapsed into mutual blame and *animadversion*.

音频

Word List 09

adorn /əˈdɔːrn/	翻 *v.* 装饰 to make (someone or something) more attractive by adding something beautiful 例 He **adorned** the sitting room with flowers and candles in anticipation of his guests' arrival. 派 adornment (n. 装饰)
duplicitous /duːˈplɪsɪtəs/	翻 *adj.* 欺骗的 deceptive in words or action 例 Only after the campaign volunteers became aware of their candidate's questionable motives could they recognize the **duplicitous** nature of his speeches. 派 duplicity (n. 欺骗)
vehement /ˈviːəmənt/	翻 *adj.* 情绪激动的 showing strong and often angry feelings 例 The activists were **vehement** in their anti-war protests and picketed in front of Congress.
revive /rɪˈvaɪv/	翻 *v.* 使…复苏 to make (someone or something) strong, healthy, or active again 例 The government is hoping to diversify the economy, **revive** manufacturing and generate employment to help boost growth.
antediluvian /ˌæntɪdɪˈluːviən/	翻 *adj.* 极为过时的 very old or old-fashioned 例 The library's computer system has been called **antediluvian** because it has not been updated in so many years. 近 archaic
facet /ˈfæsɪt/	翻 *n.* （事物的）方面 a part or element of something 例 Remembering to schedule regular oil changes is a **facet** of responsible car ownership.
ponderous /ˈpɑːndərəs/	翻 *adj.* 笨重的 slow or awkward because of weight and size 例 A trained ballerina looks weightless whereas a beginner tends to be slow and **ponderous**. 反 gossamer 翻 *adj.* 无聊的 very boring or dull 例 By the end of the **ponderous** lecture, the entire audience was snoring loudly.

detract
/dɪˈtrækt/

略 *v.* 贬低 to diminish the importance, value, or effectiveness of something

例 They feared that the bad publicity surrounding him would *detract* from their own election campaigns.

近 deprecate

派 detractor（n. 诋毁者）

specific
/spəˈsɪfɪk/

略 *adj.* 独特的 relating to a particular person, situation, etc.

例 Although the name of the suspect was not yet released by the police, the newspaper article detailed the *specific* person in custody.

略 *adj.* 清晰的，明确的 clearly and exactly presented or stated

例 I am confused how you could have ruined the pasta sauce when the recipe offered *specific* instructions for cooking.

aggrandize
/əˈgrænˌdaɪz/

略 *v.* 夸大，吹捧 to make appear great or greater

例 Television can *aggrandize* normal people, but it can also make public figures look foolish.

略 *v.* 抬高身价，提高地位 to enhance the power, wealth, position, or reputation of

例 The king *aggrandized* himself by having 40-foot-high gold-plates statues made.

派 self-aggrandizement（n. 自我吹捧）

prospect
/ˈprɑːspekt/

略 *n.* 前景 someone or something that is likely to succeed or to be chosen

例 When he was a young baseball *prospect*, Eddie was expected to star in the major leagues, but his recurring knee injury kept him in the dugout.

chagrin
/ʃəˈgrɪn/

略 *n.* 苦恼，烦恼 a feeling of being frustrated or annoyed because of failure or disappointment

例 Edgar's *chagrin* at having bungled the simple assignment was clear from his trembling lips and teary eyes.

近 vexation

略 *v.* 使烦恼 to vex or unsettle by disappointing or humiliating

例 *Chagrined* by the repeated insults of the neighborhood bully, Jack began taking a different route to school each morning.

seclusion
/sɪˈkluːʒn/

略 *n.* 隔离，隐居 the act of placing or keeping someone away from other people; the act of secluding someone

例 During the loud storm, the cocker spaniel sought *seclusion* in the closet to avoid the sound of the thunder.

略 *n.* 偏僻之处 a secluded or isolated place

例 Some men build a "man cave" as a place of *seclusion* away from their wives and adult responsibilities.

| **commence** /kəˈmens/ | **v.** 开始 to begin |
| | The new cookie company is getting its storefront ready and will be **commencing** sales within a week. |

mordant /ˈmɔːrdnt/	**adj.** 尖酸刻薄的 expressing harsh criticism especially in a way that is funny
	The television interviewer is known to traumatize politicians with his **mordant** sense of humor.
	acerbic
	genial

| **disconcerting** /ˌdɪskənˈsɜːrtɪŋ/ | **adj.** 令人不安的 causing an emotional disturbance |
| | While the idea of laser surgery to correct vision may be **disconcerting**, studies suggest it is safe. |

| **embellish** /ɪmˈbelɪʃ/ | **v.** 装饰 to make beautiful with ornamentation |
| | The carpenter decided to **embellish** the plain, wooden chair with elaborate carvings. |

pugnacious /pʌɡˈneɪʃəs/	**adj.** 好争斗的 showing a readiness or desire to fight or argue
	Edwards's angry tone was emblematic of her **pugnacious** approach to politics.
	belligerent, truculent

exacerbate /ɪɡˈzæsərbeɪt/	**v.** 使⋯恶化 to make (a bad situation, a problem, etc.) worse
	The governor concluded that the city's fiscal problems had been **exacerbated** by poor management.
	aggravate
	alleviate, mitigate

furtive /ˈfɜːrtɪv/	**adj.** 鬼鬼祟祟的 done in a quiet and secret way to avoid being noticed
	Spies provide information to enemy governments in **furtive**, secretive meetings.
	secretive

| **bewilder** /bɪˈwɪldər/ | **v.** 使⋯困惑 to confuse (someone) very much |
| | The recent series of events completely **bewildered** the young politician who was not expecting such a harsh backlash. |

| **unidimensional** /ˌjuːnɪdɪˈmenʃənl/ | **adj.** 肤浅的 lacking depth |
| | He may appear to be a simple and **unidimensional** man, but his manners disguise his wisdom. |

| **jaded** /ˈdʒeɪdɪd/ | **adj.** 厌倦的，无聊的 feeling or showing a lack of interest and excitement caused by having done or experienced too much of something |
| | Viewers might justifiably feel **jaded** when exposed to the same sights over and again. |

| **visionary** /ˈvɪʒəneri/ | **adj.** 有远见的 having or expressing clear ideas about what should happen or be done in the future |
| | As a **visionary** entrepreneur, Steve Jobs built innovative products, like the iPad, that attracted millions of consumers. |

☐ commence ☐ mordant ☐ disconcerting ☐ embellish ☐ pugnacious
☐ exacerbate ☐ furtive ☐ bewilder ☐ unidimensional ☐ jaded
☐ visionary

archetypal /ˌɑːrkiˈtaɪpl/	释 *adj.* 典型的 being a perfect example of something
	例 In the James Bond movies, every enemy is an ***archetypal*** villain with no morals and hundreds of disposable henchmen.
	近 classic

humility /hjuːˈmɪləti/	释 *n.* 谦虚 the quality or state of being humble
	例 Known for his ***humility***, Derek Jeter never bragged about his successes.

disclose /dɪsˈkloʊz/	释 *v.* 揭发，揭露 to make (something) known to the public
	例 We can be certain that our medical information will not be made public as it is illegal for doctors to ***disclose*** the medical history of their patients.

adversarial /ˌædvərˈseriəl/	释 *adj.* 敌对的 involving two people or two sides who oppose each other
	例 The ***adversarial*** relationship between the employers and employees of this company resulted in lots of strikes and disagreements.
	近 antagonistic
	派 adversary（n. 对手）

beneficiary /ˌbenɪˈfɪʃieri/	释 *n.* 受益者 a person, organization, etc., that is helped by something
	例 As the ***beneficiary*** of the record donation, the World Health Organization was able to vaccinate millions of young Africans against polio.

premature /ˌpriːməˈtʃʊr/	释 *adj.* 过早的 happening too soon or earlier than usual
	例 In 1948, the *Chicago Daily Tribune* made the ***premature*** declaration of Dewey as winner of the election, but he went on to lose.
	近 precocious

jeopardize /ˈdʒepərdaɪz/	释 *v.* 使…危险 to put (something or someone) in danger
	例 The safety of the mountain climbers may be ***jeopardized*** if detailed weather reports cannot be obtained throughout the expedition.
	近 endanger

conjure /ˈkʌndʒər/	释 *v.* 想象出 to create or imagine (something)
	例 The little boy was amazed when the wizard ***conjured*** a table filled with delicious foods with a wave of his wand.
	近 imagine

persevere /ˌpɜːrsəˈvɪr/	释 *v.* 坚持 to continue doing something or trying to do something even though it is difficult
	例 Believing that the problem could be solved with the right information, the scientist vowed to ***persevere*** in her research.

enormous /ɪˈnɔːrməs/	释 *adj.* 大量的 very great in size, amount, or degree
	例 B.F. Skinner's theories about psychology had an ***enormous*** impact when first published, but they have mostly been rejected since.
	近 magnitude
	释 *adj.* 穷凶极恶的 exceedingly wicked
	例 Jack the Ripper was known for his gruesome and ***enormous*** sins involving the murder and dissection of female victims during the Victorian times.

□ archetypal □ humility □ disclose □ adversarial □ beneficiary
□ premature □ jeopardize □ conjure □ persevere □ enormous

inverse
/ˌɪnˈvɜːrs/

释 *adj.* 相反的 opposite in order, nature, or effect
例 Everyone was surprised when the balloon did the *inverse* of what we expected and fell back to earth.

indiscriminate
/ˌɪndɪˈskrɪmɪnət/

释 *adj.* 不加区分的，不加选择的 not marked by careful distinction
例 Chinese trade may have been inspired by Western ideas but it did not adopt them in an *indiscriminate* fashion.

释 *adj.* （因为不加区别而）多样的 heterogeneous or motley
例 The pirate Blackbeard's crew was an *indiscriminate* mix of former soldiers, criminals, exiles, and orphans.

defy
/dɪˈfaɪ/

释 *v.* 不遵守，不服从，抵抗 to refuse to obey
例 I have never *defied* my mother, but this time I did because she was clearly being unreasonable.
近 disregard, flout
派 defiant（adj. 反叛的）

admonish
/ədˈmɑːnɪʃ/

释 *v.* 警告，批评 to criticize or warn gently but seriously
例 The hikers were *admonished* by the park rangers for the dangerous route that they were taking, but they continued without heeding their advice.
近 scold

释 *v.* 劝告 to give friendly advice or encouragement
例 When the boy was uncertain about riding a bicycle for the first time, his father quietly *admonished* him to get on the seat and start pedaling.

preclude
/prɪˈkluːd/

释 *v.* 阻止 to prevent (someone) from doing something
例 Genna's worries about looking foolish *precluded* her from being herself and making friends.
近 prevent, rule out

forswear
/fɔːrˈswer/

释 *v.* 放弃 to promise to give up (something) or to stop doing (something)
例 With his new focus on health, Sean *forswore* cigarettes and took up exercise.
近 eschew

solidarity
/ˌsɑːlɪˈdærəti/

释 *n.* 团结 unity (as of a group or class) that produces or is based on community of interests, objectives, and standards
例 The people in the crowd felt *solidarity* with one another in the knowledge of the hard work they had all put in to elect the new mayor.
近 camaraderie

conspicuous
/kən'spɪkjuəs/

adj. 显眼的，明显的 very easy to see or notice

William H. Johnson's paintings were seldom ***conspicuous*** in major exhibitions and were often ignored by art critics.

prominent, salient, obtrusive, marked, noticeable, remarkable, noteworthy

adj. 吸引人的 attracting attention

Stranded on the desert island, Gilligan hoped that a pilot would fly by and notice the ***conspicuous*** "SOS" written in palm fronds.

disinformation
/,dɪs,ɪnfər'meɪʃn/

n. 假情报，假消息 false information deliberately and often covertly spread

Disinformation about the candidate's infidelities spread just before the election and she had little time to refute the lies.

mendacity

preempt
/pri'empt/

v. 阻止，先发制人 to prevent (something) from happening

The early arrival of the guests ***preempted*** my plan to shower before the dinner party.

v. 取代 to take the place of

We were quite happy that the dinner guests brought an expensive bottle of wine to ***preempt*** our subpar selection.

supersede

v. 抢占 to acquire by preemption

When the fire alarm sounded, we were unable to drink the table wine and we ***preempted*** the bottle for use on the next occasion.

recapitulate
/,ri:kə'pɪtʃuleɪt/

v. 总结 to give a brief summary of something

The board members asked for the project manager's previous report be ***recapitulated*** just before the meeting as too much time had passed since the report was last presented.

paralyze
/'pærəlaɪz/

v. 使…瘫痪 to make (a person or animal) unable to move or feel all or part of the body

The snake's venom completely ***paralyzed*** his leg and he felt powerless to move.

v. 使…无效或无力 to make powerless or ineffective

When the bear reared up on its hind legs, the camping party was ***paralyzed*** with fear and did not know whether to run or play dead.

inexpressible
/,ɪnɪk'spresəbl/

adj. 无以言表的 too strong or great to be expressed or described

The ***inexpressible*** sadness that the nation felt after 9/11 was met with solemn dedications and prayers across the world.

ineffable, unutterable

absorbing
/əb'zɔ:rbɪŋ/

adj. 吸引人的 fully taking one's attention

Breaking Bad is the perfect TV show to binge-watch on a lazy Saturday afternoon as it is thoroughly ***absorbing*** and fast-paced.

□ conspicuous   □ disinformation   □ preempt   □ recapitulate   □ paralyze
□ inexpressible   □ absorbing

plethora
/ˈpleθərə/
- 释 *n.* 大量 a very large amount or number
- 例 Some psychologists argue that a **plethora** of choices can be paralyzing, since too many make it difficult to pick one.
- 选 glut, surfeit
- 反 dearth, scarce

disregard
/ˌdɪsrɪˈgɑːrd/
- 释 *v.* 无视，忽视 to ignore (something) or treat (something) as unimportant
- 例 Eliza's manager has **disregarded** her requests for a day off, even though she has sent him several e-mails.
- 选 contempt, defy

turbulent
/ˈtɜːrbjələnt/
- 释 *adj.* 混乱的，猛烈的 causing unrest, violence, or disturbance
- 例 Flights from Heathrow Airport were delayed because of **turbulent** winds and sudden hailstorms.

antagonistic
/ænˌtægəˈnɪstɪk/
- 释 *adj.* 敌对的 showing dislike or opposition
- 例 The vague border between the two properties has long been a matter of contention for the **antagonistic** neighbors.
- 选 adversarial, inimical
- 派 antagonize（v. 引起反感）

commonplace
/ˈkɑːmənpleɪs/
- 释 *n.* 平庸，普通 something that happens or appears in many places and is not unusual
- 例 Heckling during a political rally is so **commonplace** that it surprises no one, but the same behavior at a scientific conference would be very startling indeed.
- 选 pervasive

meager
/ˈmiːgər/
- 释 *adj.* 不足的，少的 deficient in quality or quantity
- 例 Professor Gray hypothesized that people dependent on external authority will inevitably falter because they have **meager** self-discipline.
- 选 insufficient, paltry

tendentious
/tenˈdenʃəs/
- 释 *adj.* 偏袒的，偏向的 strongly favoring a particular point of view in a way that may cause argument
- 例 The op-ed was a **tendentious** attack on fracking that was marred by flawed logic and biased research.
- 反 unbiased

prestige
/preˈstiːʒ/
- 释 *n.* 声望，声誉 the respect and admiration that someone or something gets for being successful or important
- 例 Winning an Academy Award gives an actor **prestige** and almost ensures that he or she will be cast in more high-profile films.
- 派 prestigious（adj. 受到尊敬的，有威望的）

burlesque
/bɜːrˈlesk/
- 释 *n.* 滑稽讽刺作品，嘲弄 mockery usually by caricature
- 例 The depiction of Alexander Hamilton as a clown in that theatrical production was so effective that I consider it to be a **burlesque** in its highest form.
- 选 caricature

attain
/ə'teɪn/

释 **v.** 达到，获得 to accomplish or achieve (something); to succeed in getting or doing (something)

例 Supreme Court justices have **attained** the highest positions in the judicial system, and thus are given the final say on high-level cases.

upsurge
/'ʌpsɜːrdʒ/

释 **n.** 增长 a rapid or sudden increase or rise

例 After the release of Pokémon Go, there was an **upsurge** in pedestrian accidents.

grouchy
/'ɡraʊtʃi/

释 **adj.** 易怒的，脾气不好的 having a bad temper

例 When his parents removed the television from the house, the cartoon-obsessed child became **grouchy** and threw a fit.

pliable
/'plaɪəbl/

释 **adj.** 易受影响的 too easily influenced or controlled by other people

例 Sue became the director's personal assistant as she was a **pliable** ally who voted according to the wishes of her boss.

释 **adj.** 容易弯曲或模制的 easily bent or moulded

例 The **pliable** substance is highly flexible and capable of assuming different shapes.

reproach
/rɪ'proʊtʃ/

释 **v.** 斥责，批评 to express disapproval or disappointment to (someone)

例 James was **reproached** by his mother for being unconcerned about his studies and consistently failing his exams.

histrionic
/ˌhɪstri'ɑːnɪk/

释 **adj.** 戏剧性的，做作的 deliberately affected

例 The boy's parents ignored his **histrionic** outburst over a paper cut.

反 unaffected

abnegate
/'æbnəˌɡeɪt/

释 **v.** 舍弃，否认 to deny or renounce

例 During the trip, Maria **abnegated** her parental responsibilities and left the children at the hotel while she partied.

释 **v.** 放弃，屈服 to relinquish or surrender

例 When the revolution came to the steps of the palace, the former king of Greece **abnegated** power and fled to England.

provoke
/prə'voʊk/

释 **v.** 激起 to cause the occurrence of (a feeling or action)

例 Excessive secrecy tends to invite excessive curiosity and thus serves to **provoke** the very impulses against which it guards.

释 **v.** 激怒 to incite to anger

例 **Provoked** by reports of animal abuse, the veterinarian wrote an angry letter to the cosmetic company.

avaricious
/ˌævə'rɪʃəs/

释 **adj.** 贪婪的 excessively acquisitive especially in seeking to hoard riches

例 It is not fair to call someone **avaricious** for wanting to make enough to live on.

近 rapacious

派 avarice（n. 贪婪）

(114)
□ attain   □ upsurge   □ grouchy   □ pliable   □ reproach
□ histrionic   □ abnegate   □ provoke   □ avaricious

brag
/bræg/

释 *v.* 吹嘘，炫耀 to talk about yourself, your achievements, your family, etc., in a way that shows too much pride

例 Everyone grew tired of Tom **bragging** about his "career" as a movie star, especially since his only credit was as an extra in a B-movie.

派 braggart（n. 吹嘘的人）

---

heed
/hiːd/

释 *v.* 留心，注意 to pay attention to (advice, a warning, etc.)

例 The undergrads did not **heed** the warning about riptides and suffered serious casualties.

派 heedful（adj. 小心的），heedless（adj. 无心的）

---

sagacious
/səˈgeɪʃəs/

释 *adj.* 聪明的，睿智的 having or showing an ability to understand difficult ideas and situations and to make good decisions

例 Socrates is now considered to be a **sagacious** philosopher with infinite wisdom, but in Ancient Athens, many considered him a phony.

---

penalty
/ˈpenəlti/

释 *n.* 惩罚 punishment for breaking a rule or law

例 Law fails to deter potential criminals if the **penalty** for crime is too light or applied too rarely.

派 penalize（v. 惩罚）

---

prefigure
/ˌpriːˈfɪgjər/

释 *v.* 预示 to show or suggest (something that will happen or exist at a future time)

例 Faure's music **prefigured** the subsequent development of Impressionistic music in France in the late nineteenth century.

选 anticipate

---

glorify
/ˈglɔːrɪfaɪ/

释 *v.* 赞美 to represent as glorious

例 The monument to Martin Luther King Jr. in Washington D.C. **glorifies** the achievements and sacrifices of the Civil Rights leader.

---

animus
/ˈænɪməs/

释 *n.* 敌意 a strong feeling of dislike or hatred

例 Ward insisted he harbored no **animus** toward Howell, but the two never spoke again.

选 hostility

---

justification
/ˌdʒʌstɪfɪˈkeɪʃn/

释 *n.* 理由 an acceptable reason for doing something

例 Rather than being upset by the cat's destruction of the chair, we were delighted to have a **justification** to go furniture shopping.

选 rationale

派 justify（v. 使…合理）

---

pertain
/pərˈteɪn/

释 *v.* 与…相关 to relate to

例 While revising case files, the judge noticed that several documents did not **pertain** to that specific trial and had been put there by accident.

反 irrelevant

释 *v.* 适用，适合 to be appropriate to something

例 The class was confused by the substitute teacher's choice of video because it did not **pertain** to the topic of world history at all.

---

aggrieve
/ə'griv/

释 *v.* 使痛苦 to give pain or trouble to; to distress
例 ***Aggrieved*** by massive debts, the family grew even more desperate when the bank repossessed their home.

释 *v.* 侵害 to inflict injury on
例 At the joust, Lancelot fought a duel against the knight who ***aggrieved*** the honor of Queen Guinevere.

dearth
/dɜːrθ/

释 *n.* 缺乏 the state or condition of not having enough of something
例 Noting a ***dearth*** of robins around his home, the bird-watcher wondered whether this reflected an overall decrease in this species' population.
选 paucity, vacuousness
反 glut, plethora

calumny
/'kæləmni/

释 *n.* 诽谤 an untrue statement that is made to damage someone's reputation
例 When you are Tweeting negative remarks about someone, you probably don't think much about your risk of being sued for ***calumny***.
选 defamatory

rampant
/'ræmpənt/

释 *adj.* 广泛的 profusely widespread
例 Laziness is ***rampant*** in the office, with people taking increasingly longer breaks.

释 *adj.* 猖獗的 growing quickly and in a way that is difficult to control
例 If there was a pesticide that could successfully control the ***rampant*** growth of weeds, its inventor would be a billionaire.
选 luxuriant

vulnerable
/'vʌlnərəbl/

释 *adj.* 易受伤害的 easily hurt or harmed physically, mentally, or emotionally
例 It was immoral for the conmen to target ***vulnerable*** elderly people living alone in this neighborhood.

pertinent
/'pɜːrtɪnənt/

释 *adj.* 相关的 having a clear decisive relevance to the matter in hand
例 When the lawyer finally presented the ***pertinent*** security camera footage, it was clear that the defendant acted in self-defense.
选 relevant

distort
/dɪ'stɔːrt/

释 *v.* 曲解 to twist out of the true meaning or proportion
例 If good judgment involves both logic and intuitive reasoning, then suppressing intuition might actually ***distort*** judgment.

释 *v.* 扭曲 to twist out of a natural, normal, or original shape or condition
例 The static in the air ***distorted*** the image on the old television and made it unwatchable.

□ aggrieve □ dearth □ calumny □ rampant □ vulnerable
□ pertinent □ distort

overextend
/ˌoʊvərɪkˈstend/

v. 过分扩展，承担过多义务 to extend or expand beyond a safe or reasonable point; especially, to commit (oneself) financially beyond what can be paid

例 The doctor was advised to sell his mansion so that he would not **overextend** his financial resources in paying for child support each month.

precocious
/prɪˈkoʊʃəs/

adj. 早熟的 exhibiting mature qualities at an unusually early age

例 Pablo Picasso was a **precocious** youth; his extraordinary artistic talent was obvious at a very early age.

近 maturity

派 precocity（n. 早熟）

repudiate
/rɪˈpjuːdieɪt/

v. 否认，拒绝 to refuse to accept or support

例 Henry **repudiated** his former racist views and insisted that he now supports equality for all.

近 recant

quirky
/ˈkwɜːrki/

adj. 奇怪的，古怪的 unusual especially in an interesting way

例 The British are known for their love of eccentricity, and Vanbrugh Castle, located in London, is certainly **quirky**.

近 unconventional

proponent
/prəˈpoʊnənt/

n. 支持者 a person who argues for or supports something

例 Edith Wharton was a true **proponent** of the short story: she fervently argued for the genre at every opportunity.

近 defender, champion

反 detractor, vilifier, belittler

reiterate
/riˈɪtəreɪt/

v. 重复强调 to repeat something you have already said in order to emphasize

例 The magazine editor **reiterated** many times that all writers should stop using so many exclamation points in their writing.

conscientious
/ˌkaːnʃiˈenʃəs/

adj. 本着良心的 very careful about doing what one is supposed to do; concerned with doing something correctly

例 Mike was a **conscientious** employee who always committed to his responsibilities and followed the orders of his superiors.

近 exacting

adj. 勤勉认真的，一丝不苟的 thoroug

例 Before handing in the math assign **conscientious** check of his work to ens

rapacious
/rəˈpeɪʃəs/

adj. 贪婪的 having or showing a str money or possess things

例 Nearly seventy years ago, the **rapa** razing many homes in the process.

近 avaricious

disquisition
/ˌdɪskwɪˈzɪʃn/

释 *n.* 演讲，报告 a long speech or written report on a subject
例 BP was required to write a long *disquisition* on the effects of the Gulf Coast oil spill on the local environment.

foretell
/fɔːrˈtel/

释 *v.* 预言，预测 to tell of or indicate beforehand
例 Although the book *1984* did not accurately *foretell* the future, its notion of the "Big Brother" remains relevant to our time and age.

understate
/ˌʌndərˈsteɪt/

释 *v.* 少说，少报 to represent as less than is the case
例 Because of the high crime rate in the city, the marketing firm *understated* the risks of moving when recruiting new clients.

释 *v.* 带有限制地表达 to state or present with restraint especially for effect
例 The activist decided to *understate* her anger about the poverty epidemic and instead strategically focus on the statistics.

discredit
/dɪsˈkredɪt/

释 *v.* 拒绝承认 to refuse to accept as true or accurate
例 Fashion is partly a search for a new language to *discredit* and challenge old norms.

释 *v.* 使被怀疑 to cause disbelief in the accuracy or authority of
例 *Discredited* by rumors of bribery and corruption, the governor was ushered out of office in a shocking recall election.

释 *v.* 破坏名声 to deprive of good repute
例 The misdeeds of individuals are often used to *discredit* the institutions of which they are a part.

underscore
/ˌʌndərˈskɔːr/

释 *v.* 强调 to emphasize (something) or show the importance of (something)
例 Clinton's campaign added a last-minute stop in Indianapolis on Sunday, thus *underscoring* their interest in the state.

predetermine
/ˌpriːdɪˈtɜːrmɪn/

释 *v.* 预先决定 to decide (something) before it happens or in advance
例 "Is life *predetermined*, or do we have full control over our destiny?", the religious scholar asked the class.

provisional
/prəˈvɪʒənl/

释 *adj.* 临时的 serving for the time being
例 As a *provisional* measure to reduce pollution, the government temporarily shut down some factories.
选 conditional

circumspect
/ˈsɜːrkəmspekt/

释 *adj.* 谨慎的 thinking carefully about possible risks before doing or saying something
例 Daniel's *circumspect* attitude toward life is holding him back; he is always scared of taking risks.
选 prudent, chary, cautious
反 rash

majestic
/məˈdʒestɪk/

释 *adj.* 庄严威武的 large and impressively beautiful

例 Inspired by the sight of the *majestic* Grand Tetons, Katherine Lee Bates penned *America the Beautiful*.

选 august

estrange
/ɛˈstreɪndʒ/

释 *v.* 使疏远 to cause someone to be no longer friendly or close to another person or group

例 The husband's infidelity *estranged* the wife and eventually led to divorce.

选 unlinked, disaffect

反 reconciliate

Word List ⏩ 10

音频

falsehood /'fɔːlshʊd/	释 *n.* 谎言，谬论 an untrue statement 例 How can we ever trust a news station that only reports ***falsehoods*** and rumors?
manipulate /mə'nɪpjuleɪt/	释 *v.* 操控 to move or control (something) with your hands or by using a machine 例 While locked in a chest and plunged into water, Harry Houdini was able to ***manipulate*** the chains and escape before running out of oxygen.
pathological /ˌpæθə'lɑːdʒɪkl/	释 *adj.* 极端的 being such to a degree that is extreme, excessive, or markedly abnormal 例 It became clear that Brian was a ***pathological*** liar who lied about even the most innocuous things. 释 *adj.* 病态的 indicative of disease 例 I encouraged my mother to visit the doctor after she complained of ***pathological*** symptoms.
circuitous /sɜr'kjuːɪtəs/	释 *adj.* 兜圈子的，不直接的 not being forthright or direct in language or action 例 By shifting his camp and taking ***circuitous*** routes, the guerilla fighter escaped his pursuers. 选 indirect
propitious /prə'pɪʃəs/	释 *adj.* 吉祥的，吉利的 likely to have or produce good results 例 It was a ***propitious*** sign when the company's stock price rose the moment the new CEO took office. 选 auspicious
insightful /'ɪnsaɪtfʊl/	释 *adj.* 有洞察力的 having or showing a very clear understanding of something; having or showing insight 例 Poe's ***insightful*** reviews of contemporary fiction often give us a new perspective of literature.
nullify /'nʌlɪfaɪ/	释 *v.* 使…无效 to cause (something) to lose its value or to have no effect 例 The government ***nullified*** the law yesterday and claimed it should never have been on the ballot in the first place. 选 disprove

☐ falsehood   ☐ manipulate   ☐ pathological   ☐ circuitous   ☐ propitious
☐ insightful   ☐ nullify

facilitate
/fəˈsɪlɪteɪt/

释 *v.* 辅助，帮助 to make easier

例 His goal was to *facilitate* the committee's deliberations and allow a decision to be reached easily.

选 speedup, expedite

反 hamper

appeal
/əˈpiːl/

释 *v.* 呼吁，恳求 to ask for something (such as help or support) in a serious way

例 With the discovery of new DNA evidence, the convicted murderer *appealed* his conviction and demanded freedom.

释 *v.* 吸引 to be pleasing or attractive to someone

例 A hot stew is what truly *appeals* to me after a long day outside in freezing temperatures.

appease
/əˈpiːz/

释 *v.* 安抚，缓和 to make (someone) pleased or less angry by giving or saying something desired

例 The author expanded the last act of her play to *appease* those critics who had called it too abrupt.

选 placate

deleterious
/ˌdeləˈtɪriəs/

释 *adj.* 有害的 damaging or harmful

例 Doctors initially feared that antibiotics would have a *deleterious* effect on health by destroying healthy tissue as well as harmful bacteria.

选 detrimental, devastating

ethereal
/iˈθɪriəl/

释 *adj.* 虚无的 lacking material substance: immaterial, intangible

例 The Orthodox service was truly an *ethereal* and indescribable experience that stimulated all of the senses.

释 *adj.* 天上的 of or relating to the regions beyond the earth

例 Even after I photographed the image of the ghost, none of my friends believed that my *ethereal* encounter was real.

rehabilitate
/ˌriːəˈbɪlɪteɪt/

释 *v.* 恢复 to restore to a former capacity

例 There is no sense trying to *rehabilitate* the reputation of the mosquito: nobody loves such a creature.

选 restore

cluster
/ˈklʌstər/

释 *v.* 聚集 to come together to form a group

例 Rainstorms tend to *cluster* together during the monsoon season and produce continuous rainfall for a prolonged period of time.

partisan
/ˈpɑːrtəzn/

释 *n.* 强硬支持者（尤指盲目的、偏见的、不理性的支持）a firm adherent to a party, faction, cause, or person; especially, one exhibiting blind, prejudiced, and unreasoning allegiance

例 Anderson was a *partisan* who had a fanatic commitment to only one political cause.

bypass
/ˈbaɪpæs/

释 *v.* 绕过 to go around or avoid (a place or area)
例 Ancient cave painters seemed to have selected certain walls and *bypassed* others for reasons that remain obscure to us.
选 circumvent, skirt

scrupulous
/ˈskruːpjələs/

释 *adj.* 小心谨慎的 very careful about doing something correctly
例 John's supervisors highly regard his *scrupulous* attitude to work as it always ensures an output of great quality.

释 *adj.* 有道德的，有良心的 acting in strict regard for what is considered right or proper
例 Although most people in the early years of the internet explored only legitimate uses of computer networks, others were less *scrupulous* and took advantage of the technology's potential for mischief.
反 dishonest

monolithic
/ˌmɑːnəˈlɪθɪk/

释 *adj.* 庞大而僵硬的 constituting a massive undifferentiated and often rigid whole
例 Startups can see a broader range of problems to address because they don't have to wear the same economic blinkers as established, *monolithic* companies.

scathing
/ˈskeɪðɪŋ/

释 *adj.* 尖酸刻薄的 very hash or severe
例 The movie got a *scathing* review in the *New York Times* for its weak dialogue and lack of plot.
选 acerbic, sarcastic

block
/blɑːk/

释 *v.* 阻碍，妨碍 to make unsuitable for passage or progress by obstruction
例 The Republicans *blocked* the passage of the Right to Choose bill, citing religious and moral reasons in their opposition.
选 hinder

off-putting
/ˈɔːf pʊtɪŋ/

释 *adj.* 令人反感的 unappealing; causing one to feel dislike of someone or something
例 When I opened the container of leftover vegetables, the *off-putting* aroma made it clear that the food had spoiled.

profligate
/ˈprɑːflɪgət/

释 *adj.* 奢侈的，花钱大手大脚的 carelessly and foolishly wasting money or other resources
例 Emilia has been thoroughly *profligate* ever since she got her first pay check in the law firm.
选 extravagant, prodigal
反 frugal

□ bypass   □ scrupulous   □ monolithic   □ scathing   □ block
□ off-putting   □ profligate

unctuous
/ˈʌŋktʃuəs/

释 *adj.* 虚情假意的 revealing or marked by a smug, ingratiating, and false earnestness or spirituality

例 The **unctuous** senator greeted the undecided voters with an insincere grin and a slap on the back.

派 unctuousness（n. 虚情假意）

释 *adj.* 油腻的 rich in oil or fat

例 Although some remove the **unctuous** gristle on the beefsteak, I relish the delicious, fatty flavor.

nimble
/ˈnɪmbl/

释 *adj.* 灵敏的，轻快的 able to move quickly, easily, and lightly

例 After looking over the CCTV video, the police determined that the thief was quite **nimble** and had climbed through the window gracefully.

选 dexterous, skillful, adroit

释 *adj.* 机敏的 able to learn and understand things quickly and easily

例 Even at 80, my grandmother's mind is **nimble** as ever; she reads a book and does a word puzzle every day.

shoddy
/ˈʃɑːdi/

释 *adj.* 劣质 poorly done or made

例 The **shoddy** workmanship of the table was not only apparent in its outward appearance, but also in its structural weakness whenever weight is applied.

heterogeneous
/ˌhetərəˈdʒiːniəs/

释 *adj.* 组成多样的，混合的 made up of parts that are different

例 Some species can camouflage themselves against any background to increase their chances of survival in a **heterogeneous** environment.

选 disparate, dissimilar

verisimilitude
/ˌverɪsɪˈmɪlɪtuːd/

释 *n.* 逼真 the quality of seeming real

例 Carrie's account may have seemed mostly fictive but it did bear traces of **verisimilitude** in some respects.

选 realism

derivative
/dɪˈrɪvətɪv/

释 *adj.* 非原创的 unoriginal

例 The dancer's performing style was mostly **derivative** and inept, and can hardly be considered to be creative or original.

反 precursory

sycophantic
/ˌsɪkəˈfæntɪk/

释 *adj.* 奉承的 fawning, obsequious

例 Her dislike of flattery made her disregard **sycophantic** people who tried to win her approval through praise.

选 obsequious, adulator

派 sycophant（n. 拍马屁的人）

circumvent
/ˌsɜːrkəmˈvent/

释 *v.* 绕过，回避 to avoid being stopped by (something, such as a law or rule)

例 Eager to enlist as a soldier during the American Revolution, Deborah Sampson Gannett successfully **circumvented** the military's gender boundary by donning men's clothing and assuming a male identity.

选 bypass, skirt, sidestep

☐ unctuous ☐ nimble ☐ shoddy ☐ heterogeneous ☐ verisimilitude
☐ derivative ☐ sycophantic ☐ circumvent

rigid
/'rɪdʒɪd/

释 *adj.* 僵硬的 not flexible

例 Because there was no flexibility to the structure, the *rigid* foundation of the building cracked in the recent California earthquakes.

选 dogmatic

派 rigidity（n. 僵化）

释 *adj.* 严格精确的 precise and accurate in procedure

例 Deviating the slightest from the *rigid* surgical procedures can cause massive damage to the intestines.

释 *adj.* 思想僵化的 not willing to change opinions or behavior

例 The party leadership were *rigid* believers in centrist ideology, even when it seemed that voters did not prefer it.

plaintive
/'pleɪntɪv/

释 *adj.* 痛苦的 expressing suffering or sadness

例 *Plaintive* sobbing had been coming from Betty's room all afternoon, reflecting her sadness about the loss of the family dog.

选 elegiac

detestation
/ˌdiːte'steɪʃn/

释 *n.* 厌恶，反感 extreme hatred or dislike

例 The poet showed his *detestation* of publicity by hanging up on the interviewer and refusing to give public readings.

派 detest（v. 厌恶）

susceptible
/sə'septəbl/

释 *adj.* 易受影响的 easily affected, influenced, or harmed by something

例 Because of his allergies, David was extremely *susceptible* to illness and was sick at least once a month.

tautology
/tɔː'tɑːlədʒi/

释 *n.* 赘述 a statement in which one repeats a word, idea, etc., in a way that is not necessary

例 That rich people can afford to buy nicer things isn't a great insight, it's a *tautology*.

leaven
/'levn/

释 *v.* 使…生动，使…更有趣 to make (something) less serious and often more exciting

例 The grave and solemn talk was *leavened* by slight optimism and a sense of humor at the end.

convulsion
/kən'vʌlʃn/

释 *n.* 骚乱，动乱 a sudden change or disturbance that affects a country, organization, etc.

例 Financial conditions in the United States have recently become unpredictable, and *convulsions* in the stock markets could harm the country's economy.

选 upheaval

exorbitant
/ɪg'zɔːrbɪtənt/

释 *adj.* 过度的，超出合理范围的 going far beyond what is fair, reasonable, or expected

例 Brazilian police broke up a black-market ring that tried to illegally sell over 700 Olympic tickets at *exorbitant* prices.

☐ rigid ☐ plaintive ☐ detestation ☐ susceptible ☐ tautology
☐ leaven ☐ convulsion ☐ exorbitant

corollary /ˈkɔːrəleri/	释 *n.* 推论，结果 something that naturally follows or results from another thing 例 An unexpected *corollary* of this era of two-parent professionals is the rise of day cares and child care services.
perforce /pərˈfɔːrs/	释 *adv.* 必然地 used to say that something is necessary or must be done 例 To advocate placing such secret information in the public record was *perforce* an act of disloyalty.
proselytize /ˈprɑːsələtaɪz/	释 *v.* 劝诱，使变节 to try to persuade people to join a religion, cause, or group 例 The professor has been a believer in Apple products for years and annoys people by constantly *proselytizing* for the Mac.
fetishize /ˈfetɪʃaɪz/	释 *v.* 把…当成神物而崇拜 to make a fetish of; to treat or regard with fetishism 例 Civility in politics is nice, but we *fetishize* it when we treat it as the most important goal.
omnivorous /ɑːmˈnɪvərəs/	释 *adj.* 杂食的 eating both plants and animals 例 Some people believe chimps eat only fruit and leaves, but they are actually *omnivorous* and regularly hunt other animals. 释 *adj.* 求知若渴的 eager to learn about many different things 例 An *omnivorous* historian, Bo constantly reads books about American, Russian, British and European history.
urbane /ɜːrˈbeɪn/	释 *adj.* 礼貌的 polite and confident 例 The dinner party's host was truly *urbane* and impressed his guests with his elegant manners, discriminating taste, and broad education.
idiosyncrasy /ˌɪdiəˈsɪŋkrəsi/	释 *n.* 独特的气质 an unusual way in which a particular person behaves or thinks 例 The *idiosyncrasy* in painter Sigmar Polke's style lies in his eccentric themes and imagery. 近 distinct, atypical 派 idiosyncratic（adj. 异类的）
forthcoming /ˌfɔːrθˈkʌmɪŋ/	释 *adj.* 直白的 honest and open 例 Young people are sometimes surprised to find that older people are less than *forthcoming* when asked their age. 释 *adj.* 即将到来的 appearing, happening, or arriving soon 例 Tesla's *forthcoming* Model 3 is being marketed as something revolutionary: an electric car for the masses.
pecuniary /pɪˈkjuːnieri/	释 *adj.* 金钱的 relating to or in the form of money 例 Having to pay for travel and accommodation at academic conferences can cause *pecuniary* difficulties for graduate students. 近 economic

pathos
/ˈpeɪθɑːs/

例 *n.* 怜悯，同情 an emotion of sympathetic pity

例 The actor's performance was full of ***pathos*** and moved the whole audience to tears.

cosmopolitan
/ˌkɑːzməˈpɑːlɪtən/

例 *adj.* 见多识广的 having worldwide rather than limited or provincial scope or bearing

例 Lusia Capetillo's career was truly ***cosmopolitan*** as she also worked in Florida, New York, and Cuba after participating in the early labor union movement in Puerto Rico.

反 insular

例 *adj.* 来自四面八方的 composed of persons, constituents, or elements from all or many parts of the world

例 Although New York is not the world's largest city, its diverse population provides it with a unique ***cosmopolitan*** character.

例 *adj.* 世界各地都有的 found in most parts of the world and under varied ecological conditions

例 Mosquitoes are ***cosmopolitan*** pests that come out in the summer time all over the world.

panoply
/ˈpænəpli/

例 *n.* 大批，全副(装备) a group or collection that is impressive because it is so big or because it includes so many different kinds of people or things

例 As a vast empire of dozens of conquered people, the Persian Empire could muster a ***panoply*** of troops to extend the dominion of the king.

arboreal
/ɑːrˈbɔːriəl/

例 *adj.* 树的 of or relating to trees

例 Maple syrup is a sweet ***arboreal*** delight that is made from the sap of many trees.

例 *adj.* 树栖的 living in or often found in trees

例 As an ***arboreal*** creature, the chimpanzee has legs that evolved differently from those of upright humans.

nostalgia
/nəˈstældʒə/

例 *n.* 思乡 the state of being homesick

例 Within one day at camp, the child grew ***nostalgic*** and yearned to be home with his family immediately.

例 *n.* 怀旧，怀念 a wistful or excessively sentimental yearning for return to or of some past period or irrecoverable condition

例 The ***nostalgia*** for the sitcom *Friends* is strange as there are so many better ones from the early '90s, like *My So-Called Life* and *Roseanne*.

peremptory /pəˈremptəri/	**adj.** 不容反抗的，断然的 admitting of no contradiction
	The new teacher spoke in such a **peremptory** manner that all of us understood that she would not stand for disobedience.
	adj. 狂妄自大的 characterized by often imperious or arrogant self-assurance
	His **peremptory** manner contrasted starkly with the deeply seated insecurities that he tried to repress.
avian /ˈeɪviən/	**adj.** 跟鸟有关的 of or relating to birds
	At the **avian** exhibit, the child saw dozens of examples of brightly colored, exotic birds from the tropics.
ramshackle /ˈræmʃækl/	**adj.** 摇摇欲坠的 appearing ready to collapse
	Despite the **ramshackle** appearance of the hotel, the beds were comfortable and the view unmatched.
	adj. 制作粗糙的 not carefully made or put together
	Having started the project an hour before it was due, the student had time to make only a **ramshackle** model of Apollo 11.
quiver /ˈkwɪvər/	**v.** 战栗 to shake because of fear, cold, nervousness, etc.
	The audience could hear Jane's voice **quiver** in fear as she began her public speech.
rancor /ˈræŋkər/	**n.** 憎恨 an angry feeling of hatred or dislike for someone who has treated you unfairly
	The delegates' behavior at the convention was disgraceful and fully deserving of the **rancor** it provoked.
	acrimony
dewy-eyed /ˌduːiˈaɪd/	**adj.** 天真的，朴素的 innocent
	Having been raised in a rural community, the **dewy-eyed** girl was shocked upon arrival in Los Angeles when she saw her first skyscraper and bout of rush-hour traffic.
epitome /ɪˈpɪtəmi/	**n.** 典型 a perfect example
	Many critics of modern art saw Duchamp's *Nude Descending a Staircase* as the **epitome** of the lofty aims of Futurism.
fissure /ˈfɪʃər/	**n.** 裂缝 a narrow opening or crack
	Upon inspection of the earthquake damage, the engineers realized that a large **fissure** had divided the road in two.
	n. 分歧 a separation or disagreement in thought or viewpoint
	A personal quarrel resulted in a **fissure** that split the football team in two and affected their ability to perform collectively during games.
parley /ˈpɑːrli/	**v.** 谈判 to discuss terms with an enemy
	Battle was inevitable as the general decided not to **parley** with the enemy.

immolate
/ˈɪməleɪt/

v. 用火摧毁 to kill or destroy (someone or something) by fire

After being tortured by a poisoned blanket, Hercules built a pyre on Mt. Oete to **immolate** himself and end his suffering.

---

lassitude
/ˈlæsɪtuːd/

n. 无精打采 lack of physical or mental energy

After working out, people are usually filled with a deeply pleasurable **lassitude** and naturally feel more relaxed.

反 vigor

---

pompous
/ˈpɑːmpəs/

adj. 过于华丽的 excessively elevated or ornate

In contrast to Roman architecture, which was typically **pompous** in style, Greek architecture was austere.

近 bombastic

adj. 傲慢的，自以为是的 having or exhibiting self-importance

Despite being consistently panned by record companies and critics, the **pompous** braggart believed he was the world's greatest guitarist.

---

overreach
/ˌoʊvərˈriːtʃ/

v. 因野心勃勃而失败 to defeat (oneself) by seeking to do or gain too much

The climber **overreached** his body's capabilities and was eventually defeated in his attempt to climb all 8,000-meter peaks within a year.

v. 不自量力做… to try to do something that is beyond your ability to do

The sailor **overreached** his capabilities to sail in bad weather and inadvertently drove the boat directly into the eye of the storm.

---

demarcate
/ˈdiːmɑːrkeɪt/

v. 划分边界 to set the boundaries of; to delimit

If you cross the borders that are firmly **demarcated** between the two territories, you risk getting into trouble with the authorities.

近 line

---

evince
/ɪˈvɪns/

v. 显示 to display clearly

Ronald's report contained dozens of relevant citations that **evinced** the great amount of research he had done.

反 conceal

---

veer
/vɪr/

v. 改变方向 to change direction or course

Upon receiving information about the iceberg, the captain of the Titanic immediately tried to **veer** away from it.

---

resilient
/rɪˈzɪliənt/

adj. 能（从困境中）恢复的 able to become strong, healthy, or successful again after something bad happens

Although other European states broke apart under the stresses of political upheaval, the seventeenth-century Dutch republic proved **resilient**.

反 lack of elasticity

派 resilience（n. 适应性）

adj. 有弹性的 able to return to an original shape after being pulled, stretched, pressed, bent, etc.

After years of being coiled around the ball, the rubber band was no longer **resilient**; it was stretched and unusable.

□ immolate　　□ lassitude　　□ pompous　　□ overreach　　□ demarcate
□ evince　　□ veer　　□ resilient

revolt
/rɪˈvəʊlt/

v. 反叛，反抗 to fight in a violent way against the rule of a leader or government

The French Revolution started out with peasants demanding a change in the government and **revolting** against the monarchy.

v. 反感 to cause (someone) to feel disgust or shock

The diner was **revolted** by the appearance of lamb's brains on the menu and could not bring himself to try the local delicacy.

devolve
/dɪˈvɑːlv/

v. 衰落 to gradually go from an advanced state to a less advanced state

It's easy to complain that artists are self-indulgent, but society would **devolve** quickly if they were gone.

v. （权力、责任）移交 to pass on from one person or entity to another

The king had little choice but to accept the fait accompli: power was henceforth to **devolve** from an absolute monarchy to a parliamentary constitution.

adulation
/ˌædʒəˈleɪʃn/

n. 恭维，吹捧 excessive or slavish admiration or flattery

Brianna's dislike of **adulation** made her regard people who complimented her as phonies.

sycophant

demolish
/dɪˈmɑːlɪʃ/

v. 拆毁 to forcefully tear down or take apart (a structure)

The building was old and dangerous, so the local government decided to **demolish** it as soon as possible.

v. 破坏 to damage (something) so that it cannot be repaired

As a hideous symbol of repression, the monument of the fascist dictator was **demolished** by rebels during the Revolutionary insurgence.

timely
/ˈtaɪmli/

adj. 合时宜地 occuring at a suitable time

The workers made the **timely** decision to unionize just as management was considering cutting their pensions.

opportune

snapshot
/ˈsnæpʃɑːt/

n. 大致情况，简介 a quick view or a small amount of information that tells you a little about what someone or something is like

The short charity trip to the poor villages of Nicaragua provided Rachel with a **snapshot** of rural life in Central America.

n. 快照 an informal photograph that is taken quickly

He took a quick **snapshot** of the group of monkeys by the road as their car whizzed by.

obsequious
/əbˈsiːkwiəs/

adj. 谄媚的 too eager to help or obey someone important

Annoyed by the new employee's **obsequious** manner, the supervisor told him that no one likes a yes-man.

sycophantic

☐ revolt   ☐ devolve   ☐ adulation   ☐ demolish   ☐ timely
☐ snapshot   ☐ obsequious

gut
/gʌt/

釋 *n.* 内心深处 innermost emotional or visceral response
例 I had a *gut* feeling that the real culprit was John even though I could not prove it rationally.

釋 *v.* 摘取要点 to extract essential or major parts of
例 He was employed to *gut* the lengthy manuscript into various comprehensible papers.
近 eviscerate

hierarchy
/'haɪərɑːrki/

釋 *n.* 等级制度，有等级划分的组织 the classification of a group of people according to ability or to economic, social, or professional standing or the group so classified
例 In the European Medieval Ages, society was ruled by feudalism and had strict *hierarchies* that determined who obeyed whom.
派 hierarchical（adj. 等级制的）

釋 *n.* 权力机构 a body of persons in authority
例 The coal miners demanded a meeting with the company *hierarchy* to discuss wage reforms.

terse
/tɜːrs/

釋 *adj.* 简洁的 brief and direct in a way that may seem rude or unfriendly
例 The professor urged students toward a *terse* rather than an embellished prose style as he preferred economy of written expression.
近 curt, taciturn, laconic, succinct

abate
/ə'beɪt/

釋 *v.* 减弱 to become weaker
例 Assuming that the birds nesting in the reserve were no longer in danger from poachers, the caretakers *abated* their vigilance.
近 mitigate
反 augment
派 unabated（adj. 没有减弱的）

fluster
/'flʌstər/

釋 *v.* 使…不安 to make (someone) nervous and confused
例 The missing students completely *flustered* Tom as he knew that dire consequences awaited him.
反 calm

flatter
/'flætər/

釋 *v.* 谄媚，拍马屁 to praise (someone) in a way that is not sincere
例 Everyone in the office knew that Jerry only *flattered* his boss in order to get a raise.
近 fawn

accentuate
/ək'sentʃueɪt/

釋 *v.* 强调 to make (something) more noticeable
例 The blue dress *accentuated* Heidi's brilliant blue eyes, making them stand out in a crowd.
近 highlight

(130)
□ gut   □ hierarchy   □ terse   □ abate   □ fluster
□ flatter   □ accentuate

augment /ɔːɡ'ment/	释 **v.** 放大 to increase the size or amount of (something) 例 Florence Bascom was an accomplished geologist who **augmented** the world's knowledge of mountain formation. 选 extend, enhance 释 **v.** 补充 to supplement 例 The preservation of wild fruits helps to **augment** the fall harvest and allows the farmers to combat scurvy during the winter.
certitude /'sɜːrtɪtuːd/	释 **n.** 确信无疑 freedom from doubt 例 When **certitude** melts into uncertainty, it is hard for a former believer to decide what to think.
cachet /kæ'ʃeɪ/	释 **n.** 声望，威望 an indication of approval carrying great prestige 例 Some ambitious lawyers are willing to work on Supreme Court cases without pay as they believe that this increased **cachet** will help them succeed in the future.
contrite /kən'traɪt/	释 **adj.** 后悔的 feeling or showing regret for bad behavior 例 The office sandwich thief was **contrite**, issuing an apology and promising that such an incident wouldn't happen again. 选 penitent, remorse
unanimous /ju'nænɪməs/	释 **adj.** 意见一致的 having the same opinion 例 The city council's **unanimous** rejection of a proposal so critical to the mayor's agenda was a shocking setback for the mayor.
neologism /ni'ɑːlədʒɪzəm/	释 **n.** 新词，新意思 a new word or expression or a new meaning of a word 例 A visioneer is a **neologism** of "visionary" and "engineer", and perfectly captures the hybrid nature of these technologists' activities. 反 archaism
aristocracy /ˌærɪ'stɑːkrəsi/	释 **n.** 贵族统治，精英统治 government by the best individuals or by a small privileged class 例 The emperor Ying Zheng created an **aristocracy** that was not hereditary and could not be passed down to the next generation. 反 menial 派 aristocratic（adj. 贵族的）
inimical /ɪ'nɪmɪkl/	释 **adj.** 有害的，不友好的 likely to cause damage or have a bad effect 例 Those protesters opposed Obama's abortion rights agenda, which they considered **inimical** to Catholic teaching. 选 antagonistic, deleterious
hallow /'hæloʊ/	释 **v.** 尊敬，崇敬 to respect greatly; to venerate 例 As she is the leading surgeon in the hospital, her expertise and advice are incredibly **hallowed**. 选 respect

annals
/ˈænlz/

n. 历史记载 historical records

The 1960s civil rights marches were some of the most inspiring events in the ***annals*** of technology.

execrate
/ˈeksɪˌkreɪt/

v. 痛斥 to dislike and criticize (someone or something) very strongly

The critic ***execrated*** Hoffman's novel and said that slamming it shut was the only pleasure it provided.

unexampled
/ˌʌnɪɡˈzæmpld/

adj. 史无前例的 without precedent

During a period of ***unexampled*** intellectual ferment in physics, Oppenheimer published papers on every major issue in his field.

novel

tug
/tʌɡ/

v. 用力拉 to pull something with a quick, forceful movement

It was only when he felt the boy ***tug*** at his pants that the man realized there were children in the crowded room.

n. 斗争 a struggle between two people or opposite forces

In the meeting, there was a real ***tug*** of war between members of the design team about whether to include gaudy rims on the new convertible.

claustrophobic
/ˌklɔːstrəˈfoʊbɪk/

adj. 狭小而引起不适的 uncomfortably closed or hemmed in

It was not the tornado that Walt feared; it was being stuck in the ***claustrophobic*** storm shelter for hours.

atavism
/ˈætəˌvɪzəm/

n. 重现 the return of a trait or recurrence of previous behavior after a period of absence

Despite having been self-sufficient for ten years, Bob allowed his parents to wait on him hand and foot whenever he returned home, thus demonstrating a form of ***atavism*** that surprised others.

n. 返祖现象 the reappearance of a characteristic in an organism after several generations of absence, usually caused by the chance recombination of genes.

Because neither his parents nor his grandparents were redheads, it was clear that Don's fiery looks were an ***atavism*** from ancestors who lived generations before.

prepossessing
/ˌpriːpəˈzesɪŋ/

adj. 有吸引力的 appealing or attractive

Jane was very plain and far from ***prepossessing*** in appearance, but her wit and charm made people pay attention to her.

perfidious
/pərˈfɪdiəs/

adj. 不可信赖的 not able to be trusted

The general was so widely suspected of being ***perfidious*** during the war that his name eventually became synonymous with disloyalty.

loyal

perfidy（n. 背信弃义，欺诈）

音频

jubilation /ˌdʒuːbɪˈleɪʃn/	释 *n.* 高兴，喜悦 great happiness or joy 例 There was great *jubilation* in the room when my sister announced that she was expecting. 近 enthusiasm
peregrination /ˌperəɡrɪˈneɪʃn/	释 *n.* 长途旅行，游历 a voyage, especially an extensive one 例 Jose went on frequent *peregrinations* in the course of writing his travel novel.
retribution /ˌretrɪˈbjuːʃn/	释 *n.* 惩罚 punishment for doing something wrong 例 The informer did not want to give his surname for fear of *retribution* against his school-age children or his businesses.
charlatan /ˈʃɑːrlətən/	释 *n.* 骗子 a person who falsely pretends to know or be something in order to deceive people 例 Concerned about protecting investors from *charlatans*, bad ideas and their own poor judgment, the agency spent years drafting its proposed rules.
malinger /məˈlɪŋɡər/	释 *v.* 装病以逃避工作 to feign illness or other incapacity in order to avoid duty or work 例 One doctor who treated the supposed chronic fatigue sufferer suspected he might be *malingering*, since he could not describe his symptoms.
halcyon /ˈhælsiən/	释 *adj.* 岁月静好的，安宁的 very happy and successful 例 The 1990s were *halcyon* years for the organization: the staff was happy, customers were satisfied, and profits were excellent. 反 miserable
predominant /prɪˈdɑːmɪnənt/	释 *adj.* 最显著的，主导的 more important, powerful, successful, or noticeable than other people or things 例 Angry Birds had success at a time when the *predominant* way to make money from games was to charge a small fee up front.
evocative /ɪˈvɑːkətɪv/	释 *adj.* 唤起的 bringing thoughts, memories, or feelings into the mind 例 Halle Berry's portrayal of Dorothy Dandridge is powerfully *evocative*: it calls forth the qualities that made Dandridge a legend.
nonchalant /ˌnɑːnʃəˈlɑːnt/	释 *adj.* 漠不关心的 relaxed and calm in a way that shows that one does not care or is not worried about anything 例 Clowns are haunting and creepy for some people, but I am rather *nonchalant* about them and cannot care less. 近 insouciant

☐ jubilation ☐ peregrination ☐ retribution ☐ charlatan ☐ malinger
☐ halcyon ☐ predominant ☐ evocative ☐ nonchalant

ennoble
/ɪˈnoʊbl/

释 *v.* 使…崇高 to make (someone or something) better or more worthy of admiration

例 Chuck's first victory at the Indy 500 on the eve of his retirement **ennobled** him even more to racing fans.

反 abase

eradicate
/ɪˈrædɪkeɪt/

释 *v.* 根除 to remove (something) completely

例 Traditions are so tenacious and hard to **eradicate** that they often survive for generations, through countless social and historical changes.

prodigal
/ˈprɑːdɪgl/

释 *adj.* 奢侈浪费的 characterized by profuse or wasteful expenditure

例 She is frugal in business matters but notoriously **prodigal** in her private life.

选 profligate, extravagant

反 penurious

派 prodigality（n. 挥霍）

释 *adj.* 多产的，大量的 yielding abundantly

例 Winter is bleak, but spring immediately gives us the impression that nature is **prodigal** with its gifts.

disengage
/ˌdɪsɪnˈgeɪdʒ/

释 *v.* 使解脱 to release from something that engages or involves

例 Matt suddenly **disengaged** his hand from his girlfriend's to swat a fly.

rebound
/rɪˈbaʊnd/

释 *v.* 从挫败中恢复 to recover from setback or frustration

例 Last July, Microsoft introduced Windows 10 and raised some hopes that the industry would **rebound** in PC sales.

释 *v.* 弹回 to bounce back off something after hitting it

例 The basketball players braced themselves to catch the ball as it **rebounded** off the rim.

adhere
/ədˈhɪr/

释 *v.* 依附于…，坚持 to stick to something

例 The country's leader has consistently rejected any criticism of its human rights record, saying it **adheres** to the rules of law.

反 detach

unilateral
/ˌjuːnɪˈlætrəl/

释 *adj.* 单方面的 involving only one group or country

例 Without consulting its allies, Canada made a **unilateral** agreement to invade Alaska.

equable
/ˈekwəbl/

释 *adj.* 平静的 tending to remain calm

例 In spite of the potential dangers, Gretta remained **equable** while searching for her runaway daughter.

释 *adj.* 稳定不变的 free from sudden or harsh changes

例 Is it better for the economy if the stock market remains **equable** or if it swings between highs and lows?

instantiate
/ɪnˈstænʃiˌeɪt/

释 *v.* 举例，例证 to represent (an abstraction) by a concrete instance

例 The problem of police brutality is **instantiated** by shocking incidents like the shooting of Philando Castillo by Minnesota police officers.

□ ennoble □ eradicate □ prodigal □ disengage □ rebound
□ adhere □ unilateral □ equable □ instantiate

diverse /daɪ'vɜːrs/	释 *adj.* 多样的，不同的 different from each other 例 Congress is having difficulty developing a consensus on energy policy because the policy objectives of various members of Congress rest on such *diverse* assumptions. 选 varied, divergent
protean /'proʊtiən/	释 *adj.* 多样的 displaying great diversity or variety 例 Turn-of-the-century actress Sarah Bernhardt had so *protean* a talent that she convincingly portrayed many different types of characters. 选 versatile
pillory /'pɪləri/	释 *v.* 批评 to publicly criticize (someone) in a very harsh way 例 While her father was being *pilloried* throughout Latin America, the actress was given the celebrity treatment on the cover of a Colombian magazine. 选 vilify 反 exalt
exuberant /ɪg'zuːbərənt/	释 *adj.* 过量的 extreme or excessive in degree, size, or extent 例 The *exuberant* wealth of the aristocrats results in levels of repugnance in me. 释 *adj.* 热情洋溢的 filled with energy and enthusiasm 例 The abstract painting's bright colors and *exuberant* brushstrokes create a joyful feeling.
plunder /'plʌndər/	释 *v.* 掠夺 to steal things from (a place, such as a city or town) especially by force 例 Early American settlers are portrayed as heroes, but they *plundered* land and other goods from the Native Americans.
ennui /ɑːn'wiː/	释 *n.* 无趣，无聊 a lack of spirit, enthusiasm, or interest 例 Living in a suburb surrounded by bland suburbs and strip malls can inspire a sense of *ennui*.
conceive /kən'siːv/	释 *v.* 构想，创造 to think of or create (something) in the mind 例 She was unable to *conceive* of a decent solution to the problem despite thinking hard for the whole day. 选 imaginable
devoid /dɪ'vɔɪd/	释 *adj.* 缺乏的 being without 例 The annual company picnic appeared to be *devoid* of all fun, with each employee silently sitting and checking their phones.
sophisticated /sə'fɪstɪkeɪtɪd/	释 *adj.* 精于世故的，老练的 having or showing a lot of experience and knowledge about the world and about culture, art, literature, etc. 例 Growing up in a *sophisticated* family of opera singers, Giuseppe regularly attended art openings and museum exhibits. 反 naïve 释 *adj.* 高度复杂的 highly developed and complex 例 By the standards of the day, the computer on board Apollo 11 space shuttle was *sophisticated*; by today's standards, it has the power of a modern calculator.

☐ diverse   ☐ protean   ☐ pillory   ☐ exuberant   ☐ plunder
☐ ennui   ☐ conceive   ☐ devoid   ☐ sophisticated

conclusive
/kən'kluːsɪv/

释 *adj.* 终结的，最终的 putting an end to debate or question especially by reason of irrefutability

例 The inscription found beside the tomb provided *conclusive* evidence that King Tut was buried inside.

enlighten
/ɪn'laɪtn/

释 *v.* 启迪，开导 to give knowledge or understanding to (someone)

例 The 18th-century philosopher and novelist William Godwin attempted to *enlighten* his contemporaries on feminist ideas.

methodology
/ˌmeθə'dɑːlədʒi/

释 *n.* 方法论 a set of methods, rules, or ideas that are important in a science or art; a particular procedure or set of procedures

例 It is important to have a well-developed and logical *methodology* to ensure that the experiment is repeatable and the results reliable.

tectonic
/tek'tɑːnɪk/

释 *adj.* 建筑的 relating to construction or building

例 For many cultures, mud bricks are essential *tectonic* ingredients used by construction workers.

释 *adj.* 地壳构造的 of or relating to changes in the structure of the Earth's surface

例 When the *tectonic* plates shifted, the earth trembled and produced an earthquake near San Jose.

释 *adj.* 影响广泛的 having a strong and widespread impact

例 The atomic bombs that fell on Japan had a *tectonic* effect on warfare for years to come.

monogamy
/mə'nɑːɡəmi/

释 *n.* 一夫一妻制 the state or practice of being married to only one person at a time

例 By taking his marriage vows, Andrew agreed to practice *monogamy* with his partner and not seek relationships outside the marriage.

pathogen
/'pæθədʒən/

释 *n.* 病原体 a specific causative agent (as a bacterium or virus) of disease

例 A deadly *pathogen*, HIV caused an international health scare in the 1980s and 1990s.

depict
/dɪ'pɪkt/

释 *v.* 描述 to describe (someone or something) using words, a story

例 The painting by Rubens *depicts* Prometheus bound to a rock with an eagle pecking out his liver.

dismissive
/dɪs'mɪsɪv/

释 *adj.* 轻视的，无视的 serving to dismiss

例 The president refused to answer any questions and addressed the crowd with a *dismissive* gesture.

近 ignorant

派 dismiss（v. 不再考虑）

释 *adj.* 轻蔑的 showing indifference or disregard

例 Paul is so *dismissive* of his friend Amy that onlookers may see it as rude and contemptuous.

□ conclusive □ enlighten □ methodology □ tectonic □ monogamy
□ pathogen □ depict □ dismissive

invertebrate
/ɪnˈvɜːrtɪbrət/

adj. 软弱无力的 lacking in strength or vitality

Bill's *invertebrate* attempts to defend himself against the bully's insults were so timid that the bully ignored them.

n. 无脊椎动物 an animal, such as an insect or a mollusk, that lacks a backbone or spinal column

As an *invertebrate*, the spider joins a whole class of animals that have exoskeletons instead of interior bones.

discrepancy
/dɪsˈkrepənsi/

n. 差异 a difference especially between things that should be the same

There is a major *discrepancy* between the financial accounts in the company's books and the amount of money in its bank account.

incongruity

demographic
/ˌdeməˈɡræfɪk/

adj. 与人口统计有关的 of or relating to the study of changes that occur in large groups of people over a period of time: of or relating to demography

Marketing firms rely heavily on *demographic* information such as statistical data about the size, growth, and distribution of human populations.

forage
/ˈfɔːrɪdʒ/

v. 寻找（食物）to search for something (such as food or supplies)

Although the ground is littered with leaves during the fall season, squirrels successfully *forage* for acorns and other nuts scattered on the ground.

synchronous
/ˈsɪŋkrənəs/

adj. 同时的 happening, moving, or existing at the same time

Unlike the Georgian calendar, the Islamic lunar calendar is *synchronous* with the phases of the moon.

hagiography
/ˌhæɡiˈɑːɡrəfi/

n. （夸大的）传记 traditionally, an account of a saint's life; an idealized biography

The biography of Woodrow Wilson was a true *hagiography* that praised his good deeds and ignored his racism.

hagiographic（adj. 过于谄媚的）

monochromatic
/ˌmaɪnəkroʊˈmætɪk/

adj. 单调的 lacking variety, creativity, or excitement

Other than the good food, the festival was a *monochromatic* affair of identical, slow, and depressing shoegaze bands.

employ
/ɪmˈplɔɪ/

v. 使用 to make use of

Some employers want to supplement the hiring process by *employing* graphologists to study applicants' handwriting for character analysis.

v. 雇佣 to give a job to

Having been *employed* by Honda for many years, I received a discount on my automobile purchases.

indigenous
/ɪnˈdɪdʒənəs/

概 *adj.* 当地的 originating and growing or living in an area or environment; native

例 The Venus flytrap plant is **indigenous** to coastal areas of North and South Carolina; it grows naturally only in this region.

概 *adj.* 与生俱来的 innate or inborn

例 Cats do not have to be taught to pounce and play with small objects; it is an **indigenous** behavior.

反 acquired

insurrection
/ˌɪnsəˈrekʃn/

概 *n.* 造反 a usually violent attempt to take control of a government

例 While the new policy could cause threats of **insurrection**, it is more likely that most employees would obey.

ideology
/ˌaɪdiˈɑːlədʒi/

概 *n.* 思想体系，意识形态 the set of ideas and beliefs of a group or political party

例 The anarchist **ideology** calls for the elimination of a central government.

segregate
/ˈsegrɪgeɪt/

概 *v.* 分离，隔离 to separate groups of people because of their particular race, religion or other trait

例 In the past, African Americans were **segregated** from white Americans in the American South and attended different schools.

概 *v.* 强制隔离 to not allow people of different races to be together in (a place, such as a school)

例 The civil rights movement fought against practices that **segregated** blacks and whites.

propound
/prəˈpaʊnd/

概 *v.* 提出…供考虑 to offer for discussion or consideration

例 Professor Jackson **propounded** his pet theory to anyone who would listen, even before finding evidence to support it.

adulterate
/əˈdʌltəreɪt/

概 *v.* 掺假 to make (something, such as a food or drink) impure or weaker by adding something of poor quality

例 In 2011, the University of California at Davis found that about 69% of the olive oil sold in the United States is **adulterated** with other oils.

概 *adj.* 伪造的 spurious; adulterated

例 The pharmacist was convicted of selling **adulterate** drugs in order to maximize profits.

expository
/ɪkˈspɑːzətɔːri/

概 *adj.* 解释的，阐释的 used to describe writing that is done to explain something

例 The killer's "manifesto" was a 1000-page **expository** rant that described his bizarre justifications for hatred.

anemia
/əˈniːmiə/

概 *n.* 缺乏活力 lack of vitality

例 Her performance at work has been marked by **anemia** due to complex familial problems that have been sapping her energy.

□ indigenous   □ insurrection   □ ideology   □ segregate   □ propound
□ adulterate   □ expository   □ anemia

excavate /ˈekskəveɪt/	释 **v.** 开凿，挖出 to uncover (something) by digging away and removing the earth that covers it 例 While **excavating** a sanctuary, the archaeologists discovered the buried remains of a cult statue to Jupiter.
acerbic /əˈsɜːrbɪk/	释 **adj.** （语言）辛辣尖刻的 expressing harsh or sharp criticism in a clever way 例 Frank is known for his **acerbic** personality and willingness to speak freely. 选 mordant, caustic, cutting, scathing 反 sweet
resurgence /rɪˈsɜːrdʒəns/	释 **n.** 复苏 a growth or increase that occurs after a period without growth or increase 例 Following the success of Pokémon Go, there was a **resurgence** of nostalgic video games from the 1990s. 选 recrudescent 派 resurgent（**adj.** 复活的）
colloquial /kəˈloʊkwiəl/	释 **adj.** 口头的，非正式的 using conversational style 例 The physicist realized she needed to translate her ideas into **colloquial** English if she wanted non-physicists to understand what she was researching.
interjection /ˌɪntərˈdʒekʃn/	释 **n.** 插话 the act of uttering exclamations; something interjected, as a remark 例 Harvey's girlfriend accused him of interrupting, but he said his **interjections** were just meant to express agreement.
hoodwink /ˈhʊdwɪŋk/	释 **v.** 欺骗 to deceive or trick (someone) 例 Email scammers **hoodwink** people by making them think they are going to receive a large sum of money by wire transfer.
analogous /əˈnæləgəs/	释 **adj.** 相似的 similar in some way 例 The mental process that creates an original poem or drama is **analogous** to the one that creates scientific discoveries, since both require a creative breakthrough. 选 comparable
latent /ˈleɪtnt/	释 **adj.** 潜藏的，潜在的 present but not visible or active 例 Although it was a surprise to the rest of the world, the coup was in fact provoked by **latent** dissatisfaction within the country.
boycott /ˈbɔɪkɑːt/	释 **v.** 抵制 to refuse to buy, use, or participate in (something) as a way of protesting 例 After seeing the horrifying documentary on the poultry industry, many Americans **boycotted** chicken. 反 patronize

sentimental /ˌsentɪ'mentl/ ▬▬▬▬▬	释 *adj.* 感情用事的 resulting from feeling rather than reason or thought 例 The ring was a cheap plastic bauble, but it was a ***sentimental*** reminder of Jill's first love. 释 *adj.* 多愁善感的 marked or governed by feeling, sensibility, or emotional idealism 例 Although the movie lacked a discernible plot, it was a ***sentimental*** ode to childhood that resonated with many in the audience.
castigate /'kæstɪgeɪt/ ▬▬	释 *v.* 严厉批评 to criticize (someone) harshly 例 Citing evidence of corruption, the investigating committee ***castigated*** the senator for his misconduct and told him not to do it again. 选 chastise
preeminent /ˌpriː'emɪnənt/ ▬▬▬▬	释 *adj.* 杰出的，独一无二的 better than others 例 With its large circulation, *Essence* magazine has enjoyed a ***preeminent*** presence among black women.
terminology /ˌtɜːrmə'nɑːlədʒi/ ▬▬▬▬	释 *n.* 术语 the special words or phrases that are used in a particular field 例 Writing guides advise academics to avoid specialized ***terminology*** and technical language when it is possible to make a point without them.
domesticate /də'mestɪkeɪt/ ▬▬▬▬	释 *v.* 驯服 to breed or train (an animal) to need and accept the care of human beings; to tame (an animal) 例 Some believe that monkeys and chimps learn new skills from being ***domesticated***, but others argue these animals would learn even more if left in the wild.
pedagogical /ˌpedə'gɑːdʒɪkl/ ▬▬▬▬▬▬	释 *adj.* 教育学的 of or relating to teachers or education 例 The teacher adopted the Socratic Method as his primary ***pedagogical*** approach in the small classroom and always intensely questioned students about their ideas.
skew /skjuː/ ▬▬▬	释 *v.* 歪曲，曲解 to change (something) so that it is not true or accurate 例 Polling only voters who use a landline phone can ***skew*** the poll results in favor of one candidate. 派 askew (adj. 歪的，斜的)
static /'stætɪk/ ▬▬▬▬	释 *adj.* 静态的 showing little or no change, action, or progress 例 If an artist tries to duplicate another artist's style, the resulting pieces will be ***static*** and lifeless. 选 invariable
discrete /dɪ'skriːt/ ▬▬▬▬▬	释 *adj.* 分开的，分离的 separate and different from each other 例 Rejecting the idea that city and suburb are ***discrete*** entities, the writer insisted that they are socially and economically interdependent. 反 continuous

☐ sentimental ☐ castigate ☐ preeminent ☐ terminology ☐ domesticate
☐ pedagogical ☐ skew ☐ static ☐ discrete

corrode
/kəˈroʊd/

释 **v.** 削弱，破坏 to weaken or destroy gradually
例 Proper car maintenance ensures that minor problems will not **corrode** the integrity of the automobile over time.

释 **v.** 腐蚀 to slowly break apart and destroy (metal, an object, etc.) through a chemical process
例 Avoid spilling the acidic solution, because it will **corrode** any surface it touches!

protagonist
/prəˈtægənɪst/

释 **n.** 重要人物 the main character in a narrative or work of fiction
例 F. Scott Fitzgerald tends to develop conflicted **protagonists** who are both the heroes of the story and morally flawed.

释 **n.** 支持者 a supporter or champion
例 Malcolm X was a **protagonist** of the Civil Rights movement and was murdered for his beliefs upon returning from a hajj to Mecca.

forerunner
/ˈfɔːrʌnər/

释 **n.** 先驱 someone or something that comes before another
例 The crude animated effects created by projected images from seventeenth-century lantern slides were **forerunners** of modern film animation.
近 precursor

释 **n.** 预兆 a sign of something that is going to happen
例 Ten-inch floppy discs look ridiculous now, but they were the **forerunners** of today's USB drives.

clutch
/klʌtʃ/

释 **v.** 抓住 to hold onto (someone or something) tightly with your hand
例 As Maria walked down the dark street, she **clutched** her purse and looked around nervously for muggers.

straggle
/ˈstrægl/

释 **v.** 迷路 to wander from the direct course or way
例 While the tour group moved on, the window-shoppers **straggled** and fell behind.

释 **v.** 散乱 to move away or spread out from others in a disorganized way
例 The student volunteers were instructed to clear up the piles of trash and debris **straggled** along the coast.

rhetorical
/rɪˈtɔːrɪkl/

释 **adj.** 有说服力的 of, relating to, or concerned with the art of speaking or writing formally and effectively especially as a way to persuade or influence people
例 Although Demosthenes had the **rhetorical** abilities to command a crowd, he was handicapped as a public speaker by his speech impediment.

equilibrium
/ˌiːkwɪˈlɪbriəm/

释 **n.** 平衡 a state in which opposing forces or actions are balanced so that one is not stronger or greater than the other
例 The different branches are supposed to remain in **equilibrium** and maintain a balance of power, not create gridlock.

□ corrode   □ protagonist   □ forerunner   □ clutch   □ straggle
□ rhetorical   □ equilibrium

quintessential
/ˌkwɪntɪ'senʃl/

释 *adj.* 精华的，典型的 of, relating to, or having the nature of a quintessence; being the most typical
例 According to Larry's wife, he is a *quintessential* self-made man who started his own business at 18.

regimen
/'redʒɪmən/

释 *n.* 统治，政府统治 governmental rule or control
例 The new party's *regimen* over the country proved to be disastrous and led to protests and strikes in no time.

objective
/əb'dʒektɪv/

释 *adj.* 客观的 dealing with facts without allowing personal feelings to confuse them
例 Personally distanced from the quarrel, the judge served as an *objective* arbitrator in the bitter divorce.
选 fair

postulate
/'pɑːstʃəleɪt/

释 *v.* 假设，假定 to suggest (something, such as an idea or theory) especially in order to start a discussion
例 Galileo was one of the first scientists who *postulated* that the Earth revolved around the Sun, and he was later discovered to be correct.
反 deny as false

onset
/'ɑːnset/

释 *n.* 开始 the beginning of something
例 Sleep actually occurs instantaneously, though one may receive clues signaling its *onset* for several minutes before one falls asleep.

impinge
/ɪm'pɪndʒ/

释 *v.* 猛烈撞击 to strike or dash especially with a sharp collision
例 I heard the huge raindrops *impinge* upon the earth during the heavy thunderstorm.

释 *v.* 影响 to have an effect or make an impression
例 The paperwork requirements in this office are annoying, but they should not *impinge* on your ability to finish your work.

释 *v.* 妨碍，侵犯 to encroach or infringe
例 As the trees grew, they *impinged* more and more on the power lines.

thrive
/θraɪv/

释 *v.* 兴旺发达 to grow or develop successful
例 If there's one lesson we should learn from our economic success over three centuries, it is that we *thrive* on competition.

milieu
/miː'ljɜː/

释 *n.* 环境 the physical or social setting in which something occurs or develops
例 With the culture of free love and peace, the social *milieu* of the 1960s starkly contrasted with the conservative, post-war 1950s.

paradoxical
/ˌpærə'dɑːksɪkl/

释 *adj.* 不寻常的 not being the normal or usual kind
例 Large in stature, Bartolo Colon was the *paradoxical* athlete who was not outwardly fit, but was an incredible pitcher.

释 *adj.* 悖论的，矛盾的 of the nature of a paradox
例 The *paradoxical* nature of Brandon's utterance "all Brandons are liars" left us laughing hysterically.

□ quintessential   □ regimen   □ objective   □ postulate   □ onset
□ impinge   □ thrive   □ milieu   □ paradoxical

iterate
/ˈɪtəreɪt/

释 *v.* 重说一遍，重做一遍 to say or state or run again
例 A good essay should find a way to develop a point, not just *iterate* it over and over.

prophetic
/prəˈfetɪk/

释 *adj.* 预言的 correctly stating what will happen in the future
例 Grover Pease Osborne's 1893 economics treatise was remarkably *prophetic* since it foresaw that technological advances would increase the availability of natural resources.
选 prescient

delineate
/dɪˈlɪnieɪt/

释 *v.* 描绘轮廓 to mark the outline of
例 Before founding a new city, the Romans would *delineate* its boundaries with a deep trench that they dedicated to the gods.

释 *v.* 详细描述 to clearly describe
例 The professor made it easy for me to learn from my mistakes by *delineating* all the areas that need improvement in my essay.

condone
/kənˈdoʊn/

释 *v.* 原谅，认可 to forgive or approve (something that is considered wrong)
例 Having grown up in a tough, violent community, Gil's father *condoned* fighting as a means to avenge any injury.
选 excuse

acumen
/əˈkjuːmən/

释 *n.* 机智，精明 keenness and depth of perception, discernment, or discrimination especially in practical matters
例 The audience may not have had the theoretical knowledge to understand the new play, but they certainly had the *acumen* to appreciate it.
选 shrewdness

agonize
/ˈægənaɪz/

释 *v.* 感到痛苦，挣扎 to suffer agony, torture, or anguish
例 Jefferson was playing football with his friends the whole weekend and was far from *agonizing* over his imminent deadline on Monday.

revere
/rɪˈvɪr/

释 *v.* 尊敬 to have great respect for (someone or something)
例 Quentin Tarantino is *revered* by many young filmmakers for his brilliant innovations in cinematography.
选 venerate
反 profane
派 irreverent（adj. 不尊敬的）

reckless
/ˈrekləs/

释 *adj.* 粗心的，鲁莽的 not showing proper concern about the possible bad results of your actions
例 It was *reckless* of the hikers to head out on their journey into the wilderness without enough supplies or practical survival experience.

unsparing
/ʌnˈsperɪŋ/

釋 *adj.* 无情的，苛求的 not merciful or forbearing
例 Despite being in the lead by several touchdowns, the *Crimson Tide* was *unsparing* in its offensive onslaught.

釋 *adj.* 不节俭的 not frugal
例 It was surprising that the boss was so critical of Tom's plan as she is usually *unsparing* in her approval of his decisions.

belligerent
/bəˈlɪdʒərənt/

釋 *adj.* 好斗的 angry and aggressive
例 To temper the *belligerent* student's aggression, the teacher separated him from the class and encouraged him to develop his artistic talent.
选 pugnacious

taciturn
/ˈtæsɪtɜːrn/

釋 *adj.* 沉默寡言的 tending to be quiet
例 Being too *taciturn* can be a bad trait if you never say what you are really thinking.
选 terse, curt, laconic
派 taciturnity（n. 沉默寡言）

penitential
/ˌpenɪˈtenʃl/

釋 *adj.* 后悔的，忏悔的 relating to the feeling of being sorry for doing something wrong
例 After stealing a candy bar, the child was visibly *penitential* and confessed to his parents.
选 contrite

frivolous
/ˈfrɪvələs/

釋 *adj.* 无关紧要的 of little weight or importance
例 Laura's *frivolous* concerns irritated her mother, who wanted her to focus only on her grades.

釋 *adj.* 不严肃的，轻率的 silly and not serious
例 The boss refused to give anyone a raise, and told the workers they would not need it if they stopped buying *frivolous* items like lattes.
派 frivolity（n. 轻浮，无聊）

plead
/pliːd/

釋 *v.* 辩护 to argue a case or cause in a court of law
例 Betty's lawyer *pleaded* her case in court competently but the judge was not convinced.

orthodox
/ˈɔːrθədɑːks/

釋 *adj.* 主流的 accepted as true or correct by most people
例 The belief that hard work alone can bring you success is *orthodox* among the older generation.

釋 *adj.* 正统信仰的 accepting and closely following the traditional beliefs and customs of a religion
例 He was an *orthodox* follower of Buddhism until he came into contact with the extremist cults.

□ unsparing   □ belligerent   □ taciturn   □ penitential   □ frivolous
□ plead   □ orthodox

Word List 12

音频

allege /əˈledʒ/	释 **v.** 断言，宣称 to assert without proof or before proving 例 Because the teacher **alleged** that I plagiarized, I was suspended until I eventually proved otherwise.
reconcile /ˈrekənsaɪl/	释 **v.** 调和 to cause people or groups to become friendly again after an argument or disagreement 例 The couple **reconciled** after both sides apologized and came to a compromise.
improvise /ˈɪmprəvaɪz/	释 **v.** 即兴表演 to speak or perform without preparation 例 Unlike some entertainers whose performances rarely vary, Louis Armstrong frequently **improvised** during his performances, spontaneously introducing new phrasing in existing songs.
eliminate /ɪˈlɪmɪneɪt/	释 **v.** 移除，去掉 to get rid of 例 Geoffrey's corrupt dealings earned him such disgrace that any possibility of his being reelected to the city council was completely **eliminated**. 选 put to rest
disquiet /dɪsˈkwaɪət/	释 **v.** 使…不安 to take away the peace or tranquility of 例 The residents of the peaceful neighborhood were **disquieted** by the news of a huge condo development being built down the street.
predicament /prɪˈdɪkəmənt/	释 **n.** 困境 a difficult or unpleasant situation 例 She felt quite tortured when caught in the **predicament** of having to either betray her best friend or lie to her boyfriend. 选 dilemma, quandary
fester /ˈfestər/	释 **v.** 恶化 to become worse as time passes 例 Because the wound was not properly cared for, it slowly **festered** until an infection took hold of the limb. 反 heal
accord /əˈkɔːrd/	释 **n.** 和谐，一致 agreement; harmony 例 Democrats and libertarians are often in **accord** on the issue of decriminalizing drugs.
ascertain /ˌæsərˈteɪn/	释 **v.** 查明 to learn or find out (something, such as information or the truth) 例 Sally read through the entire e-mail thread but could not **ascertain** when the party was actually taking place.

☐ allege   ☐ reconcile   ☐ improvise   ☐ eliminate   ☐ disquiet
☐ predicament   ☐ fester   ☐ accord   ☐ ascertain

counterproductive
/ˌkaʊntərprəˈdʌktɪv/

释 *adj.* 起反作用的，事与愿违的 tending to hinder the attainment of a desired goal

例 Although daydreaming is generally seen as *counterproductive*, it can be surprisingly useful in helping us make progress toward long-term goals.

misnomer
/ˌmɪsˈnoʊmər/

释 *n.* 误称 a name that is wrong or not proper or appropriate

例 The term "dry cleaning" is something of a *misnomer* since this process generally involves application of perchloroethylene, a liquid chemical.

precarious
/prɪˈkerəriəs/

释 *adj.* 处境危险的 characterized by a lack of security or stability that threatens with danger

例 The life of a secret agent is *precarious* as a tiny mistake can expose his or her true identity.

选 perilous

反 safe

unrelenting
/ˌʌnrɪˈlentɪŋ/

释 *adj.* 不屈的 having or exhibiting uncompromising determination; unyielding

例 Athletes need to be disciplined at all times and especially *unrelenting* in the face of failure.

释 *adj.* 持续的，不减退的 not letting up or weakening in vigor or pace

例 While hiking, we were forced to take shelter in a cave during the *unrelenting* storm.

选 persistent

soporific
/ˌsɑːpəˈrɪfɪk/

释 *adj.* 令人昏昏欲睡的 causing a person to become tired and ready to fall asleep

例 The eager members of the audience found the lecture topic stimulating, but unfortunately the lecturer's droning voice had a *soporific* effect.

反 invigorating, stimulant

disseminate
/dɪˈsemɪneɪt/

释 *v.* 传播，散布 to cause (something, such as information) to be distributed to many people

例 Most politicians find the television indispensable to enabling their messages to be speedily and effectively *disseminated*.

选 transmit

反 garner

派 disseminator（n. 传播者）

lure
/lʊr/

释 *v.* 诱惑 to cause or persuade (a person or an animal) to go somewhere or to do something by offering some pleasure or gain

例 *Lured* by the calls of the hunter, the duck flew to his death.

反 repel

banish
/ˈbænɪʃ/

释 *v.* 驱逐 to send away

例 The king *banished* the traitor from his kingdom after he attempted to overthrow the throne.

选 expel, oust

degrade /dɪˈɡreɪd/	**v.** 贬低 to treat (someone or something) poorly and without respect
	Betty felt *degraded* by her classmates when she first got wind of the nasty rumors spreading around the school.
	v. 退化 to make the quality of (something) worse
	It is no surprise that the nuts have *degraded* in taste and freshness after they were left exposed to the air for months.
skittish /ˈskɪtɪʃ/	**adj.** 多变的 tending to change often; not dependable or stable
	The sparrow is characterized by its *skittish* flight and is usually seen darting from one direction to the other.
	adj. 易受惊吓的，易激动的 easily frightened or excited; restive
	During storms, dogs are very *skittish* and bark frequently at the lightning.
	restive, fractious
tranquil /ˈtræŋkwɪl/	**adj.** 安静的 free from commotion or disturbance
	In retrospect, the presidency of Dwight Eisenhower is perceived as a *tranquil* period because it was relatively free of domestic conflict.
	peaceful
	commotion, ferment
	adj. 心神安宁的 free from anxiety, tension, or restlessness
	On a much-deserved vacation, the newlyweds spent a *tranquil* day on the beach reading and listening to the sounds of the waves.
seemly /ˈsiːmli/	**adj.** 好看的 good-looking and handsome
	Stereotypically, the male model was *seemly*, but very unintelligent.
	adj. 得体的 conventionally proper
	It is not *seemly* to wear a bikini to a restaurant, even if you have just come from the beach.
	decorous
unkempt /ˌʌnˈkempt/	**adj.** 不整洁的，邋遢的 not neat or orderly
	You can tell which houses are occupied by college students by their *unkempt* yards and beer cans on the porch.
decorous /ˈdekərəs/	**adj.** 得体的 correct and polite in a particular situation
	The children were told to behave in a *decorous* manner at the dinner and not be rude to the guests.
	seemly
	decorum (n. 得体，礼节)
tawdry /ˈtɔːdri/	**adj.** 俗气的 cheap and gaudy in appearance or quality
	A high-quality sequined gown can look beautiful, but one from a discount store will likely just look *tawdry*.
	adj. 卑鄙的 morally low or bad
	Parents in the audience were caught off guard when the local theater turned *Othello* into a *tawdry* burlesque that was unfit for children.

décor /deɪˈkɔːr/	**n.** （装修的）格调，风格 the way that a room or the inside of a building is decorated The new homeowners were fans of modern **décor** and renovated their apartment to fit that aesthetic.
lush /lʌʃ/	**adj.** 茂盛的，郁郁葱葱的 lavishly productive The garden was a **lush** carpet of greenery by the time summer rolled in. **adj.** 奢华的 opulent or sumptuous The banquet was a **lush** affair with food from around the world, expensive tableware, and impeccable service.
acidic /əˈsɪdɪk/	**adj.** 酸的，尖酸刻薄的 having a very sour or sharp taste The sommelier grimaced at the **acidic** taste of the near-vinegar beverage and spit it out immediately.
coarse /kɔːrs/	**adj.** 粗糙的 having a rough quality Using sandpaper, the carpenter smoothed the **coarse** surface of the wood. **adj.** 粗鲁的 rude or offensive When traveling, it is important to remember that behavior that is normal in one place may be **coarse** and offensive in another.
impoverished /ɪmˈpɑːvərɪʃt/	**adj.** 贫瘠的，贫乏的 represented by few species or individuals The once enormous buffalo population became **impoverished** due to over-hunting.
threshold /ˈθreʃhould/	**n.** 阈值，临界点 the point or level at which something begins or changes The petition has reached its goal of 100,000 signatures, which is the **threshold** for a direct response from the White House.
disparage /dɪˈspærɪdʒ/	**v.** 鄙视 to insult someone or something, or describe it negatively Although Isaac is very good at math, he should not **disparage** others by mocking them for being bad at it. slight
invalidate /ɪnˈvælɪdeɪt/	**v.** 削弱，使……无效 to weaken or destroy the effect of (something) When it was discovered that Barry Bonds used performance-enhancing drugs, his homerun record became **invalidated**.
hackneyed /ˈhæknid/	**adj.** 陈词滥调的 not interesting, funny, etc., because of being used too often The comedian's **hackneyed** jokes did not earn much laughter from the audience; they had heard too many jokes about airline food and women's love of shopping. unoriginal original, fresh
ruminate /ˈruːmɪneɪt/	**v.** 仔细思考 to think carefully and deeply about something Rosario **ruminated** on the problem at length, but could not figure out whether to take the new job.

□ décor   □ lush   □ acidic   □ coarse   □ impoverished
□ threshold   □ disparage   □ invalidate   □ hackneyed   □ ruminate

meander
/mi'ændər/

法 *v.* 迂回曲折，漫无目的地走动 to move or cause to move in a sinuous, spiral, or circular course

例 The countryside landscape is often beautiful, with broad grasslands and rivers that *meander* through them.

bucolic
/bjuː'kɑːlɪk/

法 *adj.* 乡间生活的 of or relating to the country or country life

例 Thomas Hardy's novels are described as *bucolic* because of their interest in daily life in rural and agricultural settings.

近 pastoral

pastoral
/'pæstərəl/

法 *adj.* 乡间生活的 of or relating to the countryside or to the lives of people who live in the country

例 Betty looked down from the hill at the *pastoral* view of grass, hedges and trees.

近 bucolic

hard-nosed
/'hɑːrd,noʊzd/

法 *adj.* 顽强的，不讲情面的 being tough, stubborn, or uncompromising

例 Even the most *hard-nosed* teachers agreed that students should not be penalized for taking a sick day.

法 *adj.* 精明而讲究实际的 concerned with or involving practical considerations

例 The *hard-nosed* coach was unaffected by his athletes' complaints about the heat.

petty
/'peti/

法 *adj.* 不重要的，次要的 not very important or serious

例 Despite the *petty* nature of the argument about the missing $2, the brothers refused to speak to each other for a decade.

法 *adj.* 小气的 marked by or reflective of narrow interests and sympathies

例 People who will only vote for a candidate of their gender or race are letting *petty* concerns outweigh the greater good.

近 small-minded

opportunistic
/,ɑːpərtuː'nɪstɪk/

法 *adj.* 机会主义的，投机的 taking advantage of chances for personal benefit as they arise

例 During the economic collapse, the *opportunistic* investor bought companies at a fraction of their previous values.

menace
/'menəs/

法 *v.* 威胁 to threaten harm to (someone or something)

例 *Menaced* by the serial killer for months, the community prayed that the cops would find the criminal.

painstaking
/'peɪnzteɪkɪŋ/

法 *adj.* 勤奋努力的 need or showing diligent care and effort

例 Among scientists, Doudna is known for her *painstaking* attention to detail, which she often harnesses to solve problems that other researchers have dismissed as unsolvable.

近 meticulous

humanitarian
/hjuː,mænɪ'teriən/

adj. 人道的，博爱的 relating to or characteristic of people who work to improve the lives and living conditions of other people

Today, the International Red Cross is the world's most admired **humanitarian** group.

predispose
/,priːdɪ'spoʊz/

v. 使…易受感染 to make susceptible or liable

Having pneumonia **predisposes** you to a number of other medical complications.

eminent
/'emɪnənt/

adj. 杰出的 successful, well-known and respected

If you read the letters of **eminent** people, you will see that they have the same trivial problems as everyone else.

famous

eminence（n. 卓越）

declamatory
/dɪ'klæmətɔːri/

adj. 演说般的，慷慨激昂的 expressing feelings or opinions in a way that is loud and forceful

A good essayist avoids **declamatory** prose and instead makes his or her points through subtle suggestions.

ascetic
/ə'setɪk/

adj. 生活朴素的 relating to or having a strict and simple way of living that avoids physical pleasure

The millionaire decided to live an **ascetic** life free of luxuries after he had a near-death experience.

libertine

safeguard
/'seɪfgɑːrd/

v. 保护 to make (someone or something) safe or secure

The Constitution **safeguards** the rights of every American citizen.

preserving

sinister
/'sɪnɪstər/

adj. 邪恶的 frightening; having an evil appearance

The internet may be helpful and informative, but it has a **sinister** side that conceals many dark dealings.

adj. 不吉利的 presaging ill fortune or trouble

The witch uttered a **sinister** incantation that spelled doom for the enemy.

convincing
/kən'vɪnsɪŋ/

adj. 有说服力的 causing someone to believe that something is true or certain

The engineers regarded the claims about the new software with skepticism, but the demonstration of the software was so **convincing** that it won them over.

peak
/piːk/

n. 顶点，顶峰 the highest level or greatest degree

Aaron Boone's game-winning homerun in the World Series was the **peak** of his otherwise lackluster baseball career.

unrivaled
/ʌn'raɪvld/

adj. 无法匹敌的 better than anyone or anything else

Germans say their country's beer and chocolate are so good they are quite simply **unrivaled**.

rival（n. 敌人）

☐ humanitarian　　☐ predispose　　☐ eminent　　☐ declamatory　　☐ ascetic
☐ safeguard　　☐ sinister　　☐ convincing　　☐ peak　　☐ unrivaled

pivotal
/ˈpɪvətl/

adj. 非常重要的 very important

Doing a final proofread is not an afterthought but a *pivotal* part of the essay-writing process.

recondite
/ˈrekəndaɪt/

adj. 难懂的 difficult or impossible for one of ordinary understanding or knowledge to comprehend

Comparative Literature is considered an obscure and *recondite* major at State University; only two people are majoring in it.

esoteric, arcane, abstruse

widely understood

morbid
/ˈmɔːrbɪd/

adj. 不健康的 not healthy or normal

Some are turned off by *morbid* drawings of skeletons while others think they look cool.

adj. （话题）不愉快的 relating to unpleasant subjects

It may be *morbid* to think about death, but many young people facing terminal illnesses are forced to do so quite frequently.

staple
/ˈsteɪpl/

adj. （食物、商品等）必要的 used, needed, or enjoyed constantly by many people

In the ancient Mediterranean, grain, wine, and olive oil were the *staple* foodstuffs for all people.

adj. 重要的，主要的 principal, chief

Oil is the world's *staple* fuel source.

herald
/ˈherəld/

n. 前兆 a sign that something will happen

Laocoon warned the Trojans that the Greek horse was not a dedication, but a *herald* of the destruction that would meet the city.

v. 预示 to be a sign of

Revelations says that the rise of an Anti-Christ will *herald* the end of days.

harbinger

cure-all
/ˈkjʊrɔl/

n. 万能灵药 a cure or solution for any illness or problem

Although probiotics are not a digestive *cure-all*, they can be beneficial to both kids and adults.

panacea

ruthless
/ˈruːθləs/

adj. 无情的，残忍的 having no pity

Ruthless to the end, the Spartans pursued their opponents to achieve final victory.

scorn
/skɔːrn/

v. 鄙视，嘲笑 to show disdain or derision

Pit bulls are *scorned* because they are most often owned by poor people.

deride

scornful（adj. 轻蔑的）

acquisitive /əˈkwɪzətɪv/	释 *adj.* 贪婪的 having a strong desire to own or acquire more things 例 Brandon's ***acquisitive*** nature pushed almost everyone away from him, since he cared more about profit than about his friends.
clangorous /ˈklæŋgərəs/	释 *v.* 叮当响的，响亮的 having a loud resonant metallic sound 例 When the church bell fell from its fitting, it made a ***clangorous*** noise that echoed through the entire belfry.
rejuvenate /rɪˈdʒuːvəneɪt/	释 *v.* 使…重新有活力 to give new strength or energy to 例 Far from exhausting him, the harder work schedule seems to have ***rejuvenated*** the recovering patient.
obsess /əbˈses/	释 *v.* 沉迷于… to think and talk about someone or something too much 例 The man was ***obsessed*** over beanie babies in the 1990s and now owns 2000 stuffed animals that suddenly seem worthless to him.
canonical /kəˈnɑːnɪkl/	释 *adj.* （书籍等在某个领域）经典之作的 of or relating to the group of books, plays, poems, etc., that are traditionally considered to be very important 例 Many ***canonical*** works of literature were considered cheap and lowbrow when first published. 派 canonize（v. 奉为经典，推崇）
undo /ʌnˈduː/	释 *v.* 撤销 to stop the effect of 例 It is hard to ***undo*** the effects of saying something cruel to a friend.
obsolete /ˌɑːbsəˈliːt/	释 *adj.* 过时的 no longer used because something newer exists 例 The floppy disc is now ***obsolete***; no new computer has a drive to insert them in. 近 outmoded, fusty
quotidian /kwoʊˈtɪdiən/	释 *adj.* 普通的 everyday; commonplace 例 Foreigners may view life in Morocco as exotic and extraordinary, but its residents would likely find it mundane and ***quotidian***. 近 workaday 反 extraordinary, unusual
pathetic /pəˈθetɪk/	释 *adj.* 可怜的 causing feelings of sadness and sympathy 例 The cat was a ***pathetic*** sight when it first arrived at the shelter, but after months of care, it looks absolutely handsome. 释 *adj.* 差劲的，不足的 pitifully inferior or inadequate 例 The professor scorned his student for her ***pathetic*** attempt at an essay.
bathetic /bəˈθetɪk/	释 *adj.* 陈腐的 marked by exceptional commonplaceness; overly sentimental 例 The teenager's diary entries about her breakup were serious to her, but would have seemed ***bathetic*** to any adult who read them.

veracious
/vəˈreɪʃəs/

adj. 真实的 marked by truth
例 The witness offered a **veracious** account of the burglary that stood up to interrogation in court.
近 truth
派 veracity (n. 真实)

adj. 精确的 accurate; precise
例 The nursing records were detailed and **veracious** as they were recorded and checked meticulously by a team of dedicated staff.

voracious
/vəˈreɪʃəs/

adj. 贪婪的 excessively eager
例 Annabelle is a truly **voracious** leader who manages to get even the most passive member to start cheering enthusiastically.
近 insatiable

adj. 贪吃的 having a huge appetite
例 The castaways had **voracious** appetites that seemed impossible to satiate as they had gone hungry for three full days before being rescued.
近 prodigious

exploit
/ɪkˈsplɔɪt/

v. 充分利用 to make productive use of
例 Educators can **exploit** children's interest in dinosaurs to teach them about the history of life on Earth.

v. 剥削 to make use of meanly or unfairly for one's own advantage
例 When his opponent failed to capture his queen, Gary Kasparov **exploited** the advantage to move into "checkmate".

n. 成就，功绩 an act or deed, especially a brilliant or heroic one
例 Most of Herakles's **exploits** are well-known, but few know that he also destroyed the city of Troy.

retrofit
/ˈretroʊfɪt/

v. 翻新 to provide (something) with new parts that were not available when it was originally built
例 In Cuba, it is necessary to **retrofit** the old cars with new parts because of the trade embargo.

witty
/ˈwɪti/

adj. 机智幽默的 funny and clever
例 Their **witty** banter had Angela and Charles laughing all night.

provocative
/prəˈvɑːkətɪv/

adj. 引起争论的，启发的 causing discussion, thought, argument, etc.
例 Mary's **provocative** outfit spiked a heated discussion among the family members about whether fishnet stockings were appropriate for church.
近 inflammatory, controversial

adj. 刺激的 causing excitement
例 The new water brand stirred up interest with a **provocative** and shocking ad campaign.
近 stimulating

impecunious
/ˌɪmpɪˈkjuːniəs/

🔢 *adj.* 贫穷的 having little or no money

📝 Even for the habitually *impecunious*, it is hard to resist spending money on luxury items.

🔄 indigent

🔄 wealthy

assiduous
/əˈsɪdʒuəs/

🔢 *adj.* 努力的 showing great care, attention, and effort

📝 Bill has received much praise from his supervisors for his *assiduous* attitude and optimistic perspective.

🔄 industrious

tacit
/ˈtæsɪt/

🔢 *adj.* 不言而喻的，心照不宣的 expressed or understood without being directly stated

📝 Rose smiled approving, giving the child *tacit* permission to pet her dog.

transgress
/trænzˈgres/

🔢 *v.* 违反，违背 to disobey a command or law

📝 Some readers find the crime novels of Patricia Highsmith to be immoral because her villains are not always punished for their *transgressions*.

abstruse
/əbˈstruːs/

🔢 *adj.* 难以理解的 difficult to comprehend

📝 Though the principles of the banking trade may appear somewhat *abstruse*, the practice is capable of being reduced to strict rules.

🔄 esoteric, arcane, recondite

embed
/ɪmˈbed/

🔢 *v.* 嵌入 to place or set (something) firmly in something else; to make something an integral part of

📝 In the 19th century, many parts of society were *embedded* in the complex and brutal economy of slavery.

🔄 excise

render
/ˈrendər/

🔢 *v.* 使…进入某种状态 to cause (someone or something) to be in a specified condition

📝 The simple fact is that too many Americans are *rendering* themselves voiceless by failing to participate in the political process.

🔢 *v.* 复制 to produce a copy or version of

📝 Unlike *Nicholas Nickleby* which slavishly attempted to *render* its entire source, *Les Miserables* skips many parts of the book.

🔄 reproduce, regurgitate

alter
/ˈɔːltər/

🔢 *v.* 改变 to change (something)

📝 With the arrival of rain, we had to *alter* our plans for the class field trip to an indoor activity.

penchant
/ˈpentʃənt/

🔢 *n.* 倾向 a strong liking for something or a strong tendency to behave in a certain way

📝 Despite his *penchant* for rich food, the chef was able to change his habits when his diet became threatening to his health.

🔄 dislike

□ impecunious   □ assiduous   □ tacit   □ transgress   □ abstruse
□ embed   □ render   □ alter   □ penchant

tailor
/ˈteɪlər/

v. 修改 to make or change (something) so that it meets a special need or purpose

We make sure to ***tailor*** lesson plans to each student with our customized tutoring services!

n. 裁缝 one that makes, repairs, and alters garments such as suits, coats, and dresses

Because Jane bought the dress without trying it on, she had to take it to a ***tailor*** when she realized that it did not fit properly.

homogeneous
/ˌhoʊməˈdʒiːniəs/

adj. 同种的，相似的 of the same or similar nature or kind

Although Lucky Charms promises hearts, stars, clovers, and moons, the marshmallows in my bowl of cereal were a ***homogeneous*** group of moons.

uniform, unvaried, resemblance

disparate

immense
/ɪˈmens/

adj. 巨大的 very great in size or amount

The Atlantic Ocean is an ***immense*** basin filled with an enormous amount of water.

colossal

kindred
/ˈkɪndrəd/

adj. 相关的，相似的 closely related or similar

Upon learning that Betty was also a fan of obscure 1990s music, I knew we were ***kindred*** spirits who would get along.

affiliated

affiliate
/əˈfɪlieɪt/

v. 附属 to closely connect (something or oneself) with or to something (such as a program or organization) as a member or partner

Although David looks like a normal person, he is in fact ***affiliated*** with a dangerous mafia.

kindred

run-of-the-mill
/ˌrʌnəvðəˈmɪl/

adj. 平凡的 average or ordinary

Even if the culprits are ***run-of-the-mill*** criminals, the pet store theft is one of the most unusual crimes we've seen in years.

refuge
/ˈrefjuːdʒ/

n. 避难所 a place that provides shelter or protection

During the blizzard, we took ***refuge*** inside and played video games until the storm passed.

oasis

oratorical
/ˌɔːrəˈtɔːrɪkl/

adj. 口才的 of or relating to the skill or activity of giving speeches

Barack Obama's ***oratorical*** skills and experience as a president will make him an expensive public speaker after his term expires.

incense
/ˈɪnsens/

v. 激怒 to arouse the extreme anger or indignation of

Incensed by the bully's harassment, Peter punched him in the face.

☐ tailor ☐ homogeneous ☐ immense ☐ kindred ☐ affiliate
☐ run-of-the-mill ☐ refuge ☐ oratorical ☐ incense

mortify /ˈmɔːrtɪfaɪ/	v. 使…尴尬 to cause (someone) to feel very embarrassed and foolish Kathy was **mortified** when she found out that her mom had read her diary and found out about her crush on a classmate. embarrass
heterodox /ˈhetərədɑːks/	adj. 异端邪说的，非主流观点的 not agreeing with established beliefs or standards While she was originally doubted, Nobel laureate Barbara McClintock has lived to see the triumph of her once **heterodox** scientific theories. iconoclastic
doctrinaire /ˌdɑːktrəˈner/	adj. 空谈理论的，教条的 of, relating to, or characteristic of a person inflexibly attached to a practice or theory; dictatorial Joining a political party does not mean you have to support all their positions in a **doctrinaire** way. dogmatic n. 教条主义者（不顾实际而一味坚持某一经验或理论的人）a person inflexibly attached to a practice or theory without regard to its practicality Jack was a true **doctrinaire** who tried to establish a branch of the libertarian political party with no money or followers.
sporadic /spəˈrædɪk/	adj. 不规律的，偶发的，随机的 occurring occasionally, singly, or in irregular or random instances Kate would have **sporadic** flashbacks of her terrible childhood even as an adult. fitful, scanty
dictate /ˈdɪkteɪt/	v. 掌控，支配 to control or command Common sense **dictates** that you should wash your hands after shaking hands with a sick person.
buoyant /ˈbɔɪənt/	adj. 愉悦的 happy and confident Chris Porter's new composition is rather schizophrenic as it swings from a **buoyant** to a menacing mood within a few bars. adj. 漂浮的，可浮起来的 able to float or able to cause things to float The ship provides dozens of **buoyant** life vests to keep the passengers afloat in the event of accident.

□ mortify   □ heterodox   □ doctrinaire   □ sporadic   □ dictate
□ buoyant

Word List 13

音频

premonitory /prɪˈmɑːnɪtɔːri/	■ *adj.* 警告的 giving warning
	例 Televisions give off a ***premonitory*** siren if there is severe weather approaching.
abreast /əˈbrest/	■ *adj.* 与时俱进的 up to a particular standard or level especially of knowledge of recent developments
	例 When the Zulu hunters learned of the other tribe's movements, they ran back to their village to keep the chief ***abreast*** of the developments.
	■ *adv.* 平行地，并列 side by side
	例 They marched in orderly ranks, three ***abreast***, like emperor penguins in a nature film.
	■ *adv.* 不落后于 up to date with
	例 I encourage you to join the international psychology association to stay ***abreast*** of the latest developments in the field of positive psychology.
obstinate /ˈɑːbstɪnət/	■ *adj.* 固执的 refusing to change one's behavior or ideas
	例 Blake was ***obstinate*** in his decision to move to China and refused to change his mind.
	反 tractable
redeem /rɪˈdiːm/	■ *v.* 赎罪 to atone for
	例 After serving 200 hours of community service, Julio had ***redeemed*** himself for illegally spray-painting the wall of the pizza shop.
	■ *v.* 赎回 to buy back
	例 For a limited time, you can ***redeem*** 20 UPC codes from the bottom of the milk carton for another free carton!
debacle /deɪˈbɑːkl/	■ *n.* 大灾难 a great disaster
	例 Greed is behind every ***debacle*** in the Wall Street.
	反 success
	■ *n.* 彻底失败 a complete failure
	例 Microsoft's first attempt at the Surface RT was a complete ***debacle***, but the newer Surface Pros are lauded as great devices.
	选 fiasco

omit
/əˈmɪt/

v. 省略，忽略 to not include or to leave undone

The book's final chapter on Mildred Imach Cleghorn is incomplete as it crucially **omits** Cleghorn's years as an Apache tribal leader.

include

omission (n. 省略)

boon
/buːn/

n. 好处，福利 a benefit or advantage

Although mosquitoes are a **boon** to local ecosystems, they are a nuisance to all humans.

benefit

hidebound
/ˈhaɪdbaʊnd/

adj. 守旧的 not willing to accept new or different ideas

Henry Clay was a Kentucky slave owner who accepted the **hidebound** racial views of the time, yet looked forward to a day when the nation's enslaved blacks would be freed.

sullen
/ˈsʌlən/

adj. 阴郁的，生气的 showing a brooding ill humor or silent resentment; morose or sulky

Geniuses can be **sullen** introverts like Michelangelo or talkative extroverts like Titian.

surly, grumpy

adj. 阴沉灰暗的 gray and dark

The **sullen** skies warned of a coming storm.

prudent
/ˈpruːdnt/

adj. 谨慎的 marked by circumspection

Because farmers were not **prudent** in their agricultural practices, the droughts of the 1930s had an even worse effect on the land than they otherwise would have.

circumspect

foolhardy

imprudent (adj. 不谨慎的)

adj. 节省的 provident or frugal

We were **prudent** with our purchases and avoided name-brand food products as we were on a strict budget.

provident

adj. 睿智的，精明的 marked by wisdom or judiciousness

The sage was a **prudent** man who dispensed wisdom freely to those who listened.

juxtapose
/ˌdʒʌkstəˈpoʊz/

v. 并排放置 to place two or more things side by side

Maxine Hong Kingston's *The Woman Warrior* **juxtaposes** contrasting stories of women who are triumphant and victimized.

noxious
/ˈnaːkʃəs/

adj. 有害的 harmful to living things

We bought the carbon monoxide detector as it could detect **noxious** fumes in very small amounts.

obnoxious
/əbˈnɑːkʃəs/

adj. 极其令人反感的 odiously or disgustingly objectionable

I find frogs utterly *obnoxious* creatures as they croak all night long and keep the neighborhood up.

laborious
/ləˈbɔːriəs/

adj. 费力的 requiring a lot of time and effort

Until now, researchers had the tools to genetically manipulate only a small selection of animals, and the process was often inefficient and *laborious*.

arduous

adj. 勤奋的 devoted to labor

With hopes of becoming rich, the investment banker invested all his time in *laborious* office work and avoided social affairs.

rhapsody
/ˈræpsədi/

n. 慷慨激昂的说辞 a written or spoken expression of great enthusiasm, praise, etc.

Upon her retirement, the professor was given a *rhapsody* by the English department praising her service to the community.

stanch
/stæntʃ/

v. 阻止 to stop or check in its course

The dam *stanched* the flow of the Colorado River and provided power to millions.

v. 止血 to stop blood from flowing

By wrapping his arm in a towel, Buck hoped to *stanch* the blood from the gunshot wound.

divert
/daɪˈvɜːrt/

v. 分散，转移（注意力、精神）to distract

Diverted by the 80% clearance sale, Jessie forgot about her nail appointment and went shopping.

v. 通过转移注意力使人愉悦 to give pleasure to especially by distracting the attention from what burdens or distresses

After her recent break-up, Jill asked her friends to go dancing to *divert* her mind from the sadness.

entertain

diverting（*adj.* 有趣的）

bungle
/ˈbʌŋɡl/

v. 搞砸 to not do (something) well or successfully

Rita *bungled* her entire book report assignment by spilling coffee onto her computer and losing the file.

pendulum
/ˈpendʒələm/

n. 摇摆不定的局势（或事态）something (as a state of affairs) that alternates between opposites

As a bipolar sufferer, Andy requires medicine to keep the *pendulum* of his emotions in check.

fixate
/ˈfɪkˌseɪt/

v. 注视，全神贯注 to give all of your attention to something

When Adam *fixated* on a new research project, all of his other cares were ignored.

aghast
/ə'gæst/

释 *adj.* 吃惊的 shocked and upset

例 Mary was *aghast* when she realized that she had failed all her exams, even though she had been studying hard for months.

obdurate
/'ɑːbdərət/

释 *adj.* 固执的 stubbornly persistent in wrongdoing

例 Linda is *obdurate* in matters large and small: she is inflexible in her opinions and will not listen to opposing views.

选 intransigence, fortitude

反 flexible, complaisant

foresight
/'fɔːrsaɪt/

释 *n.* 远见 the ability to see what will or might happen in the future

例 Aleksandr Solzhenitsyn's *foresight* proved keenest when he accurately predicted that his books would someday appear in his native Russia.

glamorous
/'glæmərəs/

释 *adj.* 有吸引力的 very exciting and attractive

例 Everyone imagines the *glamorous* lifestyle of a movie star, but they do not realize the hard work necessary to act and promote films.

relegate
/'relɪɡeɪt/

释 *v.* 降低 to assign to a place of insignificance or of oblivion

例 During the 1950s, talented African American actresses like Dorothy Dandridge were often marginalized and *relegated* to playing mostly stereotypical roles.

apostle
/ə'pɑːsl/

释 *n.* 狂热的支持者 an ardent supporter

例 A controversial figure, Marilyn Manson was hated by parents, but adored by his young *apostles*.

foreground
/'fɔːrɡraʊnd/

释 *v.* 强调 to make (something) more important

例 The search for alternative energy became *foregrounded* in the national consciousness due to increased newspaper coverage.

pious
/'paɪəs/

释 *adj.* 信仰虔诚的 deeply religious

例 Most modern popes are *pious* figures, but many Medieval popes were immoral and power hungry.

释 *adj.* 假虔诚的，伪善的 marked by false devoutness; solemnly hypocritical

例 The false prophet was a *pious* sham who could not tell what time it was, much less predict the future.

self-righteous
/ˌself'raɪtʃəs/

释 *adj.* 自以为是的 convinced of one's own righteousness especially in contrast with the actions and beliefs of others

例 As the epitome of *self-righteous* celebrities, Kanye West is the greatest believer in his own artistic greatness.

brandish
/'brændɪʃ/

释 *v.* 炫耀 to display ostentatiously

例 He *brandished* his enormous Rolex watch in an attempt to make his friends envious.

选 boast

释 *v.* 挥舞 to shake or wave (as a weapon) menacingly

例 *Brandishing* his long sword, the Viking charged into the enemy fortress.

erroneous
/ɪˈroʊniəs/

adj. 错误的 not correct

True vertigo is not mere dizziness but an involuntary, **erroneous** perception that one is moving.

inaccurate

feasible
/ˈfiːzəbl/

adj. 可行的 possible to do

Telescopes have become so inexpensive that astronomy is now **feasible** as a hobby and accessible to almost anyone.

practicable

schism
/ˈsɪzəm/

n. 分裂 division or separation

The conflicting views that the issue sparked within the scientific community were so pronounced that they nearly amounted to a **schism**.

factiousness

notorious
/noʊˈtɔːriəs/

adj. 臭名昭著的 well-known or famous especially for something bad

Nutrition studies can be misleading; they are often based on food questionnaires that are **notorious** for being inaccurate.

infamous

notoriety (*n.* 臭名昭著)

providential
/ˌprɑːvɪˈdenʃl/

adj. 幸运的，凑巧的 happening at a good time because of luck

The hero's arrival just in time to save the day was **providential**.

tumultuous
/tuːˈmʌltʃuəs/

adj. 混乱的 involving a lot of violence, confusion, or disorder

The foreign correspondent was accustomed to completing his assignments under **tumultuous** conditions, so writing on the subway was not a problem for him.

panache
/pəˈnæʃ/

n. 炫 dash or flamboyance in style and action

Saul exhibits **panache** by dressing in flamboyant patterns and driving attention-grabbing sports cars.

gawky
/ˈgɔːki/

adj. 笨拙的 awkward and clumsy

Ever the **gawky** teen, Terry could not walk up the stairs without bumping into something.

virulent
/ˈvɪrjələnt/

adj. 有害的，有毒的 extremely dangerous and deadly and usually spreading very quickly

Cholera was once a **virulent** disease that killed millions throughout Europe.

adj. 恶毒的 full of malice

The **virulent** speech spewed out of the demagogue's mouth, spreading hate against the good people of his country.

□ erroneous   □ feasible   □ schism   □ notorious   □ providential
□ tumultuous   □ panache   □ gawky   □ virulent

malignant
/məˈlɪgnənt/

adj. 有害的 tending to produce death or deterioration

Elephants don't get cancer as frequently as humans do, even though their bodies contain many more cells that could potentially become **malignant**.

adj. 恶毒的 passionately and relentlessly malevolent

Jessie is known as the **malignant** scourge of the classroom due to his constant fighting and arguments with the teachers.

benign
/bɪˈnaɪn/

adj. 无害的 not causing harm or damage

Nuclear engineer Meena Mutyala argues that nuclear power is an environmentally **benign** technology as it operates with essentially no emissions.

innocuous, anodyne

adj. 温和的，善良的 showing kindness and gentleness

Myrtle was a **benign** old lady who volunteered at the homeless shelter every day and donated her money to various charities.

abridge
/əˈbrɪdʒ/

v. 缩短 to shorten by leaving out some parts

The film was **abridged** from its original cut as the festival director found it too long for the program.

synoptic

lurid
/ˈlʊrɪd/

adj. 令人震惊的，耸人听闻的 causing shock or disgust

Newscasts are routinely filled with such sensational stories that the public is seldom shocked by even the most **lurid** ones.

sensational

copious
/ˈkoʊpiəs/

adj. 大量的 very large in amount or number

The second edition of the textbook provides **copious** footnotes as the editors have apparently collected a great deal of background data since the previous edition.

abundant

negligent
/ˈneglɪdʒənt/

adj. 疏忽大意的 failing to take proper or normal care of something or someone

A forthcoming report concludes that **negligent** government regulators allowed corrupt practices to drive Mexico's banking system into bankruptcy.

lax, careless

sartorial
/sɑːrˈtɔːriəl/

adj. 与衣服相关的 of or relating to a tailor or to clothing

Unlike the loose-fitting clothing that was popular in the 1990s, the **sartorial** trend of our time is tight and body conscious attire.

supersede
/ˌsuːpərˈsiːd/

v. 淘汰，取代 to take the place of (someone or something that is old, no longer useful, etc.)

If a child is a guest in someone's home, their rules **supersede** those enforced by the child's parents

preempt

162
□ malignant   □ benign   □ abridge   □ lurid   □ copious
□ negligent   □ sartorial   □ supersede

thrill /θrɪl/	*v.* 使…兴奋 to cause (someone) to feel very excited or happy Scientists were **thrilled** by the wealth of information that Voyager II sent back from Neptune twelve years after leaving Earth.
approbate /'æprə,beɪt/	*v.* 支持，赞成 to approve or sanction Even though the president **approbated** the attack on the terrorist organization, he was saddened to know that it would result in hundreds of deaths. condemn
relinquish /rɪ'lɪŋkwɪʃ/	*v.* 放弃 to give up (something) Pope Ratzinger is the second Pope in history to have **relinquished** his powers as the leader of the Catholic Church. cede, abandon
replenish /rɪ'plenɪʃ/	*v.* 补充，修复 to fill or build up again Henry asked the server to **replenish** his glass with a second serving of coke.
curtail /kɜːr'teɪl/	*v.* 削减 to reduce or limit (something) City leaders practiced austerity out of respect for taxpayers by **curtailing** the number of new public projects.
fabricate /'fæbrɪkeɪt/	*v.* 编造，捏造 to make up for the purpose of deception The consultants repeatedly managed to dupe the team of scientists by **fabricating** data. forge *v.* 生产，制造 to construct or manufacture When one is traveling, handcrafts **fabricated** by the hands of locals are better souvenirs than cheap, plastic knick-knacks.
manacle /'mænəkl/	*v.* 限制 to restrain from movement, progress, or action **Manacled** by one party's refusal to compromise, Congress could not pass a single bill during their most recent session.
rein /reɪn/	*n.* （马的）缰绳 a strap fastened to a bit by which a rider or driver controls an animal Pulling the horse back with its **reins**, the rider stopped just before the horse was about to trip on the hole in the road. *v.* 限制，阻止 to check or stop by or as if by a pull at the reins When the teacher raised her voice, the students knew they had to **rein** in their rambunctious energy and pay attention.

bridle
/'braɪdl/

v. 限制，抑制 to restrain, check, or control with or as if with a bridle

Even though he kept losing money, Joe refused to **bridle** his passion for gambling.

inhibit

unbridled（*adj.* 不受控制的）

n. 马勒 the headgear with which a horse is governed and which carries a bit and reins

Among the many types of **bridles**, the gag **bridle** is the most common for polo matches because they have the most severe action.

grant
/grænt/

v. 承认 to admit (something) although it does not agree with or support one's previous opinion

"I **grant** you that we did not make a profit last quarter, but if we stay the course, we will see major profits in the future," the financial analyst told his boss.

v. 授予 to bestow or transfer formally

Students who are **granted** extra responsibilities will respond by acting more mature.

v. 允许 to agree to do, give, or allow (something asked for or hoped for)

After years of asking to play football, the son was finally **granted** permission by his mother, even though she was aware of the dangers of the sport.

digress
/daɪ'gres/

v. 偏题，跑题 to speak or write about something that is different from the main subject being discussed

The art professor was never one to **digress**: she always stuck closely to the subject of every lecture.

entrench
/ɪn'trentʃ/

v. 牢固地确立 to establish firmly or solidly

Despite its patent implausibility, this belief has become so **entrenched** that no amount of rational argument will suffice to get rid of it.

entrenched（*adj.* 根深蒂固的）

prowess
/'praʊəs/

n.（超凡的）技巧，能力 great ability or skill

A school's **prowess** in sports does not matter if it cannot provide a good education to all its students.

secular
/'sekjələr/

adj. 世俗的 of or relating to the physical world and not the spiritual world

Many devout followers commit themselves to the teachings of their religions and place their spiritual needs above their **secular** wants.

adj. 非宗教的 not religious

Many European countries are **secular** states in which religion does not play an active role in shaping the government.

ecstatic /ɪkˈstætɪk/	释 *adj.* 特别高兴的 very happy or excited 例 She was *ecstatic* about her first pregnancy and was seen beaming with excitement. 近 euphoric 反 disgruntled, crestfallen
euphoria /juːˈfɔːriə/	释 *n.* 特别高兴 a feeling of great happiness and excitement 例 When the professor received the grant to build his chemistry lab, he had a sense of *euphoria* knowing that his hours writing grant proposals had paid off. 近 ecstasy 派 euphoric（*adj.* 特别高兴的）
disgruntle /dɪsˈɡrʌntl/	释 *v.* 使…不高兴 to make ill-humored or discontented 例 *Disgruntled* by his sudden firing, the Burger King employee spray-painted obscene messages on the walls of his former employer. 近 crestfallen
gracious /ˈɡreɪʃəs/	释 *adj.* 有礼貌的 very polite in a way that shows respect 例 They were *gracious* hosts who offered us endless food and a comfortable home to stay in for three days. 释 *adj.* 优雅的 graceful 例 Never seeming flustered by any situation, Sophia Lauren is the paradigm of a *gracious* actress.
humdrum /ˈhʌmdrʌm/	释 *adj.* 无聊的，千篇一律的 not interesting or dull 例 The old man lived such a *humdrum* life consisting of a daily routine of watching reality TV, eating and sleeping. 近 dull 反 unrepeated
polarize /ˈpoʊləraɪz/	释 *v.* 使…两极化 to break up into opposing factions or groupings 例 The introduction of the intelligent and provocative team member completely *polarized* the existing team into likers and haters.
hand-wringing /ˈhændˌrɪŋɪŋ/	释 *n.* 焦虑的、绝望的言谈举止 an overwrought expression of concern or guilt 例 When Jeff was romantically rejected by his best friend, he was utterly embarrassed and went through a lot of *hand-wringing* at the bleak prospect of seeing her again.
prime /praɪm/	释 *v.* 使…准备好 to make (someone) ready to do something 例 *Priming* his musket with gunpowder, the soldier added the bullet, pulled the gun to his shoulder, and fired at the enemy line. 释 *adj.* 最重要的 most important 例 The Chrysler building is a *prime* example of the influence that the discovery of King Tut's tomb had on Art Deco.

vanquish
/ˈvæŋkwɪʃ/

v. 打败，战胜 to defeat (someone) completely in a war, battle, etc.

The two knights were equally powerful and skilled, but it was Arthur who eventually **vanquished** his opponent.

triumph
/ˈtraɪʌmf/

n. 胜利，成就 a great or important victory

The movie *Birdman* was a **triumph** of cinematography and experimentation as proven by its recent win of the Best Picture award at the Oscars.

forge
/fɔːrdʒ/

v. 伪造，造假 to make or imitate falsely especially with intent to defraud

Jeb was arrested for **forging** signatures on stolen checks and withdrawing the cash from the bank.

fabricate

v. 努力形成 to form or bring into being especially by an expenditure of effort; to sharp (metal) by heating and hammering

The swordsmith **forged** a razor-sharp sword that was both durable and light for the samurai warrior.

garrulous
/ˈgærələs/

adj. 话多的 very talkative

Steven's **garrulous** nature annoys almost everyone in the office; he talks on and on for hours about whatever is on his mind.

loquacious

taciturn

garrulity（*n.* 啰嗦）

prevaricate
/prɪˈværɪˌkeɪt/

v. 搪塞，闪烁其词 to avoid telling the truth by not directly answering a question

The White House spokesman seemed to **prevaricate** when the other delegates asked about the situation in Iraq.

eclectic
/ɪˈklektɪk/

adj. 多元的 including things taken from many different sources

The new novels draws on several different genres and so can rightly be termed **eclectic**.

haughty
/ˈhɔːti/

adj. 高傲的，傲慢的 blatantly and disdainfully proud

After winning the award, Phillip adopted a **haughty** pose, treating even his best friends in a snooty manner.

dismantle
/dɪsˈmæntl/

v. 拆开 to take to pieces, to tear down

During the night of November 9, 1989, crowds of Germans began **dismantling** the Berlin Wall—a barrier that for almost 30 years had symbolized the Cold War division of Europe.

v. 破坏 to destroy (something) in an orderly way, to take to pieces

When the battleship was decommissioned, it was **dismantled** and its metal sold for scrap.

propagate
/ˈprɑːpəɡeɪt/

v. 宣扬，宣传 to foster growing knowledge of, familiarity with, or acceptance of (as an idea or belief)

Many cult leaders are able to acquire bands of trusting followers by **propagating** the idea that our days on Earth are coming to an end.

caricature
/ˈkærɪkətʃər/

n. 讽刺画 a drawing that makes someone look funny or foolish because some part of the person's appearance is exaggerated

The media image of Bush as a bumbling idiot is a **caricature**, not literal reality.

abrade
/əˈbreɪd/

v. 磨损 to damage (something) by rubbing, grinding, or scraping

After thousands of miles of driving, tires become **abraded** by friction and need to be changed.

v. （在精神上）折磨 to wear down in spirit

The years-long siege **abraded** the morale of the Frenchmen and they surrendered their castle to their English adversaries.

blight
/blaɪt/

v. 破坏 to impair the quality or effect of

The long drought in California has **blighted** the countryside, turning it into a dark brown mass of dead vegetation.

pristine
/ˈprɪstiːn/

adj. 原始的 belonging to the earliest period or state

The **pristine** copies of the manuscript are highly valued and cannot be accessed by the general public.

adj. 未被破坏的 not spoiled, corrupted, or polluted and left in its natural state

Many are attracted to the **pristine** nature of National Parks.

undisturbed

corrupted by civilization

apposite
/ˈæpəzɪt/

adj. 合适的，相关的 highly pertinent or appropriate

If you knew where I had last put my wallet, why didn't you offer this **apposite** piece of information when we were searching?

fitting, germane

irrelevant

germane
/dʒɜːrˈmeɪn/

adj. 相关的 relating to a subject in an appropriate way

The history teacher often went on tangents that referred to other periods of history and were not **germane** to the day's lesson.

relevant, apposite

fitful
/ˈfɪtfl/

adj. 不规律的，一阵阵的 not regular or steady

The **fitful** ferry service between Santa Rosa Island and the mainland makes it difficult for tourists to plan a trip to the island in advance.

sporadic

imperturbable
/ˌɪmpər'tɜːrbəbl/

释 *adj.* 镇定的，冷静的 very calm

例 The Prime Minister handled the crisis calmly and dispassionately, thereby enhancing his reputation for being *imperturbable*.

选 unflappable

反 volatile

exigent
/'ɛksɪdʒənt/

释 *adj.* 紧急的 requiring immediate attention

例 Although the rules of the pool state "no running", the child's injury was an *exigent* circumstance that allowed the rule to be ignored.

选 pressing

反 deferrable

surrogate
/'sɜːrəgət/

释 *adj.* 代理的 appointing as a successor, deputy, or substitute for oneself

例 Because Jan was infertile, she and her husband had to find a *surrogate* mother to carry their baby to the end of term.

erstwhile
/'ɜːrstwaɪl/

释 *adv.* 过去 in the past

例 Ernest now works in a corporate job making millions of dollars a year and has abandoned the hippy life, which *erstwhile* defined him.

选 onetime

onetime
/'wʌn,taɪm/

释 *adj.* 过去的，之前的 having been someone or something specified in the past

例 The *onetime* NFL All-Star OJ Simpson now sits in prison for a number of crimes.

选 erstwhile

florid
/'flɔːrɪd/

释 *adj.* 过分修饰的，花哨的 elaborately decorated

例 In contrast to writers who employ a *florid* style, Hemingway is known for prose that is spare and direct.

释 *adj.* 红润的 having a red or reddish color

例 Kate had a *florid* appearance from the high fever that had kept her in bed for three days.

defame
/dɪ'feɪm/

释 *v.* 贬损，玷污 to hurt the reputation of (someone or something) especially by saying things that are false or unfair

例 Media reports alleged that the candidate's campaign strategy was designed to hobble her opponent's chances for election by *defaming* his reputation.

派 defamatory（*adj.* 诽谤的）

inveigle
/ɪn'veɪgl/

释 *v.* 诱骗 to persuade (someone) to do something in a clever or deceptive way

例 By offering his spacious SUV, Sam *inveigled* his way into the trip to the beach with the "cool" kids.

反 request directly

□ imperturbable　　□ exigent　　□ surrogate　　□ erstwhile　　□ onetime
□ florid　　□ defame　　□ inveigle

timorous
/ˈtɪmərəs/

adj. 胆小的 easily frightened

Brian's *timorous* personality and lack of confidence made it really hard for him to get a job.

diffident

反 intrepid

omniscient
/ɑːmˈnɪsiənt/

adj. 无所不知的 knowing everything

Regulators are not the *omniscient* judges that legislation so often presumes as they often fall short too.

interminable
/ɪnˈtɜːrmɪnəbl/

adj. 持续的，没完没了的 continuing for a very long time

Students were all bored by the *interminable* lecture, which went an hour over the scheduled time.

posture
/ˈpɑːstʃər/

n. 态度，立场 state or condition at a given time especially with respect to capability in particular circumstances

Upon seeing the downtrodden *posture* of the opposing team, the Little League Vikings knew they were going to win the football game before the game even began.

v. 装腔作势 to assume an artificial or pretended attitude

Adam *postured* supreme confidence during his date with the beautiful model, but his insecurity and low self-esteem still showed.

反 behave naturally

narcissism
/ˈnɑːrsɪsɪzəm/

n. 自恋 egoism; egocentrism

Carl's *narcissism* was his worst enemy because he believed that anyone who criticized him was a fool.

self-flattery

substantiate
/səbˈstænʃieɪt/

v. 证明 to prove the truth of (something)

By citing data from nations where female scientists earn less than male counterparts, the author attempted to *substantiate* the claim that discrimination still exists.

反 disprove

Word List 14

音频

---

snare
/sner/

🔲 *n.* 陷阱 a position or situation from which it is difficult to escape
🔲 Great renown is frequently a **snare** for growing companies as they become obsessed with it and lose sight of what really matters at the heart of their business.

🔲 *v.* 捕捉 to cause (something) to become caught in something
🔲 Using a hidden trap, the hunter **snared** the rabbit and took it home for dinner.

---

forestall
/fɔːrˈstɔːl/

🔲 *v.* 阻止 to stop (something) from happening
🔲 David tried to **forestall** a breakup by apologizing to his girlfriend and buying her gifts.
🔲 avert, prevent
🔲 precipitate

---

beholden
/bɪˈhoʊldən/

🔲 *adj.* 亏欠的 being under obligation for a favor or gift
🔲 In Medieval Europe, serfs were **beholden** to their lords for the land that they were given to till.

---

indebted
/ɪnˈdetɪd/

🔲 *adj.* 感激的 owing gratitude or recognition to another
🔲 Our modern view of the world and present exploration of the universe are profoundly **indebted** to Kepler and Newton's insights.
🔲 beholden
🔲 indebtedness（*n.* 受恩惠）

---

impute
/ɪmˈpjuːt/

🔲 *v.* 归罪于，归咎于 to say or suggest that someone or something has or is guilty of (something)
🔲 Although Rick was just trying to help, bad motives were **imputed** to him.

---

brazen
/ˈbreɪzn/

🔲 *adj.* 厚颜无耻的，臭不要脸的 acting or done in a very open and shocking way without shame or embarrassment
🔲 Viktor was **brazen** about cheating and openly looked up test answers on his phone.

---

nettle
/ˈnetl/

🔲 *v.* 使…生气 to make (someone) angry
🔲 **Nettled** by the poor customer service he received at Target, Larry took to twitter to tell all of his friends not to shop there anymore.
🔲 nettlesome（*adj.* 烦人的）

☐ snare ☐ forestall ☐ beholden ☐ indebted ☐ impute
☐ brazen ☐ nettle

contemptuous /kən'temptʃuəs/	*adj.* 鄙视的 feeling or showing deep hatred or disapproval Galileo's writing is energetic and contains ***contemptuous*** attacks on lesser minds. disdainful contempt（*n.* 轻蔑）
objurgation /'ɑbdʒər,geɪʃən/	*n.* 斥责，非难 a harsh rebuke The teacher's ***objurgation*** had no effect on the student, who continued being disruptive every day.
nascent /'næsnt/	*adj.* 初始的 beginning to exist During the ***nascent*** years of IBM, the company struggled due to the lack of interest in computers. budding, unformed
token /'toʊkən/	*n.* 象征 something that signifies or evidences authority, validity, or identity The Harvard study suggested that long-term happiness is a ***token*** of positive human relationships. *adj.* 象征性的 done as an indication or a pledge On many television shows, actors with minority racial backgrounds are added as ***token*** characters to boost the show's diversity.
residual /rɪ'zɪdʒuəl/	*adj.* 剩余的，残留的 leaving a residue that remains effective for some time As the slug crawled across the pavement, it left a trail of ***residual*** slime pointing in the direction it came from. *n.* 剩余，残渣 the part that is left when the other people or things are gone, used An error had clearly occurred as the ***residual*** that remained after all preceding steps did not tally with the accounts recorded.
deft /deft/	*adj.* 灵巧的 able to do something quickly and accurately This biographer provides several family trees for reference, but the textual description of the family lineage is so ***deft*** that the charts are rather unnecessary.
eloquent /'eləkwənt/	*adj.* 能说会道的，能言善辩的 having or showing the ability to use language clearly and effectively In 2004, Barack Obama gave an ***eloquent*** speech at the Democratic National Convention that brought hope and inspired millions for change in the USA. rhetoric
adroit /ə'drɔɪt/	*adj.* 灵巧的 very clever or skillful Some interactive computer games are so difficult and complex that only the most ***adroit*** player can master them. dexterous, nimble, skillful, defy, acumen maladroit（*adj.* 笨拙的）

plentiful
/ˈplentɪfl/

▓ *adj.* 慷慨的 giving or providing many desired things
▓ Agricultural jobs were ***plentiful*** in the rural town in the south, but few in the highly educated village deemed themselves worthy of these lower-paying positions.

bountiful
/ˈbaʊntɪfl/

▓ *adj.* 丰富的 given or provided abundantly
▓ It was a ***bountiful*** harvest that produced record amounts of strawberries for the farm.
▓ fertile

▓ *adj.* 慷慨的 liberal in bestowing gifts or favors
▓ Growing up, we loved spending the holidays at our grandparents' house because they were ***bountiful*** with presents.

clearheaded
/ˈklɪrˈhedɪd/

▓ *adj.* 思路清晰的 having or showing an ability to think clearly
▓ The electronics store owner had a ***clearheaded*** understanding of how hard it would be to turn a profit.

interweave
/ˌɪntərˈwiːv/

▓ *v.* 混合 to mix or blend together
▓ ***Interweaving*** rock, pop, and experimental music, the Beatles were a groundbreaking band that remains highly influential.

impolitic
/ɪmˈpɑːlətɪk/

▓ *adj.* 不明智的 unwise
▓ "It would be ***impolitic*** to condemn the demands of the masses if you want to be re-elected," the political advisor warned the representative.
▓ tactless

feeble
/ˈfiːbl/

▓ *adj.* 衰弱的，虚弱的 very weak
▓ ***Feeble*** from several round of chemotherapy, the elderly lady could not climb the stairs in her house and was forced to move to an elders' home.
▓ enfeeble（*v.* 使衰弱）

prerogative
/prɪˈrɑːgətɪv/

▓ *n.* 特权 a right or privilege
▓ The executive exercised his ***prerogative*** to buy stock options and invested most of his income into his own business.

vigilant
/ˈvɪdʒɪlənt/

▓ *adj.* 警惕的 carefully noticing problems or signs of danger
▓ It is paramount for a cycling tourist to be ***vigilant*** as situations that require a cyclist to be alert and keen-witted inevitably arise.

clumsy
/ˈklʌmzi/

▓ *adj.* 笨拙的 lacking dexterity, nimbleness, or grace
▓ The praying mantis is a ***clumsy*** creature that cannot walk straight and looks perpetually drunk.

fringe
/frɪndʒ/

▓ *adj.* 次要的，边缘的，不重要的 something that is marginal, additional, or secondary to some activity, process, or subject
▓ The existence of ancient aliens is a ***fringe*** theory explaining the construction of ancient structures like the pyramids; it receives little support from mainstream scholars.
▓ marginal, peripheral
▓ center

172
□ plentiful   □ bountiful   □ clearheaded   □ interweave   □ impolitic
□ feeble   □ prerogative   □ vigilant   □ clumsy   □ fringe

denigrate /ˈdenɪɡreɪt/	*v.* 攻击，贬损 to attack the reputation of In recent years, carbohydrates have been **denigrated** by nutritionists as a primary contributor to Americans' weight problem.
implore /ɪmˈplɔːr/	*v.* 恳求，哀求 to ask or beg for (something) in a very serious or emotional way Having **implored** her parents for months, the three-year-old was ecstatic when she received a new Barbie doll for her birthday.
supplicate /ˈsʌplɪˌkeɪt/	*v.* 恳求 to make a humble entreaty Seeking revenge for his conquered fiefdom, the petty lord **supplicated** the king for an army to help retake his land. entreat, solicit supplication（*n.* 恳求）
willful /ˈwɪlfl/	*adj.* 固执任性的 refusing to change your ideas or opinions or to stop doing something There was conflict between the **willful** Ph. D. student and her advisor because the student refused to incorporate her professor's advice into the dissertation. *adj.* 故意的 done deliberately The **willful** alternation of his team's lineup during the games ensured a swift victory for the football manager.
entreaty /ɪnˈtriːti/	*n.* 恳求 a serious request for something Following international protocols, Mexico made an official **entreaty** to Nicaragua to return the escaped convicts. supplication entreat（*v.* 恳求）
notwithstanding /ˌnɑːtwɪθˈstændɪŋ/	*prep.* 尽管 prep. despite **Notwithstanding** the burnt rice, the dinner was a delicious success!
insipid /ɪnˈsɪpɪd/	*adj.* 无聊的 not interesting or exciting The soup was utterly **insipid** and can be best described as a bland concoction less flavorful than water. bland
modish /ˈmoʊdɪʃ/	*adj.* 时髦的 fashionable or stylish Chanel has reached international fame for its clothing by setting the benchmark in **modish** design.
salubrious /səˈluːbriəs/	*adj.* 有益健康的 making good health possible or likely For centuries, the locals have praised the **salubrious** benefits of the natural sulfur spa on joint pain, gout, and other ailments. unhealthful

treacherous
/ˈtretʃərəs/

adj. 不可靠的，背叛的 not able to be trusted
Sally is a **treacherous** girl who makes friends, then betrays them.
faithful

adj. 危险的 marked by hidden dangers, hazards, or perils
Without a guardrail, the road carved a **treacherous** path up the sheer sides of the mountain.

objectionable
/əbˈdʒekʃənəbl/

adj. 令人反感的 causing people to be offended
Suzie found the comedian's show **objectionable** due to his repeated jokes about genocides and famines.

recrudesce
/ˌriːkruːˈdes/

v. 复发 to break out or become active again
After months in the cocoon, the caterpillar **recrudesces** as a butterfly and flies away from its former home.

tangible
/ˈtændʒəbl/

adj. 可感知的，实实在在的 able to be touched or felt
The gun they found in the suspect's house is **tangible** proof of his guilt, no one now doubts he is the murderer.

nebulous
/ˈnebjələs/

adj. 模糊的，不清楚的 not clear
Frustrated with the **nebulous** plans "to get drinks sometime", Willie made concrete arrangements with his friends to meet this Saturday.
vague

utter
/ˈʌtər/

adj. 完全的 complete, absolute or entire
If the sun turned into a supernova, it would cause the **utter** destruction of all life.

v. 发出声音 to send forth as a sound
During the moment of silence in memory of the armed forces, no one **uttered** a sound.

aberrant
/æˈberənt/

adj. 不正常的 deviating from the usual or natural type
Terry was usually polite, so his teachers regarded his loud conduct at the assembly as **aberrant**.
anomalous

doom
/duːm/

v. 注定（失败）to make certain the failure or destruction of
From the beginning, the Belgian resistance to the movement of German troops **doomed** the German war plan to invade France in World War I.
doomsday（*n.* 世界末日）

slender
/ˈslendər/

adj. 缺少的，不足的 limited or inadequate in amount or scope
The lawyer's closing remarks summed up the **slender** thread of evidence for the accused's guilt.

adj. 窄的，瘦的 thin, very narrow or not wide
Never before had the chef seen such delicate and **slender** noodles as the thin pasta that was typical of the Italian mountain village.

☐ treacherous   ☐ objectionable   ☐ recrudesce   ☐ tangible   ☐ nebulous
☐ utter   ☐ aberrant   ☐ doom   ☐ slender

garner
/ˈɡɑːrnər/

v. 收集 to collect or gather (something)

The police department struggled to **garner** enough evidence to convict the murder suspect, and finally had to let him go.

v. 通过努力获得… to acquire by effort

The pop fan had **garnered** quite a collection of singers' autographs.

recruit
/rɪˈkruːt/

v. 招募 to find suitable people and get them to join a company, an organization, the armed forces, etc.

Ever in need of new troops, the army often **recruits** at local high schools and career fairs.

provision
/prəˈvɪʒn/

n. 预备，预先采取的措施 something that is done in advance to prepare for something else

Mrs. Wenger had made **provision** for her retirement with early career investments and long-term insurance plans.

n. 提供，供应 the act or process of supplying or providing something

The **provision** of transport by the government in rural areas is usually scarce and sketchy, so you will be better off with your own car.

prompt
/prɑːmpt/

v. 促进，激起 to serve as the inciting cause of

The economic crisis that hit Europe **prompted** Greece to default on its loans.

adj. 敏捷的，迅速的 of or relating to prompting actors

To make sure that the actors did not forget their lines, a staff member used **prompt** cards that listed the sentences for each actor.

assail
/əˈseɪl/

v. 批评，攻击 to attack or criticize (someone or something) in a violent or angry way

David was **assailed** by doubts and questions about his future shortly after he quit his job.

endow
/ɪnˈdaʊ/

v. 赋予 to freely or naturally provide (someone or something) with something

The Declaration of Independence states that all men are **endowed** with certain inalienable rights, such as "life, liberty, and the pursuit of happiness".

v. 捐赠 to give a large amount of money to a school, hospital, etc. , in order to pay for the creation or continuing support of (something)

Upon Malcolm's death, Yale will be **endowed** with a billion-dollar donation from his estate.

intrude
/ɪnˈtruːd/

v. 闯入 to come or go into a place where you are not wanted or welcome

Thieves are more likely to **intrude** on your home if they think no one is there.

designate
/ˈdezɪɡneɪt/

🔲 *adj.* 指定的，选定的 chosen for a particular job but not officially doing that job yet

🔲 When Tom Carney announced his retirement from the nightly news, Jon Powers became the replacement *designate*.

🔲 *v.* 指定，指派 to officially choose (someone or something) to do or be something

🔲 After donating millions of dollars to the presidential campaign, the wealthy dentist was *designated* the ambassador of Ecuador after an election victory.

tackle
/ˈtækl/

🔲 *v.* 着手处理 to begin working on

🔲 Having decided to *tackle* the chapters in order, the graduate student began writing the introduction to her thesis.

🔲 *v.* 抓住并摔倒 to seize and throw (a person) to the ground

🔲 When the running back broke free from the scrum, a safety dashed over to try to *tackle* the man with the football.

prosecute
/ˈprɑːsɪkjuːt/

🔲 *v.* 从事 to engage in

🔲 The advocacy group were less concerned with helping a party get elected than with *prosecuting* their own agenda.

🔲 *v.* 起诉，检举 to bring legal action against for redress or punishment of a crime or violation of law

🔲 Shoplifters will be handed over to the police and duly *prosecuted* in court.

abolish
/əˈbɑːlɪʃ/

🔲 *v.* 废除，废止 to officially end or stop (something, such as a law)

🔲 During the Civil War, Abraham Lincoln *abolished* slavery in the USA.

bestow
/bɪˈstoʊ/

🔲 *v.* 授予，给予 to give (something) as a gift or honor

🔲 The Queen *bestowed* the Prime Minister with the privilege of governing the country.

compile
/kəmˈpaɪl/

🔲 *v.* 编辑 to collect and edit into a volume

🔲 All of Shakespeare's sonnets have been *compiled* in a single volume for easy reference.

requisite
/ˈrekwɪzɪt/

🔲 *adj.* 必要的 needed for a particular purpose

🔲 Mario is unable to advance to the next level in the video game until he collects the *requisite* number of mushrooms.

🔲 essential

splendor
/ˈsplendər/

🔲 *n.* 光辉，壮丽 great and impressive beauty

🔲 It is easy to spend hours staring at the natural *splendor* of Yosemite.

176
☐ designate ☐ tackle ☐ prosecute ☐ abolish ☐ bestow
☐ compile ☐ requisite ☐ splendor

exempt /ɪgˈzempt/	*adj.* 被免除的 not required to do something that others are required to do Because Big Brother/Big Sister is a nonprofit organization, it is ***exempt*** from paying taxes to the government. *v.* 免除 to say that (someone or something) does not have to do something that others are required to do The teacher ***exempted*** Chris from the weekly homework assignment after he was injured in a car crash.
invoke /ɪnˈvoʊk/	*v.* 引述 to appeal to or cite in support or justification In most legal systems, the insanity defense is rarely ***invoked*** because it is difficult to prove someone's mental state. *v.* 恳求，祈求 to make an earnest request for When the immense Macedonian army invaded Greece, the Thebans ***invoked*** the name of Zeus and called on him to give them victory.
entrust /ɪnˈtrʌst/	*v.* 委托，托付 to give someone the responsibility of doing something or of caring for someone or something Upon her deathbed, the grandmother ***entrusted*** the family Bible to her oldest granddaughter in order to safeguard it for the future.
alliance /əˈlaɪəns/	*n.* 联盟，联合 the state of being joined in some activity or effort Microsoft and Google entered into an ***alliance*** to build superior hardware and combat the growing power of Apple.
periodical /ˌpɪriˈɑːdɪkl/	*adj.* 周期的 happening regularly over a period of time The ***periodical*** return of mosquitoes in summer time is the bane of an otherwise pleasant time of year.
spacious /ˈspeɪʃəs/	*adj.* 宽敞的 having a large amount of space Although it is only a studio, the arrangement of the furniture helped make the apartment seem more ***spacious*** than it is.
eligible /ˈelɪdʒəbl/	*adj.* 合格的 able to be chosen for something Not all the students who apply for a scholarship are ***eligible*** to obtain one, since some do not meet the requirements.
strenuous /ˈstrenjuəs/	*adj.* 费力的 requiring or showing great energy and effort Years of ***strenuous*** lifting of heavy furniture had left him too debilitated to be able to stand up for long periods of time. *adj.* 活跃的 vigorously active The "My Little Pony" message board was a forum for ***strenuous*** discussion, and visitors were startled by the heated tone of its debates. vigorous
adjacent /əˈdʒeɪsnt/	*adj.* 相邻的 close or near It was impossible to find my car in the parking lot because it had the same make, model, and color as all the ***adjacent*** cars.

wrench
/rentʃ/

v. 猛扭 to move with a violent twist

Liam grabbed the assailant's weapon and ***wrenched*** it out of his hands before the man could fight back.

v. 歪曲，曲解 to distort

The tapestry was no longer recognizable after it became lodged in the van door during the move and was ***wrenched*** out of shape.

confiscate
/'kɑːnfɪskeɪt/

v. 没收 appropriated by the government

At an event this past week, workers destroyed 662kg of ***confiscated*** ivory in a symbolic gesture showing the country's commitment to fighting African elephant poaching.

ferocious
/fəˈrouʃəs/

adj. 凶猛的，残忍的 very fierce or violent

Although the kickball game started out friendly, competitive team members turned it into a ***ferocious*** contest with arguing and fighting.

adj. 十分强烈的 very great or extreme

During the Lenten fast, the priest could not ignore his ***ferocious*** appetite and thoughts of hamburgers consumed his mind.

velocity
/vəˈlɑːsəti/

n. 速度，迅速 quickness of motion

In the sky, no bird can match the ***velocity*** of the peregrine falcon and its 200+ mile per hour speed.

consign
/kənˈsaɪn/

v. 委托，转交 to give, transfer, or deliver into the hands or control of another

Michael had to leave home for a month-long business trip, so he ***consigned*** his dog to his next-door neighbor's care.

grapple
/ˈgræpl/

v. 抓住 to seize with or as if with a grapple

The children watched intently as they controlled the toy machine to ***grapple*** the nemo plush with its hooks.

v. 握紧 to bind closely

Passers-by ***grappled*** with the man after the attack.

deviate
/ˈdiːvieɪt/

v. 脱离，偏离 to do something that is different or to be different from what is usual or expected

Financial crises arise when the financial system ***deviates*** too far from the equilibrium or fair price.

mislead

prodigious
/prəˈdɪdʒəs/

adj. 惊人的 amazing or wonderful, very impressive

While traveling near the Sun, the comet Hale-Bopp produced a ***prodigious*** amount of dust, much more than the comets Halley or Hyakutake.

preternatural

slight

adj. 巨大的 very big

The ***prodigious*** stack of papers on the professor's desk showed how much grading he had to do before the end of the semester.

☐ wrench　　☐ confiscate　　☐ ferocious　　☐ velocity　　☐ consign
☐ grapple　　☐ deviate　　☐ prodigious

induce
/ɪnˈduːs/
- 译 *v.* 诱导 to lead or move, as to a course of action, by influence or persuasion
- 例 Three weeks after the expected due date of the baby, labor was *induced* by the doctors with medicine so that the child could be born.

assimilate
/əˈsɪməleɪt/
- 译 *v.* 吸收 to learn (something) so that it is fully understood and can be used
- 例 It takes time to *assimilate* a shocking new fact into your understanding of the world.

- 译 *v.* 使同化 to make similar
- 例 Some immigrants easily *assimilate* into their new cultures, but others never learn the new language or culture.

encroach
/ɪnˈkroʊtʃ/
- 译 *v.* 侵占 to gradually move or go into an area that is beyond the usual or desired limits
- 例 Drivers who don't look where they're going are likely to *encroach* on someone else's lane.

embody
/ɪmˈbɑːdi/
- 译 *v.* 体现 to represent (something) in a clear and obvious way
- 例 Mr. Obama seemed to *embody* the America that the world admires and envies: a country of optimism and confidence.
- 派 embodiment（*n.* 体现，化身）

coincide
/ˌkoʊɪnˈsaɪd/
- 译 *v.* 碰巧 to happen at the same time as something else
- 例 Because the Orthodox and Catholic calendars are different, the Easters of the two branches of Christianity *coincide* irregularly.

- 译 *v.* 与…相一致 to agree with something exactly
- 例 On some issues our opinions *coincide*, while on others they diverge, but thankfully our friendship remains unaffected throughout these fluctuations.

confer
/kənˈfɜːr/
- 译 *v.* 授予，给予 to give (as a property or characteristic) to someone or something
- 例 Willie Mays was invited to the commencement ceremony by the university, during which an honorary doctorate degree will be *conferred* upon him.

- 译 *v.* 协商 to discuss something important in order to make a decision
- 例 The judges *conferred* among themselves to decide what score the gymnast should receive.

subdue
/səbˈduː/
- 译 *v.* 征服，打败 to get control of (a violent or dangerous person or group) by using force, punishment, etc.
- 例 The man planned to shoot up the train but was *subdued* by three Americans.

fatal
/ˈfeɪtl/
- 译 *adj.* 致命的 causing death
- 例 Struck in the head by the ax, the Viking quickly died from the *fatal* wound.

☐ induce   ☐ assimilate   ☐ encroach   ☐ embody   ☐ coincide
☐ confer   ☐ subdue   ☐ fatal

dwell /dwel/	**释** *v.* 居住 to live in a particular place **例** According to Norse mythology, dwarves are tiny creatures that ***dwell*** inside mountains. **释** *v.* 持续地谈论 to speak or write insistently **例** The magazine writer has always been obsessed with traveling and is known to ***dwell*** on descriptions of exotic locales.
comprise /kəmˈpraɪz/	**释** *v.* 构成 to be made up of (something) **例** The museum ***comprises*** two buildings: one for traveling exhibitions, and the other for permanent collections. **释** *v.* 包含 to include; contain **例** Compiling the various documents that ***comprise*** the design is a real problem with a large project, but it is critical.
vicinity /vəˈsɪnəti/	**释** *n.* 周边环境 the area around or near a particular place **例** Signs warned against straying off the roads in Kosovo because landmines could still be buried in the ***vicinity***. **释** *n.* （距离）近 the quality or sate of being near **例** Although she did not provide the correct answer, the student got partial credit because she was in the ***vicinity*** of solution.
tentative /ˈtentətɪv/	**释** *adj.* 试探性的，临时的 not fully worked out, concluded, or agreed on; provisional **例** He set a ***tentative*** date of September 15th for the launch of his website. **释** *adj.* 犹豫的，不确定的 hesitant and uncertain **例** As with any ***tentative*** project, it's very possible the proposed system will never be developed.
pillage /ˈpɪlɪdʒ/	**释** *v.* 掠夺 to plunder ruthlessly **例** During World War II, Japanese soldiers often ***pillaged*** Chinese towns by killing locals and stealing their valuables.
pinnacle /ˈpɪnəkl/	**释** *n.* 顶点 the highest point of development or achievement **例** Many see the 1950s as the ***pinnacle*** of American car culture, with its cheap gas and eye-catching designs.
ailment /ˈeɪlmənt/	**释** *n.* 疾病 a sickness or illness **例** A vigorous man in his youth, David was struck by a deadly ***ailment*** in his 20's that sapped his strength and ability to walk. **选** illness

□ dwell   □ comprise   □ vicinity   □ tentative   □ pillage
□ pinnacle   □ ailment

apprentice
/əˈprentɪs/

🔲 *n.* 新手 an inexperienced person
🔲 As an *apprentice* in the construction industry, Cal made many mistakes and only slowly learned the trade.

🔲 *n.* 学徒 a person who learns a job or skill by working for a fixed period of time for an expert in that job or skill
🔲 Hoping to become a blacksmith, the *apprentice* worked closely with the master to learn all aspects of the trade through careful observation and practice.

preoccupied
/priˈɑːkjupaɪd/

🔲 *adj.* 专注的 thinking about something a lot or too much
🔲 Adolescent boys are often *preoccupied* with building muscle and toning their physiques.

exhale
/eksˈheɪl/

🔲 *v.* 呼出 to breathe out
🔲 Ticks are amazing hunters and can smell the *exhaled* carbon dioxide of a mammal five minutes after the mammal has passed by.

rebuke
/rɪˈbjuːk/

🔲 *v.* 指责，非难 to speak in an angry and critical way to (someone)
🔲 David's mum had *rebuked* him for drinking too much and neglecting his studies.

cavalier
/ˌkævəˈlɪr/

🔲 *adj.* 随便的，轻蔑的 marked by or given to offhand and often disdainful dismissal of important matters
🔲 When companies are *cavalier* with their customers' data, they make it more likely that it will be hacked.
🔲 capricious

hereditary
/həˈredɪteri/

🔲 *adj.* 遗传的 passing from a person who has died to that person's child or younger relative
🔲 A large part of his wealth is *hereditary* and not acquired through his own means.

shallow
/ˈʃæloʊ/

🔲 *adj.* 肤浅的 lacking depth of intellect, emotion, or knowledge
🔲 The plan was so *shallow* and impractical that no serious attempt was ever made to realize it.
🔲 profound

deflect
/dɪˈflekt/

🔲 *v.* 使…偏离，改变方向 to cause (something that is moving) to change direction
🔲 The object of the game in air hockey is to *deflect* the puck away from your goal using a sliding paddle.

🔲 *v.* 使不受到…的影响 to keep (something, such as a question) from affecting or being directed at a person or thing
🔲 When asked about her recent divorce, Madonna *deflected* the question in order to avoid the recent emotional pain.
🔲 shrug off

☐ apprentice   ☐ preoccupied   ☐ exhale   ☐ rebuke   ☐ cavalier
☐ hereditary   ☐ shallow   ☐ deflect

finesse

/fɪˈnes/

n. 技巧高超 skillful handling of a situation

例 Although he played the violin well as an amateur, he lacked the *finesse* that would make him a top class player.

反 heavy-handedness

v. 躲避 evade or skirt

例 Knowing that Katie Holmes's time as a scientologist was a sore subject, David Letterman was not surprised when she *finessed* questions away from her faith.

v. 巧妙地处理 to handle, deal with, or do (something) in an indirect and skillful or clever way

例 Because they have to deal with many strong personalities, directors need the ability to *finesse* personal disagreements.

belated

/bɪˈleɪtɪd/

adj. 晚的，迟的 happening or coming very late or too late

例 Reminded of her cousin's birthday two days after it happened, Kelly sent *belated* congratulations in a Facebook message.

Word List 7 15

音频

sheer /ʃɪr/	释 *adj.* 完全的 complete and total
	例 Overwhelmed by the ***sheer*** number of stray dogs, we were unable to enjoy the pantheon for much longer than five minutes.
	释 *adj.* 陡峭的，几乎垂直的 marked by great and continuous steepness
	例 Towering over us were ***sheer*** cliffs that seemed impossible to climb.

levity /ˈlevəti/	释 *n.* 不严肃，轻浮 a lack of seriousness
	例 Despite his attempts to bring ***levity*** to the sad situation, the tone of the conversation failed to lighten up.
	反 gravity

insidious /ɪnˈsɪdiəs/	释 *adj.* 阴险的，暗中为害的 causing harm in a way that is gradual or not easily noticed
	例 Cancer is an ***insidious*** disease; it spreads slowly in the patient's body without the patient knowing.

amass /əˈmæs/	释 *v.* 积聚，积累 to come together
	例 Holding interviews and focus groups with your staff will allow you to ***amass*** an understanding of what they are thinking.
	近 glean

ostensible /ɑːˈstensəbl/	释 *adj.* 表面的，虚假的 seeming or said to be true or real but very possibly not true or real
	例 Her ***ostensible*** explanation for her actions concealed its truly wicked intentions.

somber /ˈsɑːmbər/	释 *adj.* 严肃的，悲伤的 very sad and serious
	例 Many forget that Memorial Day is a ***somber*** occasion to remember the fallen soldiers who protected the nation.
	近 solemn
	释 *adj.* 昏暗的 having a dull or dark color
	例 Although the colors of the Fall leaves are brilliant for a month, they quickly turn to ***somber*** ruddy tones as the leaves fall to the earth and decay.

☐ sheer ☐ levity ☐ insidious ☐ amass ☐ ostensible
☐ somber

profound
/prəˈfaʊnd/

▫ *adj.* 深刻的 having or showing great knowledge or understanding
▫ Kaiser Kuo's *profound* knowledge of the internet and of social media landed him a great job as the communication manager at Baidu.
▫ trenchant
▫ superficial, shallow

▫ *adj.* 强烈的 very strongly felt
▫ After cheating on the test, Bobby had a *profound* sense of guilt and he immediately confessed to the teacher.

contour
/ˈkɑːntʊr/

▫ *n.* 轮廓 the outline or outer edge of something
▫ The elevations of mountains are depicted on maps by *contour* lines that mark regular intervals of elevation gain.

chaos
/ˈkeɪɑːs/

▫ *n.* 混乱 complete confusion and disorder
▫ When the stock market crashed in 1929, the American economy was thrown into utter *chaos* as everyone withdrew their bank accounts and sold their stocks.
▫ chaotic（*adj.* 混乱的）

voluminous
/vəˈluːmɪnəs/

▫ *adj.* 巨大的，大量的 very large
▫ Despite *voluminous* books on linguistics existing in many institutions, even most college-educated people know little about this discipline.

revile
/rɪˈvaɪl/

▫ *v.* 辱骂，斥责 to speak about (someone or something) in a very critical or insulting way
▫ Since the so-called American Dream is about making money and being successful, to revile the rich is to *revile* the American Dream.

corporeal
/kɔːrˈpɔːriəl/

▫ *adj.* 肉体的，有实体存在的 having or consisting of a physical body or form
▫ An essential dispute between the sects of Christianity is whether God ever held a *corporeal* form or is only a spiritual being.

oscillate
/ˈɑːsɪleɪt/

▫ *v.* 犹豫不决 to vary between opposing beliefs, feelings, or theories
▫ *Oscillating* between political parties, the fiscally conservative but socially liberal man finally settled on Libertarianism.
▫ waver

▫ *v.* 摇摆 to swing backward and forward like a pendulum
▫ The speed at which a pendulum *oscillates* depends on its weight and length.

monarchy
/ˈmɑːnərki/

▫ *n.* 君主政体 a form of government in which a country is ruled by a monarch
▫ With the Queen as the head of state, England is one of the few remaining *monarchies* in the world.

☐ profound   ☐ contour   ☐ chaos   ☑ voluminous   ☐ revile
☐ corporeal   ☐ oscillate   ☐ monarchy

inoculate
/ɪˈnɑːkjuleɪt/

释 *v.* （给某人）灌输，注入（想法）to introduce something into the mind of

例 Christian parents sometimes try to *inoculate* their children's minds with Biblical ideas.

释 *v.* 注射疫苗 to inject a material (as a vaccine) into to protect against or treat a disease

例 *Inoculating* individuals with cowpox would prevent children from acquiring smallpox in the future.

subsist
/səbˈsɪst/

释 *v.* 维持生存，生存下去 to exist or continue to exist

例 Once the animal uses up its usual sources of nourishment, it will have to *subsist* on acorns.

suffrage
/ˈsʌfrɪdʒ/

释 *n.* 选举权 the right to vote in an election

例 Women in the United States gained *suffrage* long after Black American men did, but Black citizens had greater difficulty exercising their new voting rights.

patron
/ˈpeɪtrən/

释 *n.* 赞助人 a person who gives money and support to an artist, organization, etc.

例 The Medicis were famous *patrons* of the arts who sponsored the works of Michelangelo and Leonardo Da Vinci, among others.

exile
/ˈeksaɪl/

释 *n.* 流放，放逐 a situation in which you are forced to leave your country or home and go to live in a foreign country

例 Nearly half of the deportees died in the first year of *exile* due to disease or starvation.

释 *v.* 流放，放逐 to banish or expel from one's own country or home

例 After losing power to the military coup, the former king of Greece was *exiled* to the UK.

inhospitable
/ˌɪnhɑːˈspɪtəbl/

释 *adj.* 不友好的 not generous and friendly to guests or visitors

例 Menacing clouds and a sudden drop in temperature signaled the onset of *inhospitable* weather.

释 *adj.* 贫瘠的，荒凉的 having an environment where plants, animals, or people cannot live or grow easily

例 *Inhospitable* to all but the most robust animals, the Sahara Desert is one of the most oppressive environments in the world.

oblique
/əˈbliːk/

释 *adj.* 间接的 not straightforward

例 He seems to have answered the direct question in an *oblique* manner rather than unequivocally.

释 *adj.* 倾斜的 having no right angle

例 Many centuries ago, the Anasazi Indians built their stone houses facing south to capture the *oblique* rays of a winter sun.

bequeath
/bɪˈkwiːð/

释 *v.* 遗赠 to give or leave by will (used especially of personal property)
例 Gretta **bequeathed** her gold necklace to her daughter in the hope that she would treasure the precious heirloom.

释 *v.* 留下，传下 to hand down
例 Though many medieval women possessed devotional books that had belonged to their mothers, formal written evidence of women **bequeathing** books to their daughters is scarce.
派 bequest（*n.* 遗产）

retention
/rɪˈtenʃn/

释 *n.* 保留 the act of keeping someone or something
例 Duke basketball prides itself on the **retention** of its players, with most entering the NBA only after they graduate.

ramify
/ˈræməˌfaɪ/

释 *v.* 使分叉 to split up into branches or constituent parts
例 Approximately 6 million years ago, the primate family tree **ramified** to produce several different mammals, including the forerunners of humans.

prescribe
/prɪˈskraɪb/

释 *v.* 规定 to set down as a rule or guide; enjoin
例 Apart from introducing a set of beliefs, religion also **prescribes** a way of life and a set of rituals to be enacted by its followers.

deprive
/dɪˈpraɪv/

释 *v.* 使丧失，剥夺 to take something away from
例 Many countries do not have taxpayer-funded schooling, and so children there are **deprived** of education.

necessitate
/nəˈsesɪteɪt/

释 *v.* 使成为必要 to make (something) necessary
例 For old people, spending time with their grandchildren is enjoyable but exhausting, and usually **necessitates** a restorative nap.

inhale
/ɪnˈheɪl/

释 *v.* 吸入 to breathe in
例 Winding his way past noisy slot machines and crowded gaming tables, Jack dashed for the exit as he was desperate to **inhale** fresh air and see the sky.

dexterity
/dekˈsterəti/

释 *n.* 灵巧，敏捷 skill and grace in physical movement, especially in the use of the hands; adroitness
例 Her **dexterity** at the piano is clearly indicative of great musical talent.

释 *n.* 聪明，伶俐 skill and grace in physical movement, especially in the use of the hands; adroitness
例 It takes great mental **dexterity** to solve a Rubik's cube consistently, much less to do it in under 10 seconds!

ooze
/uːz/

释 *v.* 渗出 to flow out slowly
例 Blood continued to **ooze** from the cut in Paul's arm even after he had pressed a gauze against it for 15 minutes.

释 *v.* 表现，显示 to show (a quality, emotion, etc.) very clearly or strongly
例 After winning the Science Fair, the student **oozed** confidence and seemed to think he was the smartest person in the world.

□ bequeath   □ retention   □ ramify   □ prescribe   □ deprive
□ necessitate   □ inhale   □ dexterity   □ ooze

patronize
/ˈpeɪtrənaɪz/

▦ *v.* 赞助 to give money or support to (someone or something)
例 As a supporter of the arts, John Vanderbilt *patronized* the Metropolitan Museum of Art by donating large sums to them.

▦ *v.* 摆出高人一等的态度对待 to talk to (someone) in a way that shows that you believe you are more intelligent or better than other people
例 After receiving his Ph.D. , Joe could not talk to the blue-collar workers in his hometown without *patronizing* them.

▦ *v.* 经常光顾 to be a frequent or regular customer or user of
例 Embarrassed by her taste for Nancy Drew novels, Pauline donned a wig and *patronized* a bookstore three towns away.

eject
/iˈdʒekt/

▦ *v.* 驱逐，逐出 to force (someone) to leave
例 Daniel was *ejected* from the party for being too loud and turning violent after a few drinks.

▦ *v.* 喷出，发出 to push out
例 When the plane was struck by a missile, the pilot *ejected* himself from the cockpit and descended to the ground safely.

overdue
/ˌoʊvərˈduː/

▦ *adj.* 延误的，拖延的 not appearing or presented by a stated, expected, or required time
例 Changing the culture and policy on gun violence is long *overdue*; we cannot continue to do nothing as more Americans are killed every day.

brusque
/brʌsk/

▦ *adj.* 唐突的，无礼的 talking or behaving in a very direct, brief, and unfriendly way
例 Brittany is considered by many to be a *brusque* person because she is very impatient and easily irritated.

prose
/proʊz/

▦ *adj.* 平凡的，乏味的（同prosaic）dull or ordinary
例 The clerk set out to type the *prose* reports just as he has every single day for the past decade.

▦ *n.* 散文 writing that is not poetry
例 In Greek literature, Herodotus wrote the first *prose* work to describe the Persian Wars in plain speech rather than poetry.

uprising
/ˈʌpraɪzɪŋ/

▦ *n.* 起义，叛乱 a usually violent effort by many people to change the government or leader of a country
例 After welfare was cut, there was an *uprising* against the totalitarian government.

touchstone
/ˈtʌtʃstoʊn/

▦ *n.* 检验标准 something that is used to make judgments about the quality of other things
例 With the rising popularity of social media, the opinions of others have become the *touchstone* of the mass's political beliefs and social issues.

☐ patronize   ☐ eject   ☐ overdue   ☐ brusque   ☐ prose
☐ uprising   ☐ touchstone

purveyor /pər'veɪər/	释 **n.** 供应商 a person or business that sells or provides something 例 As a **purveyor** of the finest fish, the fishmonger had clients among the city's top sushi chefs. 派 purvey（v. 供给）, purveyance（n. 供应）
parody /'pærədi/	释 **n.** 拙劣的模仿 a literary or musical work in which the style of an author or work is closely imitated for comic effect or in ridicule 例 Many "Saturday Night Live" are **parodies** of current news that are intended to demonstrate the absurdity of real life.
decimate /'desɪmeɪt/	释 **v.** （严重地）破坏 to destroy a large number of (plants, animals, people, etc.) 例 Fortunately, the hurricane was spared, averting the catastrophe many feared would **decimate** the city.
decipher /dɪ'saɪfər/	释 **v.** 解释，破译 to find the meaning of (something that is difficult to read or understand) 例 With the help of the secret key, the children were able to **decipher** the clues given by the radio station and read the secret message.
amenable /ə'miːnəbl/	释 **adj.** 愿意的，服从的 willing to agree or to accept something that is wanted or asked for 例 Mark was a true professional who was **amenable** to criticism and desired only to improve at his job. 反 recalcitrant
siphon /'saɪfn/	释 **v.** 抽走（资金，资源）to take and use (something, such as money) for your own purpose 例 The greedy treasurer **siphoned** money from the ALS foundation into his own personal bank account.
annotate /'ænəteɪt/	释 **v.** 注释 to add notes or comments to (a text, book, drawing, etc.) 例 In illuminated manuscripts, many monks **annotated** the Bible with entertaining drawings of devils and evil creatures.
procure /prə'kjʊr/	释 **v.** 获得 to get (something) by some action or effort 例 When exploring options for **procuring** technology for your organization, don't focus on the provider's current product, but on where they're headed.
hiatus /haɪ'eɪtəs/	释 **n.** 间歇 a period of time when something (such as an activity or program) is stopped 例 The U. S. resumed conducting navigation operations in the South China Sea last fall after a four-year **hiatus**. 选 break
cantankerous /kæn'tæŋkərəs/	释 **adj.** 易怒的 often angry and annoyed 例 Although aging brings about changes, it does not change who you are; a grumpy thirty-year-old will probably still be **cantankerous** at seventy.

escalate
/ˈeskəleɪt/

释 *v.* 加剧，恶化 to become worse or to make (something) worse or more severe

例 The debate over shocking content in movies will likely **escalate** as advocates of free speech continue to confront those who regulate entertainment.

释 *v.* 升高，提升 to become greater or higher or to make (something) greater or higher

例 Tension **escalated** among the diners in the restaurant as a couple loudly fought in the corner.

bombard
/bɑːmˈbɑːrd/

释 *v.* （如炸弹般）攻击（人或事物）to hit or attack (something or someone) constantly or repeatedly

例 American consumers, **bombarded** with advertising, are buying vitamin and mineral supplements at an unprecedented rate.

vernacular
/vərˈnækjələr/

释 *adj.* 口头语的，俗语的 of, relating to, or using the language of ordinary speech rather than formal writing

例 The poet's publisher cautioned her against overusing **vernacular** language, but the poet preferred the lively, informal dialect of her hometown.

prevail
/prɪˈveɪl/

释 *v.* 流行 to be usual, common, or popular

例 Common sense **prevailed** when the proposition to end the sale of bread was voted down.

scenario
/səˈnærioʊ/

释 *n.* 情形 a description of what could possibly happen

例 Although the coach described what to do in this **scenario**, we failed to execute the Hail Mary at the end of the game and lost.

hitherto
/ˌhɪðərˈtuː/

释 *adv.* 至今 until now

例 Greg, who had **hitherto** remained quiet, spoke up in the meeting to express his opinion.

vertiginous
/vɜːrˈtɪdʒɪnəs/

释 *adj.* 令人眩晕的 causing or likely to cause a feeling of dizziness especially because of great height

例 Since climbing the steep mountainside could make even the most experienced climbers **vertiginous**, I would not advise novices to try their luck.

近 dizzying

bravado
/brəˈvɑːdoʊ/

释 *n.* 装作勇敢 a pretense of bravery

例 In Don Quixote's mind, it was a great show of **bravado** to joust the windmill, but in reality, there was no danger to his well-being.

释 *n.* 莽撞 the quality or state of being foolhardy

例 With the **bravado** of a reckless teen, Tim ran across the street blindfolded to impress his friends with his fearlessness.

steadfast
/ˈstedfæst/

释 *adj.* 坚定不移的 firm in belief, determination, or adherence

例 He cites his **steadfast** devotion to his religion as the one constant motivation throughout his life.

近 unfaltering

☐ escalate   ☐ bombard   ☐ vernacular   ☐ prevail   ☐ scenario
☐ hitherto   ☐ vertiginous   ☐ bravado   ☐ steadfast

oblivious
/ə'blɪviəs/

释 *adj.* 无意识的，遗忘的 not conscious or aware of someone or something
例 Most drivers are *oblivious* to the fact that cars have contained powerful computers for decades.

refractory
/rɪ'fræktəri/

释 *adj.* 不服管的，难处理的 resisting control or authority
例 The stables had adopted a new pony that proved to be extremely *refractory* and took over a month to train.

释 *adj.* 难治愈的 resistant to treatment
例 Treatment for itchy eyes consists of eyelid hygiene, lubricant eye drops, and systemic antibiotics for *refractory* cases.

resign
/rɪ'zaɪn/

释 *v.* 接受 to accept something as inevitable
例 *Resigned* to a career as a janitor, Jim sought fulfillment in his hobby of building model airplanes.

释 *v.* 辞职 to give up one's office or position
例 When the football coach learned that his daughter had a fatal illness, he *resigned* from his position to spend more time with his family.

abiding
/ə'baɪdɪŋ/

释 *adj.* 长期的 continuing for a long time
例 Although he began training as an accountant, magic remained his *abiding* passion in life.
近 stable

dull
/dʌl/

释 *adj.* 无聊的 not exciting or interesting
例 Despite the critics' love of the movie, *Boyhood* was a *dull* affair that lacked any excitement or engaging plot structure.

释 *adj.* 笨的 mentally slow
例 Many of his teachers thought that the *dull* boy had a learning disability, but his mother refused to have him tested.

debonair
/,debə'ner/

释 *adj.* 彬彬有礼的 suave; urbane
例 The prince's *debonair* mannerism is what helped him charm the Duchess of Cambridge during their courtship.

释 *adj.* 欢乐的，无忧无虑的 carefree and gay; jaunty
例 I sometimes stop at Rosey Jekes café for a cappuccino if I am feeling particularly *debonair* and in the mood to people-watch.

infuriate
/ɪn'fjʊrieɪt/

释 *v.* 使…愤怒 to make (someone) very angry
例 The captain had very high expectations of the men and was easily *infuriated* by their disobedience.

crestfallen
/'krestfɔːlən/

释 *adj.* 沮丧的 very sad and disappointed
例 The teacher was *crestfallen* upon learning that the entire class had failed the test, since he had taken a lot of time to prepare them for it.
近 disgruntle

(190)
□ oblivious   □ refractory   □ resign   □ abiding   □ dull
□ debonair   □ infuriate   □ crestfallen

wistful /ˈwɪstfl/	释 *adj.* 渴望的，思念过去的 full of yearning or desire tinged with melancholy 例 "I am obviously attached to the place, I was born there," he said with a ***wistful*** smile.
concur /kənˈkɜːr/	释 *v.* 同意 to express agreement 例 Everyone in the room ***concurred*** that it would be best for the company to go public as soon as possible. 反 dissent, gainsay 释 *v.* 同时发生 to happen together 例 In a rare event, a solar eclipse ***concurred*** with the winter solstice.
boast /boʊst/	释 *v.* 吹嘘 speak vaingloriously 例 Jon enjoys ***boasting*** about his successful climb of Mt. Everest and telling everyone that he is the best athlete in Chicago. 释 *v.* 拥有 have or contain 例 Although Pete Rose is not in the Hall of Fame, he ***boasts*** an all-time record of over 4000 hits.
extrapolate /ɪkˈstræpəleɪt/	释 *v.*（依据已知信息）推测 to form an opinion or to make an estimate about something from known facts 例 The researchers thought it was too difficult to ***extrapolate*** any conclusions from the data available, since the data did not follow any pattern.
resemble /rɪˈzembl/	释 *v.* 与…相似 to be like or similar to 例 Bharara ***resembles*** his predecessors in his professional background, but differs from them in style and execution. 选 homogeneity 派 resemblance（*n.* 相似）
ordain /ɔːrˈdeɪn/	释 *v.* 命令 to order by virtue of superior authority; decree or enact 例 Upon reaching brewing capacity, Budweiser ***ordained*** the construction of a new brewery. 释 *v.* 注定 to prearrange unalterably; predestine 例 After years of education in the seminary, Father John was finally ***ordained*** a priest by the bishop.
mirth /mɜːrθ/	释 *n.* 欢乐 happiness and laughter 例 The performance produced much ***mirth*** among the audience. 选 jovial 派 mirthful（*adj.* 欢乐的）
jovial /ˈdʒoʊviəl/	释 *adj.* 高兴的 full of happiness and joy 例 The expedition's leader was unfailingly ***jovial***, and this good-humored attitude proved to be infectious. 选 mirthful

cajole
/kə'dʒoʊl/
- *v.* 哄骗 to persuade with flattery or gentle urging especially in the face of reluctance
- The teacher **cajoled** his students with extreme flattery in an attempt to persuade them to do research projects for extra credit.
- coax

baneful
/'beɪnfl/
- *adj.* 有害的 seriously harmful
- Despite the instant pleasures of drugs, they are **baneful** substances that can have serious health, social, and economic implications.

identical
/aɪ'dentɪkl/
- *adj.* 完全一样的 exactly the same
- The highly detailed model of the ship looked **identical** to the actual ship in all but size.

proscribe
/proʊ'skraɪb/
- *v.* 禁止 to not allow
- Censorship laws directly **proscribe** free expression by determining and governing the kind of art and literature available to people.
- forbid, enjoin
- sanction
- proscriptive (*adj.* 禁止的)

arguably
/'ɑːrgjuəbli/
- *adv.* 可以这样说地 it can be argued
- Michael Jordan is **arguably** the best basketball player of all time, but he was certainly the most important global ambassador for the sport.

obstreperous
/əb'strepərəs/
- *adj.* 不服管的，桀骜不驯的 difficult to control and often noisy
- To call Carlos **obstreperous** would be to mistake his natural self-confidence and youthful high spirits for defiance.

volition
/və'lɪʃn/
- *n.* 自愿选择，自行决定 the power to make your own choices or decisions
- Rumor has it that Janice was forced to resign after losing the Coca Cola account, but, in reality, she left of her own **volition** to start a new marketing company.

hectic
/'hektɪk/
- *adj.* 非常忙碌的 very busy and filled with activity
- CEOs of large companies have such **hectic** business schedules, no wonder they are barely at home and rarely get to spend time with their families.

sumptuous
/'sʌmptʃuəs/
- *adj.* 奢侈的，华丽的 extremely costly, rich, luxurious, or magnificent
- The **sumptuous** mansion was filled with fancy cars, marble floors, and gold adornment.
- lavish

gravitate
/'grævɪteɪt/
- *v.* 被吸引到···，倾向 to be attracted to or toward something
- Children should be allowed to try the things they **gravitate** toward.

particularize
/pər'tɪkjələraɪz/
- *v.* 详细阐述 to give specific details or examples of
- Greg talked only in vague terms about his party, refusing to **particularize** any component that might ruin the surprise.

☐ cajole ☐ baneful ☐ identical ☐ proscribe ☐ arguably
☐ obstreperous ☐ volition ☐ hectic ☐ sumptuous ☐ gravitate
☐ particularize

albeit
/ˌɔːlˈbiːɪt/

释 *conj.* 即使 conj. although
例 Herschel was a brilliant child in school, ***albeit*** lacking in common sense.

abet
/əˈbet/

释 *v.* 怂恿，支持，教唆（犯罪）to help, encourage, or support someone in a criminal act
例 By sending her fugitive son $100 over the transfer wire, she committed a crime by ***abetting*** a criminal.
选 instigate
反 frustrate

anodyne
/ˈænədaɪn/

释 *adj.* 不惹人厌烦的 not likely to offend or upset anyone
例 As a quiet, bookish fellow, Norman was an ***anodyne*** member of the party who would not cause a stir.
选 benign

释 *adj.* 缓解疼痛的 serving to alleviate pain
例 Sean regularly used aspirin as an ***anodyne*** for his recurring back pain.

credulous
/ˈkredʒələs/

释 *adj.* 易受欺骗的 too ready to believe things
例 The ancient Greek writer Herodotus was very ***credulous***, accepting wildly improbable legends as historical facts.
选 trusting
派 credulity（*n.* 轻信）

asunder
/əˈsʌndər/

释 *adj.* 分裂的 into parts
例 Their deteriorating relationship was finally torn ***asunder*** after she confessed that she never loved him.
反 linked

petulant
/ˈpetʃələnt/

释 *adj.* （说话，行为）粗鲁无礼的 insolent or rude in speech or behavior
例 The ***petulant*** behavior of the child was not checked by his mother, who allowed him to speak however he pleased.
派 potulance（*n.* 任性）

释 *adj.* 易怒的，脾气坏的 having or showing the attitude of people who become angry and annoyed when they do not get what they want
例 A nightmare of a customer, Pat became loudly ***petulant*** with the waitress when the service was not prompt.

winnow
/ˈwɪnoʊ/

释 *v.* 筛选 to narrow or reduce
例 Universities have strict requirements to help ***winnow*** the best candidates, otherwise narrowing down the pool of applicants would be very time-consuming.

yearn
/jɜːrn/

释 *v.* 强烈渴望 to feel a strong desire or wish for something or to do something
例 Yeats ***yearned*** to become an author from a young age and penned his first poem at the age of 17.

☐ albeit   ☐ abet   ☐ anodyne   ☐ credulous   ☐ asunder
☐ petulant   ☐ winnow   ☐ yearn

indulgent /ɪnˈdʌldʒənt/	释 *adj.* 纵容的 willing to allow someone to have or enjoy something even though it may not be proper, healthy, appropriate, etc. 例 The bratty child is spoiled because her parents are too *indulgent* with her, buying her whatever she wants and never punishing her for being mean at school. 释 *adj.* 享乐的 done or enjoyed as a special pleasure 例 Typically stingy, Ms. Henderson allowed herself a single, *indulgent* vice: monthly massages.
preside /prɪˈzaɪd/	释 *v.* 主持，负责 to be in charge of something (such as a trial) 例 *Presiding* over the O. J. Simpson court case brought Judge Ito fame throughout the world.
meretricious /ˌmerəˈtrɪʃəs/	释 *adj.* 俗里俗气的 attractive in a cheap or false way 例 Although the *meretricious* writing style of Dan Brown appeals to the masses, his books will certainly not enter the pantheon of great literature.
burgeon /ˈbɜːrdʒən/	释 *v.* 繁荣，快速增长 to grow or develop quickly 例 Popular interest in medicinal plants has *burgeoned* over the past years despite the lack of easy-to-use field guides. 选 expansion, flourish 反 subside, wither
flourish /ˈflɜːrɪʃ/	释 *v.* 繁荣 to be very successful 例 The tiny start-up has grown strength in strength and *flourished* into a huge business over the past years.
gigantic /dʒaɪˈɡæntɪk/	释 *adj.* 极大的 extremely large 例 After the magic beans were planted, Jack was confronted by a *gigantic* beanstalk that reached to the sky.
snub /snʌb/	释 *v.* 怠慢，不理睬 to ignore (someone) in a deliberate and insulting way 例 In the political debate, the Republican candidate *snubbed* the Democratic candidate because he did not think a Democrat could provide any valid suggestions on running the country. 选 slight
underplay /ˌʌndərˈpleɪ/	释 *v.* 轻描淡写，低估 to make (something) seem less important than it actually is 例 *Underplaying* his ability at pool, the hustler intentionally lost his first game and then raised the bet for the second so that he could "earn his money back".
obliterate /əˈblɪtəreɪt/	释 *v.* 抹去，使…消失 to destroy (something) completely so that nothing is left 例 Scientists predict that humans will be able to *obliterate* their most painful memories with future technological advancements.

□ indulgent ☐ preside ■ meretricious ☐ burgeon ☐ flourish
□ gigantic ☐ snub ☐ underplay ☐ obliterate

Word List 16

音频

seethe /siːð/	**v.** 强压怒火，生闷气 to suffer violent internal excitement During the Arab Spring, dissent that had **seethed** under the surface of many North African countries erupted into revolution. **v.** 攒动 to move constantly and without order While the pot was boiling, the bubbles **seethed** under the tightly closed lid.
morph /mɔːrf/	**v.** 变形 to change the form or character of When Merlin wished to escape notice, he would **morph** from his human form into a frog.
subservient /səb'sɜːrviənt/	**adj.** 服服帖帖的，奉承的 very willing or too willing to obey someone else Some actors have complained that the unreasonable director dominated them and expected them to be **subservient**.
obtuse /əb'tuːs/	**adj.** 愚钝的，笨的 stupid or unintelligent Each successive generation of the robot vacuums has been less **obtuse** than the previous—but just a bit. **adj.** 难懂的 difficult to comprehend James Joyce's novel *Ulysses* is an **obtuse** piece of writing that is very difficult to understand without the aid of a commentary.
trenchant /'trentʃənt/	**adj.** 尖酸刻薄的 caustic The food critic was very **trenchant** in his remarks about the new restaurant, criticizing the restaurant's décor as well as the blandness in all the main courses. **adj.** 犀利的，一针见血的 sharply perceptive An editorialist should not repeat campaign talking points, but have **trenchant** insight into politicians' dishonesty. profound, incisive
instigate /'ɪnstɪgeɪt/	**v.** 激起，挑起 to cause (something) to happen or begin Butch's mean remarks about Vinnie's mother **instigated** the fight between the two. abet

☐ seethe ☐ morph ☐ subservient ☐ obtuse ☐ trenchant
☐ instigate

fusty
/'fʌsti/

adj. 过时的，守旧的 very old-fashioned
The **fusty** old lady still believed in arranged marriages and traditional roles of women!
obsolete, outmoded

adj. 腐臭的 full of dust and unpleasant smells
When I opened the old trunk in the attic, a **fusty** aroma from the plume of dust shot out.

cease
/siːs/

v. 停止 to stop doing
Upon being stopped by the police, it is best to **cease** what you are doing and follow their directions.

implicate
/'ɪmplɪkeɪt/

v. 牵涉 to show to be connected or involved
Many believed Don Corleone was **implicated** in the death of Giuseppe Caroni, but the FBI was never able to prove the connection.

vituperate
/vaɪ'tuːpə,reɪt/

v. 辱骂 to abuse or censure severely or abusively
Hughes's outrage turned out to be a little disproportionate as he had **vituperated** on what turned out to be a passing and insignificant fad.
vituperative (*adj.* 谩骂的)

rattle
/'rætl/

v. 扰乱 to upset (someone) especially to the point of loss of poise and composure
Rattled by the news of the car accident, Janice forgot about her meeting and immediately rushed to the hospital.

molder
/'mouldər/

v. 腐烂，退化 to decay slowly
Cars are meant to be driven, not **molder** in a showroom.

transmogrify
/,trænz'mɑːgrɪfaɪ/

v. 使…变形 to change or alter greatly and often with grotesque or humorous effect
In the new age, online platforms have **transmogrified** word of mouth into a powerful dynamic called "user-generated content".

choreograph
/'kɔːriəgræf/

v. 精心安排 to arrange or direct the movements, progress, or details of
All the con artist's victims agree that his disappearance was a spontaneous act of desperation rather than some carefully **choreographed** plot.

v. 编舞 to decide how a dancer or group of dancers will move during a performance
A traditionalist, Vladimir **choreographed** the "Dance of the Sugarplum Fairy" according to the style of the Russian Ballet.

incipient
/ɪn'sɪpiənt/

adj. 开始的 beginning to develop or exist
There is an **incipient** movement to change the rules of football in order to prevent concussions.

☐ fusty   ☐ cease   ☐ implicate   ☐ vituperate   ☐ rattle
☐ molder   ☐ transmogrify   ☐ choreograph   ☐ incipient

antiquarian
/ˌæntɪˈkweriən/

释 *adj.* 古文物研究的 relating to the collection and study of valuable old things (such as old books)

例 As a collector of *antiquarian* oddities, Franco had hundreds of unusually shaped books and reading spectacles from the eighteenth and nineteenth centuries.

boisterous
/ˈbɔɪstərəs/

释 *adj.* 吵闹的 very noisy and active in a lively way

例 After several months of training, the *boisterous* young spaniel was finally docile enough to be walked safely without a leash.

近 uproarious

反 quiet

renounce
/rɪˈnaʊns/

释 *v.* 拒绝，否认 to give up, refuse, or resign usually by formal declaration

例 The country *renounces* its right to favor locally owned business by pledging to give equal or better treatment to global corporations that come only to extract profits.

compartmentalize
/kəmˌpɑːrtˈmentəlaɪz/

释 *v.* 分门别类，划分 to separate (something) into sections or categories

例 Breaking down overall budgets into easy-to-remember categories can cause us to behave in irrational ways, as we *compartmentalize* our decisions and lose sight of the larger picture.

maelstrom
/ˈmeɪlstrɑːm/

释 *n.* 混乱，动乱 a powerful often violent whirlpool sucking in objects within a given radius

例 Charybdis was a violent *maelstrom* in the Strait of Messene that drew Odysseus's ships into its sucking whirlpool.

captious
/ˈkæpʃəs/

释 *adj.* 挑剔的，吹毛求疵的 marked by an often ill-natured inclination to stress faults and raise objections

例 The *captious* supervisor offered no support to her student and only highlighted the most petty of her writing errors.

vulgar
/ˈvʌlgər/

释 *adj.* 粗俗的 not having or showing good manners, good taste, or politeness

例 David's grandmother is a woman of little education, poor taste, and bad manners, so everyone in the family thinks she is quite *vulgar*.

释 *adj.* 普通大众的 relating to the common people or the speech of common people

例 In the fourth century A. D. , the Bible was translated into *vulgar* Latin so that it could be understood by the general populace.

fealty
/ˈfiːəlti/

释 *n.* 忠诚 loyalty to a person, group, etc.

例 The German king demanded that all of his subjects swear *fealty* to him as their supreme ruler.

bristle
/ˈbrɪsl/

释 *v.* 生气，愤怒 to become angry

例 As the biggest Toronto Maple Leafs fan, Guy *bristles* with frustration each year when his team does not win the Stanley Cup.

---

await /əˈweɪt/	释 *v.* 等待 to wait for (someone or something) 例 Because we spent so much time **awaiting** the bill at Denny's, our parking meter expired and we received a ticket.
languish /ˈlæŋgwɪʃ/	释 *v.* 衰落，不活跃 to continue for a long time without activity or progress in an unpleasant or unwanted situation 例 Jean Valjean planned every detail of his escape in his mind while **languishing** in prison.
nugatory /ˈnuːgətɔːri/	释 *adj.* 不重要的 of little or no consequence 例 The chance of winning money on card games can seem tempting compared to the **nugatory** returns from investing in index funds. 反 consequential
inept /ɪˈnept/	释 *adj.* 无能的 generally incompetent 例 It took only a year before he was fired by the company's board for his **inept** performance. 释 *adj.* 不恰当的，不合适的 not suited to the occasion 例 It was an **inept** wardrobe choice by the teen to wear a t-shirt to the prom.
spartan /ˈspɑːrtn/	释 *adj.* 简朴的 marked by simplicity, frugality, or avoidance of luxury and comfort 例 While his prison cell was **spartan**, Mr. Bae said he was content as long as he had his books.
ancillary /ˈænsəleri/	释 *adj.* 辅助的 providing something additional to a main part or function 例 The exercise book is **ancillary** to the main material and contains explanations of some obscure points of grammar. 近 supplementary
sequester /sɪˈkwestər/	释 *v.* 分离，隔离 to keep (a person or group) apart from other people 例 After both sides of the trial rested, the jury was **sequestered** from the public in order to debate the case without outside interference.
hasty /ˈheɪsti/	释 *adj.* 快速的，仓促的 done or made very quickly or too quickly 例 When his computer broke, Tim made a **hasty** choice at the electronics store, not wanting to waste time finding the best deal for the replacement. 近 impulsively, rapidly 释 *adj.* 易怒的 prone to anger 例 Sensitive about his small stature, Dan was **hasty** in becoming offended whenever someone mentioned his height.
budding /ˈbʌdɪŋ/	释 *adj.* 新出现的 being in an early stage of development 例 The ten-year-old participated in the science fair as a **budding** scientist to demonstrate his volcano model. 近 nascent

☐ await   ☐ languish   ☐ nugatory   ☐ inept   ☐ spartan
☐ ancillary   ☐ sequester   ☐ hasty   ☐ budding

vainglory /ˌveɪnˈɡlɔːri/	*n.* 极度夸耀，虚荣 excessive or ostentatious pride especially in one's achievements Even years after retiring, the **vainglorious** swimmer still wore his gold medals in public.
consummate /ˈkɑːnsəmət/	*adj.* 完满的，圆满的 complete in every detail Veronica's mastery of sophisticated laboratory instruments makes her a truly **consummate** research technician. *v.* 圆满完成 to make (something) perfect or complete Frequently, business deals are **consummated** with a handshake.
like-minded /ˈlaɪkˌmaɪndɪd/	*adj.* 思维相似的，想法一致的 having similar opinions and interests Newspaper owners and publishers tend to hire **like-minded** people to write editorials.
ecumenical /ˌiːkjuːˈmenɪkl/	*adj.* 多元的，普遍的 involving people or things from different kind; of worldwide scope or applicability The Camp board of directors is **ecumenical** and composed of representation from throughout Northern Indiana.
ardent /ˈɑːrdnt/	*adj.* 热衷的，热情的 characterized by warmth of feeling typically expressed in eager zealous support or activity Martin Luther King's speech was an **ardent** defense of peace and freedom, his passionate talk inspired millions.
rescind /rɪˈsɪnd/	*v.* 废除（法律）to end (a law, contract, agreement, etc.) officially Lawmakers are considering legislation to **rescind** sales tax on tampons and other feminine hygiene products, because they believe it is unfair to tax these necessary products. abrogate levy
distend /dɪˈstend/	*v.* 膨胀 to become larger and rounder because of pressure from inside Rob's belly **distended** slowly but surely throughout the dinner until he had to unbutton his pants. constrict, compress
self-regard /ˈselfrɪˈɡɑːrd/	*n.* 自私自利 regard for or consideration of oneself or one's own interests Seeing her child trapped in the burning house, the mother ignored all **self-regard** and jumped into the inferno to help.
subterfuge /ˈsʌbtərfjuːdʒ/	*n.* 诡计 the use of tricks especially to hide, avoid, or get something Her eyes have an innocent clarity that suggests no **subterfuge**. chicanery
agglomerate /əˈɡlɑːməreɪt/	*v.* 聚集 to gather into a ball, mass, or cluster All the dust and clothing lint **agglomerate** in the filter of the drier after several uses and should be removed for more efficient use.

goad
/goʊd/

班 **v.** 刺激 to urge or force (someone) to do something

例 You cannot **goad** a woman into dating you by being annoyingly persistent.

反 curb

surfeit
/'sɜːrfɪt/

班 **n.** 过量 an amount that is too much or more than you need

例 After ordering 12 pizzas and 3 boxes of breadsticks, the teenagers had a **surfeit** of food for their slumber party.

选 glut, plethora

transitory
/'trænsətɔːri/

班 **adj.** 短暂的 lasting only for a short time

例 Vernal pools are among the most **transitory** of ponds: they form as a result of snowmelt and a high water table in winter, and then they evaporate by late summer.

选 ephemeral, evanescent

prolix
/'proʊlɪks/

班 **adj.** 冗长的 using too many words

例 Ernest Hemingway was famous for his blunt, straightforward prose which made a statement against **prolix** writing styles.

选 verbose, long-winded

反 brief

派 prolixity（n. 啰嗦）

exactitude
/ɪɡ'zæktɪtuːd/

班 **n.** 准确 the quality or state of being accurate and correct

例 Seymour worked with immense thoroughness and made sure that every step of the complex project was carried out with **exactitude**.

chastise
/tʃæ'staɪz/

班 **v.** 谴责 to criticize (someone) harshly for doing something wrong

例 Mary was **chastised** for dropping her entire dinner on the ground and causing a huge mess.

选 castigate

protract
/proʊ'trækt/

班 **v.** 延长 to prolong in time or space

例 The President knew that one wrong move would **protract** the war, making it continue for months or years.

stymie
/'staɪmi/

班 **v.** 阻碍 to present an obstacle to

例 It does really **stymie** an investigation when a victim refuses to provide any details.

反 foster

seminal
/'semɪnl/

班 **adj.** 非常有影响力的 very important and influential

例 Although Daubigny was a **seminal** influence on Impressionist painters, his role has largely been overlooked.

authoritarian
/ə,θɔːrə'teriən/

班 **adj.** 专制的 expecting or requiring people to obey rules or laws

例 The mayor has become increasingly secretive and **authoritarian**, claiming that he should be able to do whatever he wants without journalists questioning him.

leap /liːp/	释 *v.* （话题、言论）跳跃 to pass abruptly from one state or topic to another 例 Unable to stick to the topic at hand, Andy *leapt* from politics to gardening in the same conversation. 释 *v.* 跳跃 to jump from a surface 例 The cat *leapt* from the ground to the countertop in one fluid motion.
tepid /'tepɪd/	释 *adj.* 冷淡的，不热情的 not energetic or excited 例 The proposal drew a *tepid* response from the committee as it neither elicited opposition nor enthusiasm.
malodor /mæl'oʊdər/	释 *n.* 恶臭 an offensive odor 例 Stinkbugs, as their name suggests, are capable of secreting a *malodor* which wards off predators. 选 noisome
senescence /sɪ'nesns/	释 *n.* 衰老 the state of being old or the process of becoming old 例 Memory loss is a consequence of *senescence* and is possibly related to loss of a certain type of brain cell. 选 decrepitude
decrepitude /dɪ'krepɪtuːd/	释 *n.* 衰老 the state of being old and in bad condition or poor health 例 Shocked at the *decrepitude* of the hotel, we demanded a refund so that we could book at the Hilton across the street. 选 senescence 反 sturdiness
self-styled /'self'staɪld/	释 *adj.* 自称的 called a particular thing by yourself 例 The *self-styled* "gentleman" wore a monocle and top hat in an attempt to match his nineteenth century state of mind.
cognizant /'kɑːgnɪzənt/	释 *adj.* 知道的，有意识的 aware of something 例 Many people are not *cognizant* of the benefits of a low-carb diet.
conversant /kən'vɜːrsnt/	释 *adj.* 熟悉的 having knowledge or experience 例 Although Chinese director Jia Zhangke is obviously *conversant* with the European art film, he has carved out his own ways of making cinematic meaning.
tribulation /ˌtrɪbju'leɪʃn/	释 *n.* 痛苦（的经历）unhappiness, pain, or suffering or an experience that causes someone to suffer 例 With the *tribulations* of chemotherapy behind her, Jen was eager to regain her energy and begin kayaking again.
open-ended /'oʊpən'endɪd/	释 *adj.* 开放的 allowing people to talk in a way that is not planned or controlled 例 Mary was greeted by the psychologist who encouraged the *open-ended* exploration of her psyche and motivations during the therapy session.

falsify
/ˈfɔːlsɪfaɪ/

v. 篡改，伪造 to change (something) in order to make people believe something that is not true

The witness was charged with perjury when the documents proved that he had *falsified* his account of the night's events.

panorama
/ˌpænəˈræmə/

n. 全面展示 a comprehensive presentation of a subject

Although it is not an in-depth guide to Medieval politics, the textbook offers a suitable *panorama* of the subject for an introductory college course.

n. 全景 a full and wide view of something

The peak of the Mt. Washington offers a 360-degree *panorama* of the New Hampshire wilderness.

beleaguer
/bɪˈliːgər/

v. 困扰，骚扰 to harass; beset

The success of the space program came as a pleasant surprise to a nation that had been *beleaguered* by political turmoil and social unrest.

v. 围攻 to surround with troops; besiege

The army finally came to the aid of the *beleaguered* city and freed its trapped citizens.

incumbent
/ɪnˈkʌmbənt/

n. 在职官员 one that occupies a particular position or place

As the *incumbent* president, Barack Obama was expected to endorse a candidate in the election.

adj. 义不容辞，有责任的 obligatory

After many years of tradition, it is *incumbent* upon banks to offer candy to children.

hermetic
/hɜːrˈmetɪk/

adj. 密闭的 closed tightly so that no air can go in or out

It is important to keep leftover food in containers with *hermetic* lids to prevent any form of cross contamination that could happen in the fridge.

adj. 难懂的 relating to or characterized by occultism or abstruseness

His abstract images are never *hermetic* and instead relate to our everyday lives in a direct and straightforward fashion.

反 comprehensible

adj. 退隐的，孤寂的 recluse or solitary

Despite their *hermetic* interests, Jess and Duncan were visible and influential cultural figures.

encapsulate
/ɪnˈkæpsjuleɪt/

v. 简要概括 to show or express the main idea or quality of (something) in a brief way

Although the essay David wrote was very long, the conclusion was *encapsulated* in just a paragraph.

v. （如胶囊一样）封装 to enclose in or as if in a capsule

An M&M is a convenient chocolate treat that is *encapsulated* in a hard shell to prevent the candy from melting.

interdisciplinary /ˌɪntərˈdɪsəplɪneri/	**adj.** 交叉学科的 involving two or more disciplines NASA engineer Gloria Yamauchi uses an **interdisciplinary** approach to research that draws on physics, aerodynamics, mathematics, and other fields.
impunity /ɪmˈpjuːnəti/	**v.** 免于处罚，免罪 freedom from punishment, harm, or loss The manager felt that she could say anything that she wanted with **impunity**, but some of the workers reported her bad attitude to the head of the department.
reprisal /rɪˈpraɪzl/	**n.** 报复 a retaliatory act With the failure of the military coup, the dictator made **reprisals** against his enemies and imprisoned thousands.
myopic /maɪˈɑːpɪk/	**adj.** 缺乏远见的 a lack of foresight or discernment De Grey's **myopia** in considering the larger context of his work has resulted in social and ethical implications. myopia (n. 近视)
tarnish /ˈtɑːrnɪʃ/	**v.** 玷污 to damage or ruin the good quality of Charlie Sheen has such a bad reputation that he is **tarnishing** the president's reputation by defending him.
sublime /səˈblaɪm/	**v.** 超群出众 to render sublime The ice cream started melting in the boot of the car as the dry ice around it had long **sublimed**. **n.** 崇高 something sublime The gap between the **sublime** and ridiculous is usually thin and utterly tenuous. **adj.** 卓越的，出众的 not to be excelled; supreme Sitting on the beach in the Caribbean with no worries on my mind, I was in a state of **sublime** relaxation. **adj.** 令人崇敬的 characterized by nobility; majestic When Isabelle stepped into the cathedral, she was overwhelmed by the **sublime** architecture.
remonstrate /rɪˈmɑːnstreɪt/	**v.** 反对，抗议 to present and urge reasons in opposition Many consider Facebook an appropriate forum to **remonstrate** with people of opposite political beliefs.
commiserate /kəˈmɪzəreɪt/	**v.** 哀悼，同情 to express sadness or sympathy for someone who has experienced something unpleasant When my best friend and I both lost our fathers within the space of a week, we were able to **commiserate** together. sympathize
expostulate /ɪkˈspɑːstʃuleɪt/	**v.** 争论，反驳 to disagree with something or argue against it In America, the Democratic Party always **expostulates** with the Republican Party. remonstrate

☐ interdisciplinary   ☐ impunity   ☐ reprisal   ☐ myopic   ☐ tarnish
☐ sublime   ☐ remonstrate   ☐ commiserate   ☐ expostulate

anneal
/əˈniːl/

释 *v.* 加固 strengthen or toughen

例 Plunging the scorching blade into the fire *anneals* the iron so that it can stand up to the pressures of battle.

vicissitude
/vɪˈsɪsɪtuːd/

释 *n.* 变迁，变化 the quality or state of being changeable

例 Investors are hugely dependent on the decisions of central banks; in turn, the central bankers react to the *vicissitudes* of the market.

piecemeal
/ˈpiːsmiːl/

释 *adv.* 一次少量地，一件一件地 by a small amount at a time; in stages

例 The Habitat for Humanity crew managed to finish the construction of the house by building it *piecemeal* over three summers.

释 *adj.* 逐个完成的 accomplished or made in stages

例 Although it can take a few months of continuous work to restore a vintage auto, Bob invested five years of *piecemeal* effort into his 1967 Ford Mustang.

verbose
/vɜːrˈboʊs/

释 *adj.* 冗长的 using more words than are needed

例 In Hardy's most *verbose* novels, too much fine writing and too many long sections distract from the story.

选 prolix, long-winded

派 verbosity (*n.* 啰嗦)

polyglot
/ˈpaːliglaːt/

释 *adj.* 多语的 knowing or using several languages

例 Armenian was hardly the only language of the *polyglot* Ottoman Empire as Greek, Turkish, Arabic and German were also routinely spoken.

释 *adj.* 混杂的 made up of people or things from different cultures, countries, etc.

例 Walking the Roosevelt Avenue is to see New York as it has been for over 300 years, a *polyglot* city with many immigrants from multiple countries.

machination
/ˌmæʃɪˈneɪʃn/

释 *n.* 诡计 a scheming or crafty action or artful design intended to accomplish some usually evil end

例 *House of Cards* was compulsively watchable because the endless political *machinations* of the main character begged viewers to find out what happened next.

flee
/fliː/

释 *v.* 逃脱，逃跑 to run away from danger

例 Upon hearing the explosion, all the patrons *fled* the mall to seek safety.

nefarious
/nɪˈferiəs/

释 *adj.* 邪恶的 evil or immoral

例 The police are cracking down on the *nefarious* activities of the drug-dealing ring.

派 nefatiousness (*n.* 极度的邪恶)

lachrymose
/'lækrɪmoʊs/

🔸 *adj.* 催泪的，悲伤的 tending to cause tears
🔹 It is a challenge for a writer to express deep feeling without becoming *lachrymose*.

🔸 *adj.* 爱哭的 tending to cry often
🔹 After the death of her husband, Melissa became *lachrymose* at the faintest reminder of her soulmate.

enmity
/'enməti/

🔸 *n.* 恶意，憎恶 a very deep unfriendly feeling
🔹 Although he felt that Steven was antagonistic, Mark did not sense that Steven's ill will amounted to outright *enmity*.

indignant
/ɪn'dɪgnənt/

🔸 *adj.* 非常愤怒的 very angry
🔹 Martin Luther King was *indignant* at the conditions of the African-American population in the United States.

confront
/kən'frʌnt/

🔸 *v.* 反抗 to oppose or challenge (someone) especially in a direct and forceful way
🔹 College professors must *confront* the reality that there is racism and sexism in most fields.

🔸 *v.* 面对 to meet face-to-face
🔹 It is an essential freedom for every American to *confront* his or her accuser in court and answer to the charges directly.

minutia
/mɪ'nuʃiə/

🔸 *n.* 细节，小事 a minute or minor detail
🔹 Frustrated by the *minutia* of peeling potatoes and carrots, the sous chef quit his job to start his own restaurant.

commensurable
/kə'menʃərəbl/

🔸 *adj.* 可用共同标准测量的 measurable by a common standard
🔹 Many believe it is in the USA's best interests to have units of measure that are *commensurable* with the rest of the world.

🔸 *adj.* 相称的，成比例的 commensurate; proportionate
🔹 When the college graduate quit his job at McDonalds to start a career in marketing, he was excited to receive a salary *commensurable* with his education.

discriminatory
/dɪ'skrɪmɪnətɔːri/

🔸 *adj.* 不公平的，歧视的 not fair
🔹 Although larger households use more water, charging them more per gallon for the same water is *discriminatory*.

sabotage
/'sæbətɑːʒ/

🔸 *v.* 故意破坏 to cause the failure of something deliberately
🔹 The surprise birthday party for Molly is a secret; please do not *sabotage* my plans by telling her.

commend
/kə'mend/

🔸 *v.* 赞美 to praise (someone or something) in a serious and often public way
🔹 Although some traffic-camera tickets were issued to Metrobus drivers, such a record should be *commended*, not criticized, since hundreds of Metrobuses run thousands of routes every day.

gossamer
/ˈɡɑːsəmər/

adj. 轻而薄的，虚无缥缈的 extremely light, delicate, or tenuous

例 Dickinson is often portrayed as some white *gossamer* recluse, completely divorced from the world outside her bedroom—but that is not really true.

反 ponderous

lenient
/ˈliːniənt/

adj. 宽容的 allowing a lot of freedom and not punishing bad behavior in a strong way

例 The staff members' previous supervisor had been especially *lenient* and understanding, so they were put off by the authoritarian style of the new director.

派 leniency（*n.* 宽厚，仁慈）

rectitude
/ˈrektɪtuːd/

n. 正直 the quality of being honest and morally correct

例 Professor McConnell always encouraged her students to live lives of *rectitude* and be honest about everything.

enamor
/ɪˈnæmər/

v. 使…喜爱 to cause (someone) to be loved or admired

例 As *enamored* as advertisers are with digital media, TV's ability to quickly reach many people still has value.

近 favor, captivated, hooked on

immure
/ɪˈmjʊr/

v. 囚禁 imprison

例 *Immured* in prison for many years, Nelson Mandela became a symbol of the resistance against apartheid.

v. （像嵌在墙上一样）封闭 to enclose within or as if within walls

例 With the growing threat from the Gauls, the Roman army *immured* their camp behind a tall palisade.

impudent
/ˈɪmpjədənt/

adj. 无礼的 very rude

例 He was very *impudent* to his grandmother and said some really hurtful things to the elderly lady.

反 respectful

□ gossamer □ lenient □ rectitude □ enamor □ immure □ impudent

音频

| **insolent** | **adj.** 无礼的 rude or impolite |
| /'ɪnsələnt/ | Screaming and yelling, the **insolent** child disrupted the entire airport with his antics. |

irenic
/aɪ'renɪk/

adj. 和平的 favoring, conducive to, or operating toward peace, moderation, or conciliation

Some citizens encouraged the president to back out of the peace deal, but his **irenic** spirit did not forsake him.

shear
/ʃɪr/

v. 剪（动物）毛 to cut the hair from

We decided it was time to **shear** our poodle's coat after it had gone without a haircut for a year.

v. 剥夺 to deprive of something as if by cutting

Shorn of his power, the deposed king went into exile.

coruscate
/'kɔːrəskeɪt/

v. 闪烁，闪光 sparkle

The knight's armor was visible for miles as it **coruscated** in the sunlight.

v. 焕发魅力 to be brilliant or showy in technique or style

The violinist **coruscated** through his pieces with such virtuosity that the audience gave him a standing ovation.

hideous
/'hɪdiəs/

adj. 丑陋吓人的 very ugly or disgusting

Aunt Priscilla gave Mary such a **hideous** sweater as a Christmas present that she doubts she will ever wear it.

adj. 可恶的，令人难以忍受的 morally offensive

Stealing and cheating at whim, the sociopathic girl was expelled from the university for her **hideous** behavior.

trumpet
/'trʌmpɪt/

v. 鼓吹 to praise (something) loudly and publicly especially in a way that is annoying

The company spent a lot of time at the conference **trumpeting** the sophistication of its security systems, but its reassurances sounded hollow and unconvincing.

☐ insolent   ☐ irenic   ☐ shear   ☐ coruscate   ☐ hideous
☐ trumpet

strident
/'straɪdnt/

释 *adj.* 尖锐的，刺耳的 sounding harsh and unpleasant

例 The critic noted that the *strident* tone that characterizes much of the writer's work stands in stark contrast to his gentle dispositions.

释 *adj.* （表达意见）令人不悦的 expressing opinions or criticism in a very forceful and often annoying or unpleasant way

例 When it became clear that the Senator was a *strident* opponent to the civil rights of women, he lost the election.

muckrake
/'mʌkˌreɪk/

释 *v.* 揭露丑闻 to search out and publicly expose real or apparent misconduct of a prominent individual or business

例 The magazine divided its coverage between serious *muckraking* investigations and paparazzi-style exposés of the private lives of local celebrities.

proffer
/'prɑːfər/

释 *v.* 提供 to offer or give (something) to someone

例 A person who knows nothing about a subject should not *proffer* advice about it.

revel
/'revl/

释 *v.* 陶醉 to take intense pleasure or satisfaction

例 The college graduates were so happy that school was over that they *reveled* in drinking and dancing at the graduation party.

释 *n.* 吵闹的狂欢 a noisy and wild celebration

例 In *Beowulf*, the *revels* at the mead hall are interrupted by an attack from Grendel the monster.

predicate
/'predɪkət/

释 *v.* 基于，取决于 to found or base something on

例 Many people are calling for a future *predicated* on solar and wind power rather than fossil fuels.

释 *v.* 断言，断定 to declare or affirm (something) as true or existing

例 Upon receipt of the newest signal from the Mars Rover, NASA *predicated* that the vehicle had successfully landed on the planet.

prophylactic
/ˌproʊtə'læktɪk/

释 *adj.* 预防性的 acting to defend against or prevent something, especially disease; protective

例 Getting vaccinated is a *prophylactic* measure that makes you less likely to catch a disease.

选 preventive

释 *n.* 预防类物品 a prophylactic agent, device, or measure, such as a vaccine or drug

例 Iodized salt cannot be used as a *prophylactic* as its miniscule amount of iodine is nowhere near what's recommended for exposure to radiation.

□ strident   □ muckrake   □ proffer   □ revel   □ predicate
□ prophylactic

pilfer /ˈpɪlfər/	释 **v.** 盗用 to steal things that are not very valuable or to steal a small amount of something 例 The spotted bowerbird loves shiny objects and will enter houses to **pilfer** cutlery, coins, thimbles, nails, screws, and even car keys. 选 appropriation 派 pilferage（*n.* 盗窃）
constrict /kənˈstrɪkt/	释 **v.** 限制 to prevent or keep (something or someone) from developing freely 例 Voter turnout was **constricted** by the limited early voting hours. 选 constrain 释 **v.** 压缩 to become narrower, smaller, or tighter 例 During her asthma attack, Betty's lungs **constricted** and she wheezed with difficulty in breathing. 反 dilate, distend
imbibe /ɪmˈbaɪb/	释 **v.** 喝 to drink (something) 例 At their dinner parties, the ancient Greeks preferred to **imbibe** wine mixed with honey and water. 选 quaff
quaff /kwɑːf/	释 **v.** 大口喝，痛饮 to drink a large amount of (something) quickly 例 The dwarf **quaffed** a hearty mug of ale to wash down his steak dinner. 选 imbibe
crumble /ˈkrʌmbl/	释 **v.** 崩溃，瓦解 to break down completely : to stop functioning 例 After the family abandoned their wooden home, it **crumbled** into a derelict eyesore in a matter of months. 选 disintegrate
disintegrate /dɪsˈɪntɪɡreɪt/	释 **v.** 瓦解 to break apart into many small parts or pieces 例 The gingerbread house **disintegrated** when it was left out in the rain. 选 crumble 反 synthesize
brook /brʊk/	释 **v.** 容忍，忍受 to stand for; tolerate 例 With the recent rash of violence, many have **brooked** openly for gun control. 选 tolerate
muddle /ˈmʌdl/	释 **v.** 使困惑 to cause confusion in (someone or someone's mind) 例 The surveillance footage **muddled** public opinion on the matter because it conflicted with the reports of both the police and the victim. 选 confuse
unerring /ʌnˈɜːrɪŋ/	释 **adj.** 一贯准确的 committing no mistakes; consistently accurate 例 It seemed that the anatomy professor was **unerring** until we saw him mistake the third for the fourth vertebrae. 选 settled

☐ pilfer ☐ constrict ☐ imbibe ☐ quaff ☐ crumble
☐ disintegrate ☐ brook ☐ muddle ☐ unerring

provenance
/ˈprɑːvənəns/

🔊 *n.* 出处，起源 the origin or source of something
📝 The ***provenance*** of these videos may be a little dubious but the content looks genuine.
🔄 origin

inscrutable
/ɪnˈskruːtəbl/

🔊 *adj.* 难以理解的 difficult to understand : causing people to feel curious or confused
📝 Sitting in the meeting, we were unable to read the ***inscrutable*** expression on the client's face and understand his concerns.
🔄 uninformative, impenetrable, abstruse

genial
/ˈdʒiːniəl/

🔊 *adj.* 友好的 marked by or diffusing sympathy or friendliness
📝 Unlike the typical depiction of a burly bouncer, the doorman was a ***genial*** fellow who preferred to calm down angry people with humor.
🔄 friendliness
🔁 mordant, saturnine
🔀 geniality（*n.* 和蔼）

reluctant
/rɪˈlʌktənt/

🔊 *adj.* 不情愿的 feeling or showing doubt about doing something; not willing or eager to do something
📝 When I found out that skydiving was planned for the trip, I was ***reluctant*** to go because of my fear of heights.
🔄 loath, unwillingly
🔀 reluctantly（*adv.* 不情愿地）

supple
/ˈsʌpl/

🔊 *adj.* 灵活的 readily adaptable or responsive to new situations
📝 With its patented memory foam, the new mattress is a ***supple*** "sleep experience" that conforms uniquely to each person.
🔄 flexible

contravene
/ˌkɑːntrəˈviːn/

🔊 *v.* 违反 to fail to do what is required by (a law or rule)
📝 Providing military aid to illegitimate organizations ***contravenes*** the principles of international law: we should back only legal government entities.
🔄 violate

ungainly
/ʌnˈɡeɪnli/

🔊 *adj.* 笨拙的 moving in an awkward or clumsy way : not graceful
📝 The guinea pig was an ***ungainly*** creature better characterized as a bumbling mass of fur than a graceful pet.
🔄 awkward

ludicrous
/ˈluːdɪkrəs/

🔊 *adj.* 滑稽可笑的 amusing or laughable through obvious absurdity, incongruity, exaggeration, or eccentricity
📝 Dan's ***ludicrous*** idea got us into a lot of trouble; I have no idea why I agreed to participate in his foolish plan.
🔄 risible

☐ provenance ☐ inscrutable ☐ genial ☐ reluctant ☐ supple
☐ contravene ☐ ungainly ☐ ludicrous

dispatch /dɪˈspætʃ/	英 *n.* 迅速 promptness and efficiency in performance or transmission 例 Recognizing that time was a critical factor, the paramedics responded to the call with ***dispatch***. 选 celerity 反 leisureliness
handicap /ˈhændɪkæp/	英 *n.* 障碍 a disadvantage that makes achievement unusually difficult 例 Emily always believed that her inability to drive was something of a ***handicap***, because she needed to rely on the inefficient public transportation system to get around the city. 选 hindrance
chimera /kaɪˈmɪrə/	英 *n.* 幻想 something that exists only in the imagination and is not possible in reality 例 Without freedom, particularly freedom of expression, democracy is a ***chimera***. 选 illusion
ominous /ˈɑːmɪnəs/	英 *adj.* 不吉利的 suggesting that something bad is going to happen in the future 例 Despite international efforts to stop the rise, the CO_2 concentration has steadily grown near the ***ominous*** benchmark. 选 inauspicious
limpid /ˈlɪmpɪd/	英 *adj.* 清澈透明的 marked by transparency; pellucid 例 It is an unforgettable experience to dive into the ***limpid*** waters off Indonesia's resort island of Bali. 选 pellucid 反 turbid
forsake /fərˈseɪk/	英 *v.* 放弃 to give up or leave (someone or something) entirely 例 Muhammad was a devout Muslim and promised he would never ***forsake*** his religion. 选 neglect
exonerate /ɪgˈzɑːnəreɪt/	英 *v.* 免罪，免责 to prove that someone is not guilty of a crime or responsible for a problem, bad situation, etc. 例 Once the principal realized that the fire alarm had been set off by accident, she apologized to the suspected students and announced that they had been ***exonerated***. 选 absolve 派 exoneration（*n.* 免罪）
annihilate /əˈnaɪəleɪt/	英 *v.* 毁灭，毁坏 to destroy (something or someone) completely 例 When the Black Death arrived in Europe, populations across many towns were completely ***annihilated***. 选 destroy

surmise /sər'maɪz/	**v.** 猜测 a thought or idea based on scanty evidence: conjecture 例 The lack of documents has led historians to **surmise** the motives of the rulers of Crete. 近 infer
rapprochement /ˌræprouʃ'maːn/	**n.** 友好，和谐 the development of friendlier relations between countries or groups of people who have been enemies 例 The two pandas Mrs. Nixon greeted were a high-profile symbol of diplomatic **rapprochement** between the United States and China, brokered under her husband's administration. 近 reconciliation
exert /ɪg'zɜːrt/	**v.** 使用 to use (strength, ability, etc.) 例 The weightlifter **exerted** all of his strength to achieve his personal best in the clean-and-jerk. 近 wield
wield /wiːld/	**v.** 使用 to have and use (power, influence, etc.) 例 A gang of thieves entered the bank **wielding** different kinds of weapons; the leader was holding a shotgun, while the other members were either holding a pistol or a knife. 近 exert
guzzle /'gʌzl/	**v.** 狂饮 to drink (something, such as beer or liquor) quickly or in large amounts 例 Absolutely parched, the distance runner **guzzled** a gallon of water after her run in the summer heat. 近 swill
kinfolk /'kɪnfouk/	**n.** 亲戚 a person's relatives 例 In the small village in West Virginia, many of the residents are the **kinfolk** of a single extended family. 近 relative
divergent /daɪ'vɜːrdʒənt/	**adj.** 不同的 differing from each other or from a standard 例 In his essay, writer Rudolfo Anaya strives to combine his Mexican and American identities, blending **divergent** worldviews to create one unique vision. 近 incongruous, disparate 反 enclosed
vestige /'vestɪdʒ/	**n.** 遗迹,遗留 the last small part that remains of something that existed before 例 The **vestiges** of the kiwi bird's wings are merely rudiments that have remained over the course of evolution and no longer serve any function. 近 relic
profusion /prə'fjuːʒn/	**n.** 大量 a large amount of something 例 Despite the **profusion** of books written about Greta Garbo, she ultimately remains a mysterious personality. 近 wealth

forebode /fɔːrˈboʊd/	释 **v.** 担忧 to have an inward conviction of (as coming ill or misfortune) 例 "The dull ache in my knee **forebodes** the coming of cold weather," the old man explained. 选 concern 释 **v.** 预示 foretell, portend 例 The gray clouds **foreboded** the impending hurricane.
calamity /kəˈlæməti/	释 **n.** 大灾难 an event that causes great harm and suffering 例 The disintegration of the Roman Empire may have been a **calamity**, but it nevertheless presented some constructive aspects. 选 disaster, catastrophic 派 calamitous（ *adj.* 灾难性的）
beget /bɪˈget/	释 **v.** 导致 to cause (something) to happen or exist 例 It is clear that severe drug addiction can **beget** homelessness and crime. 选 create
reprehensible /ˌreprɪˈhensəbl/	释 **adj.** 应受指责的 very bad; deserving strong criticism 例 Greg's **reprehensible** actions upset his wife; she could not understand why he wasted their savings on gambling. 选 deplorable 派 reprehend（ *v.* 指责）
divest /daɪˈvest/	释 **v.** 剥夺 to deprive or dispossess, especially of property, authority, or title 例 Once the judge had been found guilty of corruption, it was not long before he was **divested** of his position. 选 strip
wondrous /ˈwʌndrəs/	释 **adj.** 奇异的 causing wonder or amazement ; very beautiful or impressive 例 The color of the fall leaves in Vermont is a **wondrous** sight, with the mountains blanketed by a fiery hue. 选 amazing
recalcitrant /rɪˈkælsɪtrənt/	释 **adj.** 顽固的 stubbornly refusing to obey rules or orders 例 **Recalcitrant** to the end, the old man refused to take his prescribed medicines. 选 headstrong 反 submissive, amenable
succinct /səkˈsɪŋkt/	释 **adj.** 简洁的 using few words to state or express an idea 例 Responding to criticism that the script was rambling and muddled, the new screenwriter revised the dialogue to make it **succinct**. 选 concision 派 succinctness（ *n.* 简明）
recrudescent /ˌriːkruːˈdesnt/	释 **adj.** 复发的 breaking out again; renewing 例 At the end of the hibernation, the **recrudescent** bear emerges from his shelter to eat. 选 resurgent

□ forebode   □ calamity   □ beget   □ reprehensible   □ divest
□ wondrous   □ recalcitrant   □ succinct   □ recrudescent

frugal /ˈfruːgl/	释 *adj.* 节俭的 careful about spending money unnecessarily; using money or supplies in a very careful way 例 Households have been *frugal* recently by cutting back on purchases of automobiles despite cheap gasoline. 近 thrift 派 frugality（*n.* 节约）
unseemly /ʌnˈsiːmli/	释 *adj.* 不得体 not proper or appropriate for the situation; not seemly 例 It is *unseemly* to share the details of your dating life at the office. 近 indecorous
preternatural /ˌpriːtərˈnætʃrəl/	释 *adj.* 异乎寻常的 surpassing the normal or usual; extraordinary 例 Darren's sensitivity to his celebrity clients is nothing short of *preternatural*: he is able to anticipate their needs before they themselves are fully aware of them. 近 prodigious 释 *adj.* 超自然的 transcending the natural or material order; supernatural 例 Many interpret the white light in near-death experiences as originating from a *preternatural* order.
provident /ˈprɑːvɪdənt/	释 *adj.* 节俭的 frugal; economical 例 Jason started becoming overly *provident* ever since he had to provide for himself and would not even treat himself to an ice cream over the weekend. 释 *adj.* 有远见的 making provision for the future: prudent 例 She took up an insurance plan as a *provident* measure to safeguard her family in case anything happened to her.
interlope /ɪnˈtɜːrloʊp/	释 *v.* 入侵，干涉 to intrude or interfere 例 *Interloping* plant species from other lands often cause environmental damage by outcompeting the locals.
coterie /ˈkoʊtəri/	释 *n.* 小团体 an intimate and often exclusive group of persons with a unifying common interest or purpose 例 China is home to a *coterie* of contemporary painters whose works fetch millions of dollars at international auctions.
aplomb /əˈplɑːm/	释 *n.* 自信沉着，泰然自若 complete and confident composure or self-assurance: poise 例 Though Judd is typically reserved in social gatherings, he spoke and acted with unusual *aplomb* at last night's reception.
bemoan /bɪˈmoʊn/	释 *v.* 哀悼，悲伤 to express deep grief or distressove 例 *Bemoaning* the lack of coffee at the conference, the presenter stormed out and went to Starbucks. 释 *v.* 抱怨，不满 to regard with displeasure, disapproval, or regret 例 Nostalgic fans *bemoan* the crassness of sports today for its associations with lying, cheating, and commercialism.

☐ frugal　　　☐ unseemly　　　☐ preternatural　　　☐ provident　　　☐ interlope
☐ coterie　　　☐ aplomb　　　☐ bemoan

mediate
/ˈmiːdieɪt/

🔈 *v.* 调解 to interpose between parties in order to reconcile them

📖 Because she had assumed that the disputes between the parties could be successfully *mediated*, the attorney had not prepared herself for a long, drawn-out public trial.

🔈 *v.* 影响 to have an effect or influence in causing (something) to happen

📖 Our eating habits are rooted in our physiology but they are, nonetheless, also *mediated* by the culture in which we grow up.

🔀 influence

exposé
/ɪkˈspoʊz/

🔈 *n.* 揭露黑暗的报道 a news report or broadcast that reveals something illegal or dishonest to the public

📖 In the chilling *exposé* on the meat industry, CNN revealed the horrid conditions under which chickens are kept on large poultry farms.

reticent
/ˈretɪsnt/

🔈 *adj.* 沉默寡言的 inclined to be silent or uncommunicative in speech : reserved

📖 Despite Paul's occasional desire to show off, he remained at heart a very *reticent* person.

🔈 *adj.* 有保留的 restrained in expression, presentation, or appearance

📖 Wanting to look professional, Ashley was *reticent* about wearing bright clothing to the job interview.

myriad
/ˈmɪriəd/

🔈 *adj.* 大量丰富的 both numerous and diverse

📖 Texas is known for its wild orchids, whose diversity is evident in their *myriad* colors: 52 species have been catalogued, ranging from pure white to bright red.

expurgate
/ˈekspərgeɪt/

🔈 *v.* 删除（令人反感的内容） to change (a written work) by removing parts that might offend people

📖 The editor removed large portions of the manuscript and *expurgated* entire paragraphs that were offensive.

🔀 censor

triumvirate
/traɪˈʌmvərət/

🔈 *n.* 三足鼎立 government by three persons or by a coalition of three parties

📖 The first *triumvirate* of ancient Rome was a secret alliance formed by Caesar, Pompey and Crassus.

indefatigable
/ˌɪndɪˈfætɪgəbl/

🔈 *adj.* 不知疲倦的 incapable of being fatigued: untiring

📖 Michael Scott told his employees he would be *indefatigable* in his attempts to prevent the branch from being shut down.

paean
/ˈpiːən/

🔈 *n.* 赞美 a work that praises or honors its subject

📖 Judy Chicago's *The Dinner Party* is a *paean* to women's achievements throughout history.

hallmark /'hɔːlmɑːrk/	释 *n.* 特征 a distinguishing characteristic, trait, or feature 例 One *hallmark* of turtles is their endurance, as exemplified in the moral story of the rabbit and the turtle. 反 characteristic feature
potent /'poʊtnt/	释 *adj.* 有权势的，有权力的 having great control or authority 例 The Bible portrays King Solomon as a *potent* leader who used his power wisely. 派 impotent（*adj.* 无力的），omnipotent（*adj.* 全能的） 释 *adj.* 强有力的 possessing inner or physical strength; powerful 例 Be careful when drinking hard liquor; it is more *potent* than beer and can lead to bad judgement.
lopsided /ˌlɑːp'saɪdɪd/	释 *adj.* 不均衡的 uneven or unequal 例 The president has recognized the consequences of the country's *lopsided* economical development which has left rural villages poorer and cities much richer.
subtle /'sʌtl/	释 *adj.* 难以理解的 difficult to understand or perceive 例 Class struggle is a *subtle* subtext that covertly structures many of Dickens's novels. 反 obvious 释 *adj.* 灵巧的，精湛的 highly skillful; expert 例 With his *subtle* craftsmanship, Nick could carve intricate and beautiful designs on a wooden tabletop. 释 *adj.* 聪明的 clever and indirect; not showing your real purpose 例 When the spies encountered each other on the streets of Moscow, they gave a *subtle*, knowing glance at each other and continued walking.
adamant /'ædəmənt/	释 *adj.* 固执的 not willing to change an opinion or decision; very determined 例 Sonia was *adamant* about joining the military; for weeks, her parents tried to change her mind, but they could not.
melancholy /'melənkɑːli/	释 *n.* 忧伤 a sad mood or feeling 例 As the day began its descent into evening, I couldn't help but feel a bit *melancholy*.
unalloyed /ˌʌnə'lɔɪd/	释 *adj.* 纯粹的，完全的 complete; unqualified 例 Marriage should be a union where two people are in full and *unalloyed* sympathy and accord. 反 adulterated
spew /spjuː/	释 *v.* 喷出，涌出 to send or cast forth with vigor or violence or in great quantity 例 Yesterday, Blair noticed that a factory just outside the city was *spewing* out a never-ending black cloud of pollution.

☐ hallmark ☐ potent ☐ lopsided ☐ subtle ☐ adamant
☐ melancholy ☐ unalloyed ☐ spew

maze /meɪz/	释 *n.* 迷宫 a complicated and confusing system of connected passages 例 In *The Shining*, Jack chases his son through a *maze* of hedges and quickly becomes lost.
misfeasance /mɪsˈfiːzəns/	释 *n.* 过失，不法行为 trespass, specifically the performance of a lawful action in an illegal or improper manner 例 Billy only wanted to retrieve the ball from his grumpy neighbor's yard, but he was cited by the police for *misfeasance*.
rebellious /rɪˈbeljəs/	释 *adj.* 反抗的，难控制的 refusing to obey rules or authority or to accept normal standards of behavior, dress, etc. : having or showing a tendency to rebel 例 The government did not like the group's *rebellious* acts and feared that they would lead to a civil war.
durable /ˈdʊrəbl/	释 *adj.* 持久的，耐用的 staying strong and in good condition over a long period of time 例 Many bomb shelters are stocked with *durable* foodstuffs that will not spoil for many years. 反 evanescent
varnish /ˈvɑːrnɪʃ/	释 *v.* 装饰 adorn, embellish 例 The general tried to *varnish* his reputation by telling stories of heroism.
labyrinthine /ˌlæbəˈrɪnθaɪn/	释 *adj.* 复杂的 of, relating to, or resembling a labyrinth; intricate, involved 例 It was a struggle to read the book because its *labyrinthine* plot was impossible to follow.
mar /mɑːr/	释 *v.* 损毁，损伤 to ruin the beauty or perfection of (something) ; to hurt or damage the good condition of (something) 例 The spectacular Alpine valley was *marred* by the oil-burning monstrosity that served electricity to the region.
platitude /ˈplætɪtuːd/	释 *n.* 陈词滥调 a banal, trite, or stale remark 例 Hoping to get votes, the presidential candidate offered *platitudes* to the voters about "change" without providing any details.
exclusive /ɪkˈskluːsɪv/	释 *adj.* 独有的，排外的 not shared; available to only one person or group 例 Apple has won an *exclusive* streaming deal with Taylor Swift to show a concert film from her world tour. 派 exlude (*v.* 阻止，驱逐)
acclaim /əˈkleɪm/	释 *v.* 欢呼，喝彩 to praise (someone or something) in a very strong and enthusiastic way 例 Taylor Swift's new album has been greatly *acclaimed* by the media, with reviewers praising her talent.
meld /meld/	释 *v.* 混合 merge, blend 例 For mayonnaise to come out right, egg yolks and vinegar must be *melded* together into a smooth mixture. 近 combine

tremendous /trə'mendəs/	释 *adj.* 巨大的 very large or great 例 The growing concern with customer-tailored products creates *tremendous* challenges for product manufacturers in terms of costing and profitability.
scatter /'skætər/	释 *v.* 分散 to separate and go in different directions 例 The geese *scattered* after the child threw a ball into the pond.
concise /kən'saɪs/	释 *adj.* 简洁的 using few words; not including extra or unnecessary information 例 Because he tended to write long-winded essays, Simon worked to be more *concise*. 近 brief
oracle /'ɔːrəkl/	释 *n.* 预言 an authoritative or wise statement or prediction 例 After ten spot-on predictions at previous Super Bowls, all future predictions made by the physicist and his computer algorithm were considered *oracles*. 派 oracular（*adj.* 预言的） 释 *n.* 先知 a person considered to be a source of wise counsel or prophetic opinions 例 Sitting on a tripod, the *oracle* at Delphi uttered confusing prophecies to the ancient Greeks. 近 prophetic
extenuate /ɪk'stenjuˌeɪt/	释 *v.* 减轻 to lessen or to try to lessen the seriousness or extent of by making partial excuses: mitigate 例 The police officer considered the impending birth of a child to be an *extenuating* circumstance for speeding and let Matt off with a warning.
viable /'vaɪəbl/	释 *adj.* 可行的 capable of being done or used 例 Attending college is a *viable* option only for those who can afford it. 释 *adj.* 可以存活的 capable of living or of developing into a living thing 例 While undergoing fertility treatment, the couple hoped one of the *viable* embryos would be accepted by the woman's body.
midst /mɪdst/	释 *n.* 当中 the interior or central part or point: middle 例 In the *midst* of a hurricane, there is always a calm "eye" in the storm.
abuse /ə'bjuːs/	释 *v.* 滥用 to use (something) wrongly 例 When it was discovered that the teacher had *abused* his power to force students into unlawful acts, he was promptly fired and blacklisted.
cliché /kliː'ʃeɪ/	释 *n.* 陈词滥调 a hackneyed theme, characterization, or situation 例 Most music in any period relies on *cliché*, with only a few artists being truly original.

(218)
□ tremendous □ scatter □ concise □ oracle □ extenuate
□ viable □ midst □ abuse □ cliché

contiguous
/kənˈtɪɡjuəs/

adj. 临近的 used to d
immediately next to each other
Although there are 50 states in the USA, ͻ
Alaska and Hawaii are geographically separated from the re ͻ.

endanger
/ɪnˈdeɪndʒər/

v. 危害 to cause (someone or something) to be in a dangerous place
or situation
While riding in the car, we felt **endangered** by the lack of working
seat beats.

boorish
/ˈbʊrɪʃ/

adj. 粗鲁的，粗野的 resembling or befitting a boor (as in crude
insensitivity)
Because of his **boorish** behavior, Jon was never invited to client dinners
for fear of offending the client.
chivalrous

high-minded
/haɪˈmaɪndɪd/

adj. 高尚的 having or showing intelligence and a strong moral
character
As a **high-minded** moralist, the Senator refuses to vote in line with his
political party when the stance conflicts with his personal beliefs.

de-emphasize
/diˈemfəsaɪz/

v. 降低…的重要性 to reduce in relative importance
When applying for the job at the bank, Gary had to **de-emphasize** a
criminal history that was very much in his past.

poise
/pɔɪz/

v. 使平衡 to hold (something) in a balanced and steady position
Walking through the restaurant, the waitress skillfully **poised** six plates
on her forearm.

quandary
/ˈkwɑːndəri/

n. 困境 a situation in which you are confused about what to do
The movie portrays people making impossible choices in which each
option will harm someone; it is one moral **quandary** after another.
dilemma, predicament
certainty

ploy
/plɔɪ/

n. 策略 a clever trick or plan that is used to get someone to do
something or to gain an advantage over someone
Unbeknownst to the opposition, the short kickoff was a **ploy** to cause a
fumble and recover the ball.

n. 诱惑 a strong urge or desire to have or do something

例 Susan could not resist the **temptation** to devour her mom's chocolate cake even though she was not supposed to touch it.

adj. 压迫的 unreasonably burdensome or severe

例 In the desert, the **oppressive** daytime heat makes it impossible to work between 11:00 AM and 5:00 PM.

perbole
/haɪˈpɜːrbəli/

n. 夸张 language that describes something as better or worse than it really is

例 "We know you were hungry, John, but it is a **hyperbole** to say that you could eat an entire cow!"

反 understatement

派 hyperbolize (v. 夸张)

trickster
/ˈtrɪkstər/

n. 骗子 someone who tricks or deceives people especially in order to get something

例 The truth is, **tricksters** are like burglars; if they are really determined to do you in, there's always a way.

genteel
/dʒenˈtiːl/

adj. 有教养的，彬彬有礼的 having a quietly appealing or polite quality

例 The entire neighborhood was shocked when it was discovered that Sam, who was known for his **genteel** demeanor, was a serial killer.

impassioned
/ɪmˈpæʃnd/

adj. 充满激情的 showing or feeling very strong emotions

例 **Impassioned** by the speech of the demagogue, the people took to the streets and attacked opposing voters.

deduce
/dɪˈduːs/

v. 推断 to use logic or reason to form (a conclusion or opinion about something) ; to decide (something) after thinking about the known facts

例 Although you never said you were going to the concert, I **deduced** it from your clothing and the tickets sticking out of your pocket.

flip
/flɪp/

v. 翻动 to cause (something) to turn or turn over quickly

例 In order to settle the bet, Mark **flipped** a coin and called a side before it landed.

infinite
/ˈɪnfɪnət/

adj. 无限的 having no limits

例 The amount of matter in the universe is not **infinite**, even though it is too big to conceive of.

adj. 极大的 extremely large or great

例 In the **infinite** limits of space, billions of galaxies exist, each containing billions of stars.

diffident
/ˈdɪfədənt/

adj. 缺乏自信的，胆怯的 lacking confidence; not feeling comfortable around people

例 Extremely **diffident**, Saul preferred to stay inside his house rather than encounter people he did not know.

□ temptation □ oppressive □ hyperbole □ trickster □ genteel
□ impassioned □ deduce □ flip □ infinite □ diffident

neutralize
/ˈnuːtrəlaɪz/

▪ *v.* 抵消，使无效 to stop (someone or something) from being effective or harmful

▪ With the enemy's anti-aircraft capabilities ***neutralized***, the bombers moved into position to protect the advancing troops.

controvert
/ˈkɑːntrəvɜːrt/

▪ *v.* 争论，辩论 to dispute or oppose by reasoning

▪ The baseball coach insisted that the ball was fair and ***controverted*** the umpire's call on the field.

succumb
/səˈkʌm/

▪ *v.* 屈服 to stop trying to resist something

▪ Luna was determined to lose weight, but it was hard for her not to ***succumb*** to her cravings for chocolate, pizza, and ice cream.

▪ yield

fury
/ˈfjʊri/

▪ *n.* 狂怒，暴怒 violent anger

▪ In the ***fury*** over the death of his friend Patroklus, Achilles showed no mercy while slaughtering the Trojans.

▪ infuriate（*v.* 激怒）

severe
/səˈvɪr/

▪ *adj.* 严厉的 very harsh

▪ Many think that 20-year prison sentences are far too ***severe*** for non-violent drug crimes.

conspire
/kənˈspaɪər/

▪ *v.* 共谋，协力 to secretly plan with someone to do something that is harmful or illegal

▪ In order to overthrow the dictator, many of the Roman senators ***conspired*** to stab Caesar when he entered the Senate.

gleam
/gliːm/

▪ *n.* 微光 a small, bright light

▪ Despite their massive size, stars appear as tiny ***gleams*** in the nighttime sky.

imperial
/ɪmˈpɪriəl/

▪ *adj.* 帝国的 of or relating to an empire or an emperor

▪ By order of ***imperial*** decree, the Roman emperor requires all citizens to return to their place of birth for the census.

paraphernalia
/ˌpærəfəˈneɪliə/

▪ *n.* 行头，装饰品 objects that are used to do a particular activity; objects of a particular kind

▪ In some country, anyone who gives tobacco or tobacco ***paraphernalia*** to someone under age 21 could be found guilty of a misdemeanor crime.

cast-iron
/ˈkæstˈaɪərn/

▪ *adj.* 坚固的，顽强的 very strong or tough

▪ The ***cast-iron*** regulations of the establishment meant that no compromises to the contract could be made.

detritus
/dɪˈtraɪtəs/

▪ *n.* 碎石，残余物 the pieces that are left when something breaks, falls apart, is destroyed, etc.

▪ Large plastic bags filled with radioactive topsoil and ***detritus*** dot the abandoned fields.

☐ neutralize ☐ controvert ☐ succumb ☐ fury ☐ severe
☐ conspire ☐ gleam ☐ imperial ☐ paraphernalia ☐ cast-iron
☐ detritus

rivalry
/ˈraɪvlri/

释 *n.* 竞争，对抗 a state or situation in which people or groups are competing with each other

例 The Yankees-Red Sox *rivalry* is one of the oldest and bitterest competitions in sports.

派 rival（*n.* 对手）

halt
/hɔːlt/

释 *v.* 停止 stop

例 Upon seeing the stop sign, Fran *halted* her car at the intersection.

释 *v.* 踌躇 to stand in perplexity or doubt between alternate courses: waver

例 *Halted* by the vague instructions, Kathy misassembled the dresser.

avant-garde
/ˌævɑ̃ˈɡɑːrd/

释 *n.* 先锋派，前卫派 a group of people who develop new and often very surprising ideas in art, literature, etc.

例 The *avant-garde* of the art world often fail to attract mainstream attention, but their creativity and influence are often recognized many years after.

释 *adj.* 前卫的，先锋的 of or relating to an avant-garde

例 Even as a musician who favors *avant-garde* music, I have to say that Aaron's recital on Wednesday was truly adventurous.

stipulate
/ˈstɪpjuleɪt/

释 *v.* 规定 to specify as a condition or requirement (as of an agreement or offer)

例 Eva *stipulated* precise financial conditions that would protect herself before agreeing to marry her fiancé.

释 *v.* 保证 to give a guarantee of

例 The hockey player's contract secures his financial well-being for the future as it *stipulates* a guaranteed payment even after injuries.

dispense
/dɪˈspens/

释 *v.* 分配，分发 to give or provide (something)

例 The old man was always eager to *dispense* wisdom and talked to anyone who would listen.

派 dispense with（放弃）

leach
/liːtʃ/

释 *v.* 被冲走，滤去 to remove (nutritive or harmful elements) from soil by percolation

例 Years of acid rain *leached* the nutrients from the soil resulting in fields that were essentially sterile.

brackish
/ˈbrækɪʃ/

释 *adj.* 令人恶心的 distasteful; unpalatable

例 If the pipes in an area are corroded, the tap water will be discolored, *brackish* and undrinkable.

malodorous
/ˌmælˈoʊdərəs/

释 *adj.* 难闻的，恶臭的 having a bad smell

例 While camping in the wilderness, one dreams of washing *malodorous* clothing with a real washing machine.

redolent /ˈredələnt/	释 *adj.* 芬芳的 having a strong smell; full of a fragrance or odor
	例 When Jan sprayed perfume, the room became ***redolent*** with the pleasant aroma.

noisome /ˈnɔɪsəm/	释 *adj.* 有害的，恶臭的 very unpleasant or disgusting
	例 The heavy metal concert was ***noisome*** to the musicians' parents and turned them off with its disturbing lyrics and dissonant sounds.
	反 fragrant

adjudicate /əˈdʒuːdɪkeɪt/	释 *v.* 裁定，宣判 to make an official decision about who is right in a dispute
	例 During the divorce proceedings, the judge ***adjudicated*** alimony and child support between the couple.

eschew /ɪsˈtʃuː/	释 *v.* 避免 to avoid (something) especially because you do not think it is right, proper, etc.
	例 Tom ***eschewed*** drinking alcohol because he knew it was bad for his health.
	反 seek

abbreviate /əˈbriːvieɪt/	释 *v.* 缩短 to make (something) shorter; especially ; to reduce (a word or name) to a shorter form
	例 Many words in our everyday use are usually ***abbreviated*** for convenience: "math" for mathematics, and "exam" for examination are just two examples.
	反 extend

contingent /kənˈtɪndʒənt/	释 *adj.* 依情况而定的 dependent on conditions or occurrences not yet established; conditional, dependent
	例 Using hormones to treat human beings is ***contingent*** on whether hormones that work in the laboratory can affect whole organisms in predictable ways.
	释 *n.* 偶然的 happening by chance or accident; fortuitous
	例 Every undogmatic historian is aware of the multitude of ***contingent*** events that entered into the victory of the Bolshevik revolution.

auspicious /ɔːˈspɪʃəs/	释 *adj.* 吉兆的，幸运的 showing or suggesting that future success is likely
	例 Lobster is commonly served during Chinese festivals and at weddings as its bright red color is considered ***auspicious***.
	近 favorable

essential /ɪˈsenʃl/	释 *adj.* 重要的，必要的 extremely important and necessary
	例 Even though Mestel's account is rather simplified in parts, on the whole it captures the ***essential*** aspects of the physics of white dwarf evolution.
	近 indispensable

bootless /ˈbuːtlɪs/	释 *adj.* 无用的 useless, unprofitable
	例 The young squire was crushed to discover that his attempts to woo the duke's proud daughter were ***bootless***.

posit /'pɑːzɪt/	释 *v.* 假定，假设 to suggest (something, such as an idea or theory) especially in order to start a discussion 例 The office manager ***posited*** that a possible reason for the fire was a cheese pita that had been heated in the microwave for too long.
accrete /ə'krit/	释 *v.* 逐渐增长 to cause to adhere or become attached; also : accumulate 例 After the ship sat in the harbor for years, its hull became ***accreted*** with urchins and other marine animals.
adjunct /'ædʒʌŋkt/	释 *n.* 附属物 something that is joined or added to another thing but is not an essential part of it 例 In Germany, any addition to beer that is not water, yeast, grain, and hops is an unlawful ***adjunct***.
abound /ə'baʊnd/	释 *v.* 富于，充满 to be present in large numbers or in great quantity 例 Our country ***abounds*** with sites, cities and natural beauty, and a family road trip is one of the best ways to explore it all.
subsequent /'sʌbsɪkwənt/	释 *adj.* 后来的，随后的 happening or coming after something else 例 In this case, initial tests proved the foot was human, but ***subsequent*** forensic examination found very little DNA.
heretofore /ˌhɪrtu'fɔːr/	释 *adv.* 迄今为止 until this time : before now 例 Smart phones are relatively new inventions; ***heretofore***, people could only use the internet on their personal computers.
preponderance /prɪ'pɑːndərəns/	释 *n.* （数量上的）优势 a superiority or excess in number or quantity 例 The lawyer managed to convince the jury of the defendant's guilt by offering a ***preponderance*** of evidence, including DNA and video surveillance.
uncompromising /ʌn'kɑːmprəmaɪzɪŋ/	释 *adj.* 不妥协的，坚定的 not willing to change a decision, opinion, method, etc. : not willing to make or accept a compromise 例 Although in public life Simone de Beauvoir's feminist stance was ***uncompromising***, her personal life revealed a greater degree of ideological flexibility.
moralistic /ˌmɔːrə'lɪstɪk/	释 *adj.* 说教的 having or showing strong opinions about what is right behavior and what is wrong behavior 例 The ***moralistic*** teacher dictated proper behaviors to his congregation and angrily disapproved of any disobedience.
benevolent /bə'nevələnt/	释 *adj.* 仁慈的，慈善的 kind and generous 例 God is often portrayed as a ***benevolent*** figure who would do anything to please and encourage His followers. 近 magnanimous, altruistic 反 antipathetic, truculent
impose /ɪm'poʊz/	释 *v.* 把…强加于 to force someone to accept (something or yourself) 例 The High School ***imposed*** strict measures on the students including an entire ban on soft drinks.

☐ posit　　　☐ accrete　　　☐ adjunct　　　☐ abound　　　☐ subsequent
☐ heretofore　　☐ preponderance　　☐ uncompromising　　☐ moralistic　　☐ benevolent
☐ impose

224

resume /rɪ'zuːm/	释 **v.** 恢复 to begin again or go on with again after interruption 例 When Jeff returned from the bathroom, we pressed "play" to **resume** the movie.
stalemate /'steɪlmeɪt/	释 **n.** 僵局 a drawn contest; deadlock 例 The argument ended in a **stalemate** and the sisters were not able to come to a common understanding.
insatiable /ɪn'seɪʃəbl/	释 **adj.** 无法满足的 always wanting more and not able to be satisfied 例 The dog had an **insatiable** appetite and would eat any food placed in front of it. 近 quenchless 派 satiate（v. 充分满足）
snappish /'snæpɪʃ/	释 **adj.** 厉声说话的，暴躁的 feeling or showing irritation 例 Distracted by her work and money problems, Kim developed a bad temper that resulted in her being **snappish** with the rest of her family.
peccadillo /ˌpekə'dɪloʊ/	释 **n.** 小过失 a small mistake or fault that is not regarded as very bad or serious 例 The opposition will use Senator Tankerbell's **peccadilloes** and immoral actions against him.
reparation /ˌrepə'reɪʃn/	释 **n.** 修理 something that is done or given as a way of correcting a mistake that one has made or a bad situation in the past 例 Realizing that I had forgotten to pay for my newspaper, I went back to the store to make **reparations** for my inadvertent theft. 释 **n.** 赔偿 money that a country or group that loses a war pays because of the damage, injury, deaths, etc., it has caused 例 After World War II, Germany was forced to pay **reparations** for all the damages it caused to the Allied forces.
inextricable /ˌɪnɪk'strɪkəbl/	释 **adj.** 纠缠不清的，无法解脱的 impossible to separate; closely joined or related 例 Humor is often **inextricable** from culture: if you are not familiar with a culture, you will not get their jokes.
impregnable /ɪm'pregnəbl/	释 **adj.** 坚固的 not able to be captured by attack; very strong 例 The US basketball team put up an **impregnable** defense, not allowing their rivals to score a single point.
impotent /'ɪmpətənt/	释 **adj.** 无力的，无效的 lacking power or strength 例 Although the Porsche knock-off looked very fast, its inferior design made it **impotent** on the race track.
precede /prɪ'siːd/	释 **v.** 领先，在…之前 to happen, go, or come before (something or someone) 例 The athlete has the potential to be as good as, or better, than anybody who **preceded** him. 近 predate, antedate

supplant
/səˈplænt/

☐ **v.** 取代 to take the place of (someone or something that is old or no longer used or accepted)

☐ Recently, many newspapers have claimed that digital publications have **supplanted** paperback volumes.

encounter
/ɪnˈkaʊntər/

☐ **v.** 遭遇，遇到 to have or experience (problems, difficulties, etc.)

☐ Whenever I **encountered** huge difficulties in completing the task, I immediately consulted my advisor who was able to give me pointed advice on how to proceed.

beset
/bɪˈset/

☐ **v.** 困扰 to cause problems or difficulties for (someone or something)

☐ Brazil, which has been **beset** by political crises, is forecast to see its economy shrink by 3. 8%, the same amount as last year.

fatigue
/fəˈtiːg/

☐ **n.** 疲劳 the state of being very tired : extreme weariness

☐ Sleep disorders can lead to **fatigue**, anxiety, depression and poor daytime performance in both physical and mental tasks.

offish
/ˈɔːfɪʃ/

☐ **adj.** 冷漠的 somewhat cold and reserved

☐ Avoiding the **offish** police offer, Dan asked the friendly one for directions to Time Square.

jockey
/ˈdʒɑːki/

☐ **v.** 不择手段地谋取有利地位 to do something in an effort to get an advantage

☐ After **jockeying** for an inside position in the race, the speed skater shaved valuable seconds off her time.

perceptive
/pərˈseptɪv/

☐ **adj.** 有洞察力的，敏锐的 having or showing an ability to understand or notice something easily or quickly

☐ Highly **perceptive**, Sue realized I was a little sad at the concert despite my efforts to appear happy.

shortcut
/ˈʃɔːrtkʌt/

☐ **n.** 捷径 a quicker or easier way to do something

☐ There is no **shortcut** to writing a novel; one must compose all elements of the story.

jubilant
/ˈdʒuːbɪlənt/

☐ **adj.** 喜悦的 feeling or expressing great joy; very happy

☐ The students were **jubilant** after the team's name was announced, and relieved to have continued the school's winning tradition.

sensuous
/ˈsenʃuəs/

☐ **adj.** 赏心悦目的 highly appreciative of the pleasures of sensation

☐ The massage was a deeply **sensuous** experience that completely relaxed my body and brought utter pleasure.

controversial
/ˌkɑːntrəˈvɜːrʃl/

☐ **adj.** 有争议的 relating to or causing much discussion, disagreement, or argument; likely to produce controversy

☐ Ishmael Reed has a knack for being different and **controversial**, as suggested by his book title *Writing Is Fighting*.

☐ supplant ☐ encounter ☐ beset ☐ fatigue ☐ offish
☐ jockey ☐ perceptive ☐ shortcut ☐ jubilant ☐ sensuous
☐ controversial

seamy
/'siːmi/

adj. 丑恶的 of or relating to unpleasant and usually illegal things (such as crime, drugs, etc.)

例 The magazine *Vice* explores the **seamy** underbelly of modern society, including stories of drugs, crimes, and sex.

反 decent, respectable

pledge
/pledʒ/

v. 保证，许诺 to formally promise to give or do (something)

例 Grace **pledged** to finish the marathon and donate all the money sponsored through door-to-door donations to an ALS charity.

retain
/rɪˈteɪn/

v. 保持 to keep (someone) in a position, job, etc.

例 During the downsizing of the paper company, only a small number of people were **retained** as workers in the one remaining branch.

反 discard

disproportionate
/ˌdɪsprəˈpɔːrʃənət/

adj. 不成比例的 having or showing a difference that is not fair, reasonable, or expected; too large or too small in relation to something

例 The blame directed to you was completely **disproportionate** to the minor role that you played in the execution of the crime.

temper
/'tempər/

v. 调和，使缓和 to make (something) less severe or extreme

例 The new survey, in which people report being unhappy with their jobs and lives, shows that optimism about the future of the country has **tempered**.

选 moderate, mitigate, neutralize

outdo
/ˌaʊtˈduː/

v. 超过，胜过 to do better than (someone or something); to be more successful than (someone or something)

例 With the desire to be the greatest player of all time, Barry Bonds **outdid** Mark McGwire's home record with 73.

abash
/əˈbæʃ/

v. 使羞愧，使困窘 to destroy the self-possession or self-confidence of: disconcert

例 **Abashed** by the critic's review of my book, I locked myself inside and refused to participate in the book tour.

unexceptional
/ˌʌnɪkˈsepʃənl/

adj. 普通的 not unusually good, interesting, etc. ; not exceptional

例 For some consumers, the packaging and branding were enough to elevate otherwise **unexceptional** products.

obtrusive
/əbˈtruːsɪv/

adj. 显著的，突兀的 undesirably noticeable

例 The **obtrusive** waiter stood too close to our table and kept staring at us as we ate our meals.

impasse
/'ɪmpæs/

n. 僵局 a situation in which no progress seems possible

例 Negotiations between the two groups soon became so heated that agreement was inconceivable: they have reached an **impasse**.

superficial
/ˌsuːpərˈfɪʃl/

释 *adj.* 表面的 presenting only an appearance without substance or significance

例 The interview revealed that her understanding of the field is merely *superficial* and not in-depth at all.

释 *adj.* 肤浅的 concerned only with the obvious or apparent: shallow

例 The author of the celebrity biography hopes readers can find connections with these famous people whom we all know at a *superficial* level.

近 shallow

moderate
/ˈmɑːdərət/

释 *v.* 使缓和 to lessen the violence, severity, or extremeness of

例 The men's rights activist writes sexist rants on his blog, but *moderates* his views when he gives interviews.

近 temper

释 *adj.* 适度的，有节制的 being within reasonable limits; not excessive or extreme

例 Florida winters are generally *moderate* and usually require just a light jacket and sometimes a hat.

派 immoderate (*adj.* 无节制的，过度的)

decode
/ˌdiːˈkoʊd/

释 *v.* 破译，解码 to find or understand the true or hidden meaning of (something)

例 When the human genome was *decoded* in the early 2000s, some scientists predicted that victory over many diseases was at hand.

vagary
/ˈveɪɡəri/

释 *n.* 反复无常 an extravagant or erratic notion or action; caprice

例 There are many *vagaries* in Ben's behavior; he will go from happy to irritated and nervous with no warning.

近 caprice, whim

evangelist
/ɪˈvændʒəlɪst/

释 *n.* 狂热支持者 an enthusiastic advocate

例 As an *evangelist* for the paleo diet, Beth talked about the horrors of grains and other processed foods.

释 *n.* 福音传教士 one who practices evangelism

例 The enthusiastic *evangelist* has recently taken to popular social media platforms to encourage others to join him in his faith.

pedigree
/ˈpedɪɡriː/

释 *n.* 血统，门第 the origin and history of something especially when it is good or impressive

例 Because of its *pedigree* as the offspring of a Kentucky Derby winner, the horse was quite easy to sell.

prominent
/ˈprɑːmɪnənt/

释 *adj.* 著名的 widely known; eminent

例 Abraham Lincoln was a *prominent* lawyer before he became president, and earned much fame in that profession.

释 *adj.* 显著的 immediately noticeable; conspicuous

例 The gaudy and bright painting was displayed in a *prominent* position just above the mantle and could not be ignored.

近 salient

☐ superficial   ☐ moderate   ☐ decode   ☐ vagary   ☐ evangelist
☐ pedigree   ☐ prominent

enforce /ɪn'fɔːrs/	**v.** 实施，强制 to make (a law, rule, etc.) active or effective; to make sure that people do what is required by (a law, rule, etc.) 例 With the installation of the traffic camera, the police were able to **enforce** the red light laws without being physically present.
amid /ə'mɪd/	**prep.** 在···之中 prep. in or into the middle of (something) 例 **Amid** the excitement of the party, my girlfriend broke up with me.
boost /buːst/	**v.** 增加，促进 to increase the force, power, or amount of (something) 例 Government investments can often **boost** the economy and create greater employment opportunities.
stagger /'stægər/	**v.** 使···震惊 to shock or surprise (someone) very much 例 The extensive destruction of the San Francisco Earthquake **staggered** many of its residents who had believed their buildings were earthquake-proof.
	v. 跌跌撞撞地走 to move on unsteadily 例 After the robber was shot by the police, he **staggered** for a short distance before eventually falling to the ground.
imperil /ɪm'perəl/	**v.** 使处于危险 to put (something or someone) in a dangerous situation 例 Reading text messages while driving is not only dangerous to the driver, but **imperils** everyone in the car and other cars.

piety
/ˈpaɪəti/

> *n.* 虔诚 devotion to God; the quality or state of being pious
>
> Known for his great **piety**, Pope John Paul II was a representative of the Church and its faith.

flair
/fler/

> *n.* 天资，天分 an unusual and appealing quality or style
>
> Fiona always dressed with originality and **flair** and never followed prevailing fashion trends.
>
> virtuosity

braggadocio
/ˌbræɡəˈdoʊtʃioʊ/

> *n.* 自夸，吹牛大王 the annoying or exaggerated talk of someone who is trying to sound very proud or brave
>
> The mayoral candidate is a narcissist, and he can't read a scripted speech without swerving off into **braggadocio**.

hurtle
/ˈhɜːrtl/

> *v.* 猛冲，猛烈碰撞 to cause (something or someone) to move or go with great speed and force
>
> After the rollercoaster crested the steep slope, we **hurtled** to the ground at a rapid pace.

savor
/ˈseɪvər/

> *v.* 享受 to enjoy (something) for a long time
>
> Knowing that the meal cost several hundred dollars, we **savored** every bite and prolonged the dining experience.

eviscerate
/ɪˈvɪsəreɪt/

> *v.* 使…失去力量 to deprive of vital content or force
>
> After showing up to the debate unprepared, Talbot was **eviscerated** by the skilled debater on the opposite team.
>
> gut

mince
/mɪns/

> *v.* 装腔作势 to utter or pronounce with affectation
>
> He **minced** every single one of Sally's words in an exaggerated way to mock her usual condescending tone of speaking.
>
> *v.* 委婉表达 to restrain (words) within the bounds of decorum
>
> Though Fine uses humor and playfulness in her writing, she can be critical, **mincing** no words in her judgements of other scientists' work.

exterminate
/ɪkˈstɜːrmɪneɪt/

> *v.* 使灭绝，消除 to destroy or kill (a group of animals, people, etc.) completely
>
> The husband was given clear orders by his wife to **exterminate** all mice in the house using traps and poison.
>
> terminate (*v.* 终止)

intact /ɪnˈtækt/	▣ *adj.* 完整的 not broken or damaged; having every part ▣ The bombing of Dresden in 1945 completely destroyed the city and left behind nothing ***intact***.
belittle /bɪˈlɪtl/	▣ *v.* 轻视，贬低 to describe (someone or something) as little or unimportant ▣ Mary constantly ***belittled*** her colleagues in front of her boss, who did not appreciate her rudeness. ▣ vilify
obstruct /əbˈstrʌkt/	▣ *v.* 阻碍，妨碍 to slow or block the movement, progress, or action of (something or someone) ▣ During the storm, a tree fell onto the road and ***obstructed*** traffic in both directions.
proximity /prɑːkˈsɪməti/	▣ *n.* 距离近 the state of being near ▣ Naturally, ***proximity*** makes friendships easier: the people we live near to or interact with frequently are more likely to become our friends.
harness /ˈhɑːrnɪs/	▣ *v.* 利用 to use (something) for a particular purpose ▣ By ***harnessing*** the power of the sun, we can power the world. ▣ utilize, exploit
spurious /ˈspjʊriəs/	▣ *adj.* 假的 not genuine, sincere, or authentic ▣ On Antiques Roadshow, the expert on Ming Dynasty pottery immediately noticed that the jug was ***spurious***. ▣ implausible
apocryphal /əˈpɑːkrɪfl/	▣ *adj.* 被人们普遍接受却不正确的，假的 well-known but probably not true ▣ Odds are the news is ***apocryphal***, but it continues to circulate because it's entirely believable.
applaud /əˈplɔːd/	▣ *v.* 赞美，支持 to express approval of or support for (something or someone) ▣ Loving the theatrical performance of the Lion King, the entire audience stood up to ***applaud***.
bifurcate /ˈbaɪfərkeɪt/	▣ *v.* 一分为二 to cause to divide into two branches or parts ▣ When the Nile reaches the mountains in central Africa, it ***bifurcates*** into two rivers.
cacophony /kəˈkɑːfəni/	▣ *n.* 刺耳的声音，不和谐的声音 harsh or discordant sound ▣ I could barely sleep as the drunk youngsters were causing such a ***cacophony*** on the streets. ▣ mellifluous ▣ cacophnous (*adj.* 刺耳的)
catastrophe /kəˈtæstrəfi/	▣ *n.* 灾难 a terrible disaster ▣ After the collapse of the bridge, the city vowed that a similar ***catastrophe*** would never occur again. ▣ catastrophic (*adj.* 大灾难的)

circumlocution
/ˌsɜːrkəmləˈkjuːʃn/

释 *n.* 绕圈的话语 the use of an unnecessarily large number of words to express an idea

例 Ben's constant use of *circumlocution* annoys his managers, who have told him over and over again to be direct.

派 circumlocutory (*adj.* 迂回的，委婉曲折的)

clairvoyance
/kleˈvɔɪəns/

释 *n.* 洞察力 ability to perceive matters beyond the range of ordinary perception

例 Many superstitious people have consulted the fortune-teller as her *clairvoyance* is reputed to have helped many people avert disasters in the future.

cloying
/ˈklɔɪɪŋ/

释 *adj.* 令人腻烦的 disgusting or distasteful by reason of excess

例 When the top fell off of the sugar shaker and the sugar poured into the coffee, the drink became a *cloying* mess that was impossible to drink.

collude
/kəˈluːd/

释 *v.* 同谋 to work with others secretly especially in order to do something illegal or dishonest

例 Behind closed doors, the executives from Macy's and Nordstrom *colluded* to fix prices on clothing to make extra money.

concord
/ˈkɑːŋkɔːrd/

释 *n.* 意见一致 a state of agreement

例 An unprecedented 100 nations signed a *concord* agreeing to reduce harmful emissions by 2020.

反 dissonance

cosset
/ˈkɑːsɪt/

释 *v.* 溺爱 to give (someone) a lot of care and attention or too much care and attention

例 With his leg broken and unable to do many normal tasks, Aaron felt *cosseted* by his grandmother who wouldn't even let him leave his bed.

counterbalance
/ˌkaʊntərˈbæləns/

释 *n.* 平衡，抵消 any force or influence that balances or offsets another

例 The accused's right to silence was a vital *counterbalance* to the powers of the police.

选 offset

释 *v.* 平衡，抵消 to offset

例 The loss of income from the failing website company was *counterbalanced* by the profits from his hardware division.

covet
/ˈkʌvət/

释 *v.* 渴求 to feel immoderate desire for that which is another's

例 Upon seeing Chip's Ferrari, I immediately *coveted* it and began saving money to buy my own.

选 envy

cursory
/ˈkɜːrsəri/

释 *adj.* 草率的，仓促的 performed rapidly with little attention to detail

例 The draft seemed good during a *cursory* read-through, but an in-depth analysis revealed its many flaws.

选 casual, perfunctory

weary
/ˈwɪri/

圖 *adj.* 令人厌烦的 having one's patience, tolerance, or pleasure exhausted

例 ***Weary*** from months of traveling, I was happy to return home and sleep in my own bed for a change.

圖 *adj.* 疲劳的 lacking strength, energy, or freshness because of a need for rest or sleep

例 Running an ultramarathon can make even the best athletes ***weary*** and exhausted.

allegory
/ˈæləgɔːri/

圖 *n.* 象征 a symbolic representation

例 The painting of river nymphs was an ***allegory*** for the coming of spring.

圖 *n.* 寓言 a story in which the characters and events are symbols that stand for ideas about human life or for a political or historical situation

例 Although seemingly a story about barn animals, *Animal Farm* is an ***allegory*** for the Russian Revolution.

peripheral
/pəˈrɪfərəl/

圖 *adj.* 不重要的 not relating to the main or most important part

例 Until it became a state, Alaska was a ***peripheral*** region in the USA with a small population.

perspicacious
/ˌpɜːrspɪˈkeɪʃəs/

圖 *adj.* 有洞察力的 of acute mental vision or discernment

例 Dr. Watson was chosen by Sherlock Holmes because the detective found him quite ***perspicacious*** and able to observe situations.

perspicuous
/ˌpɜːrspɪkjuəs/

圖 *adj.* 清晰的，易懂的 plain to the understanding especially because of clarity and precision of presentation

例 By removing any confusing prose or concepts, the professor made her speech ***perspicuous*** to even the most unlearned listener.

派 perspicuity（*n.* 清楚明了）

sleazy
/ˈsliːzi/

圖 *adj.* 低俗的，龌龊的 dishonest or immoral

例 Stereotypically, the used car salesman was a ***sleazy*** businessman who looked for every opportunity to rip off his clients.

近 sordid

indemnify
/ɪnˈdemnɪfaɪ/

圖 *v.* 赔偿 to make compensation to for incurred hurt, loss, or damage

例 Car insurance is necessary to ***indemnify*** any losses incurred during an accident.

eyesore
/ˈaɪsɔːr/

圖 *n.* 碍眼的事物 something offensive to view

例 Critics say the many cranes and construction sites in the fast-growing city are an ***eyesore***.

archive
/ˈɑːrkaɪv/

圖 *v.* 存档，保存 to file or collect in or as if in an archive

例 In order to make space for the new books, the library ***archived*** the old manuscripts in a separate building.

xenophobic
/ˌzenəˈfoʊbɪk/

釋 *adj.* 排外的，仇视外国的 marked by unduly fearful of what is foreign and especially of people of foreign origin

例 Believing that migrants were "taking the jobs of the locals", the **xenophobic** mayor called for stricter measures against immigration.

ineffable
/ɪnˈefəbl/

釋 *adj.* 难以言表的 too great, powerful, beautiful, etc., to be described or expressed

例 Great movies, like great songs, illustrate the **ineffable** and express what can't be put into words.

fluid
/ˈfluːɪd/

釋 *adj.* 流动的 characterized by or employing a smooth easy style

例 It was effortless to read the **fluid** prose of the author and I kept turning the pages to read more.

釋 *adj.* 多变的，不固定的 available for various uses

例 The computer is a **fluid** instrument that can be used for writing, statistical analysis or graphic design.

despotic
/dɪˈspɑːtɪk/

釋 *adj.* 独裁的，专制的 marked by absolute power and authority

例 As a **despotic** ruler, the dictator of Libya was called before the UN to answer for his oppression and crimes against humanity.

capitulate
/kəˈpɪtʃuleɪt/

釋 *v.* 投降 to stop fighting an enemy or opponent

例 Rather than **capitulate**, McCrory decided to roll the dice in federal court.

近 submit

abominate
/əˈbɑːmɪneɪt/

釋 *v.* 憎恶，憎恨 to feel great hatred for (someone or something)

例 **Abominated** by all, cockroaches are nuisances that many seek to exterminate completely.

反 esteem

派 abomination（*n.* 憎恨）

accommodate
/əˈkɑːmədeɪt/

釋 *v.* 调解 to bring into agreement or concord

例 By **accommodating** all North American countries in the treaty, we can encourage trade among the nations.

釋 *v.* 帮助 to provide what is needed or wanted for (someone or something)

例 In order to **accommodate** the less wealthy, colleges issue scholarships that attract highly qualified candidates.

釋 *v.* 提供住处 to make room for

例 When our best friend visited us, we **accommodated** her in our extra bedroom.

mandate
/ˈmændeɪt/

釋 *v.* 命令 to officially demand or require (something)

例 Title IX **mandates** that women have equal access to education as men.

□ xenophobic　　□ ineffable　　□ fluid　　□ despotic　　□ capitulate
□ abominate　　□ accommodate　　□ mandate

saturate
/'sætʃəreɪt/

v. 填满 to fill (something) completely with something

例 **Saturated** with profanity, the television show was unable to be broadcasted on cable television.

v. 浸泡 to make (something) very wet

例 I left my sweatshirt outside and it became fully **saturated** in the nighttime rain.

反 dehydrate

untoward
/ʌn'tɔːrd/

adj. 不利的 adverse or inauspicious

例 Manchester City's self-goal was an **untoward** sign of their catastrophic play to come.

反 favorable

adj. 不得体的 not proper or appropriate

例 Although Maria made it clear that she was not interested in George romantically, he still made **untoward** advances to her.

adj. 不服管理的 difficult to guide, manage, or work with

例 Refusing to work any additional shifts, the **untoward** McDonald's employee was fired after several months of difficult employment.

peruse
/pə'ruːz/

v. 仔细读 to examine or read (something) in a very careful way

例 Unable to read the entire newspaper, I just **perused** the headlines to find the stories that interested me.

enthrall
/ɪn'θrɔːl/

v. 吸引 to hold the attention of (someone) by being very exciting, interesting, or beautiful

例 **Enthralled** by *Planet Earth*, we sat on the couch and watched the beautiful scenes of nature and wildlife.

emphatic
/ɪm'fætɪk/

adj. 着重强调的 said or done in a forceful or definite way

例 Bayern's 7-0 victory in the Champions League finals was an **emphatic** statement that they were the best team in the league.

派 emphasize（*v.* 强调）

nonplus
/ˌnɑːn'plʌs/

v. 使困惑，使不知所措 to perplex

例 While not completely **nonplussed** by the audience's heckling, he was a little thrown off.

phlegmatic
/fleg'mætɪk/

adj. 性格冷淡的 not easily upset, excited, or angered

例 Always **phlegmatic** at the sight of blood, Lenny unsurprisingly entered the medical profession.

antidote
/'æntidoʊt/

n. 解药 something that corrects or improves the bad effects of something

例 For many, a big mug of coffee and a greasy breakfast are indulgent **antidotes** for a morning's hangover.

impersonal
/ɪmˈpɜːrsənl/

释 *adj.* 没有人情味的 not engaging the human personality or emotions
例 Many people hate the ***impersonal*** robotic voices that large companies use on their customer service hotlines and prefer real human contact.

释 *adj.* 客观的 having no personal reference or connection
例 Although Jim and Jane "dated" for several years online, Jim grew tired of the ***impersonal*** relationship and wished to meet her in real life.

ensue
/ɪnˈsuː/

释 *v.* 紧随其后 to come afterward
例 Even if a surgery goes well, the blood clots that ***ensue*** may be dangerous.

gore
/ɡɔːr/

释 *n.* 血，血块 blood, especially clotted blood
例 Many horror films include so much blood and ***gore*** that the over-the-top special effects become almost comical.

释 *n.* 毛骨悚然 gruesomeness depicted in vivid detail
例 The sensationalism that characterizes Edna O'Brien's new novel marks a change for O'Brien, who in the last couple of decades has demonstrated a marked taste for ***gore***.

fallow
/ˈfæloʊ/

释 *adj.* 休耕的 left uncultivated or unplanted
例 After several years of planting, fields must be left ***fallow*** so that their nutrients can be restored.
选 sterile

unruly
/ʌnˈruːli/

释 *adj.* 不服管理的，难以控制的 not readily ruled, disciplined, or managed
例 At a reading in New York last month, Pulitzer Prize-winning novelist Jane Smiley faced an ***unruly*** crowd that could not stop talking amongst themselves.
选 insubordinate, intractable, obstreperous

synoptic
/sɪˈnɑːptɪk/

释 *adj.* 摘要的 presenting a general view or summary
例 The sheer bulk of data from the mass media seems to overpower us and drive us to ***synoptic*** accounts for an easily and readily digestible portion of news.
选 abridged

conviction
/kənˈvɪkʃn/

释 *n.* 信念 a strong belief
例 With strong religious ***convictions***, Jeb openly chastised others whom he thought were "sinning."
选 certainty

释 *n.* 定罪 a convicting or being convicted
例 With his federal ***conviction*** for theft, Ace was shut out from voting for certain offices.

patrimony
/ˈpætrɪmoʊni/

释 *n.* 继承，世袭 property that is inherited by a person from their father
例 The wicked young nobleman had spent his ***patrimony*** within two years of his father's death.
派 patrimonial（*adj.* 祖传的）

vicarious /vaɪˈkeriəs/	**adj.** 身临其境的 felt or experienced by watching or reading about somebody else doing something, rather than by doing it oneself 例 Although a homebody, Hope lived **vicariously** through the lives of others by watching reality television.
ductile /ˈdʌktaɪl/	**adj.** 易被影响的 capable of being readily persuaded or influenced; tractable 例 The manager was caught off-guard by a surprising strike organized by usually **ductile** white-collar employees. **adj.** 可塑的 easily molded or shaped; malleable 例 Lead is **ductile** and can be flattened out into thin sheets, but it is not a very tough material.
dolorous /ˈdoʊlərəs/	**adj.** 悲伤的 very sorrowful or sad 例 The depression of the main characters cast a **dolorous** mood over the entire movie.
antiquated /ˈæntɪkweɪtɪd/	**adj.** 老旧的，过时的 old-fashioned and no longer suitable for modern conditions 例 The tradition of not wearing white after Labor Day is now **antiquated**. 选 old-fashioned, outdated
wayward /ˈweɪwərd/	**adj.** 任性的 following one's own capricious, wanton, or depraved inclinations 例 Ever the **wayward** teen, Jeff left home at a young age to follow his desire to be a wandering musician. 选 errant **adj.** 无法预料的 following no clear principle or law 例 Senator Tankerbell was a **wayward** political who agreed with any position that might be the most popular. 选 unpredictable
errant /ˈerənt/	**adj.** 随意的 moving about aimlessly or irregularly 例 Having been abandoned, the **errant** dog wandered the streets looking for a new owner. 选 wayward **adj.** 错误的 behaving wrongly 例 As an **errant** teen, I shoplifted once, but quickly turned my life around during college.
cannibalize /ˈkænɪbəlaɪz/	**v.** 采用…作为主要来源 to draw on as a major source; to exploit 例 Banking practices like credit default swaps do not add value to the economy, but **cannibalize** existing assets. **v.** 剥夺（关键成分用于别处）to deprive of vital elements or resources, such as personnel, equipment, or funding, for use elsewhere 例 After merging with Microsoft, our small AI department was **cannibalized** by the larger hardware division.

□ vicarious □ ductile □ dolorous □ antiquated □ wayward
□ errant □ cannibalize

discordant
/dɪs'kɔːrdənt/

释 *adj.* 不一致的 being at variance : disagreeing

例 Although the couple seemed to get along in public, they were quite *discordant* on ordinary matters, such as who would do the dishes.

释 *adj.* 不和谐的 disagreeable in sound; harsh or dissonant.

例 When the bassist dropped his instrument, it let out a *discordant* sound that made us cringe.

insinuate
/ɪn'sɪnjueɪt/

释 *v.* 暗示（表不满）to introduce (as an idea) gradually or in a subtle, indirect, or covert

例 Although Ann never told us she had a new boyfriend, she *insinuated* it with many comments about "going out" and "her friend".

释 *v.* 巧妙地介入（表不满）to introduce (as oneself) by stealthy, smooth, or artful means

例 When I heard that the other group was talking about stocks, I *insinuated* myself into the conversation to brag about my recent windfall.

slinky
/'slɪŋki/

释 *adj.* 鬼鬼祟祟的 stealthy, furtive, and sneaking

例 Unknown to the rat, the *slinky* cat was stalking him furtively.

attune
/ə'tuːn/

释 *v.* 使协调一致 to bring into harmony

例 It is often pleasant to go for long walks in the wilderness in order to *attune* your mind to the peacefulness of nature.

bluster
/'blʌstər/

释 *v.* （虚张声势地）恐吓 to talk or act with noisy swaggering threats

例 When he was fired from his job, Mark *blustered* around the office with empty threats of revenge.

释 *n.* 咆哮 loud, arrogant speech, often full of empty threats

例 The conservative's claim that he would "grab his musket" if his candidate lost was just *bluster*.

nonsensical
/nɑːn'sensɪkl/

释 *adj.* 无意义的 lacking intelligible meaning

例 The baby loved having the baby book read to her although it was mostly *nonsensical* sounds and pictures.

选 illogical

释 *adj.* 愚蠢的 foolish; absurd

例 After seeing the art house film, I was convinced it was a *nonsensical* mess, but everyone else thought it was a masterpiece rife with meaning.

villainous
/'vɪlənəs/

释 *adj.* 极坏的，恶劣的 appropriate to a villain, as in wickedness or depravity

例 One of D. W. Griffith's early films tells the story of a *villainous* speculator who grabs control of the entire wheat market, sending bread prices out of reach for the poor.

□ discordant   □ insinuate   □ slinky   □ attune   □ bluster
□ nonsensical   □ villainous

drudgery /'drʌdʒəri/	释 *n.* 苦工 tedious, menial, or unpleasant work 例 The ***drudgery*** of data entry is necessary in order to analyze the data collectively.
millstone /'mɪlstoʊn/	释 *n.* 重担 a heavy weight; a burden 例 Betty's criminal background was a true ***millstone*** that prevented her from finding a lucrative career. 选 encumbrance
canard /kə'nɑːrd/	释 *n.* 谣言 an unfounded or false, deliberately misleading story 例 While designing the puzzle, Frank left a number of ***canards*** to distract people from the correct answers.
accolade /'ækəleɪd/	释 *n.* 赞美 an expression of approval; praise 例 After setting the single season scoring record, Wayne received ***accolades*** by both his team and the NHL. 选 laurel 释 *v.* 赞扬 to praise or honor 例 Although she was panned online for her critique of the war in Iraq, the professor was ***accoladed*** by many thinkers.
laurel /'lɔːrəl/	释 *n.* 荣誉 honor and glory won for great achievement 例 Her Emmy Lifetime Achievement Award was a final ***laurel*** to cap an illustrious acting career. 选 accolade 释 *v.* 授予荣誉 to honor, especially with an award or a prize 例 When news was released that Joss received the book award, his academic department ***laureled*** him with a congratulatory party.
intimidate /ɪn'tɪmɪdeɪt/	释 *v.* 恐吓 to make (someone) afraid 例 As a 7-foot-tall, burly man, Mitch ***intimidated*** most people, but he was truly sweet and gentle. 选 scary
temerity /tə'merəti/	释 *n.* 鲁莽 the quality of being confident and unafraid of danger or punishment especially in a way that seems rude or foolish 例 Jess had the ***temerity*** to ask the bus driver to pull over so he could stop for beer.
assemblage /ə'semblɪdʒ/	释 *n.* 混合 a group of people or things 例 A close examination of the ***assemblage*** of pottery reveals minor changes to decoration over time.

embattle
/ɪm'bætl/

釋 *v.* 备战 to prepare for battle
例 ***Embattled*** with armor and weapons, the knights lined up opposite their enemy.

釋 *v.* 设防于…，加强巩固 to fortify
例 The small town took pains to completely ***embattle*** itself as a measure of defense against potential attacks by neighboring towns.

desultory
/'desəltɔːri/

釋 *adj.* 漫无目的的 marked by lack of definite plan, regularity, or purpose
例 The entire group made a ***desultory*** promise to "stay in touch" and "get together some time".

釋 *adj.* 散漫的 done without serious effort
例 With no financial motivation to play well, Lenny Dykstra gave ***desultory*** efforts on the baseball field when it was not his contract year.

expunge
/ɪk'spʌndʒ/

釋 *v.* 去除 to remove (something) completely
例 For most juvenile crimes, all traces on the permanent record are ***expunged*** upon their 18th birthday.
选 erase

jaundice
/'dʒɔːndɪs/

釋 *n.* 嫉妒 a state or feeling of negativity or bitterness arising especially from envy or world
例 When his rival was chosen for the executive position, Greg suffered from bitter ***jaundice*** at the thought of taking orders from his new boss.

dainty
/'deɪnti/

釋 *adj.* 小巧精致的 delicately beautiful or charming and usually small
例 The miniature cupcakes were ***dainty*** edible works of art.

obloquy
/'ɑːbləkwi/

釋 *n.* 诋毁，谩骂 abusively detractive language or utterance
例 When the public learned of the pastor's theft, the congregation uttered ***obloquies*** against him and his crime.

remiss
/rɪ'mɪs/

釋 *adj.* 粗心的，疏忽大意的 not showing enough care and attention
例 It would be ***remiss*** of the Nalgene Company not to address any quality concerns if they hope to maintain their customers

balkanize
/'bɔːlkənaɪz/

釋 *v.* 使割据 to divide or compartmentalize
例 The company has become ***balkanized***, with Marketing and Customer Retention having no contact or communication.

oxymoron
/ˌɑːksɪ'mɔːraːn/

釋 *n.* 矛盾修饰法 a combination of words that have opposite or very different meanings
例 Although we all know what you mean by "jumbo shrimp", the opposite meanings of the two words make it an ***oxymoron.***

gaiety
/'geɪəti/

釋 *n.* 欢快 a happy and lively quality
例 The ***gaiety*** of the party quickly dipped when Jeff became ill with food poisoning.

□ embattle   □ desultory   □ expunge   □ jaundice   □ dainty
□ obloquy   □ remiss   □ balkanize   □ oxymoron   □ gaiety

altercate /ˈɔːltəkeit/	🔊 **v.** 争吵 to dispute angrily or noisily 📝 Our neighbors **altercated** loudly in the driveway about the appropriate place on the street to park their respective vehicles. 🔁 quarrel
coerce /kouˈɜːrs/	🔊 **v.** 强制 to make (someone) do something by using force or threats 📝 With the gun to my back, I was **coerced** into providing the thief with my bank card and PIN.
gregarious /grɪˈgeriəs/	🔊 **v.** 群居的，好交际的 enjoying the company of other people 📝 Ever the **gregarious** socialite, Donna was the life of the party, providing hilarious banter. 🔁 social
squander /ˈskwaːndər/	🔊 **v.** 浪费，挥霍 to use (something) in a foolish or wasteful way 📝 It is not uncommon to hear about lottery winners who **squander** all of their wealth and end up poorer than before their win. 🔀 squanderer（*n.* 挥霍者）
congruent /ˈkaːŋgruənt/	🔊 **adj.** 相一致的 matching or in agreement with something 📝 Much to their dismay, Wanda and Rita were wearing **congruent** pink sweaters on the same day at work. 🔁 consistent
wallow /ˈwaːlou/	🔊 **v.** 沉溺于 to spend time experiencing or enjoying something without making any effort to change ones' situation 📝 Instead of **wallowing** in self-pity, we should be proactive and do something to fix things.
derelict /ˈderəlɪkt/	🔊 **adj.** 被遗弃的 abandoned especially by the owner or occupant 📝 It caught us by surprise when we saw a man leave his house and start the **derelict** car—it had not moved from that spot in years! 🔊 **adj.** 不负责任的，玩忽职守的 lacking a sense of duty 📝 The soldier was **derelict** of his duty when he fell asleep on post.
dilapidate /dɪˈlæpɪdeɪt/	🔊 **v.** 使…破败 to bring into a condition of decay or partial ruin 📝 Having been **dilapidated** by years of abandonment, the roof of the old house collapsed in a recent storm.
invert /ɪnˈvɜːrt/	🔊 **v.** 颠倒，倒置 to reverse the values or positions of multiple entities 📝 The idea that fast food clerks and waiters do more real work than executives **inverts** what many people assume.
introspect /ˌɪntrəˈspekt/	🔊 **v.** 自省 to examine one's own thoughts, motives and beliefs 📝 If you are going to make political change, you need to get out and organize, not just **introspect** about your own privilege. 🔁 self-analysis

repertoire
/ˈrepərtwɑːr/

释 *n.* 全部节目 a collection of material that one can perform, such as a musician's songs
例 After 15 minutes, the high school band had run through their ***repertoire***, but the audience asked for an encore so they played their songs again.

释 *n.* 全部才能，全部本领 all the things that a person is able to do
例 She is such a competent lab technician that her entire ***repertoire*** where lab work is concerned far exceeds most others.

solace
/ˈsɑːləs/

释 *v.* 安慰 to give comfort in grief or misfortune : console
例 She was ***solaced*** by the good memories that those photograph albums had captured of her now crumbling marriage.

释 *n.* 安慰，慰藉 comfort or support in a distressing situation
例 The losing team took ***solace*** in the fact that their opponent was undefeated, so they weren't the only ones to lose to them.

inquisitive
/ɪnˈkwɪzətɪv/

释 *adj.* 好奇的 tending to ask questions and seek out information
例 Children are naturally ***inquisitive*** about science unless teachers make it so boring that they lose their interest.

figment
/ˈfɪɡmənt/

释 *n.* 虚构的事物 something that is imagined but not real
例 "Death panels" were just a ***figment*** of people's imagination, not a real part of Obamacare.

intermittent
/ˌɪntərˈmɪtənt/

释 *adj.* 间歇的，断断续续的 not occurring continuously; happening at irregular intervals
例 The ***intermittent*** sound of the car alarm prevented Janine from ever really concentrating on studying for the chemistry test.

impervious
/ɪmˈpɜːrviəs/

释 *adj.* 不能渗透的 not allowing something (such as water or light) to enter or pass through
例 Diamond is ***impervious*** to water and can last for an extremely long period of time.

释 *adj.* 不受影响的 not vulnerable to being affected
例 All his friends told the bodybuilder to stop taking steroids, but he was ***impervious*** to persuasion.

Inappropriate
/ˌɪnəˈproupriət/

释 *adj.* 不适当的，不合适的 not right or suited for some purpose or situation : not appropriate or suitable
例 It was completely ***inappropriate*** of you to enter the lecture more than half an hour late without apologizing to the lecturer.
选 unacceptable

indiscernible
/ˌɪndɪˈsɜːrnəbl/

释 *adj.* 不明显的 impossible to see, hear, or know clearly
例 O'Brien's smile was so thin it was almost ***indiscernible*** even to those standing right next to him.
选 imperceptible

□ repertoire　　□ solace　　□ inquisitive　　□ figment　　□ intermittent
□ impervious　　□ inappropriate　　□ indiscernible

disreputable
/dɪsˈrepjətəbl/

adj. 声名狼藉的 not respected or trusted by most people : having a bad reputation

Many people may regard my brother to be **disreputable** due to recent reports of his misbehavior, but to me, he will always be my most beloved brother.

plebeian
/pləˈbiːən/

n. 平民，粗俗的人 a common person

It confounds me why the whole community regards the mayor as some higher being when in reality, he is just a **plebeian**.

adj. 普通的 crude or coarse in manner or style : common

Suzy was bemused when her first date led her to a rather **plebeian** restaurant filled with greasy tables and worn-out tiles.

clairvoyant
/klerˈvɔɪənt/

adj. 有洞察力的 having clairvoyance : able to see beyond the range of ordinary perception

The **clairvoyant** fortune teller predicted that Ming would soon meet with a disaster simply by sensing the negative aura that permeated him.

hallucinogen
/həˈluːsɪnədʒən/

n. 迷幻剂 a substance (such as a drug) that causes people to see or sense things that are not real: a substance that causes hallucinations

Hallucinogens, such as LSD, tend to produce illusions in people and elevate them to a different order of reality.

halluxinogenic (adj. 引起幻觉的)

voyeur
/vwaɪˈɜːr/

n. 好刺探他人隐私者 a person who likes seeing and talking or writing about something that is considered to be private

Smith may look very much the proper gentleman, but he is actually a **voyeur** who enjoys prying into people's private affairs and exposing their little secrets.

voyeuristic (adj. 爱刺探别人隐私的)

boredom
/ˈbɔːrdəm/

n. 厌倦 the state of being weary and restless through lack of interest

The **boredom** that confronted me during those long periods of study led me to binge eating and uncontrolled drinking.

apogee
/ˈæpədʒiː/

n. 最高点 the highest point of something

Even though a major part of the American troops had already withdrawn by that point, the war continued to rage at its **apogee**.

acme

acme
/ˈækmi/

n. 最高点 the highest point of something

After years of toiling at his start-up, his fame was finally at its **acme** when *Time* magazine regarded him as the top businessman in the world.

apogee

precursor
/priːˈkɜːrsər/

📝 *n.* 先驱 something that comes before something else and that often leads to or influences its development

📖 Pointillism opened up doors of creativity previously unexplored in painting and was the ***precursor*** to Impressionism that took over a huge part of the late nineteenth century.

🔄 forerunner

civil
/ˈsɪvl/

📝 *adj.* 公民的 of or relating to the people who live in a country

📖 All her children ended up being ***civil*** servants who took on different roles in the ministry of education.

📝 *adj.* 有礼貌的 polite but not friendly : only as polite as a person needs to be in order to not be rude

📖 I could tell that they did not share any intimate relations as she greeted him in a very ***civil*** manner when he entered the room.

peaceable
/ˈpiːsəbl/

📝 *adj.* 和平的，温顺的 not liking or wanting to fight or argue

📖 A ***peaceable*** settlement has finally been reached after both sides of the army were exhausted from fighting.

unfaltering
/ʌnˈfɔːltərɪŋ/

📝 *adj.* 坚定的 not wavering or weakening : firm

📖 They took a ***unfaltering*** stand against drugs in the school.

🔄 steadfast

superfluous
/suːˈpɜːrfluəs/

📝 *adj.* 多余的 beyond what is needed : not necessary

📖 She gave him such a curt look that any form of apology would have been ***superfluous***.

uncertainty
/ʌnˈsɜːrtnti/

📝 *n.* 不确定，不可靠 something that is doubtful or unknown : something that is uncertain

📖 Her eyes widened with fear and ***uncertainty*** as she gingerly approached the creaking door.

cautious
/ˈkɔːʃəs/

📝 *adj.* 小心谨慎的 careful about avoiding danger or risk

📖 Having been let down by previous business partners, James has learnt to be ***cautious*** when choosing new members to join his team.

🔄 guarded

□ precursor   □ civil   □ peaceable   □ unfaltering   □ superfluous
□ uncertainty   □ cautious

音频

cater
/ˈkeɪtər/

v. 迎合 to supply what is required or desired

Catering to the tourist crowd, the Dutch restaurant offered menus in several different languages.

clot
/klɑːt/

v. 凝固结块 to become thick and partly solid

When the blood **clotted**, it was no longer necessary to place a bandage over the wound because the blood flow was already stanched.

elate
/iˈleɪt/

v. 使兴奋，使高兴 to make (someone) very happy and excited

Elated by my acceptance to Harvard, I invited my friends over for a congratulatory party.

delight

avert
/əˈvɜrt/

v. 阻止 to prevent (something bad) from happening

The car accident was fortunately **averted** due to the driver's fast thinking and quick reaction time.

forestall

fad
/fæd/

n. 一时流行的事物 a fashion that is taken up with great enthusiasm for a brief period of time; a craze

I wonder if the paleo diet is a temporary **fad**, or a long-term shift in the way people choose to eat?

faddish (adj. 时髦的)

ape
/eɪp/

v. （笨拙的）模仿 to imitate or mimic in an inept way

Aping the sound of the dog, the infant barked at all passers-by.

irk
/ɜːrk/

v. 使…厌烦 to annoy

The musician hoped to get exposure by playing a set at the coffeeshop, but he just seemed to **irk** the people there trying to study.

irksome (adj. 烦人的)

ebb
/eb/

v. 衰落 to reduce in intensity

Opposition to the war never went away; it just **ebbed** as the amount of active troops was cut.

declining, waning

v. 退潮 to fall back from the flood stage

During the hurricane, the high waters **ebbed** just enough so that stranded citizens could be rescued.

yen
/jen/

释 *n.* （强烈的）渴望 a strong desire or propensity
例 A *yen* for smoked meat amongst Southerners has created a booming market for BBQ businesses in the South.
选 craving, longing

opt
/ɑːpt/

释 *v.* 选择 to make a choice
例 Jerry *opted* to move to China because he wanted to learn Chinese.
派 option（*n.* 选择）

curb
/kɜːrb/

释 *v.* 限制，控制 to check, restrain, or control
例 European economic development has been *curbed* by the 2008 crisis, which limited trade opportunities, as well as all other kinds of economic endeavors.

释 *n.* 限制 something that checks or restrains
例 Demarcating the side of the road and directing rain water, the *curb* is a common sight on the side of US roads.

curt
/kɜːrt/

释 *adj.* 语言简练的 sparing of words
例 We knew that the university president's *curt* email was due to his busy schedule rather than dismissiveness.
选 terse, taciturn, laconic

释 *adj.* 说话简短而粗鲁的 rudely brief or abrupt in speech
例 Upset by poor service, James gave *curt*, one-word responses to the customer service rep's questions.

snag
/snæg/

释 *n.* 故障，问题 an unexpected problem or difficulty
例 Our travel plans hit a *snag* when our connecting flight to Belgium was delayed.
选 hitch

glut
/glʌt/

释 *n.* 过量 an excessive quantity
例 There was a *glut* of food at the Christmas party, with not one dish empty by the end of the evening.
选 plethora, surfeit
反 dearth

释 *v.* 暴饮暴食 to fill, especially with food, to satiety
例 *Glutted* with pie, I could barely get off the couch.
派 gluttonous（*adj.* 贪婪的，贪吃的）

woo
/wuː/

释 *v.* 吸引 to try to attract
例 After being *wooed* with free cars and parties, I decided to accept the position at the hedge fund.

coax
/koʊks/

释 *v.* 诱骗 to influence or gently urge by caressing or flattering
例 The teacher *coaxed* his students into doing extra work for the project assigned.
选 cajole

bent
/bent/

adj. 有倾向的 strongly inclined

例 It was not surprising that Isaac's first novel dealt with aliens and future technology as he has been naturally **bent** towards science fiction since he was a boy.

n. 才能，爱好 a special inclination or capacity

例 John decided to pursue analytic philosophy as his major given his **bent** in logical thinking and deduction.

balk
/bɔːk/

v. （突然地）拒绝 to refuse abruptly

例 Since Qing was used to public speaking, she did not **balk** when asked to take the microphone and voice the concerns on behalf of all the parents.

avid
/'ævɪd/

adj. 非常渴望的，贪婪的 desirous to the point of greed

例 The young businessman was **avid** for success and had put aside all commitments that would not lend themselves to furthering his financial aims.

反 indifferent

agog
/ə'gɑːg/

adj. 急切渴望的 full of intense interest or excitement

例 I was **agog** with excitement when I discovered that my favorite band was coming to town.

tout
/taʊt/

v. 兜售 to promote or praise energetically

例 While drug manufacturers **tout** the supposed advantages of their proprietary brands, generic versions of the same medications often work just as well.

选 peddle

反 cast aspersion on

choke
/tʃoʊk/

v. 抑制 to check or hinder the growth, development, or activity of

例 The merger between the world's two largest brewers could stifle consumer choice and **choke** off America's beer renaissance.

选 strangle, suffocate

erect
/i'rekt/

adj. 笔直的 straight up and down

例 Sitting **erect** in his chair, Mike seemed professional and confident in his job interview.

awry
/ə'raɪ/

adj. 错误的 away from the correct course

例 The robot was designed to dance on command, but its electrical circuits went **awry** and smoke came out of its ears.

quip
/kwɪp/

n. 机智幽默的评论 a clever, witty remark

例 Always with a clever **quip** at hand, Hector was the life of the dinner party by bringing humor and fun.

aver
/ə'vɜːr/

v. 断言 to say (something) in a very strong and definite way

例 Because he said it so confidently, I did not argue with Jon when he **averred** that a Ford car holds the speed record, even though I did not believe it.

选 assert

反 deny

□ bent   □ balk   □ avid   □ agog   □ tout
□ choke   □ erect   □ awry   □ quip   □ aver

quash
/kwɑːʃ/

释 *v.* 废止，使无效 to annul or put an end to
例 After the commercial disaster, Microsoft *quashed* the Zune and no longer sold it.

释 *v.* 镇压，平息 to suppress or extinguish completely
例 *Quashing* the rebellion, the king put to death all the plotters against his rule.

glib
/glɪb/

释 *adj.* 即兴的 performed with a natural, offhand ease
例 When asked about the causes of the widening income gap in the city, the mayor dismissed it with a *glib* comment and a wave of his hand.
反 labored

释 *adj.* 油嘴滑舌的 marked by ease and fluency in speaking or writing often to the point of being insincere or deceitful
例 Mary was concerned she would sound too *glib*, but in fact, she really cared for Jane and really valued her thoughts.

roil
/rɔɪl/

释 *v.* 使…混乱 to cause to be in a state of agitation or disorder
例 When the instant replay showed that the umpire made the incorrect call, the stadium *roiled* in anger at the injustice.

rant
/rænt/

释 *v.* 辱骂 to speak or write in an angry or emotionally charged manner
例 Adam Carolla is famous for being able to *rant* angrily on almost any topic on his podcast.
选 diatribe

lull
/lʌl/

释 *v.* 使平静 to cause to sleep or rest
例 The gentle rocking of the sea *lulled* me quietly to sleep.

释 *n.* 暂时的平静，间歇 a relatively calm interval
例 There is always a noticeable *lull* in the traffic in New York between 3:00 and 5:00 AM, during which one can drive quickly to any destination.
选 respite
反 increased activity

avow
/əˈvaʊ/

释 *v.* 承认 to acknowledge or declare openly and unashamedly
例 *Avowing* his intent for revenge, Achilles entered the fray and decimated his Trojan opponents.

trio
/ˈtriːəʊ/

释 *n.* 三足鼎立，三个一组 a group of three
例 *The Three Musketeers* are a paradigmatic *trio* of bantering fighters.

sage
/seɪdʒ/

释 *adj.* 智慧的 very wise
例 Taking the *sage* advice of the professor emeritus, I decided to change my dissertation to a more marketable topic.
派 sagacious (*adj.* 睿智的，精明的)

释 *n.* 智者 one distinguished for wisdom
例 In hunter-gatherer societies, the oldest person is often a venerated *sage* who has accumulated vast amounts of knowledge that are valuable to the tribe.

248
□ quash   □ glib   □ roil   □ rant   □ lull
□ avow   □ trio   □ sage

lurk
/lɜːrk/

🈁 *v.* 潜藏 to exist unobserved or unsuspected
📝 I did not notice that the cat was *lurking* behind me, and inadvertently stepped on his tail when I took a step back.

🈁 *v.* 暗中行动 to move furtively
📝 *Lurking* in the shadows, Jack the Ripper would only come out unseen to kill his victims.

hoax
/hoʊks/

🈁 *v.* 欺骗 to deceive or cheat
📝 He *hoaxed* the old woman into believing that she had won the lottery prize so that he could gain access to her bank account.

flit
/flɪt/

🈁 *v.* 快速移动 to move quickly from one condition or location to another
📝 A social butterfly, Cara *flitted* from one group to the next all evening at the party.
🈺 plod

apex
/'eɪpeks/

🈁 *n.* 最高点，顶峰 the highest point or the highest level
📝 Since Laura is at the *apex* of the engineering profession, she is in demand by all architecture firms in the country.

spur
/spɜːr/

🈁 *v.* 刺激 to incite or stimulate
📝 Frances Keller's 1904 expose of abuses of immigrants by employers *spurred* the Progressive Party to work toward legislation to fix the situation.
🈺 foster

scant
/skænt/

🈁 *adj.* 稀缺的 inadequately supplied
📝 With water in *scant* supply, the shipwrecked crew grew quite desperate concerning their hopes of survival.
🈺 limited
🈺 profuse

abhor
/əb'hɔːr/

🈁 *v.* 厌恶 to dislike very much
📝 Like many unions, the United Steel workers *abhor* two-tier contracts as they are convinced these contracts sell out future generations and sow tensions between older and younger workers.
🈺 admire
🈺 abhorrent（*adj.* 令人厌烦）

prone
/proʊn/

🈁 *adj.* 有倾向的 having a tendency or inclination
📝 Women are obviously more *prone* to getting breast cancer than men are.

usurp
/juː'zɜːrp/

🈁 *v.* 篡夺 to seize and hold in possession by force without right
📝 The Ottoman Empire *usurped* the Byzantine Empire in 1453 when the army of the Ottoman empire entered the Byzantine Capital and conquered it.
🈺 abdicate

☐ lurk ☐ hoax ☐ flit ☐ apex ☐ spur
☐ scant ☐ abhor ☐ prone ☐ usurp
249

pithy
/ˈpɪθi/

■ *adj.* 简洁有力的 forceful and brief
■ Only three minutes long, Lincoln's Gettysburg Address is known to be one of the most powerful and *pithy* speeches delivered in history.
■ pith (*n.* 精髓，核心)

tonic
/ˈtɑːnɪk/

■ *adj.* 有益健康的 restorative or stimulating to health or well-being
■ A century ago, cocaine was regularly administered as a cure-all *tonic* drug for the middle and lower classes.
■ restorative

niche
/niːʃ/

■ *n.* 小众市场 a special area of demand for a product or service
■ By constructing a camera that can take detailed close-ups of objects, Nikon sold a device that filled a specialty photographic *niche*.

■ *n.* 称心如意的活动、工作等 a situation or activity specially suited to a person's interests, abilities, or nature
■ Although collecting wolverine carvings is a *niche*, it is quite lucrative for the two artisans who cater to it.

trite
/traɪt/

■ *adj.* 陈词滥调的 not evoking interest because of overuse or repetition
■ That the Earth revolves around the Sun might now seem obvious and *trite*, but when Galileo thought of it, few believed him.

stoic
/ˈstoʊɪk/

■ *adj.* 不以苦乐为意的，淡泊的 seemingly indifferent to or unaffected by pleasure or pain; impassive
■ Ever the *stoic* man, Stan seemed unperturbed by the sirens and excitement around him.

murky
/ˈmɜːrki/

■ *adj.* 昏暗的 dark or dim
■ Unnoticed by the swimmers, several great white sharks swam close by in the *murky* water.

■ *adj.* 难懂的，不清晰的 not clearly known, understood, or expressed
■ Without forensic evidence or footage, the precise happenings of the crime will always remain *murky*.

blunt
/blʌnt/

■ *adj.* 直率的 abrupt and often disconcertingly frank in speech
■ Jerry is always very *blunt*, speaking the first things that come to his mind.

■ *adj.* 反应迟钝的 obtuse in understanding or discernment
■ With his text rejected by the publisher, the graduate student worked to clarify his *blunt* text and argumentation.

■ *adj.* 钝的，不锋利的 having a dull edge or end; not sharp
■ It is difficult to cut vegetables easily with a *blunt* knife.

flout
/flaʊt/

■ *v.* 蔑视，鄙视 to treat with contemptuous disregard
■ Jacob constantly *flouted* the law, such as driving without wearing a seatbelt while drinking a gin and tonic.
■ disregard, defy

□ pithy   □ tonic   □ niche   □ trite   □ stoic
□ murky   □ blunt   □ flout

rue /ruː/	**n. 后悔** regret, sorrow 例 Knowing that it was the last episode, fans of *The Wire* felt **rue** upon watching the series finale.
rote /rəʊt/	**n. 死记硬背** the use of memory usually with little intelligence 例 The more familiar you are with the terminology, the less you'll have to rely on **rote** memorization after you enter medical school.
dire /'daɪər/	**adj. 可怕的，严重的** very bad; causing great fear or worry 例 The family gathered around the bedside of Grandma the moment doctors warned us of her situation getting progressively **dire**.
snob /snɑːb/	**n. 势利小人** someone who tends to criticize, reject, or ignore people who come from a lower social class, have less education, etc. 例 In the court of popular opinion, all writers are guilty of being **snobs** until proved innocent.
shun /ʃʌn/	**v. 躲避** to avoid 例 Native American potters often **shun** the shortcuts offered by modern technology (such as the use of commercial clay, pigments, or kiln firing), instead adhering to the traditional methods of their ancestors. 选 eschew 反 seek
idle /'aɪdl/	**adj. 空闲的** not working, active, or being used 例 Having been **idle** for months after the car accident, Aaron could only run a mile on his first day of training. 反 active **adj. 没有价值的** having no value, use, or significance 例 Despite being an **idle** trinket, the thimble was a reminder of Sally's grandmother and her love of sewing.
crass /kræs/	**adj. 粗鲁的** so crude and unrefined as to be lacking in discrimination and sensibility 例 Use of **crass** language is not permitted in the school by teachers or students. 反 refined **adj. （用于贬义词加强语气的）非常的** used as a pejorative intensifier 例 He had removed her from that **crass** monied Middle Atlantic society where she had seemed stilted and fragile.

apt
/æpt/

adj. 合适的 exactly suitable

The place name for the town of Peculiar, Missouri, does not seem evidently **apt** since there is nothing particularly odd about it.

adj. 有倾向的 having a natural tendency

Apt with musical instruments, Chuck did not need to practice to be the best saxophonist in his high school.

adj. 聪明的，灵巧的 quick to learn or understand

In only two weeks, the **apt** student managed to grasp all the concepts of organic chemistry.

---

hone
/hoʊn/

v. 磨炼（技能）to perfect or make more intense or effective

According to some political analysts, the candidate's occasionally rambling responses to questions suggest that her debating skills need to be **honed**.

近 enhance

反 blunt

---

veto
/ˈviːtoʊ/

v. 否决 to reject (a proposed law) officially

The mayor there is currently deciding whether to sign or **veto** that bill.

---

blur
/blɜːr/

v. 使…模糊不清 to make (something) unclear or difficult to see or remember

The drama was so close to reality that the lines between fiction and reality were almost entirely **blurred**.

---

verge
/vɜːrdʒ/

n. 边缘 an area along the edge of a road, path, etc.

While mountain biking, Ryan's tire hit a rock and he fell over the **verge** and into the wilderness.

n. 临界点 brink or threshold

After taking a wrong turn in New York City, we knew that the rough neighborhood we entered had put us on the **verge** of danger.

---

swift
/swɪft/

adj. 快速的 happening or done quickly or immediately

Apple Pay launched in the UK last summer, and made relatively **swift** progress adding banks.

adj. 反应灵敏的 smart or intelligent

As a world chess champion, Gary Kasparov was known for his **swift** and strategic moves.

---

sever
/ˈsevər/

v. 打碎，分裂 to divide into parts

In order to share the pie between the group, it was necessary to **sever** it into six equal pieces.

v. 切掉 to cut off (a part) from a whole

In the movie *127 Hours*, the main character had to **sever** his own arm with a knife after being trapped in a rocky crevice.

□ apt □ hone □ veto □ blur □ verge □ swift □ sever

extol /ɪkˈstoʊl/	🔹 *v.* 赞美 to praise highly 🔹 Act according to your company values, treat customers well and do good in the world, and you will have a following *extolling* your virtues.
exalt /ɪgˈzɔːlt/	🔹 *v.* 赞美 to praise, or honor 🔹 The nominee's speech *exalted* the president's policies to reduce poverty and income inequalities. 🔹 valorize 🔹 *v.* 提升 to raise in rank, character, or status 🔹 *Exalted* by the queen, Sir Elton John now holds a knighthood in the UK.
tweak /twiːk/	🔹 *v.* 拧 to twist sharply 🔹 When I lost control of the horse, its jerking *tweaked* the arm that held the reins. 🔹 *v.* 略微调整 to make usually small adjustments in 🔹 "All we have to do is *tweak* the code to get the final bugs out of the program," the computer programmer said to his team.
verve /vɜːrv/	🔹 *n.* 热情, 活力 great energy and enthusiasm 🔹 Isabel Allende invokes the spirit of her family with *verve*, recreating lively incidents with prose that is vital and exuberant.
coy /kɔɪ/	🔹 *adj.* 腼腆的 having a shy or sweetly innocent quality 🔹 Playing *coy* and hard to get, Ann tried not to show her true affection for Bruce. 🔹 *adj.* 含糊其辞的 showing reluctance to make a definite commitment 🔹 Alex Rodriquez was *coy* about the Yankees' offer so that he could try to shop for more lucrative contracts elsewhere. 🔹 frank
whit /wɪt/	🔹 *n.* 少量 a very small amount 🔹 I opened the rubber cement jar, but it was dried up with not a *whit* of liquid left inside.
pine /paɪn/	🔹 *v.* 渴望 to yearn intensely and persistently especially for something unattainable 🔹 After being deprived for months in Europe, Kyle *pined* for a good American cheeseburger. 🔹 *v.* 憔悴 to become thin and weak because of sadness or loss 🔹 Juliet *pined* so much for her Romeo that she was only a shell of her former self.
demur /dɪˈmɜːr/	🔹 *v.* 反对 to voice opposition; object 🔹 When evidence is conjectural, reasonable people may *demur*, but when firm scientific proof has been supplied, they should reconsider their opposition.

belie
/bɪˈlaɪ/

释 *v.* 掩盖 to give a false impression of
例 Jessica's smile *belied* her sorrow, hiding her feelings from everyone except those who knew her best.

释 *v.* 与…相矛盾 to run counter to
例 The infidelity and lying of the preacher *belied* his profession as a representative of God.
选 contradict

释 *v.* 证明…为假 to show (something) to be false or wrong
例 Although Adam stated that he was an expert in ancient Egyptian art, his inability to identify depictions of Akhenaten *belied* his claims.
反 aver

spike
/spaɪk/

释 *v.* （短期大幅）上升 to increase greatly in a short period of time
例 During the summer months, the use of electricity *spikes* in Florida with the increased use of air conditioning.

quell
/kwel/

释 *v.* 压制，镇压 to end or stop (something) usually by using force
例 The controversial tax fueled a sustained uprising that could not be *quelled* by the Prime Minister's impassioned speeches.
反 ferment

vapid
/ˈvæpɪd/

释 *adj.* 无聊的 lacking liveliness
例 Put off by her *vapid* date, Zelda left dinner early to meet her friends for drinks and a fun evening.
选 jejune

venal
/ˈviːnl/

释 *adj.* 贪污的 open to bribery
例 Accused of stealing taxpayers' money, the state legislators were condemned for their *venal* behavior.

hitch
/hɪtʃ/

释 *n.* （隐形的）问题，难题 a hidden problem that makes something more complicated or difficult to do
例 Upon learning of the *hitch* in our plan—that no one in our group had an international driver's license—we were forced to take the train.
选 snag

rebut
/rɪˈbʌt/

释 *v.* 驳斥 to refute by offering opposing evidence or arguments
例 The candidate *rebutted* the media's charge of political inexperience by citing his broad background in both local and state government.

delve
/delv/

释 *v.* 搜寻，挖掘 to search deeply and laboriously
例 After hearing about a big corruption case, several journalists of the *New York Times* decided to *delve* deeper into the issue and discover all there is to know about the people involved.

释 *v.* 深入探讨 to discuss or explain a subject in detail
例 With the rise of the internet, it is easy to *delve* into any subject or interest.

totem
/ˈtoʊtəm/

圉 *n.* 标志，象征 a venerated emblem or symbol
例 Ray Treacy was regarded as a ***totem*** in sport and many reacted to his passing with great sadness.
派 totemic（*adj.* 图腾的）

edify
/ˈedɪfaɪ/

圉 *v.* 启迪 to instruct especially so as to encourage intellectual, moral, or spiritual improvement
例 Ines and Juanita were much ***edified*** by the inspiring sermon delivered by the new pastor.

grip
/ɡrɪp/

圉 *v.* 吸引 to get and hold the interest or attention of (someone)
例 Film *Noir* manages to ***grip*** the audience's attention through great suspense, absorbing drama and stinging social comment.

crave
/kreɪv/

圉 *v.* 极度渴望 to have a very strong desire for (something)
例 Acupuncture can affect your mindset such that you no longer ***crave*** unhealthy food and are more inclined to make healthier food choices.
派 craving（*n.* 渴望）

mimic
/ˈmɪmɪk/

圉 *v.* 模仿 to imitate or copy
例 Young painters in the seventeenth century usually ***mimicked*** the masters before they attempted to fashion their own style.
近 camouflage, replicate
派 mimicry（*n.* 模仿）

gauge
/ɡeɪdʒ/

圉 *v.* 评估，判断，衡量 to evaluate or estimate
例 The ballet teacher could ***gauge*** how much potential a dancer had after watching him or her for a few seconds.
近 reckon

deter
/dɪˈtɜːr/

圉 *v.* 阻止 to prevent (something) from happening
例 The police officers tried to ***deter*** the juvenile delinquent from ever stealing again by warning him of all the consequences that would result if he did not stop his bad behavior.
近 constrain

bogus
/ˈboʊɡəs/

圉 *adj.* 假的 not real or genuine
例 When we took the painting to the appraiser, we were shocked to learn that it was a ***bogus*** Picasso and worthless.

cloak
/kloʊk/

圉 *v.* 伪装，掩盖 to hide or disguise
例 ***Cloaked*** by dark shadows, the ninja moved stealthily and unseen.

aloof
/əˈluːf/

圉 *adj.* 冷漠的，疏远的 removed or distant either physically or emotionally
例 After the breakup with her boyfriend, Krissy was ***aloof*** and distant in social situations.

akin
/əˈkɪn/

圉 *adj.* 相似的，相关的 essentially similar, related, or compatible
例 Although the bright pink birds seem ***akin*** to the ones we usually see in the park, they are in reality two separate species.

☐ totem ☐ edify ☐ grip ☐ crave ☐ mimic
☐ gauge ☐ deter ☐ bogus ☐ cloak ☐ aloof
☐ akin

croon /kruːn/	释 *v.* 低吟浅唱 to sing in a low soft voice 例 Vivien swooned when her lover ***crooned*** Frank Sinatra in her ear. 选 warble
bland /blænd/	释 *adj.* 无聊的 dull or insipid 例 Upon seeing the ***bland*** apartment, we immediately rejected it as a future home because it lacked any character or architectural appeal. 选 insipid 释 *adj.* 温和的 pleasant in manner 例 The orchestral composition was a ***bland*** piece that made for a relaxing concert.
surly /'sɜːrli/	释 *adj.* 傲慢的，粗暴的 sullenly ill-humored; gruff 例 Sarah is always ***surly*** when she does not get enough sleep, and drives people away by snapping at them. 选 sullen
probe /proʊb/	释 *v.* 仔细调查 to search into and explore very thoroughly 例 After the accusations of tax fraud, the FBI and IRS ***probed*** into the financial accounts of Al Capone.
hoard /hɔːrd/	释 *v.* 贮藏 to collect and hide a large amount of 例 After reports came out of a broken gas pipeline, people began ***hoarding*** gas out of fear that the city would run out.
sap /sæp/	释 *n.* 活力 vitality 例 The ***sap*** of any government is the social contract between the people and the institutions. 释 *v.* 使…失去活力 to deplete or weaken gradually 例 The oppressive heat ***sapped*** all of my strength and I was unable to work in the garden.
rive /raɪv/	释 *v.* 劈开 to divide into pieces 例 Heresy and schism are not restricted to theologians: science also has its share of fields that are ***riven*** by sectarianism.
riot /'raɪət/	释 *n.* 暴乱 a situation in which a large group of people behave in a violent and uncontrolled way 例 When Nero cut off the supply of free bread, the Roman citizens took to the streets in a violent ***riot***.
glum /glʌm/	释 *adj.* 悲伤的 sad or depressed 例 ***Glum*** about the death of his beloved dog, Jim could barely get out of bed.

☐ croon   ☐ bland   ☐ surly   ☐ probe   ☐ hoard
☐ sap   ☐ rive   ☐ riot   ☐ glum

whet
/wet/

>>> **v.** 削尖 to make sharper or stronger
例 A bite of the free bread was enough to **whet** my appetite for the remaining three courses of the dinner.

>>> **v.** 使…更灵敏 to make keen or more acute
例 Many blind people say that their other senses are **whetted** to complement the lack of vision.

plod
/plɑːd/

>>> **v.** （勤奋而单调地）工作 to work laboriously and monotonously
例 After **plodding** through my days at the office for a year, I decided to quit and run a marathon.
近 slog
反 gambol

>>> **v.** （缓慢或无聊地）进行 to proceed slowly or tediously
例 With the heavy rains, the French army could only **plod** through the muddy fields en route to Russia.

gloat
/gloʊt/

>>> **v.** 洋洋自得，幸灾乐祸 to show pride in an improper or selfish way
例 Though proud to win the game, Cody was careful not to **gloat** lest he appear too self-satisfied.

loath
/loʊθ/

>>> **adj.** 不情愿的 unwilling to do something
例 **Loath** to go running, I decided to take a nice walk instead.
近 reluctant, disinclined

chic
/ʃiːk/

>>> **adj.** 时尚的 fashionable style
例 Making soup stock from bones was once an old-fashioned pursuit, but it has become downright **chic**.
近 elegant

sham
/ʃæm/

>>> **adj.** 虚假的 not genuine
例 It was clearly a **sham** magician act as the ears of the rabbit were sticking out of the hat before the trick even began.

don
/dɑːn/

>>> **v.** 穿上 to put on
例 **Donning** his jacket, Shep walked into the cold outdoors to begin to work on his farm.

oust
/aʊst/

>>> **v.** 驱逐 to cause or force to leave a position
例 The corporation's board of directors took action and **ousted** the chief executive when it became clear that his performance would never improve.
近 expel, banish

>>> **v.** 取代 to take the place of
例 In 2008, Barack Obama **ousted** George Bush as president of the USA.

sift
/sɪft/

>>> **v.** 分离，筛选 to separate or remove
例 A book reviewer should **sift** an author's useful and thought-provoking observations from the useless and tedious.

expel /ɪkˈspel/	释 *v.* 驱逐 to officially force (someone) to leave a place or organization
	例 After Madison was caught cheating on her exam, the university *expelled* her from the school and escorted her off campus.
	近 oust, banish
loose /luːs/	释 *adj.* 松弛的 not tightly fastened, attached or held
	例 With the rapid weight loss, Chet's clothes were too *loose* to wear any more.
	派 loosen (*v.* 解开，放宽)
adept /ˈædept/	释 *adj.* 精通的 very good at doing something hard
	例 An *adept* writer, Bill could write a compelling newspaper article in only twenty minutes.
	近 proficient
lapse /læps/	释 *v.* 停止 to go out of existence
	例 Charlie's gym membership *lapsed* after a year, so he had to renew it for another year by paying a fee.
	释 *n.* 疏忽大意 a slight error usually caused by lack of attention or forgetfulness
	例 "The single instance in which I shared company secrets was a simple *lapse* of judgement rather than a pattern of immorality," Rich said.
guile /gaɪl/	释 *n.* 欺骗 deceitful cunning
	例 With great *guile*, the pickpocket distracted the tourist so that he could steal her purse.
	近 deviousness
	派 guileless (*adj.* 诚实的)
decay /dɪˈkeɪ/	释 *v.* 衰退 to decline in health, strength, or vigor
	例 After years of being left in the rain, the wooden box *decayed* to a state of near nothingness.
	近 deterioration
sloth /sloʊθ/	释 *n.* 懒惰 the quality of being lazy
	例 A couch potato is another way to describe a person overcome with *sloth* and who has little motivation to be active.
dwarf /dwɔːrf/	释 *v.* 使…变得矮小或不重要 to cause to appear smaller or to seem inferior
	例 People who are both innovative and diligent will be the new elite, and their financial achievements will *dwarf* those of today's elite.
deify /ˈdeɪɪfaɪ/	释 *v.* 奉…为神，尊敬 to treat (someone or something) like a god or goddess
	例 *Deifying* her supervisor, Janice defended his research to anyone who disagreed with his interpretations.
hoary /ˈhɔːri/	释 *adj.* 老掉牙的 extremely old
	例 The *hoary* old pine has stood as a symbol of the university since it was founded many years ago.

□ expel　　　□ loose　　　□ adept　　　□ lapse　　　□ guile
□ decay　　　□ sloth　　　□ dwarf　　　□ deify　　　□ hoary

pique
/piːk/

释 *v.* 激怒，惹怒 to make someone annoyed or angry
例 ***Piqued*** by the mean responses to my forum post, I vowed never to share my opinions online again.
派 piquant（*adj.* 刺激的，迷人的）

hubris
/ˈhjuːbrɪs/

释 *n.* 自大，傲慢 exaggerated pride or self-confidence
例 The ***hubris*** of Oedipus is clear in his assumption that he could not be responsible for the plague on the city.
选 arrogant

hew
/hjuː/

释 *v.* 遵守 to conform to or adhere
例 When a journalist always ***hews*** to the talking points of their favored party, people become suspicious that they are getting article ideas from the campaign.
选 conform

释 *v.* 砍树 to cut down (a tree)
例 The ax handle was ***hewn*** from a sturdy old pine and had lasted for generations.

tilt
/tɪlt/

释 *v.* 倾斜 slant or bias
例 The photojournalist's new book on contemporary African American life is ***tilted*** toward celebratory images, as opposed to images of suffering.
选 list

feat
/fiːt/

释 *n.*（彰显技艺等的）成就 an act or achievement that shows courage, strength, or skill
例 Magician Harry Houdini performed ***feats*** of escape so astounding that he became legendary.

marvel
/ˈmɑːrvl/

释 *v.* 震惊，惊讶 to feel great surprise, wonder, or admiration
例 Having never been to New York, we ***marveled*** at the stunning sight of the Empire State Building and the mass of skyscrapers.

释 *n.* 惊世之作 one that causes wonder or astonishment
例 Michelangelo's Laocoon is a statue that is a true ***marvel*** to admire.

leak
/liːk/

释 *v.* 泄漏信息 to give out (information) surreptitiously
例 WikiLeaks ***leaked*** the classified documents that suggested the US officials falsified information during the Iraqi War.
派 leakage（*n.* 泄露）

guild
/gɪld/

释 *n.* 协会 an organized group of people who have joined together because they share the same job or interest
例 By forming a ***guild***, the coopers were able to protect their own interests and collectively raise prices on barrels.

slur
/slɜːr/

📖 *n.* 诽谤 an insulting or disparaging remark or innuendo

例 The White House has faced tough questioning over comedian Larry Wilmore's use of a taboo racial **slur** at its annual correspondents' dinner.

选 aspersion

反 flattery

📖 *v.* 含糊不清地说 to slide or slip over without due mention, consideration, or emphasis

例 She was understandably outraged as her contributions were all **slurred** over in the annual report that her employer submitted to the company.

反 pronounce clearly

cede
/siːd/

📖 *v.* 割让 to give control of (something) to another person, group, government, etc.

例 The author aimed to show that many of the questions traditionally debated among philosophers can be **ceded** to the realm of scientific research.

shrill
/ʃrɪl/

📖 *v.* 尖叫 to utter in a shrill manner; scream

例 Lucy **shrilled** in horror when the rat ran over her feet and even paused briefly on her toe.

skim
/skɪm/

📖 *v.* 浏览 to read or glance through (a book, for example) quickly or superficially

例 While **skimming** through the ESPN magazine, I only stopped to read the pieces on college football.

wilt
/wɪlt/

📖 *v.* 萎蔫，衰弱 to lose energy, confidence, effectiveness, etc.

例 In the harsh summer heat, all of us gardeners **wilted** and lost our energy.

mete
/miːt/

📖 *v.* 分配 to distribute as deserved

例 During the mass trial for treason, the judge **meted** out sentences to each of the conspirators.

spunk
/spʌŋk/

📖 *n.* 勇气 spirit, courage, and determination

例 Holly was selected as camp counselor for her **spunk** that helped to energize everyone else in the room.

cinch
/sɪntʃ/

📖 *n.* 容易的事 something that is very easy to do

例 If we could just agree on who is invited to our party, sending out the invitations would be a **cinch**.

backwater /'bækwɔːtər/	释 *n.* 停滞或落后的地方 a place or situation regarded as isolated, stagnant, or backward 例 Lacking any bookstores, theaters or culture of any kind, the town I am from could be described as a ***backwater***.
moonshine /'muːnʃaɪn/	释 *n.* 空话，假话 empty talk; foolish or untrue words 例 Jon's threats of revenge were ***moonshine*** that no one took seriously.
brainchild /'breɪntʃaɪld/	释 *n.* （辛苦劳动的）成果，结晶 a product of one's creative effort 例 Cartoon detective Dick Tracy is the ***brainchild*** of Chester Gould, who created this comic strip hero in 1931.
deadpan /'dedpæn/	释 *adj.* 面无表情的 impassively matter-of-fact, as in style, behavior, or expression 例 It was no wonder that half the audience was asleep by the time she had finished delivering her speech with such ***deadpan*** fervor. 释 *adj.* 以面无表情的方式来传递幽默的 sounding and looking completely serious when you are saying or doing something funny 例 With his ***deadpan*** humor, it was sometimes difficult to tell whether Rich was serious or kidding.
sidestep /'saɪdstep/	释 *v.* 回避，绕过 bypass, evade 例 Postponing the court hearing temporarily ***sidesteps*** what has become a bitter clash with the world's most valuable company. 近 circumvent 反 confront directly
upshot /'ʌpʃɑːt/	释 *n.* 结局 the final result 例 While cooking, the pasta sauce seemed like a disaster, but the ***upshot*** was quite tasty.
upbeat /'ʌpbiːt/	释 *adj.* 积极乐观的，愉快的 positive and cheerful 例 Always ***upbeat***, Kris could turn almost any negative situation into a fun experience.

downsize
/ˈdaʊnsaɪz/

释 *v.* 缩小 to reduce in size
例 As empty-nesters, the middle-aged couple **downsized** their family car from a minivan to a sedan.

释 *v.* 裁员 to fire (employees) for the purpose of downsizing a business
例 With the recent economic crisis, many large companies were forced to **downsize** by laying off employees.

impressionable
/ɪmˈpreʃənəbl/

释 *adj.* 易受影响的 easy to influence
例 My favorite Harrison novels remain his early ones: I read them at an **impressionable** age, and they mean a lot to me.

personable
/ˈpɜːrsənəbl/

释 *adj.* 品貌兼优的 pleasant or amiable in person
例 Although Shannon often preferred to be alone, she was quite **personable** and outgoing in social situations.

inviting
/ɪnˈvaɪtɪŋ/

释 *adj.* 吸引人的 attractive
例 The small cottage had an **inviting** appearance that made me want to buy it immediately.

liken
/ˈlaɪkən/

释 *v.* 比较 compare
例 Some people are often **likened** to celebrities, but I do not look like any movie star.

wholesale
/ˈhoʊlseɪl/

释 *adj.* 大规模的 affecting large numbers of people or things
例 Hurricane Katrina caused the **wholesale** destruction of many of the city's wards, but the French Quarter remained largely intact.

wholesome
/ˈhoʊlsəm/

释 *adj.* 有益健康的 promoting health of body
例 Everyone should pursue a healthy lifestyle of **wholesome** food and daily exercise.

romanticize
/roʊˈmæntɪsaɪz/

释 *v.* 理想化 to think about or describe something as being better or more attractive or interesting than it really is
例 As the countryside was increasingly perceived to be under threat, people in cities **romanticized** the rural landscape as a moral and healthy antidote to urban life.
近 idealized

defining
/dɪˈfaɪnɪŋ/

释 *adj.* 非常重要的 critically important
例 Professor Jenkins's urban history course was a **defining** moment in my life because it made me realize I want to become a social worker.

telling
/ˈtelɪŋ/

释 *adj.* 有说服力的，有影响力的 carrying great weight and producing a marked effect
例 The near unanimous "election" of the dictator was **telling** of the large extent to which the election was rigged.

dour
/ˈdaʊər/

释 *adj.* 严肃的，阴郁的 gloomy, sullen
例 With the **dour** expression on Kristen's face, few thought she was welcoming or warm.

☐ downsize   ☐ impressionable   ☐ personable   ☐ inviting   ☐ liken
☐ wholesale   ☐ wholesome   ☐ romanticize   ☐ defining   ☐ telling
☐ dour

teem /tiːm/	释 **v.** 充满 to become filled to overflowing 例 For people **teeming** with hopes and dreams, the news that they have terminal cancer is impossible to accept.
backbone /ˈbækboʊn/	释 **n.** 支柱，支撑 the main support or major sustaining factor 例 The army will always remain the **backbone** of the armed forces as the most substantial fighting force.
pronounced /prəˈnaʊnst/	释 **adj.** 显著的，明显的 strongly marked 例 Neanderthals are distinguished by their **pronounced** jaw lines and robust bones.
calculated /ˈkælkjuleɪtɪd/	释 **adj.** 故意的，精打细算的 carefully planned for a particular and often improper purpose 例 It is no accident that most people find Davis' book disturbing, for it is **calculated** to undermine beliefs they have long cherished.
backfire /ˌbækˈfaɪər/	释 **v.** 事与愿违，起反作用 to have the reverse of the desired or expected effect 例 Given the recent news that a certain additive put in gasoline to reduce air pollution is actually contaminating groundwater, it comes as no surprise that many other well-intentioned fixes also **backfire**.
redoubtable /rɪˈdaʊtəbl/	释 **adj.** 令人肃然起敬的 causing or deserving great fear or respect 例 The **redoubtable** J.K. Rowling has become a literary icon after publishing the famous *Harry Pottery* series. 反 unimpressive
gridlock /ˈgrɪdlaːk/	释 **n.** 交通堵塞 a situation in which streets are so full that vehicles cannot move 例 During rush hour, the **gridlock** in LA's streets make it impossible to return home in less than two hours. 释 **n.** 僵局 a situation in which no progress can be made 例 With the bipartisan bickering, no bills were able to pass through the **gridlock** in Congress.
bookish /ˈbʊkɪʃ/	释 **adj.** 书呆子气的 interested in reading books and studying as opposed to other pursuits 例 As a boy, Harry was a **bookish** lad who eschewed sports in favor of the library.
wanting /ˈwaːntɪŋ/	释 **adj.** 有缺陷的 not being up to standards or expectations 例 The high school football player was cut from the team because his athletic prowess was found to be **wanting**. 近 flawed 反 satisfactory 派 want（*n.* 贫困）

airtight
/ˈertaɪt/

释 *adj.* 密封的，不透气的 impermeable to air or nearly so
例 In order to preserve the leftovers in the fridge, it is best to keep the containers **airtight**.

释 *adj.* 无懈可击的 having no noticeable weakness, flaw or loophole
例 After the thieves spent years designing an **airtight** plan to steal the painting, the heist went off without a hitch.

lest
/lest/

释 *conj.* 唯恐 conj. for fear that
例 We should remember the 2008 economic crisis, **lest** we assume another recession can't happen.

streamline
/ˈstriːmlaɪn/

释 *v.* 简化 to make simpler or more efficient
例 In an effort to **streamline** her writing, Lauren attempted to eliminate the wordiness and make only points that were truly necessary.

释 *v.* 使现代化 to bring up to date
例 By downloading the newest update of Windows, the computer lab was finally **streamlined** to work with the newest software.

grandstand
/ˈɡrænstænd/

释 *adj.* 博眼球的 done for show or to impress on lookers
例 The **grandstand** dance before the end zone allowed the defender to catch up and knock the football out of the player's hand.

释 *v.* 赚取眼球 to play or act so as to impress onlookers
例 Nate publicly quit his job at Walmart in order to **grandstand** and tell off his boss in front of his friends.

foreboding
/fɔːrˈboʊdɪŋ/

释 *n.* 不祥的预感 a feeling that something bad is going to happen
例 After her conversation with the teacher, Bridget had a **foreboding** sense that she was about to be rejected from the science camp.

smother
/ˈsmʌðər/

释 *v.* 使…窒息 to kill someone by covering the face so that breathing is not possible
例 The murderer **smothered** his victim by placing a pillow on his face.

释 *v.* 遏制，阻止 to try to keep from happening
例 Learning that incriminating documents about his corrupt dealings would be released, the governor tried to **smother** the leak with bribes.

effortless
/ˈefərtləs/

释 *adj.* 不费力的 showing or requiring little or no effort
例 Playing simple songs like Canon in D has become rather **effortless** for Fanny after having learnt the piano for a decade.

discerning
/dɪˈsɜːrnɪŋ/

释 *adj.* 有洞察力的 showing insight and understanding
例 Despite disgusting many, foie gras is a delicacy and a delight for the **discerning** palate.
近 perceptive, insightful

(264)
□ airtight   □ lest   □ streamline   □ grandstand   □ foreboding
□ smother   □ effortless   □ discerning

rife /raɪf/	释 *adj.* 非常普遍的 prevalent especially to an increasing degree 例 It is necessary to pick through the beans because they are *rife* with small stones. 选 pervasive 反 sparse
girth /gɜːrθ/	释 *n.* 尺寸 size 例 The *girth* of the homegrown zucchini was such that it won the state fair! 释 *n.* 围长 a measure around a body 例 Although the sun is the most massive object in the solar system, its *girth* is modest compared to that of other celestial bodies.
hard-boiled /hɑːrd'bɔɪld/	释 *adj.* 强硬的，不动感情的 devoid of sentimentality; tough 例 The *hard-boiled* soldier, grizzled by war, could no longer share compassion with his wife.
spiteful /'spaɪtfl/	释 *adj.* 恶毒的 having or showing a desire to harm, anger, or defeat someone 例 Although Mingwei was very sarcastic at times, no one believed he was a *spiteful* person who wished to intentionally harm others.
forbear /fɔːr'ber/	释 *v.* 克制，忍耐 to control oneself when provoked 例 After years of meditation, the formerly quick-to-anger brute could now *forbear* to respond when someone insulted him.
wont /wɔːnt/	释 *adj.* 有…倾向的 inclined, apt 例 A lover of sweets, Gregg was *wont* to visit the chocolate store every day after work.
enjoin /ɪn'dʒɔɪn/	释 *v.* 禁止 to tell or urge someone to do something 例 Sheila ran a marathon for charity and *enjoined* her friends to pledge money. 选 proscribe
glean /gliːn/	释 *v.* 慢慢收集 to gather or collect in a gradual way 例 Even without looking up a word, you can sometimes *glean* its meaning by seeing it in context many times. 选 obtain
glisten /'glɪsn/	释 *v.* 表面闪烁光芒的 to shine with light reflected off a wet surface 例 The rower puffed out his cheeks and his brow *glistened* with sweat.
cleave /kliːv/	释 *v.* 忠诚于… to adhere firmly and closely or loyally and unwaveringly 例 Although Brandy's mother disapproved of her best friend Evan, she *cleaved* to him, saying she would always stay loyal. 释 *v.* 劈开 to split with sharp instrument 例 The butcher *cleaved* the pig's backbone in two.

undue /ˌʌnˈduː/	**adj.** 过量的 exceeding what is appropriate or normal 例 For many countries, the death penalty is an **undue** punishment for any crime. 选 excessive
qualm /kwɑːm/	**n.** 不安 an uneasy feeling about the propriety or rightness of a course of action 例 Xavier had no **qualms** about failing a student who never showed up for class. 选 misgiving
inestimable /ɪnˈestɪməbl/	**adj.** 无法估量的 impossible to estimate or compute 例 The vastness of the universe is **inestimable**. **adj.** 无价的 invaluable 例 The heirloom necklace had **inestimable** significance to the girl who inherited it from her grandmother.
mishap /ˈmɪshæp/	**n.** 不幸 an unfortunate accident 例 Although the family had a flat tire, the **mishap** did not delay their arrival to the mountain cabin by more than an hour.
brink /brɪŋk/	**n.** （事情发生的）边缘 the point at which something is likely to begin 例 With the assassination of Archduke Ferdinand, the world was at the **brink** of the first world war. **n.** （悬崖峭壁的）边缘 the upper edge of a steep or vertical slope 例 Many have an uneasy feeling of vertigo when standing at the **brink** of a cliff.
underpin /ˌʌndərˈpɪn/	**v.** 支持，支撑 to strengthen or support (something) from below 例 The belief that everyone in the working class is exploited in similar ways **underpins** socialist politics.
bleak /bliːk/	**adj.** 阴暗的，阴郁的 gloomy and somber 例 Mansfield's short stories present a **bleak** picture of life for women negotiating social restrictions in early twentieth-century England. **adj.** 寒冷的 cold and cutting 例 In the **bleak** winter, most want to curl up inside by a fireplace and read a book near the warm light. **adj.** 荒凉的，光秃秃的 unsheltered and barren 例 The **bleak** moor offers no protection from the wind for travelers walking across it.
whisk /wɪsk/	**v.** 迅速送走（人或事物） to move something or someone to another place nimbly and quickly 例 During their whirlwind romance, Mark **whisked** Carrie away to a small island in the Caribbean.

savvy
/'sævi/

adj. 有见识的 well-informed and perceptive

Everyone first brings their computer issues to their tech-***savvy*** friends before going to a customer service rep.

n. 知识和见识 practical understanding or knowledge of something

With his cooking ***savvy***, Wilson quit his job as an accountant to train to become a chef.

buoy
/bɔɪ/

v. 使浮起来 to keep afloat or aloft

Buoyed by the life vest, the ship's passengers floated in the ocean awaiting rescue.

v. 鼓励 to hearten or inspire

Despite having been fired recently, Cal was ***buoyed*** by a new job offer with twice the salary.

makeshift
/'meɪkʃɪft/

n. 权宜之计 a temporary or expedient substitute for something else

The WordPress blog page served as a ***makeshift*** until a professionally designed website could be completed.

adj. 权宜的，临时代用的 suitable as a temporary or expedient substitute

In the ***makeshift*** tent, the survivalists awaited the end of the storm before pressing on to the final checkpoint.

forthwith
/ˌfɔːrθ'wɪθ/

adj. 马上，立刻 without delay

In order to make the deadline, it is necessary to send the application ***forthwith*** to the HR department.

cornerstone
/'kɔːrnərstoʊn/

n. 重要的基石 an indispensable and fundamental basis

For many Americans, their faith serves as a ***cornerstone*** for their system of morals and ethics.

bedrock
/'bedrɑːk/

n. 根基 the very basis

The ***bedrock*** of any relationship is trust between the two parties.

foundation

resourceful
/rɪ'sɔːrsfl/

adj. 足智多谋的 able to act effectively or imaginatively, especially in difficult situations

Although many jobs will disappear or be downgraded, there are enormous opportunities for innovative and ***resourceful*** professionals.

appreciable
/ə'priːʃəbl/

adj. 可感知的，可衡量的 capable of being perceived or measured

Given that the boat docked to the Venice marine is of such ***appreciable*** size, it must belong to some important official or government figure.

sate
/seɪt/

v. 使…厌倦，使…腻烦 to cloy with overabundance

Our thirst for musicals was ***sated*** after a full week of watching musicals in London every night.

v. 使…满足 to appease by indulging to the full

We resolved not to return to the gelateria for another week after being ***sated*** by several scoops of our favorite ice cream.

stonewall
/'stoʊnwɔːl/

释 *v.* 拒绝合作 to refuse to comply or cooperate with
例 Disliking the band's album, the record executive **stonewalled** the release of the music until he could hire a new producer.

释 *v.* 采用拖延的战术 to engage in delaying tactics
例 Because he was running late for the meeting, Jeff asked his colleague to **stonewall** the clients until he could arrive.

involuntary
/ɪn'vɑːlənteri/

释 *adj.* 无意识的 not done or made consciously
例 When one cuts off the heads of chickens, they make many **involuntary** movements and sometimes run around the room.

astronomical
/ˌæstrə'nɑːmɪkl/

释 *adj.* 巨大的 immense
例 The US has spent an **astronomical** sum on defense and military expenditures since World War II.

释 *adj.* 天文的 of or relating to astronomy
例 Galileo's **astronomical** observations proved that the Earth moves around the sun.

misgiving
/ˌmɪs'gɪvɪŋ/

释 *n.* 不安 doubt, distrust, or apprehension
例 People are starting to have **misgivings** about internet-enabled appliances after learning they can be hacked.
近 trepidation, qualm

testy
/'testi/

释 *adj.* 易怒的 irritated, impatient, or exasperated
例 After not having slept all night, Harry was **testy** and impatient with anyone who did not respond to him immediately.
反 patient

categorical
/ˌkætə'gɔːrɪkl/

释 *adj.* 绝对的，坚定的 being without exception or qualification; absolute
例 A defining quality of all scientific laws is that their application to the entire universe must be **categorical**.

recollect
/ˌrekə'lekt/

释 *v.* 记忆 to remember something
例 In the story, Joseph **recollected** his childhood and his father's struggle with unemployment.

peerless
/'pɪrləs/

释 *adj.* 无与伦比的 being such as to have no match
例 The gigantic rollercoaster is **peerless** in its height, producing a record amount of G-forces.

proofread
/'pruːfriːd/

释 *v.* 校对 to read in order to find errors and mark corrections
例 Before turning in an essay, it is necessary to **proofread** it for any errors in grammar or spelling.

heartfelt
/'hɑːrtfelt/

释 *adj.* 真诚的 deeply or sincerely felt
例 Upon learning of her best friend's loss, Grace sent a **heartfelt** email in support.
近 sincere

☐ stonewall ☐ involuntary ☐ astronomical ☐ misgiving ☐ testy
☐ categorical ☐ recollect ☐ peerless ☐ proofread ☐ heartfelt

vainglorious /ˌveɪnˈɡlɔːriəs/	释 *adj.* 自负的，自命不凡的 excessively proud of oneself 例 The **vainglorious** soldier in Plautus' play believes all women adore him.
override /ˌoʊvərˈraɪd/	释 *v.* 否决，推翻 to make (something) no longer valid 例 West Virginia lawmakers **overrode** a governor's veto last month to pass a law. 释 *v.* 凌驾于，比…更重要 to have more importance or influence than (something) 例 The university's **overriding** concern is always the safety and well-being of its students.
hereabouts /ˌhɪrəˈbaʊts/	释 *adv.* 在附近 in this vicinity 例 "I forgot where I buried the money, but it is **hereabouts** of this tree," the prospector explained.
groundless /ˈɡraʊndləs/	释 *adj.* 毫无根据的 not based on facts 例 The conclusions of this paper are **groundless** since they are based on a trivial but critical misunderstanding. 选 unwarranted
uneventful /ˌʌnɪˈventfl/	释 *adj.* 平凡的，没有大事发生的 lacking in significant events 例 In his memoir, Dylan skipped over his **uneventful** childhood years and simply told readers about his 20s.
daredevil /ˈderdevl/	释 *adj.* 鲁莽的 recklessly and often ostentatiously daring 例 Evel Knievel was a **daredevil** motorcyclist who attempted to jump over the Grand Canyon.
incomparable /ɪnˈkɑːmprəbl/	释 *adj.* 无与伦比的 better than any other 例 The one-of-a-kind Pieta by Michelangelo is **incomparable** to all other statues, with its unique, realistic expression of emotion.
towering /ˈtaʊərɪŋ/	释 *adj.* 高大的 impressively high or great 例 Even for a basketball player, Yao Ming is a **towering** man who stands taller than anyone in a room. 释 *adj.* 强烈的 reaching a high point of intensity 例 J.D. Salinger was a **towering** luminary in the literary world, but a known recluse in his private life. 释 *adj.* 过度的 going beyond proper bounds 例 Do not fly into a **towering** rage because you lost your pen; just buy a new one.
slapdash /ˈslæpdæʃ/	释 *adj.* 草率的，粗心大意的 quick and careless 例 Having put the school assignment off to the last minute, Ricky made a **slapdash** facsimile of Charlemagne that was certain to give him a poor grade.

invaluable
/ɪnˈvæljuəbl/

adj. 极具价值的 extremely valuable or useful

For anyone spending time in the wilderness, a good knife is ***invaluable*** in order to collect firewood, whittle, prepare food, and conduct many other essential tasks.

slipshod
/ˈslɪpʃɑːd/

adj. 粗心大意的 very careless or poorly done or made

Mary was very ***slipshod*** when planning her wedding, which resulted in many mistakes occurring throughout the ceremony.

heartrending
/hɑːrtˌrendɪŋ/

adj. 令人心痛的 causing great sadness or sorrow

With her father in a coma for several years, Alice had to make the ***heartrending*** decision to take him off life support.

retiring
/rɪˈtaɪərɪŋ/

adj. 羞涩的，不善交际的，谦逊的 quiet and shy; modest

Although ***retiring*** in her personal affairs, the journalist is confrontational and blunt in her articles.

self-effacing

belabor
/bɪˈleɪbər/

v. 批评 to attack or criticize

The poor student Tom kept ***belaboring*** his point about deserving a better grade even though he had only attended class once.

yardstick
/ˈjɑːrdstɪk/

n. 准绳，标准 a standard for making a critical judgement

Practice is often a coach's ***yardstick*** to determining which players will start in each Sunday's game.

downcast
/ˈdaʊnkæst/

adj. 不开心的，沮丧的 low in spirit

After breaking up with his girlfriend, Adrian was ***downcast*** and antisocial for many weeks.

telltale
/ˈtelteɪl/

adj. 泄露内情的 indicating or giving evidence of something

The sudden appearance of a cool breeze and dark clouds are ***telltale*** signs of coming rain.

n. 告密者 informer

The whole class hated Jon as he was such a ***telltale*** and would reveal all our misdeeds to the teacher.

moody
/ˈmuːdi/

adj. 喜怒无常的 given to frequent changes of mood

Chazz's ***moody*** behavior was a point of concern for his partner, Jeff, who hated his bad moods.

adj. 悲伤的 expressive of a mood, especially a sullen or gloomy mood

With the recent family tragedy, August was understandably ***moody*** when in the company of others.

discriminating
/dɪˈskrɪmɪneɪtɪŋ/

adj. 有洞察力的，有鉴别能力的 discerning, judicious

It is the job of a civil judge to be ***discriminating*** and separate fact from fiction.

collected
/kəˈlektɪd/

adj. 冷静的 self-possessed; composed

As the class president and a straight-A student, Michelle seemed like the community's most ***collected*** and composed teenager.

adj. 收集在一起的 brought or placed together from various sources

The ***collected*** prose of Virginia Woolf showcases various short stories written but unpublished throughout her life.

taxing
/ˈtæksɪŋ/

adj. 繁重的，劳累的 burdensome and wearing

Sometimes being a parent can be ***taxing***, but watching the children grow up is enough reward to continue.

arduous

demanding
/dɪˈmændɪŋ/

adj. 费力的 requiring much effort or attention

The job application had ***demanding*** requirements that went beyond the expectations of that position, such as writing samples, ten references, and a physical checkup.

adj. （对别人）高标准要求的 requiring others to work hard or meet high expectations

Jimbo Fisher is a ***demanding*** coach, but the recent national championship demonstrates that his efforts are worthwhile.

riveting
/ˈrɪvɪtɪŋ/

adj. 吸引人的 wholly absorbing or engrossing one's attention

Man on Wire was a ***riveting*** documentary that kept the audience in suspense about a high wire crossing of the Twin Towers.

celebrated
/ˈselɪbreɪtɪd/

adj. 出名的 known and praised widely

The now-***celebrated*** poet Allen Ginsburg was denigrated as obscene during his time.

pressing
/ˈpresɪŋ/

adj. 紧急的 demanding immediate attention

With the ***pressing*** developments in Syria, the president had to leave his meeting on education reform to speak with the Secretary of State.

exigent, critical

exacting
/ɪgˈzæktɪŋ/

adj. 要求高的 making severe demands

Because the history teacher was ***exacting*** with students' writing, we all improved dramatically.

proscriptive, rigorous

adj. 费力的 requiring great care, effort

Making designer purses is an ***exacting*** task that requires specially trained artisans.

demanding

earnest
/ˈɜːrnɪst/

adj. 严肃的，真诚的 showing or expressing sincerity or seriousness

Academics are serious and ***earnest*** when giving talks, but can be witty and fun at the parties afterward.

☐ collected　　☐ taxing　　☐ demanding　　☐ riveting　　☐ celebrated
☐ pressing　　☐ exacting　　☐ earnest

unfeeling /ʌnˈfiːlɪŋ/	*adj.* 冷血的，没有同情心的 not sympathetic to others People who seem **unfeeling** can suddenly act warm and tender when their pet enters the room.
whereabouts /ˈwerəbaʊts/	*n.* 行踪，下落 approximate location With the new microchip implanted in our beagle, we were able to track his **whereabouts** on our phone at any time.
uproot /ˌʌpˈruːt/	*v.* 连根拔起，消灭 to destroy or remove completely In one of the most positive trends of our time, people are using greater access to information to **uproot** corruption.
agreeable /əˈgriːəbl/	*adj.* 适合的 suitable and conformable Many diners prefer tables at restaurants, but I find booths more **agreeable** and cozy. *adj.* 宜人的，令人愉悦的 to one's liking This process can continue until both sides arrive at a mutually **agreeable** result.
composed /kəmˈpoʊzd/	*adj.* 冷静的 calm Firefighters must remain **composed** in the face of danger and act decisively to save lives during emergency situations. unperturbed, collected, coolheaded
barring /ˈbaːrɪŋ/	*prep.* 除了…以外 prep. apart from the occurrence of; excepting **Barring** any traffic, we should arrive in time for the party.
prohibitive /prəˈhɪbətɪv/	*adj.* 昂贵的 so high or burdensome as to discourage purchase or use The cost of the Jaguar was **prohibitive** for the family, so the Wilson's bought a Kia.
phenomenal /fəˈnɑːmɪnl/	*adj.* 出众的 extraordinary and outstanding After the storm, the fishers caught briny and delicious oysters that were of such **phenomenal** quality.
incisive /ɪnˈsaɪsɪv/	*adj.* 一针见血的，深刻尖锐的 impressively direct and decisive Thanks to the President's **incisive** intervention, the crisis in parliament was prevented. acuity, tronchant
amiss /əˈmɪs/	*adj.* 错误的 in the wrong way Although everything seemed fine at the store, the manager knew something was **amiss** when she saw the employees whispering among themselves.
musty /ˈmʌsti/	*adj.* 恶臭的 having a bad smell because of wetness, old age, or lack of fresh air With the collected dust and humidity, the basement quickly took on a **musty** smell that permeated everything that was stored there. stale

□ unfeeling □ wheresabouts □ uproot □ agreeable □ composed
□ barring □ prohibitive □ phenomenal □ incisive □ amiss
□ musty

needy
/'niːdi/

adj. 贫穷的 lacking the necessities of life; poor

例 Thanksgiving is a time when people are moved to donate so that *needy* people can have a turkey dinner.

canny
/'kæni/

adj. 精明的，聪明的 very clever and able to make intelligent decisions

例 Barbara is a very *canny* shopper; she saves hundreds of dollars by buying from sales.

选 shrewd

Word List 22

音频

uncanny /ʌnˈkæni/	**adj.** 奇异的 strange or unusual in a way that is surprising or difficult to understand 例 Our dog has an **uncanny** propensity to bark five minutes before anyone arrives at the door.
mighty /ˈmaɪti/	**adj.** 强大的 having or showing great strength or power 例 The **mighty** Mississippi is a large river with a strong current.
locale /loʊˈkæl/	**n.** 地点 the place where something happens 例 Gouda is a famous **locale** for the production and sale of cheese.
finale /fɪˈnæli/	**n.** 大结局 the last part of something (such as a musical performance, play, etc.) 例 The audience stood up at the **finale** of the play to applaud the entire effort.
rationale /ˌræʃəˈnæl/	**n.** 理由 the reason or explanation for something 例 Using someone else's bad actions to justify yours is a poor **rationale** that only breeds contempt and revenge. 派 rational (adj. 理性的，合理的)，rationalize (v. 使···合理)
halfhearted /hæfˌhɑːrtɪd/	**adj.** 不认真的，不热心的 feeling or showing a lack of interest or enthusiasm 例 Having just learned about the death of her grandmother, Kerry could only give a **halfhearted** performance in the school musical. 近 tepid, lukewarm
morale /məˈræl/	**n.** 士气 the feelings of enthusiasm and loyalty that a person or group has about a task or job 例 With the rumors of significant job cuts, **morale** among the employees at Pfizer was at an all-time low.
proverbial /prəˈvɜːrbiəl/	**adj.** 家喻户晓的 commonly spoken of or widely known 例 **Proverbial** sentences are well-known to native speakers, but they are difficult for new speakers to understand because their meanings do not translate directly from the words.
shorthand /ˈʃɔːrthænd/	**n.** 速记 a method of writing quickly by using symbols or abbreviations for sounds, words, or phrases 例 In order to take lecture notes more quickly, June developed a **shorthand** for many of the significant biology terms.

274
☐ uncanny ☐ mighty ☐ locale ☐ finale ☐ rationale
☐ halfhearted ☐ morale ☐ proverbial ☐ shorthand

madcap /ˈmædkæp/	释 *adj.* 鲁莽的，行为冲动的 behaving or acting impulsively or rashly; wild 例 A *madcap* driver, Steve flew down the highway while weaving in and out of cars.
leading /ˈliːdɪŋ/	释 *adj.* 最重要的 most important 例 Of all the precious stones, the diamond is the *leading* one in terms of worth and desirability. 释 *adj.* 有影响力的 having great importance, influence, or success 例 As Hollywood's *leading* man, George Clooney has no trouble being offered acting parts.
degenerate /dɪˈdʒenəreɪt/	释 *adj.* 道德败坏的 having low moral standards 例 Despite claiming to be a harmless fun-lover, Jim was a classless and *degenerate* man who simply did anything he wanted. 释 *v.* 退化 to change to a worse state or condition 例 When the levees broke during Hurricane Katrina, the flooding quickly *degenerated* into a catastrophe.
testing /ˈtestɪŋ/	释 *adj.* 费力的 difficult to deal with 例 We had a *testing* time with our cantankerous Uncle Guido who managed to leave everyone fuming.
lengthy /ˈleŋθi/	释 *adj.* 冗长的 protracted excessively 例 May Sarton had a *lengthy* career: it lasted from 1929, when Poetry magazine published her early sonnets, to 1994, when her last collection of poems came out.
materialize /məˈtɪriəlaɪz/	释 *v.* 实现 to begin to happen or exist 例 Even if the money to open Jose's designer monocle business were to *materialize*, he would still struggle to be successful. 释 *v.* 使…具体化，使…物质化 to cause to appear in bodily form 例 Unseen in person, the ghostly apparition only *materializes* on film photographs.
calculable /ˈkælkjələbl/	释 *adj.* 可计算的 subject to or ascertainable by calculation 例 Although atoms are invisible to the naked eye, their mass and size are both easily *calculable* with the proper equipment. 释 *adj.* 可靠的 that may be counted on 例 You may assign him the job without worry as his excellence for any task is *calculable*.
gainsay /ˌɡeɪnˈseɪ/	释 *v.* 否认 to deny or disagree with (something) 例 With the company's stock going up in value, no one can *gainsay* that the CEO's management style works. 反 concur

officious /ə'fɪʃəs/	释 *adj.* 爱掺和的，爱管闲事的 volunteering one's services where they are neither asked nor needed 例 A server should be helpful, but not *officious* and hover over people as they eat.
appraise /ə'preɪz/	释 *v.* 评估 to evaluate the worth, significance, or status of 例 Before donating one of his Picasso paintings to the auction, Billy asked a historian to *appraise* the painting and estimate its worth.
restless /'restləs/	释 *adj.* 不安的 not relaxed or calm 例 *Restless* in anticipation for the SAT exam, Cletus was unable to sleep. 释 *adj.* 失眠的 having little or no rest or sleep 例 While stuck in the trench, the new Doughboy had a *restless* night fearing for his life.
bighearted /bɪg'hɑːrtɪd/	释 *adj.* 慷慨的，宽大的 generous, charitable 例 As a *bighearted* philanthropist, Warren Buffett has donated millions to the Gates foundation.
artless /'ɑːrtləs/	释 *adj.* 朴实的，单纯的 sincerely simple 例 Angelina Jolie's acceptance speech was direct and *artless* in thanking her director and her team. 反 cunning 释 *adj.* 自然的 free from artificiality 例 The janitor's *artless* essay about his troubled childhood was more moving than those by the privileged college seniors. 释 *adj.* 拙劣的，粗糙的 made without skill 例 Although the child's drawing was an *artless* mess, her mother proudly hung it on the kitchen refrigerator.
pitfall /'pɪtfɔːl/	释 *n.* 陷阱 a danger or problem that is hidden or not obvious at first 例 *Pitfalls* can come with buying an old home as issues such as pest problems and decaying furniture may not be obvious at first.
hardy /'hɑːrdi/	释 *adj.* 吃苦耐劳的 capable of withstanding adverse conditions 例 Able to survive subzero temperatures, long periods of darkness, and days without food, the Arctic wolf is clearly a very *hardy* animal. 释 *adj.* 勇敢的，大胆的 audacious or brazen 例 Like her gutter talk, Lucy's pretense at being atrocious and *hardy* was clearly a front put up for others.
aback /ə'bæk/	释 *adv.* 吃惊地 by surprise 例 I was taken *aback* when an old friend unfriended me on Facebook for a mild political post.

weighty /ˈweɪti/	*adj.* 重要的 very important and serious 例 After his most recent misdeed, Bo was called into the principal's office to have a **weighty** discussion about the importance of good behavior. *adj.* 有影响力的，有说服力的 powerful and telling 例 The famous image of the downtrodden refugee is a **weighty** photograph that humanized the victims of war. *adj.* 笨重的 having a lot of weight 例 The **weighty** tome was two thousand pages long and could not be carried with one hand.
disown /dɪsˈoʊn/	*v.* 否认 to refuse to acknowledge as one's own 例 Learning that their son was a mass murderer, Sally and Joe **disowned** their child and changed their last name.
virtually /ˈvɜːrtʃuəli/	*adv.* 几乎 almost 例 **Virtually** all children have a rebellious streak at some point in their lives.
unearth /ʌnˈɜːrθ/	*v.* 揭露 to find or discover (something) that was hidden or lost 例 After **unearthing** the world's earliest known human skull, the archaeologists publicized this news with great fanfare. 选 extract 反 conceal
uptake /ˈʌpteɪk/	*n.* 理解 understanding or comprehension 例 Jake is slow on the **uptake**, but once he has learned something he does not forget it. *n.* 吸收 an act or instance of absorbing and incorporating especially into a living organism, tissue, or cell 例 The **uptake** of drugs into the system will be faster or slower depending on how much a person has eaten.
instrumental /ˌɪnstrəˈmentl/	*adj.* 重要的 very important in helping or causing something to happen or be done 例 The colors and patterns on butterflies' wings may seem merely decorative, but they are actually **instrumental** in the survival of these insects, enabling them to attract mates and to hide from predators.
reserved /rɪˈzɜːrvd/	*adj.* 沉默寡言的 not openly expressing feelings or opinions 例 Kang-hsi, emperor of China from 1661 to 1722, expressed his private thoughts with a forthrightness rarely found in the usually **reserved** rulers of great empires.
pretext /ˈpriːtekst/	*n.* 借口 a reason that you give to hide your real reason for doing something 例 David's request to borrow coffee was only a **pretext** to meet the new neighbors without being openly inquisitive.

☐ weighty ☐ disown ☐ virtually ☐ unearth ☐ uptake
☐ instrumental ☐ reserved ☐ pretext

subtext
/ˈsʌbtekst/

n. 潜台词 an underlying meaning, theme, etc.

例 The *subtext* of her forced smiles and cryptic sentences shows her intense displeasure at how things have turned out.

setback
/ˈsetbæk/

n. 挫折 a checking of progress

例 Facing only minor *setbacks*, the hunting team managed to arrive at their blinds just in time.

backlash
/ˈbæklæʃ/

n. 激烈反对 an antagonistic reaction to an earlier action

例 Susan Faludi argued that after feminism made progress in the 70s, it suffered a *backlash* from people who disapproved of the changes.

standstill
/ˈstændstɪl/

n. 静止，停滞 a state characterized by absence of motion or of progress

例 Progress in the business deal was at a *standstill* as neither party could agree to the final payment.

level-headed
/ˈlevlˌhedɪd/

adj. 头脑清晰冷静的 having or showing an ability to think clearly and to make good decisions

例 It is necessary for the president to stay *level-headed* in times of crisis so that he can guide the country in the right direction.

近 sober

byword
/ˈbaɪwɜːrd/

n. 典型，代名词 someone or something that is closely connected with a particular quality

例 "Hands up" has become a *byword* for the protests against police brutality in the USA.

one-stop
/wʌnˌstɑːp/

adj. 一站式的，全方位的 providing or offering a comprehensive range of goods or services at one location; provided or offered at such a location

例 With its comprehensive product line, Walmart has become a *one-stop* shop for all domestic items.

upright
/ˈʌpraɪt/

adj. 垂直的 perpendicular or vertical

例 After months of standing *upright*, the flower finally drooped in the cold winter wind.

adj. 正直的 marked by strong moral rectitude

例 An *upright* citizen, Josh thought it was his obligation to alert the police when he saw injustices.

acquired
/əˈkwaɪrd/

adj. 后天习得的 of or relating to a disease, condition, or characteristic that is not congenital but develops after birth

例 Type II diabetes is an *acquired* disease that often results from eating too much processed sugars.

rosy
/ˈroʊzi/

adj. 乐观的 having or producing hope for success or happiness in the future

例 It was a real tragedy when the student died in the car accident; he had a *rosy* future with hopes of becoming a doctor.

□ subtext □ setback □ backlash □ standstill □ level-headed
□ byword □ one-stop □ upright □ acquired □ rosy

becoming /bɪˈkʌmɪŋ/	🔲 *adj.*（尤指有吸引力的）得体的，合适的 attractively suitable 📖 Oversized pleated khaki pants are not ***becoming*** on most people.
sententious /senˈtenʃəs/	🔲 *adj.* 简洁的，说教的 terse, aphoristic, or moralistic in expression 📖 The class loved Mr. Hardy for all but the ***sententious*** speeches he made whenever someone committed a mistake. 🔷 didactic, homiletic, preachy 🔶 circuitous, circumlocutory, long-winded
artifice /ˈɑːrtɪfɪs/	🔲 *n.* 诡计，欺骗 dishonest or insincere behavior or speech that is meant to deceive someone 📖 Entirely lacking in ***artifice***, Zeke made his intentions to get Waldo fired clear to all.
unrest /ʌnˈrest/	🔲 *n.* 不安 a disturbed or uneasy state 📖 There was a state of civil ***unrest*** when the news that the dictator had rigged the election became public. 🔷 anxiety
deadlock /ˈdedlɑːk/	🔲 *n.* 僵局 a situation in which an agreement cannot be made 📖 With equal numbers of Republicans and Democrats in Congress, there are frequent ***deadlocks*** that make it impossible to pass any bills. 🔷 impasse
expendable /ɪkˈspendəbl/	🔲 *adj.* 多余的 not worth saving 📖 When she was packing to move to a smaller home, Gillie made sure to throw away all ***expendable*** items so that worthless goods would not take up space in her new home. 🔷 superfluous
porous /ˈpɔːrəs/	🔲 *adj.* 可渗透的 easy to pass or get through 📖 Athletes often wear ***porous*** attire so that their sweat can seep through their clothes and evaporate. 🔷 permeable
scuffle /ˈskʌfl/	🔲 *v.* 扭打 to struggle at close quarters with disorder and confusion 📖 During their argument, the two fraternity brothers ***scuffled*** on the floor and broke a table in the fight.
unnerve /ˌʌnˈnɜːrv/	🔲 *v.* 使…失去勇气 to cause to lose courage or firmness of purpose 📖 ***Unnerved*** at the first sight of death, the young soldier fled back to his barracks and refused to re-enter combat.
clueless /ˈkluːləs/	🔲 *adj.* 无知的 not having knowledge about something 📖 ***Clueless*** about the plight of the homeless, the politician railed against them using false rhetoric.

studied /ˈstʌdɪd/	释 **adj.** 深思熟虑的 carefully considered or prepared 例 The email I sent my professor was a **studied** attempt to get a better grade by flattering him. 释 **adj.** 博学的 knowledgeable or learned 例 You can maintain a clever, astute and **studied** persona regardless of whether you're an adolescent or octogenarian.
privation /praɪˈveɪʃn/	释 **n.** 贫穷，匮乏 a lack or loss of the basic things that people need to live properly 例 When the new chief came to power, his rivals faced **privation**, loss of their property and exile to a distant land. 反 plentitude
distance /ˈdɪstəns/	释 **v.** 超出，把…甩在后面 to leave far behind; outstrip 例 **Distancing** himself from the competition, Usain Bolt set a record time in the 100-meter dash. 释 **v.** 使…远离 to place or keep at a distance 例 To **distance** himself from the other politicians, Bernie Sanders pointed out that they had ties to Wall Street.
list /lɪst/	释 **n.** 倾斜 an inclination to one side; a tilt 例 The ship's **list** during the storm indicated strong winds and turbulent waves. 反 upright
passage /ˈpæsɪdʒ/	释 **n.**（事物从一个状态到另一个状态的）转变 the process of changing 例 "With the **passage** of the new bill, we can eliminate the student loan crisis," the Senator exclaimed.
sound /saʊnd/	释 **adj.** 状态良好的 in good condition 例 After inspection of the safe, we saw that it and its contents were safe and **sound** despite the fire. 释 **adj.** 明智的，合理的 showing good judgement 例 Following the **sound** wisdom of his mentor, Jeff worked his way up in the corporate ranks.
faculty /ˈfæklti/	释 **n.** 才能，本领 a talent or natural ability for something 例 Although she often described reason as the noblest **faculty**, author Ayn Rand never implied that she rejected emotion.
function /ˈfʌŋkʃn/	释 **n.** 重大聚会 an official ceremony or a formal social occasion 例 During the official state **function**, Richard Nixon was called off stage to attend to a private matter. 释 **v.** 运转 to work or operate 例 It was necessary to take the computer to a repair shop because it was not **functioning** properly.

avatar /ˈævətɑːr/	释 *n.* 化身，代表 someone who represents a type of person, an idea, or a quality 例 Many people develop fake ***avatars*** while on the internet to protect their identities.
liberal /ˈlɪbərəl/	释 *adj.* 慷慨的 tending to give freely; generous 例 At the all-you-can-eat buffet, the server offered ***liberal*** portions of each of the 25 dishes. 释 *adj.* 思想自由的 broad-minded and not bound by orthodoxy or traditional forms 例 The Democratic party typically espouses ***liberal*** ideals of social freedom and economic support.
license /ˈlaɪsns/	释 *n.* 自由 freedom to act however you want to 例 Re hired as CEO, Steve Jobs was given complete ***license*** to lead Apple according to his own vision.
latitude /ˈlætɪtuːd/	释 *n.* 自由 freedom to choose how to act or what to do 例 Montessori schools give children ***latitude*** to study what they are interested in. 释 *n.* 纬度 distance north or south of the equator measured in degrees up to 90 degrees 例 Sited at 90 degrees ***latitude***, the North Pole is the northernmost point in the world.
court /kɔːrt/	释 *v.* 招致 to behave so as to invite or incur 例 After being ***courted*** by the Alabama Crimson Tide for months, the 5 Star recruit was finally impressed by the facilities and decided to play football for that university. 释 *v.* 吸引 to attempt to gain the favor of by attention or flattery 例 Ozzy attempted to ***court*** Sue by sending flowers and inviting her to romantic dinners.
contract /ˈkɑːntrækt/	释 *v.* 招致 to acquire or incur 例 He ***contracted*** a hefty debt of $1M after the stock market crashed. 释 *v.* 患病 to become ill with (disease) 例 While in Brazil, many tourists are fearful that they will ***contract*** the Zika virus. 释 *v.* 收缩 to become reduced in size 例 Since you know that metal ***contracts*** at lower temperatures, why don't you submerge the metal cylinder into ice water so that it can be freed from its plastic cap? 近 dwindling

betray /bɪ'treɪ/	释 *v.* （无意中）显露 to make known unintentionally 例 The smirk on his face ***betrayed*** the evil intentions he secretly harbored beneath those pretensions. 释 *v.* 背叛 to give aid or information to an enemy of; commit treason against 例 When the scout was captured by the enemy troops, he was tortured until he ***betrayed*** his general's plans for attack.
qualify /'kwɑːlɪfaɪ/	释 *v.* 限制 to modify, limit or restrict, as by listing exceptions or reservations 例 It is pointless to give predictions if you ***qualify*** every conclusion with "but we could be wrong about this".
stomach /'stʌmək/	释 *v.* 容忍 to bear without overt reaction or resentment 例 When the pep rally turned to outright insults of the other school, Jay could no longer ***stomach*** the vitriol and left.
resolve /rɪ'zɑːlv/	释 *v.* 决定，决心要做 to make a definite and serious decision to do something 例 When Justin Bieber announced a concert at Madison Square Garden, many young fans ***resolved*** to get tickets for the show. 选 resolute 反 irresolute 派 resolution（*n.* 决心） 释 *v.* 解决 to find an answer or solution to 例 The crash of the online store was ***resolved*** by adding new servers to the system that could handle the traffic.
arrest /ə'rest/	释 *v.* 阻止 to bring to a stop 例 Traffic was ***arrested*** by a major accident that blocked both lines. 释 *v.* 吸引 to attract and hold the attention of 例 ***Arrested*** by the beauty of the Grand Tetons, the campers decided to spend an extra day at the campsite. 释 *v.* 逮捕 to use the power of the law to take and keep 例 After being investigated for insider trading, Martha Stewart was ***arrested*** and put on trial.
digest /daɪ'dʒest/	释 *n.* 文摘 a summation or condensation of a body of information 例 The ***digest*** of neurological illnesses is a convenient source for doctors to begin their investigations of potentially rare diseases. 释 *v.* （对信息的）消化理解 to think over so as to understand (news, information, etc.) 例 During 9/11, it took many people a long time to ***digest*** the events that were unfolding before their eyes.

□ betray □ qualify □ stomach □ resolve □ arrest
□ digest

nexus

/ˈneksəs/

释 *n.* 连接 a means of connection
例 Grand Central Station serves as a *nexus* for a number of different subway lines in New York.
反 disconnected components

释 *n.* 核心，中心 the core or center
例 Washington D.C. is the *nexus* of all political maneuverings in the USA.

kindle

/ˈkɪndl/

释 *v.* 点燃 to ignite
例 By first using small sticks and wood chippings, it is possible to *kindle* a fire without lighter fluid.

释 *v.* 激起情绪 to arouse (an emotion)
例 The touching film *kindled* sadness at the thought of the penguin's impending extinction.

waffle

/ˈwɑːfl/

释 *v.* 犹豫不决 to be unable to make a decision
例 After years of switching his stance on the Iraqi War, John Kerry was accused of *waffling* on his positions.

释 *v.* 闪烁其词 to speak, write, or act evasively about
例 For fear of retribution by his company, Andrew *waffled* about his identity when writing the vicious attack on Haliburton.

off-key

/ˈɔːfˈkiː/

释 *adj.* 出格的，不正常的 being out of accord with what is considered normal or appropriate
例 Always the *off-key* dresser, Simon wears sports shorts to every occasion, formal or otherwise.

释 *adj.* 跑调的 pitched higher or lower than the correct notes of a melody
例 Because the violins were not properly tuned, the section was *off-key* during the entire performance.

balloon

/bəˈluːn/

释 *v.* 快速上升 to increase or rise quickly
例 When Fannie broke her leg, her weight *ballooned* due to her lack of exercise and indulgent diet.
反 decrease slowly

释 *n.* 气球 a flexible, nonporous bag inflated with a gas
例 Above this contraption floated a big egg-shaped silk *balloon* of hydrogen, from which the tricycle with the incumbent Alberto were suspended.

fetch

/fetʃ/

释 *v.* 卖得（某个价格）to bring in as a price
例 In a recent auction, a Gaugin painting *fetched* a record $300 million.

释 *v.* 去拿来 to go after and bring back
例 For many dogs, a favorite game is to *fetch* a stick that has been thrown to them.

contain /kənˈteɪn/	释 **v.** 限制 to hold or keep with limits; restrain 例 Certain atmospheric gases admit incoming sunlight and **contain** heat radiated from the ground, preventing warmth from escaping. 释 **v.** 容纳 to have within; hold 例 All of the pigs were **contained** within a pen so that they could not roam unsupervised.
stem /stem/	释 **v.** 阻止，限制 to check or go counter to 例 This new government must improve facilities in rural areas to **stem** the flow of farm workers to the city. 选 check 释 **v.** 源于，因为 to develop as a consequence of 例 The collapse of several buildings **stemmed** from foundation damage inflicted by the earthquake.
check /tʃek/	释 **v.** 阻止 to hold in restraint 例 The attempts of epidemiologists to contain the infectious disease ultimately proved futile as it always found its way to emerge somewhere else the moment it could be **checked** in one community. 选 stem 反 prompt 释 **v.** 检测 to inspect so as to determine accuracy, quality, or other condition 例 Before leaving a hotel room, one must **check** every piece of furniture to ensure that personal possessions are not left behind.
still /stɪl/	释 **adj.** 静止的 lacking motion or activity 例 Flipping a series of closely shot **still** photographs gives the impression of motion. 释 **adj.** 安静的 uttering no sound 例 With everyone gone, the house was **still** and silent.
clinical /ˈklɪnɪkl/	释 **adj.** 不感情用事的，冷静的 analytical or dolly dispassionate 例 During their dispute, Mark's girlfriend accused him of treating their relationship in a **clinical** fashion rather than considering her emotions.
novel /ˈnɑːvl/	释 **adj.** 新颖的 new and different from what has been known before 例 Jack Kerouac was a **novel** poet who merged stream of consciousness with the beat culture of the 1950s to create a new writing style. 选 original, unexampled, unprecedented 释 **adj.** 原创的 original or striking especially in conception or style 例 *Toy Story* was a **novel** film at the time, but now it is remembered as only the first of many CGI productions.

□ contain   □ stem   □ check   □ still   □ clinical
□ novel

might
/maɪt/

n. 力量，权力 power to do something

With the *might* of the Roman army behind him, Augustus conquered large areas of Egypt and Europe.

mighty（*adj.* 强大的）

grave
/greɪv/

adj. 严肃的 dignified and somber in conduct or character

The principal tried to sound very *grave*, but everyone at the assembly thought the graffiti problem was funny.

v. 雕刻，铭记 to stamp or impress deeply

For many who are abused as children, their experiences are *graved* deeply on their psyche.

affect
/ə'fekt/

v. 伪装，装腔作势 to put on a false show of

The accused *affected* a nonchalant air during the police interview; he did not even insist on his innocence.

ingenuousness

affectation（*n.* 假装）

v. 喜欢 to have or show a liking for

He *affected* a liking for avant-garde art in front of his clients, when in reality, he only liked pop culture.

v. 影响 to have an influence on

Many were directly *affected* by the recent economic downturn and lost their jobs.

flag
/flæg/

v. 衰弱 to lose vigor or strength; weaken or diminish

With his strength *flagging* from the intense workout, Ken Griffey Jr. could barely lift his bat.

wax

pan
/pæn/

v. 严厉批评 to criticize or review harshly

Although universally *panned* by its critics, the movie *Good Burger* has a small cult following.

compromise
/'kɑːmprəmaɪz/

v. 妥协，让步 to arrive at a settlement by making concessions

Apple had opposed the court order, arguing that it would *compromise* the privacy of its customers and the strength of its product security.

concession

v. 降低 to reduce in quality, value, or degree

Academic education is essential and must not be *compromised*, but schools should also offer good extracurriculars.

v. 破坏 to impair, as by disease or injury

His binge drinking has really *compromised* on the proper functioning of his liver.

impair

founder /ˈfaʊndər/	释 **v.** 彻底失败 to fail utterly; collapse 例 Black Beauty is a powerful horse, but if you make her gallop for hours without stopping, she will **founder** from exhaustion. 释 **n.** 创始人，奠基人 one who establishes something or formulates the basis for something 例 As the mythological **founder** of Syracus, Archias was revered by the later inhabitants as a hero.
august /ɔːˈgʌst/	释 **adj.** 庄严的，肃穆的 respected and dignified 例 An **august** member of the local community, the social worker fought for the rights of the poor and the minorities.
assume /əˈsuːm/	释 **v.** 假装 to pretend to have 例 By **assuming** an air of confidence, you can easily convince others of your expertise and ability.
pedestrian /pəˈdestriən/	释 **adj.** 无聊的，普通的 not interesting or unusual 例 His book on the history of science is conventional and perhaps even **pedestrian**, but it is an informative work that covers a lot of ground. 选 uninspired, mundane, ordinary, prosaic 释 **n.** 行人 a person going on foot 例 The cars stopped at the intersection to allow the **pedestrians** to walk to the other side of the road using the crosswalk.
champion /ˈtʃæmpiən/	释 **n.** 支持者 an ardent defender or supporter of a cause or another person 例 Initially a **champion** of democratic rule, the president ironically began to employ the very dictatorial powers that he had once condemned. 选 defender, proponent, advocate 反 impugn 释 **v.** 支持 to defend or support 例 Bill Gates has donated over a billion dollars to his foundation as part of his efforts to **champion** complete vaccination in Africa. 选 advocate, defend, espouse
coin /kɔɪn/	释 **v.** 发明（一个新词）to devise (a new word or phrase) 例 With the advent of the internet, a number of new expressions and abbreviations have been **coined**, such as LOL and ROFL. 选 neologism 派 coinage（ *n.* 新单词的创造，家世背景）
weather /ˈweðər/	释 **v.** 渡过（危机）to come through (something) safely 例 Sound regulation of the financial sector has helped the Indian economy to **weather** the storm and emerge stronger than ever.

□ founder □ august □ assume □ pedestrian □ champion
□ coin □ weather

document
/ˈdɑːkjumənt/

v. 详细记录 to methodically record the details of

The widely *documented* correlation between these two diseases has prompted scientists to study whether treating one can ward off the other.

documentation（*n.* 证明文件）

v. 证明，支持 to support with evidence or decisive information

Most of the arguments I've encountered so far have not been *documented* and are purely anecdotal.

contest
/ˈkɑːntest/

v. 质疑，否认 to try to disprove or invalidate (something) as by argument or legal action

There has been a tendency among art historians to *contest* not only the uniqueness of the Renaissance, but its very existence.

uncontested（*adj.* 无异议的）

intrigue
/ɪnˈtriːg/

n. 密谋，诡计 the activity of making secret plans

The Roman senate was full of *intrigue*, with senators conspiring and plotting against each other.

occasion
/əˈkeɪʒn/

v. 引起 to cause something

The recent death of the king *occasioned* the rise to power of the commoner, Darius, in the Persian Empire.

effect /ɪˈfekt/	释 *v.* 引起 to bring about; make happen
	例 Unplanned demonstrations like the Stonewall Riots can *effect* social change.
spell /spel/	释 *n.* （一段）时间 a short, indefinite period of time
	例 The friendly townspeople invited the tourists to have some lemonade on the porch and sit for a *spell*.
husband /ˈhʌzbənd/	释 *v.* 节省 to carefully use or manage, to use sparingly
	例 With the poor harvest, the farmer *husbanded* all of the food so that the supplies could last the harsh winter.
industry /ˈɪndəstri/	释 *n.* 努力 the habit of working hard and steadily
	例 Because of Obama's *industry* and intelligence, he was able to earn a law degree at the prestigious Harvard Law.
	反 sloth
demonstrative /dɪˈmɑːnstrətɪv/	释 *adj.* 显露情感的 freely and openly showing emotion or feelings
	例 Cito Gaston, one of the least *demonstrative* baseball managers, surprised reporters by weeping openly after his team won the play-offs.
pursuit /pərˈsuːt/	释 *n.* 事业 an activity that one engages as a vocation, profession, or avocation
	例 Although basketball was Magic Johnson's primary *pursuit*, he also made a fortune in the cinema business.
emergent /iˈmɜːrdʒənt/	释 *adj.* 新兴的 newly formed or prominent
	例 In *emergent* marketplaces, it is necessary to nourish economic development for sustainable development.
	派 emerge（*v.* 出现）
	释 *adj.* 突然出现的 arising unexpectedly
	例 *Emergent* from the volcano were clouds of pumice that blanketed the city of Pompeii.
	释 *adj.* 紧急的 urgent, calling for prompt action
	例 The *emergent* infestation of locusts spelled disaster for the wheat business.

□ effect □ spell □ husband □ industry □ demonstrative
□ pursuit □ emergent

inform /ɪnˈfɔːrm/	释 **v.** 通知 to give information to 例 **Informed** about the flight delay well in advance, the family waited an extra hour before driving to the airport. 释 **v.** 影响 to be the characteristic quality of 例 Cognitive research into the reading process is now **informing** some literary criticism.
appropriate /əˈprəʊpriət/	释 **adj.** 合适的 suitable or compatible 例 In many cultures, it is **appropriate** to wear black as a sign of mourning at funerals. 释 **v.** 私自占有，私自挪用 to take or make use of without authority or right 例 Elvis Presley **appropriated** the blues sounds of African American musicians to help develop the beginnings of rock music. 近 borrow 反 lend 释 **v.** 为…拨（款）to set apart for or assign to a particular purpose or use 例 The treasurer typically **appropriates** a small amount of money for refreshments that are served during each week's meeting.
circumstantial /ˌsɜːrkəmˈstænʃl/	释 **adj.** 详细的 complete and particular; full of detail 例 Congress released a **circumstantial** report detailing the multi-year investigation into steroid use in professional sports. 释 **adj.** 视情况而定的 of, relating to, or depends on circumstances 例 **Circumstantial** evidence such as the defendant's absence from work is not enough to prove him guilty. 释 **adj.** 相关但不重要的 pertinent but not essential 例 Although butter is **circumstantial** to the recipe, it can be replaced by a lower-calorie alternative.
project /ˈprɑːdʒekt/	释 **v.** 投掷 to throw forward 例 Brett Favre **projected** the football to his receiver with such force that it stung his hands. 释 **v.** 投影 to cause to appear on a surface by the controlled direction of light 例 After we started the projector, an image of the computer's screen was **projected** on a white wall. 释 **v.** 预算，预测 to calculate, estimate, or predict 例 According to the recent trends, gas prices are **projected** to decline even more by the end of the summer.

subject /ˈsʌbdʒɪkt/	释 **v.** 屈服 to subjugate; subdue 例 The significance of the Magna Carta lies not in its finite provisions, but in its broader impact: it made the king **subject** to the law.
object /ˈɑːbdʒekt/	释 **v.** 反对 to present a dissenting or opposing argument 例 In the United States, social activists who strongly **object** to a particular law can attempt to obtain a constitutional amendment to repeal it. 派 objection (n. 反对)
long /lɔːŋ/	释 **v.** 渴望 to have an earnest, heartfelt desire 例 **Longing** for his homeland, John McCain kept his morale up while in a POW camp by thinking of his friends and family.
pacific /pəˈsɪfɪk/	释 **adj.** 爱好和平的 loving peace; not wanting war or conflict 例 The **pacific** hippies protested the Vietnam War with signs of peace and free love. 选 dovish 反 turbulent
involved /ɪnˈvɑːlvd/	释 **adj.** 复杂的 complicated and intricate 例 Richard Nixon's cover-up of Watergate was so **involved** that it could not have possibly worked without a hitch.
score /skɔːr/	释 **v.** 获得···成就 to achieve or accomplish 例 NASA **scored** a victory in the space race when they landed a man on the moon first.
intimate /ˈɪntɪmət/	释 **adj.** 亲密无间的 characterized by close personal acquaintance or familiarity 例 Although not related by blood, the lifetime friends were so **intimate** that they considered each other family. 释 **v.** 暗示 to say or suggest in an indirect way 例 The professor could not officially release the results of the comprehensive exam until Monday, but she **intimated** to me that I had passed.
portentous /pɔːrˈtentəs/	释 **adj.** 不吉利的 giving a sign or warning that something usually bad o unpleasant is going to happen 例 Looking into the arrangement of the bones, the shaman said that the signs were **portentous** of the chief's impending death. 释 **adj.** 自命不凡的 self-consciously solemn or important 例 During his award ceremony, the scientist warned his family to remain silent in respect for the **portentous** affair.
rail /reɪl/	释 **v.** 抨击，批评 to express objection or criticisms in bitter, harsh, or abusive language 例 The demagogue **railed** against illegal immigration and proposed building a wall to insulate the country from migrants.

☐ subject   ☐ object   ☐ long   ☐ pacific   ☐ involved
☐ score   ☐ intimate   ☐ portentous   ☐ rail

base /beɪs/	释 *adj.* 卑鄙的 having or showing a lack of decency 例 In most spy movies, the bad guy is completely *base*, with no redeeming qualities.
course /kɔːrs/	释 *n.* 过程 progression through a development or period or a series of acts or events 例 During the *course* of the Civil War, tens of thousands of American lives were taken every month.
mount /maʊnt/	释 *v.* 上升 to increase in amount 例 With the anger between the two men *mounting*, it was only a matter of time before fisticuffs were thrown.
count /kaʊnt/	释 *v.* 有重要性 to have importance 例 *Counted* as one of the greatest players of all time, Babe Ruth still holds a special place in the hearts of baseball fans. 释 *v.* 指望，相信 to believe or consider to be 例 Although Ryan is fiscally conservative, he does not *count* himself among the Republicans because he conflicts strongly with their social positions.
insulate /ˈɪnsəleɪt/	释 *v.* 绝缘，绝热，隔音 to prevent the passage of heat, electricity or sound into or out of 例 In order to keep houses warm during the winter and increase overall efficiency, all external walls are *insulated* with a foam spray. 释 *v.* （从危险的事物中）隔离 to keep separate from something unpleasant or dangerous 例 It is impossible to *insulate* one's children from the world by homeschooling alone.
row /roʊ/	释 *n.* （多人之间的）争吵 a lot of loud arguing or complaining usually involving many people 例 During their *row*, the couple argued so loud that all the neighbors could hear.
jade /dʒeɪd/	释 *v.* 使…厌烦 to become weary or dulled 例 After years of working in the entertainment industry, the once-excited actors became *jaded* with the difficulty of sustaining a career. 释 *v.* 使…疲惫不堪 to wear out by overwork or abuse 例 *Jaded* by years of 80-hour work weeks, the marketer left his firm to start a rural farm.

☐ base ☐ course ☐ mount ☐ count ☐ insulate
☐ row ☐ jade

trammel
/ˈtræml/

释 *v.* 阻碍，限制自由 to hinder the activity or free movement of

例 The power of workers to unionize has been ***trammeled*** for too long by right-to-work laws.

近 restrain

释 *n.* 束缚 something that restricts activity, expression, or progress; a restraint

例 During the high-speed chase, the police set up a series of ***trammels*** to block the fleeing criminal.

comb
/koʊm/

释 *v.* 仔细检查，仔细搜寻 to search or examine systematically

例 While ***combing*** through the old manuscripts, the archivist discovered a never-before seen letter from John Adams.

释 *n.* 梳子 a thin toothed strip, as of plastic, used to smooth, arrange, or fasten the hair

例 Gwen could not remember where she had placed her ***comb*** after using it yesterday after the shower.

jealous
/ˈdʒeləs/

释 *adj.* 死守严防的，精心守护的 vigilant in guarding a possession

例 The mother lion was ***jealous*** in guarding her cubs from foes.

释 *adj.* 妒忌的 feeling a mean anger toward someone because he or she is more successful

例 Erin was always ***jealous*** of her older sister, who overshadowed her in school, sports, and social life.

usher
/ˈʌʃər/

释 *v.* 引领…进入 to cause to enter; to introduce

例 While early biographies of Florence Nightingale tended to be quite sycophantic, this essay about her ***ushered*** in a new era and made it fashionable to criticize her.

释 *n.* 引导员 a person who leads people to their seats

例 Upon arriving at the theater, the ***usher*** led us speedily to our seats.

cow
/kaʊ/

释 *v.* 恐吓 to make someone too afraid to do something

例 The childhood nightmare of almost drowning in the sea has ***cowed*** Lucy so much that she has not dared to step into any pool since.

hedge
/hedʒ/

释 *n.* 故意模棱两可、不绝对的言论 a calculatedly noncommittal or evasive statement

例 His reply to the journalists was utterly unsatisfying as it was rampant with ***hedges*** and vague qualifications.

释 *v.* 避免（言论）过于绝对 to avoid giving a promise or direct answer

例 As he has matured as a scholar, his conclusions, which early in his career he stated as absolute, are now often ***hedged***.

obscure
/əbˈskjʊr/

释 *adj.* 不清晰的，不易辨别的 not clearly seen or easily distinguished
例 In the nighttime sky, Saturn is the most *obscure* planet, but it can occasionally be located with the naked eye.
选 unremarkable

释 *adj.* 难以理解的（也作动词…难懂）not clearly understood or expressed
例 Kelly was wont to use *obscure* English expressions that have no meaning in the modern world.

释 *adj.* 不出名的 not well-known
例 When Leo Strauss died in 1973, he was *obscure* outside the tiny academic circle that he inhabited.

释 *v.* 遮蔽 to conceal or hide
例 During storms, the peak of Mt. Denali is often *obscured* by clouds.

yield
/jiːld/

释 *v.* 投降，屈服 to surrender or submit
例 *Yielding* to his foe, Galahad lost the joust, but retained his life.
选 succumb

释 *v.* 产出 to be productive of
例 The experiment did not *yield* the decisive outcome that the scientist had hoped for; instead, the findings were unclear.
选 engender, output

skirt
/skɜːrt/

释 *v.* 回避，避开（话题）to evade, as by circumlocution
例 The politician deliberately *skirted* the complicated issue by diverting the interviewers to other topics.
选 bypass, circumvent

asset
/ˈæset/

释 *n.* 有价值的人或事 a valuable person or thing
例 As the most profitable salesman, Mel was a true *asset* to the Nissan dealership.

释 *n.* 资产 something that is owned by a person, company, etc.
例 Upon filing for bankruptcy, it is necessary to sell off all *assets* in order to repay outstanding loans.
反 liability

dense
/dens/

释 *adj.* 浓密的 thick
例 The fog was so *dense* that we could not see oncoming traffic on the road despite having our headlights on.
选 concentrated

释 *adj.* 难以理解的 difficult to understand because of complexity or obscurity
例 Confused by the *dense* prose of the article in the New Yorker, Jane threw it aside in favor of something lighter.

释 *adj.* 笨的 slow to apprehend
例 Mickey was slightly *dense* and required several hours of afterschool help in order to understand the basic concepts of geometry.
选 witless

frown
/fraʊn/

釋 *v.* 皱眉 to wrinkle the brow
例 Upon learning that her least favorite meal was about to be served, Mary *frowned* and gave a sound of disgust.

釋 *v.* 厌恶 to regard something with disapproval or distaste
例 Most modern cultures *frown* on cannibalism, but some cultures still practice it.

content
/ˈkɑːntent/

釋 *adj.* 满足的 desiring no more than what one has
例 Despite the trunk full of toys in his room, the child was entirely *content* playing with a small stick.
选 gratification
派 contentment（*n.* 满足）

釋 *n.* 内容 the substance or significance of a written work
例 Many political speeches use convincing, emotional rhetoric that lacks any real *content*.

sanction
/ˈsæŋkʃn/

釋 *v.* 支持 to give official authorization or approval to
例 Most nations did not *sanction* the country's policies, and these laws had been generating widespread disapproval for many years.
选 endorse
反 proscribe

釋 *n.* 支持（做不可数名词）official permission or approval
例 Apparently, the aide had acted without White House *sanction*.

釋 *n.* 制裁（做可数名词）the penalty for noncompliance with a law or legal order
例 After Crimea was annexed, the NATO allies created *sanctions* against Russia to harm its economy.

accent
/ˈæksent/

釋 *v.* 发重音 to pronounce with accent
例 Even after several years in the USA, the Dutch girl *accented* many sounds, such as the "ch" as "sh".

釋 *v.* 着重强调，凸显 to give prominence to
例 By adding a bold color to one wall, the interior designer hoped to *accent* the fireplace that was positioned on it.

perennial
/pəˈreniəl/

釋 *adj.* 多年生的（植物）present at all seasons of the year
例 Unlike the tulips, the common buttercups are *perennial* plants that last throughout the year.

釋 *adj.* 持续的，长期的 continuing without interruption
例 Humanity's struggle with bedbugs is *perennial*: archaeologists have recovered remains of the parasites dating back 3,500 years to the time of the Egyptian pharaohs.
选 long-standing
反 fleeting

confound
/kən'faʊnd/

释 *v.* 使困惑 to cause to become confused or perplexed
例 Even scientists are still **confounded** by many of the mysteries of the universe.
选 perplex, obscure, flummox
反 discriminate between

释 *v.* 驳斥，证明…错误 to prove (someone or something) wrong; refute
例 I was certain that tomatoes are vegetables, but a quick Wikipedia search **confounded** me and showed that they are fruits.

释 *v.* 混淆 to fail to distinguish; mix up
例 In the large crowd, the teacher **confounded** the identities of his students and repeatedly mixed up their names.

promise
/'prɑːmɪs/

释 *n.* 前景光明 an indication of future success or improvement
例 New cancer treatments like immunotherapy show **promise** to save lives in the future.

释 *v.* 预示 to show signs of
例 Johnny Manziel's early career **promised** great potential, but his decadent lifestyle prevented him from ever reaching his height.

acknowledge
/ək'nɑːlɪdʒ/

释 *v.* 感谢 to express gratitude or obligation for
例 At the awards ceremony, Leonardo DiCaprio **acknowledged** the work of the directors and other crew who helped him win.

释 *v.* 承认 to say that you accept or do not deny the truth or existence of (something)
例 Although many **acknowledge** the likelihood that aliens exist somewhere, most reject the theory that they built the pyramids.
选 concede

volume
/'vɑːljuːm/

释 *n.* 音量 the degree of loudness or the intensity of a sound
例 In Spinal Tap, the band liked their music so loud that they added a **volume** knob that is capable of turning beyond the standard "10" to "11".

释 *n.* 书卷 book
例 In the multi-**volume** science encyclopedia, researchers are able to find descriptions of thousands of natural phenomena.

释 *n.* 体积 the amount of space occupied by a three-dimensional object as measured in cubic units
例 The **volume** of an Olympic pool is much greater than that of an ordinary backyard pool.

discharge
/dɪsˈtʃɑːrdʒ/

释 **v.** 解雇 to tell (someone) officially that they can or must leave
例 Elizabeth will be **discharged** from the hospital at noon tomorrow; she can finally go home.

释 **v.** 履行（责任，义务）to do all that is required to perform or fulfil
例 The submarine crew **discharged** its duties when it completed a tour of the Black Sea.

释 **v.** 还清，偿还 to pay off (a debt)
例 After winning big in a poker game, Johnny was able to **discharge** his debts with the loan shark.

apology
/əˈpɑːlədʒi/

释 **n.** 辩护 something that is said or written to defend something that other people criticize
例 Plato wrote an **apology** defending Socrates from the slanders that were made against him.

释 **n.** 抱歉 a statement saying that you are sorry about something
例 After being caught, Alex Rodriguez issued an **apology** for illegally using performance-enhancing drugs.

patent
/ˈpætnt/

释 **adj.** 明显的 obvious or clear
例 Footage from the moon landing made it **patent** and evident that the mission was not a hoax.

fell
/fel/

释 **v.** 砍树 to cut down (a tree)
例 Paul Bunyan **felled** countless trees with his giant ax in the American north.

释 **v.** 打倒 to beat or knock down (someone or something)
例 During the MMA match, Conor MacGregor was **felled** by the underdog, Nate Diaz, and lost his title.

appreciate
/əˈpriːʃieɪt/

释 **v.** 升值 to increase the value of
例 During many economic crises, the value of gold **appreciates** because it is a reliable, hard currency.

释 **v.** 感谢 to be grateful for
例 Most grandmothers **appreciate** any gift that their grandchildren give them, even if it is homemade and inexpensive.

reliable
/rɪˈlaɪəbl/

释 **adj.** （结论、模型等）可靠的 giving the same result on successive trials
例 During the Olympic trials, Johnny Gatlin gave **reliable** results, suggesting a minimum time he would receive in the finals.
反 random

释 **adj.** 可依赖的 able to be trusted to do or provide what is needed
例 Most companies appreciate **reliable** employees who are never late and show up for work when scheduled.

☐ discharge ☐ apology ☐ patent ☐ fell ☐ appreciate
☐ reliable

abandon
/ə'bændən/

释 *n.* 放纵 a feeling or attitude of wild or complete freedom

例 With reckless **abandon**, the college students drove off into the night with no plan in mind.

选 desert

释 *v.* 放弃 to leave and never return to

例 **Abandoning** his outpost, Bo Bergdahl was captured by rebellious soldiers.

选 relinquish

harry
/'hæri/

释 *v.* 打扰，骚扰 to disturb, distress, or exhaust by repeated demands or criticism

例 The intern was consistently **harried** by his boss to deliver deadlines at an unreasonable speed.

experimental
/ɪk,sperɪ'mentl/

释 *adj.* 新颖的，创新的 using a new way of doing or thinking about something

例 For their use of new sonic landscapes and chord progressions, the Beatles are often considered the first **experimental** pop group.

选 innovative

second
/'sekənd/

释 *v.* 同意 to agree with (a suggestion or statement)

例 When Tom proposed that we order pizza, I **seconded** the suggestion and salivated at the thought of a delicious slice.

释 *v.* 帮助，支持 to give support or encouragement to

例 After John Adam's impassioned speech at the Second Continental Congress, the delegates **seconded** his vote in favor of ratifying the Declaration of Independence.

usage
/'juːsɪdʒ/

释 *n.* 对待方式 manner of treating

例 The caravan was in shambles after being subjected to very rough and frequent **usage** throughout the road trip.

autumn
/'ɔːtəm/

释 *n.* 晚年，暮年 the later part of someone's life or of something's existence

例 The **autumn** years of the writer's life were marked by a sense of doom and pessimism.

派 autumnal (*adj.* 垂暮之年)

measured
/'meʒərd/

释 *adj.* 仔细的，有分寸的 done with thought and care

例 When the actor was asked an uncomfortable question, he gave a **measured** response that did not implicate anyone.

entrance
/'entrəns/

释 *v.* 使…着迷 to fill (someone) with delight and wonder

例 The magician **entranced** everyone in the audience with his amazing card tricks.

color
/'kʌlər/

释 *v.* 扭曲，影响 to alter or influence to some degree, as by distortion or exaggeration

例 Many couples fall out of love once they realize that their relationships had been **colored** by the initial emotions of infatuation.

---

economy
/ɪ'kɑːnəmi/

释 *n.* 节省 thrifty and efficient use of material resources
例 Like cartoonists, some painters seek to communicate character in a few strokes, but this *economy* of means does not equate to artistic shallowness.
选 brevity
派 economical（*adj.* 节俭的）

释 *n.* 经济体系 the process or system by which goods and services are produced, sold, and bought in a country or region
例 The Greek *economy* has seen a sharp downturn with record unemployment, stagnating growth, and low wages.

listless
/'lɪstləs/

释 *adj.* 没精打采的 lacking energy or spirit
例 Comanche had been doing well until recently, when kidney failure caused him to stop eating and become *listless*.
选 sluggish
反 dynamic

humor
/'hjuːmər/

释 *n.* 幽默 a funny or amusing quality
例 Demonstrating his natural *humor* at a young age, George Carlin surprised no one when he became a successful comedian.

释 *n.* 脾气，秉性 characteristic or habitual disposition or bent
例 Always in a foul *humor*, the old man alienated all of his family and friends by his constant derision and insults.

complaint
/kəm'pleɪnt/

释 *n.* 抱怨 expression of grief, pain, or dissatisfaction
例 After the initial batch of faulty products, Microsoft was inundated with *complaints* from dissatisfied clients.

释 *n.* 疾病，痛苦 a bodily ailment or disease
例 Backache is a common *complaint* among aging people.

tender
/'tendər/

释 *v.* 提供 to present acceptance
例 I decided to *tender* my resignation this morning after months of deliberation over the matter.

释 *adj.* 温柔的 very loving and gentle
例 At the end of the movie *Love Actually*, there is a *tender* moment when the main characters finally kiss.

释 *adj.* 疼痛的 painful when touched
例 Several weeks after the bike injury, the leg wound was still *tender* to the touch.

anchor /ˈæŋkər/	释 **v. 使…稳定** to hold (something) firmly in place 例 In order to avoid any possible accidents, the captain **anchored** the boat to the marina before letting passengers in. 反 dislodge 释 **v. 扮演重要角色** to be the strongest and most important part of (something) 例 During the early years of Apple, the company was **anchored** by the vision and business acumen of Steve Jobs. 释 **n. 依靠，支柱** a reliable or principal support 例 Dad was the **anchor** of the family and the burden of everyone's health and well-being weighed on his shoulders.
bitter /ˈbɪtər/	释 **adj. 怨恨的，气愤的** angry or unhappy because of unfair treatment 例 In the aftermath of his **bitter** divorce, Ben could not even contemplate dating for several months. 释 **adj. 苦的** being the opposite of sweet 例 Without the addition of milk and sugar, chocolate is often quite **bitter**.
husbandry /ˈhʌzbəndri/	释 **n. 农业，畜牧业，饲养业** the activity of raising plants or animals for food 例 The rancher was in the business of animal **husbandry**, raising cows for beef. 释 **n. 节省** the management or wise use of resources 例 Conservationists argue that unconstrained exploitation of natural resources, which might deplete them forever, should be replaced with a policy of **husbandry**.
anticipate /ænˈtɪsɪpeɪt/	释 **v. 期待** to look forward to (something) 例 Many children eagerly **anticipate** the arrival of Christmas so that they can receive presents. 释 **v. （为防止…而）预先处理** to foresee and deal with in advance 例 The challenge facing public health officials is to **anticipate** an outbreak of disease and then ensure that schoolchildren are immunized. 选 foresee
hail /heɪl/	释 **n. 欢呼，赞美** the act of greeting or acclaiming 例 The debut novel received tremendous **hail** on both sides of the Atlantic and was even made into a feature film. 释 **v. 欢呼，赞美** to greet or acclaim enthusiastically 例 A pre-publication review of *Zora and Me* **hailed** the 192-page mystery novel by calling it "absolutely outstanding". 选 acclaim

anonymous
/əˈnɑːnɪməs/

释 *adj.* 不出名的 not distinct or noticeable
例 In order to cultivate new repertoire, the music industry is providing a hearing for previously **anonymous** female composers.
选 obscure

释 *adj.* 匿名的 made or done by someone unknown
例 In order to keep his identity **anonymous**, the criminal did not sign any of his letters to the police.

tend
/tend/

释 *v.* 照顾，养育 to apply oneself to the care of
例 As a hobby, many homeowners **tend** their vegetable gardens and produce food for home consumption.

释 *v.* 倾斜 to move in a particular direction
例 If the alignment of the car is not corrected, it will **tend** to one direction or the other when you are trying to drive straight.

dissipate
/ˈdɪsɪpeɪt/

释 *v.* 使…消散 to cause (something) to spread out and disappear
例 After a week of air pollution, the wind finally started to blow, which managed to **dissipate** all of the harmful particles in the air.

释 *v.* 浪费，挥霍 to use all or a lot of (something, such as money or time) in a foolish way
例 After his lavish expenditures on houses and cars, Vanilla Ice's wealth quickly **dissipated**.
选 dispersed

misuse
/ˌmɪsˈjuːs/

释 *v.* 不公平地对待 to treat (someone) unfairly
例 In order for the employees to be happy and work at peak efficiency, their managers must not **misuse** them.

释 *v.* 误用 to use incorrectly
例 **Misusing** the clutch in a car can cause long-term damage to the transmission.
选 abuse

physical
/ˈfɪzɪkl/

释 *adj.* 实体的 existing in a form that you can touch or see
例 With the production of the mustang, an affordable sports car was finally brought to **physical** form.

释 *adj.* 自然科学的 of or relating to natural science
例 All of the **physical** world is composed of atoms and smaller subatomic particles.

释 *adj.* 肉体的 relating to the body of a person instead of the mind
例 In order to gain overall health, it is best to take care of one's **physical** and mental fitness.

embrace
/ɪmˈbreɪs/

释 **v.** 接受 to accept (something or someone) readily or gladly
例 Despite thinking that his parents would be upset with him for dropping out of college, Brad was **embraced** by his family for following his passion as a woodworker.

释 **v.** 拥抱 to hold someone in your arms as a way of expressing love or friendship
例 When the couple was finally reunited after months apart, they lovingly **embraced** each other in the airport.

descendant
/dɪˈsendənt/

释 **adj.** 下降的 moving or directed downward
例 The **descendant** escalator was moving so fast that the little girl lost her balance and crashed downwards.

释 **n.** 后代 someone who is related to a person or group of people who lived in the past
例 According to legend, the Romans were the **descendants** of the Trojans who fled from the Trojan War.

abstraction
/æbˈstrækʃən/

释 **n.** 抽象，概要 the state of being abstracted
例 Although mathematics follow strict rules, many of the concepts are **abstractions** that cannot be shown in the physical world, like negative numbers.

释 **n.** 心不在焉 absence of mind or preoccupation
例 During drug-induced states, many experience a complete **abstraction** of mind that cuts them off from reality.
选 generality, divorce

substantial
/səbˈstænʃəl/

释 **adj.** 大量的 large in amount, size, or number
例 Against all odds, the 300 Spartans held off a more **substantial** Persian force at Thermopylae for several days.

释 **adj.** 坚固的 firmly constructed
例 Although the house looked ramshackle, it was a **substantial** building that had withstood countless tornadoes and windstorms.

释 **adj.** 重要的 important or essential
例 A **substantial** portion of this work relies on your intelligence and sensitivity, not brute force.
选 concrete, solid

counterpart
/ˈkaʊntərpɑːrt/

释 **n.** 等价物 someone or something that has the same job or purpose as another
例 British police are working closely with their French **counterparts** in Marseille and are trying to find and arrest any England fans causing trouble.
选 parallel

释 **n.** 补充 something that completes
例 During the race, my **counterpart** finished in the top 10%, but I had to pull out.

mirror /ˈmɪrər/	释 **v.** 与…相似 to be very similar to (something) 例 The tranquil story recounted by Ezra Jack Keats in *The Snowy Day* **mirrors** the calm presence of the book's pristine illustrations.
enterprise /ˈentərpraɪz/	释 **n.** 活动 a systematic purposeful activity 例 In order to reach the north pole, William Perry formed an exploratory **enterprise** with other scientists and adventurers. 释 **n.** 进取心 readiness to engage in daring or difficult action 例 A man with the **enterprise** to undertake any task, Ray surprised no one by attempting to climb Mt. Everest. 选 diligence 派 enterprising (*adj.* 有进取心的，创新的)
shoulder /ˈʃoʊldər/	释 **v.** 承担 to assume the burden or responsibility of 例 Often in work groups, one member **shoulders** most of the burden while everyone else relaxes.
recipe /ˈresəpi/	释 **n.** 秘诀，方法 a formula or procedure for doing or attaining something 例 The shoe company Zappos has been so successful that other companies have tried to copy its **recipe** for success.
cupidity /kjuːˈpɪdəti/	释 **n.** 贪心 a strong desire for money or possessions 例 Proclaiming morality while practicing **cupidity**, states have tried to bring in money with lotteries by increasing revenue through gambling. 选 avarice
square /skwer/	释 **v.** 符合，一致 to bring into conformity or agreement 例 Your ideas don't **square** with mine even though you keep nodding in agreement with me. 选 conform
slight /slaɪt/	释 **v.** 轻视 to treat (someone) with disrespect 例 **Slighted** by not being chosen for the All-Star team, Derek Jeter worked even harder to prove that he was the best shortstop.
finger /ˈfɪŋɡər/	释 **v.** 指出 to point out 例 In order to deceive the police about his involvement, Jerry **fingered** someone else for the crime.
muddy /ˈmʌdi/	释 **v.** 使…模糊 to cause (something) to become unclear or confused 例 When a sixth person decided to join our trip, the transport situation became **muddy** because the car only fit five people.
people /ˈpiːpl/	释 **v.** 充满 to supply or fill with people 例 The train station was quickly **peopled** with groups of children on their way to school in the early hours of the morning.

☐ mirror ☐ enterprise ☐ shoulder ☐ recipe ☐ cupidity
☐ square ☐ slight ☐ finger ☐ muddy ☐ people

immediate
/ɪˈmiːdiət/

释 *adj.* 紧靠的，最接近的 directly touching or concerning a person or thing
例 The *immediate* influence of Plato was his mentor Socrates.

释 *adj.* 当下的 of or relating to the here and now
例 The consequences of the operation were *immediate* and rapidly resulted in death within a couple of minutes.

释 *adj.* 直接的 acting or being without the intervention of another object, cause, or agency
例 During earthquakes, the *immediate* danger is falling objects.

guesswork
/ˈɡeswɜːrk/

释 *n.* 猜测 work performed or results obtained by guess
例 The physical and astronomical sciences are still too undeveloped as yet to make their theories about the end of the universe more than *guesswork*.
近 conjecture

untiring
/ʌnˈtaɪərɪŋ/

释 *adj.* 不知疲倦的 working very hard with a lot of energy for a long time
例 Their *untiring* efforts performing in Germany helped to hone the skill of the Beatles before they released their first album.

grand
/ɡrænd/

释 *adj.* 富丽堂皇的 lavish or sumptuous
例 To commemorate his coronation by the pope, Charlemagne held a *grand* banquet filled with great amounts of exotic foods.

释 *adj.* 傲慢的 pretending to social superiority
例 Putting on *grand* airs, Paula Deen put forth the image of a sweet grandmother, but recent evidence suggests otherwise.

corrosive
/kəˈroʊsɪv/

释 *adj.* （言语）讽刺的，挖苦的 bitingly sarcastic
例 In his *corrosive* diatribe against the conspirators, Cicero attacked many of the new institutions in the Roman Republic that threatened the political order.

radical
/ˈrædɪkl/

释 *adj.* 极端的，激进的 advocating extreme measures to retain or restore a political state of affairs
例 In the early first millennium CE, the Gnostics were an accepted branch of Christianity, but now they would be considered a *radical* cult.

释 *adj.* 颠覆性的 very different from the usual or traditional
例 The *radical* success of Nirvana helped to launch alternative music into the mainstream.

释 *adj.* 根本的 very basic and important
例 The *radical* components of all matter are atoms.

fuel
/ˈfjuːəl/

释 *v.* 支撑，支持 to give support or strength to (something)
例 Many important people credit their parents for *fueling* their success.

aside

/əˈsaɪd/

🈲 *n.* 跑题 a straying from the theme

🈹 The author's main topic is trilobites, but in an ***aside*** he lashes out at readers who didn't understand his previous book.

🈹 digression

Word List 24

音频

sequel /'siːkwəl/	释 ***n.*** 后续，后果 a book, movie or other work that continues the story of a previous work 例 When the kindly old wizard died at the end of the book, readers hoped that the ***sequel*** would reveal that he was not really dead.
factotum /fæk'toʊtəm/	释 ***n.*** 杂工 a person whose job involves doing many different types of work 例 Despite being hired for a specific project, the temporary employee became a ***factotum*** who moved from division to division.
disputant /'dɪspjutənt/	释 ***n.*** 争论者 a person who is involved in a dispute and especially in a legal dispute 例 In the show, Judge Judy evaluates the veracity of both ***disputants***' stories to reach a verdict for civil damages.
novice /'nɑːvɪs/	释 ***n.*** 新手 a person who has just started learning or doing something 例 Despite being a ***novice*** brewer, Gregg won first place in the state fair with his second ever brew.
tyro /'taɪroʊ/	释 ***n.*** 新手 a person who has just started learning or doing something : a beginner or novice 例 It is impossible for an artistic ***tyro*** to make a great painting; it requires many years of practice and innate creativity. 选 neophyte 反 expert
neophyte /'niːəfaɪt/	释 ***n.*** 新手 a person who has just started learning or doing something 例 The experts could not believe that a ***neophyte*** had created such an accomplished work; they found the idea implausible. 选 tyro, novice
maverick /'mævərɪk/	释 ***n.*** 标新立异之人 a person who refuses to follow the customs or rules of group 例 The ***maverick*** pilot endangered the lives of his crew by ignoring the Air Force's policies against aerial acrobatics close to mountains. 选 nonconformist
martinet /ˌmɑːrtn'et/	释 ***n.*** 要求严格纪律的人 a person who is very strict and demands obedience from others 例 The drum major was a young ***martinet*** who ruled over his band with an iron fist.

sophist
/ˈsɑːfɪst/

释 *n.* 哲学家 philosopher
例 As a *sophist*, Protagoras taught the children of Athens moral rectitude and cosmology.

释 *n.* 诡辩家 a captious or fallacious reasoner
例 As a debater, Lenny was something of a *sophist* in that he often used subtly deceptive reasoning to win points.

quibbler
/ˈkwɪblər/

释 *n.* 吹毛求疵的人 to argue or complain about small, unimportant things
例 "I'm not usually a *quibbler* when travelling, but these peanuts are too salty," the passenger complained to the flight attendant.

pedant
/ˈpednt/

释 *n.* 卖弄学问的人 a person who annoys other people by correcting small errors and giving too much attention to minor details
例 No one likes a grammatical *pedant* who corrects everyone's speech in casual conversation.
派 pedantic（*adj.* 迂腐的，学究的）

naysayer
/ˈneɪˌseɪər/

释 *n.* 否定者，怀疑者 a person who says something will not work or is not possible; a person who denies, refuses, or opposes something
例 Shaun White silenced the *naysayers* when he landed the Tomahawk, a trick that experts thought was impossible.

acolyte
/ˈækəlaɪt/

释 *n.* 助手 someone who follows and admires a leader
例 The charismatic professor had a number of *acolytes* who hung on to every word he said and did whatever he asked.

释 *n.* 侍僧 someone who helps the person who leads a church service
例 As an *acolyte*, the young priest made several mistakes during his first service.

associate
/əˈsoʊʃieɪt/

释 *n.* 同事，伙伴 a person who you work with or spend time with
例 Many enjoy spending time with their work *associates*, but some do not like socializing after work.

canary
/kəˈneri/

释 *n.* 金丝雀 a small usually yellow or green tropical bird that is often kept in a cage
例 Previously, miners took *canaries* under the earth to warn them of noxious fumes.

braggart
/ˈbrægərt/

释 *n.* 吹牛者 a person who brags a lot
例 Whenever the department *braggart* comes to the party, he smugly makes everyone aware of all of his academic accomplishments.

dictator
/ˈdɪkteɪtər/

释 *n.* 独裁者 a person who rules a country with total authority and often in a cruel or brutal way
例 While Fidel Castro was the *dictator* of Cuba, many citizens fled their island to gain freedom from oppression in the USA.
派 dictatorial（*adj.* 独裁的，专政的）

☐ sophist ☐ quibbler ☐ pedant ☐ naysayer ☐ acolyte
☐ associate ☐ canary ☐ braggart ☐ dictator

tyrant /ˈtaɪrənt/	释 *n.* 暴君 a ruler who has complete power over a country and who is cruel and unfair 例 The country's struggle for political freedom had been long and arduous, but eventually the ruler, who was a ***tyrant***, was replaced by a true democratic leader.
denizen /ˈdenɪzn/	释 *n.* 居民 a person, animal, or plant that lives in or often is found in a particular place or region 例 Not all ***denizens*** of the sea are fish; dolphins are intelligent mammals.
bishop /ˈbɪʃəp/	释 *n.* 主教 an official in some Christian religions who is ranked higher than a priest and who is usually in charge of church matters in a specific geographical area 例 In a meeting with his priests, the ***bishop*** described the changes to the service.
clergy /ˈklɜːrdʒi/	释 *n.* 神职人员，牧师 people (such as priests) who are the leaders of a religion and who perform religious services 例 All members of the Catholic ***clergy*** are responsible to the Pope.
prophet /ˈprɑːfɪt/	释 *n.* 先知，预言者 a member of some religions (such as Christianity, Judaism, and Islam) who delivers messages that are believed to have come from God 例 According to Christians, John the Baptist is a ***prophet*** of Jesus who foretold the coming of the Messiah.
virtuoso /ˌvɜːrtʃuˈoʊsoʊ/	释 *n.* 艺术品鉴赏家 one skilled in or having a taste for the fine arts 例 As a piano ***virtuoso***, Chopin was a well-known musician before his teenage years.
progeny /ˈprɑːdʒəni/	释 *n.* 子孙，后裔 a person who comes from a particular parent or family; the child or descendant of someone 例 Due to their great pedigree, all the ***progeny*** of the racehorse Seabiscuit became champion racers.
hardliner /ˌhɑːrd ˈlaɪnər/	释 *n.* 强硬分子 someone who advocates or involves a rigidly uncompromising course of action 例 As a conservative ***hardliner***, Glen Beck refuses to acknowledge any positions of the Democratic party.
dilettante /ˌdɪləˈtænti/	释 *n.* 半吊子，业余的人，一知半解的人 a person having a superficial interest in an art or a branch of knowledge 例 It was out of modesty that Professor Green, the author of several highly respected books in his field, described himself to his colleagues as a ***dilettante***.
spearhead /ˈspɪrhed/	释 *n.* 先锋部队 a person, thing, or group that organizes or leads something (such as a movement or attack) 例 As the ***spearhead*** of the Civil Rights Movement, Martin Luther King Jr. led many peaceful protests to demand rights for African Americans.

□ tyrant   □ denizen   □ bishop   □ clergy   □ prophet
□ virtuoso   □ progeny   □ hardliner □ dilettante □ spearhead

vanguard /ˈvængɑːrd/	释 *n.* 先锋 the group of people who are the leaders of an action or movement in society, politics, art, etc. 例 The **vanguard** of the music industry thought they could litigate users to stop illegally downloading music, but it took new streaming services to curtail the practice.
philistine /ˈfɪlɪstiːn/	释 *n.* 庸俗的人 a person who is guided by materialism and is usually disdainful of intellectual or artistic values 例 Helmut Kohl wanted to be seen as an international statesman, but feared he was perceived as a provincial **philistine.** 反 aesthete
polymath /ˈpɑːlimæθ/	释 *n.* 博学的人 someone who knows a lot about many different things 例 Benjamin Franklin was renowned for being a **polymath**, having delved deeply into fields as diverse as politics, business, diplomacy, statecraft, science, and publishing. 选 encyclopedic
prodigy /ˈprɑːdədʒi/	释 *n.* 神童 a young person who is unusually talented in some way 例 The gifted child-poet Minou Drouet, hailed in the 1950s as an artistic **prodigy**, now lives in relative anonymity, enjoying a privacy unavailable to her as a child.
interlocutor /ˌɪntərˈlɑːkjətər/	释 *n.* 对话者 a person who is having a conversation with you 例 At the party, I debated politics with another **interlocutor** whose name now eludes me.
spendthrift /ˈspendθrɪft/	释 *n.* 挥霍的人 a person who spends money in a careless or wasteful way 例 A notorious **spendthrift**, Francis never batted an eyelid dining at Michelin-starred restaurants every day.
monger /ˈmʌŋgər/	释 *n.* 商人，贩子 broker, dealer — usually used in combination 例 As a **monger** of fish, Cary had to rise early to sell the night's catch.
culprit /ˈkʌlprɪt/	释 *n.* 罪犯，罪魁祸首 a person who has committed a crime or done something wrong 例 After days of searching, the **culprit** who burned the school down was finally caught by police.
curator /kjʊˈreɪtər/	释 *n.* 管理者 a person who is in charge of the things in a museum, zoo, etc. 例 The **curator** of the antiquities department at the museum organized an exhibition on post-impressionism.
orator /ˈɔːrətər/	释 *n.* 演讲者 a person who makes speeches and is very good at making them 例 In recent years, Barack Obama stands out as a powerful **orator** who convinced millions that change would come.

fledgling /ˈfledʒlɪŋ/	🔤 *n.* 无经验的人 someone or something that is getting started in a new activity 📕 The **fledgling** company required new investors in order to stay in business for a second year. 🔄 experienced
cynic /ˈsɪnɪk/	🔤 *n.* 认为人性自私的人 a person who has negative opinions about other people and about the things people do, especially a person who believes that people are selfish and are only interested in helping themselves 📕 A true **cynic**, George Carlin revealed the seediness of humanity with his hilarious anecdotes and logic.
quixote /ˈkwiksət/	🔤 *n.* 爱空想的人 a quixotic person 📕 The **quixote** believed that good vibes and love were the only things necessary to bring peace to the world.
expansionist /ɪkˈspænʃənɪst/	🔤 *n.* 扩张主义者 someone who holds the belief that a country should grow larger 📕 Early in the history of the USA, **expansionist** doctrines were justified by a sense of "manifest destiny", that America should stretch from sea to sea.
electorate /ɪˈlektərət/	🔤 *n.* 选举人 the people who can vote in an election 📕 The US **electorate** is composed of millions of people, but only a fraction of these vote.
preservationist /ˌprezərˈveɪʃənɪst/	🔤 *n.* 保护主义者 someone who works to preserve something (such as a building or an area of land) 📕 Credited as the first **preservationist**, Teddy Roosevelt established the National Park Service to protect the natural resources of America.
zealot /ˈzelət/	🔤 *n.* 狂热者 a person who has very strong feelings about something (such as religion or politics) and who wants other people to have those feelings; a zealous person 📕 David Koresh was a religious **zealot** who founded a cult and committed horrible crimes against his members in the name of god.
extremist /ɪkˈstriːmɪst/	🔤 *n.* 极端主义者 someone who believes in and supports for ideas that are very far from what most people consider correct or reasonable 📕 Some vegan **extremists** refuse to enter a restaurant where meat is served. 🔀 zealot
revisionist /rɪˈvɪʒənɪst/	🔤 *n.* 修正主义者 someone who supports ideas and beliefs that differ from and try to change accepted ideas and beliefs especially in a way that is seen as wrong or dishonest 📕 *The Man in the High Castle* is a novel featuring a **revisionist** history of World War II in which the Nazis won the war.

☐ fledgling   ☐ cynic   ☐ quixote   ☐ expansionist   ☐ electorate
☐ preservationist   ☐ zealot   ☐ extremist   ☐ revisionist

mogul /ˈmoʊɡl/	释 *n.* 有权势的人 a great personage: magnate 例 As a business *mogul*, he has become synonymous with large towers and expensive real estate.
guru /ˈɡuˌru/	释 *n.* 领袖 a teacher or guide that you trust 例 In order to enter the world's elite of Scrabble, Sam hired a former champion as a *guru* to improve his game. 释 *n.* 专家 a person who has a lot of experience in or knowledge about a particular subject 例 Bill Gates and Steve Jobs remain iconic *gurus* in the tech industry for their successful businesses and longevity in the field.
tycoon /taɪˈkuːn/	释 *n.* 企业界大亨，巨头 a very wealthy and powerful business person 例 As a young *tycoon*, Mark Cuban wisely invested his sudden wealth into more successful ventures.
bellwether /ˈbelweðər/	释 *n.* 领导者 someone or something that leads others or shows what will happen in the future 例 The rapid surge of internet stocks in the late 1990s was a *bellwether* for the dot-com bubble that immediately followed.
stickler /ˈstɪklər/	释 *n.* 坚持…的人 a person who believes that something is very important and should be done or followed all the time 例 A *stickler* for grammar, the professor marked every split infinitive or dangling participle incorrect on the essay.
diehard /ˈdaɪhɑːrd/	释 *adj.* 顽固的 strongly or fanatically determined or devoted 例 *Diehard* collectors of action figures often have entire rooms filled with mint condition figures still in the boxes.
nonentity /nɑːˈnentəti/	释 *n.* 无足轻重的人 a person who is not famous or important 例 With his 10 followers, Peter thought he was internet famous, but, in reality, he was a *nonentity* who was known by no one.
imposter /ɪmˈpɑːstər/	释 *n.* 冒名顶替的人 a person who deceives others by pretending to be someone else 例 A purported member of the Vanderbilt family turned out to be an *imposter* who hoodwinked the family into supporting him.
mastermind /ˈmæstərmaɪnd/	释 *n.* 策划者 a person who plans and organizes something 例 Although the actual thieves in the art heist were captured, the *mastermind* who organized the burglary was never caught.
iconoclast /aɪˈkɑːnəklæst/	释 *n.* 提倡打破旧习的人 a person who criticizes or opposes beliefs and practices that are widely accepted 例 The new biographer of Lincoln is an *iconoclast* who portrays him as a flawed man utterly uncommitted to anti-slavery. 派 iconoclastic（*adj.* 反传统的，反崇拜的）

☐ mogul ☐ guru ☐ tycoon ☐ bellwether ☐ stickler
☐ diehard ☐ nonentity ☐ imposter ☐ mastermind ☐ iconoclast

soothsayer /ˈsuːθseɪər/	释 *n.* 预言家 a person who predicts the future by magical, intuitive, or more rational means 例 In early cultures, **soothsayers** held great influence because of their ability to commune with the gods and magic powers.
connoisseur /ˌkɑːnəˈsɜːr/	释 *n.* 鉴赏家，内行 a person who knows a great deal about something (such as art, wine, food, etc.); an expert in a particular subject 例 After many decades of trying fine wines from all over the world, Harold thought himself a **connoisseur**. 派 connoisseurship（*n.* 鉴赏力）
boor /bʊr/	释 *n.* 粗人 a rude and rough person 例 **Boors** should avoid working in customer service industry because their rudeness with customers will result in low sales.
playwright /ˈpleɪraɪt/	释 *n.* 剧作家 a person who writes plays 例 Standing out among all of the world's **playwrights**, Shakespeare is a master of both drama and comedy.
despot /ˈdespɑːt/	释 *n.* 独裁者 a ruler who has total power and who often uses that power in cruel and unfair ways 例 During World War II, a number of fascist **despots** came to power and manipulated their people into acts of war and horrible crimes.
apologist /əˈpɑːlədʒɪst/	释 *n.* 辩护人 one who speaks or writes in defense of someone or something 例 As an **apologist** for communism, the scholar argued that it failed in the Soviet Union because of the authoritarian nature of the government and not because of the system itself.
wastrel /ˈweɪstrəl/	释 *n.* 浪费的人 a person who wastes time, money, etc. 例 The internet has turned many formerly productive workers into **wastrels** who spend the day on social media.
autocrat /ˈɔːtəkræt/	释 *n.* 独裁者 a person who rules with total power 例 Many feared that Julius Caesar would become an **autocrat** after he was named dictator for life, so the Senate plotted his assassination.
oddball /ˈɑːdbɔːl/	释 *n.* 古怪的人 a person who is noticeably strange or eccentric 例 When I got to art school, I found that many of the students were **oddballs** with eccentric ways of dressing, speaking and decorating their dorms.
bore /bɔːr/	释 *n.* 无聊的人 one that causes boredom 例 Some intellectuals are perceived as **bores** in person, but their writings are frequently very interesting.
layperson /ˈleɪpɜːrsn/	释 *n.* 外行 a member of the laity 例 If you want HR to forward your resume to the hiring manager, you need to make sure a **layperson** can understand what you're talking about. 选 nonspecialist 反 authority, expert

has-been
/ˈhæz biːn/
缀 *n.* 过时的人 a person who is no longer popular or successful
例 Criticized by many as a ***has-been***, Alex Rodriguez surprised many baseball fans by leading his team in home runs.

progenitor
/prouˈdʒenɪtər/
缀 *n.* 先驱 precursor, originator
例 Max Roach is regarded as a ***progenitor*** of modern jazz drumming because he was one of the first artists to exploit the melodic, rather than merely rhythmic, possibilities of his instrument.

benefactor
/ˈbenɪfæktər/
缀 *n.* 慈善家 someone who helps another person, group, etc., by giving money
例 Many private universities depend heavily on ***benefactors***, who are generally wealthy individuals who lend their support with gifts and donations.

gourmand
/ˈɡurmaːnd/
缀 *n.* 吃货 a person who loves to eat and drink
例 Many self-styled ***gourmands*** begin food blogs to document their dining and cooking experiences.

cronyism
/ˈkrouniːzəm/
缀 *n.* 任用亲信 the unfair practice by a powerful person (such as a politician) of giving jobs and other favors to friends
例 Many politicians are accused of lining the pockets of their closest supporters, but these reports of ***cronyism*** are rarely substantiated.
选 nepotism

nepotism
/ˈnepətɪzəm/
缀 *n.* 任人唯亲 the unfair practice by a powerful person of giving jobs and other favors to relatives
例 Denying ***nepotism***, the manager argued that he gave his son a position at the company because he was the most qualified.
选 cronyism
派 nepotistic（*adj.* 任人唯亲的）

totalitarianism
/touˌtæləˈteriənɪzəm/
缀 *n.* 极权主义 centralized control by an autocratic authority
例 Few people these days advocate for ***totalitarianism***, in which every aspect of life is controlled by the government.

utilitarianism
/juːtɪlɪˈteriənɪzəm/
缀 *n.* 功利主义 the belief that a morally good action is one that helps the greatest number of people
例 In his doctrine of ***utilitarianism***, Jeremy Bentham argued that the highest moral value is doing the most good for the most people.

cynicism
/ˈsɪnɪsɪzəm/
缀 *n.* 认为人性自私 cynical beliefs; beliefs that people are generally selfish and dishonest
例 Many people who were once idealistic turn to ***cynicism*** when they see how self-interested and corrupt others can be.

chauvinism
/ˈʃouvɪnɪzəm/
缀 *n.* 盲目的爱国心 the belief that your country, race, etc., is better than any other
例 In certain parts of the USA, ***chauvinism*** is strongly embraced by the people who think foreigners are inferior to Americans.

□ has-been　　□ progenitor　　□ benefactor　　□ gourmand　　□ cronyism
□ nepotism　　□ totalitarianism　　□ utilitarianism　　□ cynicism　　□ chauvinism

egalitarianism
/i,gælɪˈteriənɪzəm/

n. 平等主义 a belief in human equality especially with respect to social, political, and economic affairs

例 Most hunter-gatherer societies are characterized by the full equality of their members in a non-structured, **egalitarian** system of rule.

altruism
/ˈæltruɪzəm/

n. 无私，利他主义 feelings and behavior that show a desire to help other people and a lack of selfishness

例 Her actions did nothing but good, but since she performed them out of self-interest, they could not be called **altruistic**.

anarchism
/ˈænərkɪzəm/

n. 无政府主义 a belief that government and laws are not necessary

例 Many alternative communities in Germany reject the role of the government and adopt **anarchism** and self-rule.

anthropocentrism
/,ænθrəpəˈsentrɪzəm/

n. 人类中心说 considering human beings as the most significant entity of the universe

例 Although rarely stating it, many humans espouse notions of **anthropocentrism** and think the world caters to the needs of man.

atheism
/ˈeɪθiɪzəm/

n. 无神论 a disbelief in the existence of deity

例 After the sudden death of his entire family, Jeb rejected religion and embraced **atheism**.

collectivism
/kəˈlektɪvɪzəm/

n. 集体主义 a political or economic system in which the government owns businesses, land, etc.

例 Mild forms of **collectivism** exist among socialist countries, but complete control of resources by the government is rare.

dualism
/ˈduːəlɪzəm/

n. 二元论 the idea or belief that everything has two opposite parts or principles

例 The philosophy of **dualism** embraces a distinction between the corporeal body and the non-physical aspects of the mind.

feminism
/ˈfemənɪzəm/

n. 女权主义 the belief that men and women should have equal rights and opportunities

例 During the 1970s, **feminism** entered the mainstream as advocates fought for equal rights of women.

hedonism
/ˈhiːdənɪzəm/

n. 享乐主义 the belief that pleasure or happiness is the most important goal in life

例 Many people think of Roman banquets as affairs of **hedonism** filled with sex, rich food, and wine, but most were rather tame until the Empire.

individualism
/,ɪndɪˈvɪdʒuəlɪzəm/

n. 个人主义 the actions or attitudes of a person who does things without being concerned about what other people will think

例 For people like TV character the Fonz, being cool required expressing complete **individualism** with little regard for how others perceived you.

nihilism
/ˈnaɪɪlɪzəm/

n. 虚无主义 the belief that traditional morals, ideas, beliefs, etc., have no worth or value

例 Espousing the concept of **nihilism**, Nietzsche wanted to cast aside all religions and morals.

☐ egalitarianism   ☐ altruism   ☐ anarchism   ☐ anthropocentrism   ☐ atheism
☐ collectivism   ☐ dualism   ☐ feminism   ☐ hedonism   ☐ individualism
☐ nihilism

teetotalism
/ˌtiːˈtoʊtəlɪzəm/

释 *n.* 禁酒主义 the principle or practice of complete abstinence from alcoholic drinks

例 Prohibition was brought about by the popularity of **teetotalism** and the belief that alcohol was the root of many of society's evils.

---

renegade
/ˈrenɪɡeɪd/

释 *n* 叛徒 a deserter from one faith, cause, or allegiance to another

例 The country still considers this area a **renegade** province to be reunited by force if necessary.

选 rebel, outlaw

---

misanthrope
/ˈmɪsənθroʊp/

释 *n.* 厌恶人类的人，愤世嫉俗的人 one who hates or mistrusts humankind

例 He is an epic **misanthrope** and equal-opportunity bigot whose every utterance is filled with invective or despair.

---

leveling
/ˈlevlɪŋ/

释 *n.* 使平等，使一致 the act of making equal or uniform

例 The **leveling** of grading criteria across all national examination boards was received with great enthusiasm by most teachers.

---

straddle
/ˈstrædl/

释 *v.* 横跨 to be on both sides of; extend over or across

例 This park **straddles** the two neighborhoods and is a convenient meeting point for all residents to congregate.

释 *v.* 观望 to appear to favor both sides of an issue

例 She gave a comment that **straddled** complete freedom of press and media censorship so as not to offend both parties involved.

---

baleful
/ˈbeɪlfl/

释 *adj.* 邪恶的，不吉利的 portending evil; ominous

例 Ming gave such a **baleful** laugh that its wickedness sent shivers down my spine.

选 sinister

释 *adj.* （意图上）恶意的，险恶的 harmful or malignant in intent or effect

例 She felt a surge of guilt when told that her actions resulted in horrendously **baleful** consequences.

---

shelve
/ʃelv/

释 *v.* 搁置 If someone shelves a plan or project, they decide not to continue with it, either for a while or permanently

例 We are forced to **shelve** this project now due to limited resources and budget.

---

scribble
/ˈskrɪbl/

释 *v.* 草率地写画 to write or draw in a hurried, careless way

例 He hurriedly **scribbled** down the license plate of the car that had knocked down the girl before it sped away.

---

abyss
/əˈbɪs/

释 *n.* 深渊（指危险的处境）a very dangerous or frightening situation

例 Ming suffered from a mental breakdown as he could no longer cope with the **abyss** of endless work and stress.

□ teetotalism □ renegade □ misanthrope □ leveling □ straddle
□ baleful □ shelve □ scribble □ abyss

stunning /ˈstʌnɪŋ/	释 *adj.* 令人印象深刻的 strikingly impressive especially in beauty or excellence 例 The architecture of the Notre Dame cathedral in France is so ***stunning*** that I stood in awe for a full hour when I first saw it in person. 选 impressive 释 *adj.* 令人吃惊的，出乎意料的 causing astonishment or disbelief 例 Ruan's lack of guilt or shame at his offence is not only confounding but utterly ***stunning***. 选 unexpected
bulwark /ˈbʊlwɜːrk/	释 *n.* 堡垒，壁垒 a wall or embankment raised as a defensive fortification; a rampart 例 The city of Zoersol did not collapse during the medieval wars due to its impenetrable ***bulwark***. 释 *v.* 为…提供防御或保护 to provide defense or protection for 例 Freedom of press ***bulwarks*** the fundamental principles of democracy and should be upheld.
showcase /ˈʃoʊkeɪs/	释 *v.* 展示 to display prominently, especially to advantage 例 The recent retrospective ***showcased*** Monet's work with great artistic sensitivity and intellectual vigor.
staunch /stɔːntʃ/	释 *adj.* 坚定的，忠诚的 steadfast in loyalty or principle 例 The ***staunch*** anti-abortion lobbyist refused to listen to opposing opinions and remained insistent on his own beliefs. 选 loyal, steadfast
untrammeled /ʌnˈtræmld/	释 *adj.* 自由的 not limited or restricted; unrestrained 例 Yin divorced her husband as she desired an ***untrammeled*** life free from obligations to a man who did not really love her. 选 unhampered, uninhibited, unrestrained
screed /skriːd/	释 *n.* 冗长、单调的说话或者文章 a long, monotonous harangue or piece of writing 例 After decades of marriage, Han has gotten used to his wife's daily morning ***screed*** and is no longer irritated by it.
stupefaction /ˌstuːpɪˈfækʃn/	释 *n.* 非常惊讶或惊慌失措 great astonishment or consternation 例 He walked into the meeting an hour late without an apology, much to the ***stupefaction*** of the board members present.
vitriolic /ˌvɪtriˈɑːlɪk/	释 *adj.* 尖酸刻薄的 bitterly scathing; caustic 例 The columnist was unforgiving in his review of Lang Lang's concert and made several unwarranted ***vitriolic*** comments. 选 acrimonious
bombastic /baːmˈbæstɪk/	释 *adj.* 夸大的，言过其实的 (of somebody's words) sounding important but having little 例 I left the lecture halfway as I was disgusted by the lecturer's use of ***bombastic*** language and flamboyant gestures.

waggish
/'wægɪʃ/

adj. 诙谐的 characteristic of or resembling a wag; jocular or witty

例 His *waggish* remark managed to draw some laughter from the crowd and avoid a potentially awkward situation from happening.

retract
/rɪ'trækt/

v. 收回，否认 to take back; disavow

例 Sam wanted to *retract* his hurtful words after he had calmed down, but the damage had already been done as his wife was inconsolable.

etch
/etʃ/

v. 铭记 to impress, delineate, or imprint clearly

例 His generosity of spirit will be forever *etched* in my memory regardless of the fate of our friendship in the future.

exultant
/ɪg'zʌltənt/

adj. 狂喜的 marked by great joy or jubilation; triumphant

例 He let out an *exultant* cry when he received news that his book proposal had just been accepted by his publisher.

音频

axiomatic /ˌæksɪə'mætɪk/	释 *adj.* 公理的，不证自明的 of, relating to, or resembling an axiom; self-evident 例 The need for an appropriate level of circumspection when interpreting scientific results seems **axiomatic**. 近 self-evident
fusion /'fjuːʒn/	释 *n.* 融合 the merging of different elements into a union 例 Los Angelels is the place where **fusion** meets **fusion**, where Asia meets America, where good marries evil then immediately begins to see other people. 近 amalgam
exegesis /ˌeksɪ'dʒiːsɪs/	释 *n.* 解释，注释 critical explanation or analysis, especially of a text 例 When the entire world is a web of signs, everything cries out for **exegesis**.
cerebral /sə'riːbrəl/	释 *adj.* 理智的 appealing to or requiring the use of the intellect; intellectual rather than emotional 例 For all her **cerebral** elements, Rowling was also a master of the mundane. 近 intellectual 反 emotional
ideologue /'ɪdɪəlɒɡ/	释 *n.* 理论家，提倡者 an advocate of a particular ideology, especially an official exponent of that ideology 例 The president is not an **ideologue**. He's a pragmatist. He's trying to get people shoulder to shoulder and execute on the plan.
slavish /'sleɪvɪʃ/	释 *adj.* 缺乏创造力的，盲目模仿的 showing no originality; blindly imitative 例 Published to coincide with what would have been Christie's 126th birthday, the book captures the essence of the originals without being a **slavish** imitation.
hands-off /ˌhændz 'ɔːf/	释 *adj.* 不干涉的，不插手的 characterized by nonintervention 例 Is the president so **hands-off** that he waited for his secretary of defense to speak? 近 noninterventionist

no-nonsense /ˌnoʊ ˈnɑːnsens/	**adj.** 直接的，不允许的，实际的 not tolerating irrelevancies; direct, efficient, and practical 例 Her cheerful, **no-nonsense** demeanor defied the industry's longstanding practice of relegating female characters to the roles of housewife or secretary. 选 businesslike
channel /ˈtʃænl/	**v.** 指导，引导 to direct or guide along some desired course 例 Most of his energy was **channeled** into writing and lecturing. 选 direct
staid /steɪd/	**adj.** 沉着的，严肃的 characterized by sedate dignity and often a strait-laced sense of propriety 例 The traditional "Happy Birthday" isn't even celebratory; it's a **staid** musical obligation in the bleak face of aging. 选 sober
spurn /spɜːrn/	**v.** 因鄙视而拒绝 to reject disdainfully or contemptuously; scorn 例 He was abruptly turned away and, like other **spurned** applicants, was never told why. 选 flout
thenceforth /ˌðensˈfɔːrθ/	**adv.** 此后，从那时开始 from that time forward; thereafter 例 The acquaintance was made, and **thenceforth** I never went to Narischkin's without calling on her, either before or after dinner.
simpleton /ˈsɪmpltən/	**n.** 呆子，傻子 a person who is felt to be deficient in judgment, good sense, or intelligence; a fool 例 Life is pitiless and strange; only **simpletons** look for neat meanings.
duel /ˈduːəl/	**v.** 反对 to oppose actively and forcefully 例 A case of **duelling** legal directories is going to trial. **n.** 斗争 a struggle for domination between two contending persons, groups, or ideas 例 The two teams are locked in a **duel** for first place.
giddy /ˈgɪdi/	**adj.** 轻浮的，轻狂的 frivolous and lighthearted; flighty 例 When I am nervous, I become **giddy** and happily talkative.
cannibalism /ˈkænɪbəlɪzəm/	**n.** 食人，嗜食同类 the usually ritualistic eating of human flesh by a human being 例 Scientists have found evidence that starving 17th century colonists in Jamestown, Virginia, turned to **cannibalism** to survive.
galactic /gəˈlæktɪk/	**adj.** 星系的 of or relating to a galaxy, especially the Milky Way 例 India hopes the **galactic** feat will show the world it is open for business in space exploration.
platitudinous /ˌplætɪˈtuːdənəs/	**adj.** 平凡的，陈腐的 dull and tiresome 例 What often seemed essentially harmless, **platitudinous** stances may suddenly take on an oppositional, even radical, dimension.

☐ no-nonsense　　☐ channel　　☐ staid　　☐ spurn　　☐ thenceforth
☐ simpleton　　☐ duel　　☐ giddy　　☐ cannibalism　　☐ galactic
☐ platitudinous

lockstep /ˈlɑːkstep/	释 *n.* 步调一致 a standard procedure that is followed mindlessly 例 After years of moving in ***lockstep***, France and Germany are growing apart at an alarming rate.
offhand /ˌɔːfˈhænd/	释 *adj.* 即时的；未经准备的 with little or no preparation or forethought 例 The idea is to be conversational and ***offhand***, so the guys improvise part of the time.
veneer /vəˈnɪr/	释 *n.* 虚饰或虚伪的外表 a deceptive, superficial show 例 Beneath Ryan's perfect ***veneer***, she's been struggling in silence, ashamed of the reality of her situation.
wooden /ˈwʊdn/	释 *adj.* 僵硬的，呆板的 stiff and unnatural 例 She gave the stranger a ***wooden*** stare.
subsume /səbˈsuːm/	释 *v.* 归入，包含 contain or include 例 It requires a willingness to ***subsume*** ego in the collective.
plaudits /ˈplɔːdɪts/	释 *n.* 鼓掌，喝彩，赞扬 enthusiastic approval 例 Despite the ***plaudits*** he received for his rookie season, Seager left unsatisfied with his own performance and unsatisfied with a second-round playoff exit.
tack /tæk/	释 *v.* 固定，附加 fasten with small flat-headed nails; attach 例 They decided to ***tack*** an amendment to the bill.
helter-skelter /ˌheltər ˈskeltər/	释 *adv.* 匆促地，忙乱地 in disorderly haste; confusedly 例 A hail of fire from us sent the enemy troops fleeing ***helter-skelter***.
acquittal /əˈkwɪtl/	释 *n.* 宣告无罪 a judgment of not guilty 例 The defence lawyer made an eloquent plea for his client's ***acquittal***. 选 exculpating
shed /ʃed/	释 *v.* 去除，除去 to rid oneself of (something not wanted or needed) 例 It's too late to change your mind now and there is no point in ***shedding*** tears. 选 abandon
rummage /ˈrʌmɪdʒ/	释 *v.* 仔细检查 to search thoroughly by handling, turning over, or disarranging the contents of 例 The idea of reporters ***rummaging*** around in celebrities' dustbins or bugging phone calls is taking the issue of public interest too far.
disapprobation /ˌdɪsˌæprəˈbeɪʃn/	释 *n.* 不赞成；非难 an expression of strong disapproval; pronouncing as wrong or morally culpable 例 she braved her mother's ***disapprobation*** and slipped out to enjoy herself. 反 jubilation

regressive /rɪˈgresɪv/	释 *adj.* 退化的 characterized by regression or a tendency to regress 例 The policy has been condemned as a ***regressive*** step.
yore /jɔːr/	释 *n.* 很久以前 time past and especially long past 例 In days of ***yore*** it was usual for cavalryment to wear suits of armour.
laggard /ˈlægərd/	释 *adj.* 缓慢的；落后的 hanging back or falling behind; dilatory 例 In village, the ***laggard*** living condition must be improved.
query /ˈkwɪri/	释 *v.* 怀疑，提出疑问 to express doubt or uncertainty about; question 例 The minister was ***queried*** about his plans for the industry.
unremitting /ˌʌnrɪˈmɪtɪŋ/	释 *adj.* 坚持不懈的，不间断的 never slackening; persistent 例 Success is attainable through ***unremitting*** hard work. 近 continuous
accretive /əˈkriːtɪv/	释 *adj.* 增积的 the state of an increase by natural growth or addition 例 The company expects the deal to be ***accretive*** to free cash flow in 2013.
plangent /ˈplændʒənt/	释 *adj.* 悲哀的 expressing or suggesting sadness; plaintive 例 A ***plangent*** sound is a deep, loud sound, which may be sad.
iridescent /ˌɪrɪˈdesnt/	释 *adj.* 色彩斑斓的；辉煌灿烂的 brilliant, lustrous, or colorful in effect or appearance 例 The macarons' uniqueness is due to their slightly ***iridescent*** colors and simple but intense flavors — coffee, speculoos, pistachio, blackberry, lemon tea, dark chocolate.
legible /ˈledʒəbl/	释 *adj.* 清楚的，易读的 possible to read or decipher 例 Today's computer programs are mysterious creations delivered whole to the user, but the old ones had a ***legible*** structure.
asperity /æˈsperəti/	释 *n.* 态度粗暴 harshness of manner; ill temper or irritability 例 This is a drama full of warmth between both women and men, yet full, too, of ***asperity*** and political scepticism.
tangential /tænˈdʒenʃl/	释 *adj.* 离题的；肤浅的 only superficially relevant; divergent 例 Most academic research is ***tangential*** to corporate needs: academics push technological frontiers, from artificial intelligence to deep learning, without considering how they will be applied.
inching /ɪntʃ/	释 *n.* 缓慢移动 advancing slowly, as if by inches 例 Prices are ***inching*** down.
recuse /rɪˈkjuːz/	释 *v.* 取消资格 disqualify oneself (as a judge) in a particular case 例 Because Mr. Sessions is ***recused***, his deputy, Rod J. Rosenstein, is the acting attorney general for that investigation.

☐ regressive ☐ yore ☐ laggard ☐ query ☐ unremitting
☐ accretive ☐ plangent ☐ iridescent ☐ legible ☐ asperity
☐ tangential ☐ inching ☐ recuse

mock-up /ˈmɑːk ʌp/	释 *n.* 伪装工事；实物模型 full-scale working model of something built for study or testing or display 例 There's a ***mock-up*** of the main street where the Goodwins go shopping.
overweening /ˌoʊvərˈwiːnɪŋ/	释 *adj.* 傲慢的，自负的 presumptuously arrogant; overbearing 例 He was ***overweening*** and displayed his slight skill before an expert on a public occasion.
holistic /hoʊˈlɪstɪk/	释 *adj.* 整体的 emphasizing the importance of the whole and the interdependence of its parts 例 She has no faith in ***holistic*** medicine.
sideshow /ˈsaɪdʃoʊ/	释 *n.* 附带事件，小事 a subordinate incident of little importance relative to the main event 例 If we didn't, Whitewater would soon look like the ***sideshow*** it was.
natter /ˈnætər/	释 *v.* 唠叨，瞎扯 talk socially without exchanging too much information 例 Conservative politicians in particular like to ***natter*** on about family values.
confide /kənˈfaɪd/	释 *v.* 吐露 to tell (something) in confidence 例 This morning, I bask in the memories of yesterday, when amazing friends ***confided*** some very personal troubles.
fiddle /ˈfɪdl/	释 *v.* 伪造，篡改 to alter or falsify (accounts, for example) for dishonest gain 例 As long as they retain current majorities in Congress, Republicans are likely to do nothing or ***fiddle*** with minor tweaks to the law.
malice /ˈmælɪs/	释 *n.* 恶意，怨恨 a desire to harm others or to see others suffer; extreme ill will or spite 例 "I intended no ***malice***. I was only trying to amuse, not to harm anyone," the actor said.
bottleneck /ˈbɑːtlnek/	释 *v./n.* 阻塞，妨碍 to slow down or impede by creating an obstruction 例 Energy storage is the main ***bottleneck*** for clean electricity, transport and portable electronics.
dismissal /dɪsˈmɪsl/	释 *n.* 免职，开除 the condition of being dismissed 例 To be insubordinate is to invite ***dismissal*** from a corporation. 选 impeachment

短语表

at a premium	稀缺的 Spacious homes are ***at a premium*** in crammed cities such as Singapore where land is scarce and expensive.
be at odds with	与…不一致, 矛盾 John's selfish behavior ***is at odds with*** his self-professed belief in altruism.
without fail	务必 Kai's mother goes to the market at six in the morning every day ***without fail***.
nothing short of	无异于… Driving down the highway at 180km/h when you are so tired is ***nothing short of*** playing with your own life. 简直就是… That she could survive that horrendous car accident is ***nothing short of*** a miracle.
keep something at bay	控制住, 牵制 It was almost impossible to ***keep*** the negative speculations of the company ***at bay*** following the sudden resignation of the entire board of directors.
on a par with	和…一样 After training for years, my swimming has finally reached a level ***on a par with*** John's.
substitute A for B	用A代替B I was forced to ***substitute*** dried peppermint ***for*** fresh leaves as the grocery store had run out of fresh herbs.
accuse somebody of something	控告某人 The company was shaken when Helen ***accused*** her boss Richard ***of*** inappropriate behavior and threatened to bring the case to court.

charge somebody with something / charge somebody with doing something	指控某人 The store-keeper *charged* the delinquent *with* theft when unpaid goods were discovered in his bag following a search. 授予权利 The student committee *charged* the residential team *with* the overall co-ordination of the new students' accommodation.
dubious distinction	名不副实的成就 Wang has the *dubious distinction* of being the first student to score zero in all subjects in the final examinations.
on top of that	另外 If you become our employee, you will receive a very competent salary and a comprehensive package of welfare benefits *on top of that*.
for all	尽管, 虽然 *For all* the great interpersonal skills that Xin displays, her academic record just does not cut it to justify our recruiting her to be the academic director.
but for	要不是，如果没有 The rack was completely stuffed with shoes and socks *but for* a tiny segment at the top corner which no one can reach.
exact a toll / exact a high(heavy) price	迫使付出代价 Working in Saudi Arabia as female foreigner reaps in great financial rewards but *exacts a toll* on one's social freedom.
collate ... into ...	合并成… The welfare director was responsible for *collating* the students' individual feedback *into* a comprehensive overall report.
some ..., others ..., and still others ...	三种不同的观点陈述 It was clear that the class could not come to a consensus on the issue as *some* strongly objected, *others* remained neutral, *and still others* enthusiastically supported.
rest on	基于…, 依靠 Whether your leave is approved *rests on* the decision of the director.
and the like	等等，以此类推 During the first year of your undergraduate degree in Engineering, you will take various courses in the natural sciences such as Physics, Chemistry *and the like*.
anything but	绝不，一点也不 The situation was *anything but* funny and none of us could fathom why Mercutio was laughing away.

all but	释 几乎（加形容词）
	例 He was **all but** efficient in completing his task and managed to stall the progress of the project for a few weeks.
	释 （后面加名词的时候）all表示"全部"，but表示"除了"
	例 **All but** Jane managed to graduate from the course as they had met all minimum criteria set by the course supervisor.
let alone	释 更不必说
	例 It is unlikely that the boss will approve my leave of two days, **let alone** your month-long vacation.
not the least	释 尤其，特别是
	例 Jane has many bizarre habits, **not the least** of which is her obsessive cleaning of door knobs.
dispense with	释 省掉，免除
	例 You should really **dispense with** all formalities with me since we have been such close friends for a long time.
turn one's back on	释 不理睬，抛弃
	例 It is never right to **turn one's back on** the poor and homeless, especially if we have the means to help them.
take issue with	释 与…争论
	例 The sociologist **takes issue with** the prevailing assumption that the elderly have a limited impact on society.
conjure up	释 使在脑海中显现
	例 The sound of the old cassette tapes **conjured up** nostalgic images of childhood and innocence.
only too ... to ...	释 非常
	例 I was **only too** happy **to** help my colleague with her tasks as I had some free time on my hands.
a far cry from	释 完全不同
	例 Her poor academic performance this year is **a far cry from** the previous years' which were marked by pure excellence.
by virtue of	释 由于
	例 Wang managed to reach his deadline **by virtue of** pure diligence and tenacity.
give way to	释 给…让路
	例 He is a strict and unpopular employer who believes that efficiency in the company is of utmost importance and should never **give way to** compassion or generosity.
bring about	释 引起
	例 These new housing policies are supposed to **bring about** greater interaction between people of different social groups.

in response to	释 响应，对…做出反应 例 The town council decided to extend its opening hours on weekends **in response to** the residents' feedback.
by and large	释 总的来说 例 The occupants of these residential areas are, **by and large**, rather wealthy expats.
at large	释 通常 例 The student community **at large** will not revolt against the authorities unless their basic rights have been revoked.
in sharp (stark) contrast to	释 形成鲜明对比 例 **In sharp contrast to** the party animal Tom, Jane prefers to be alone and away from crowds.
run-of-the-mill	释 普通的，不出众的 例 This may be the most expensive silverware in the whole country, but to the average diner, it is just some **run-of-the-mill** utensil.
state-of-the-art	释 使用最先进技术的 例 This university has **state-of-the-art** science laboratories and some of the best international researchers.
step down	释 辞职 例 Richard Nixon is best remembered as the only US president to have **stepped down** during his term.
a minor rash of	释 少量的 例 Even though the town has only seen **a minor rash of** robberies in the past week, authorities have decided to step up security to make residents feel safer.
pertain to	释 与…有关 例 Your actions may be valid, but they are not really relevant as they do not **pertain to** the matter at hand.
be central to	释 对…重要的 例 Your participation **is central to** the success of the conference as we need you to anchor the discussions.
be peripheral to	释 对…次要的 例 The excellence of the food may be a positive element of the conference, but **is** really rather **peripheral to** its success.
be accountable for	释 对…负责 例 She may not be the most intelligent employee, but she most certainly is the most dependable as she **is** always **accountable for** her actions.
stem from / spring from	释 起源于 例 These student protests **stem from** deep dissatisfaction with education policies within the country.

as somebody puts it	释 正如某人所说 例 I suppose we will have to wait for the next outing and give this one a miss, or **as** Miss Dryer **puts it**, "take a rain check on it".
prop up	释 支持 例 The social infrastructure of the city was in shambles following the downfall of the reigning power, and in its last days was solely **propped up** by mere remnants of the authorities.
be attributed / attributable to	释 归因于 例 The low efficiency of the team can **be attributed to** poor management skills and low morale.
caution against doing	释 警告，告诫 例 His doctors **cautioned** him **against taking** long haul flights due to his weak heart and low blood pressure.
stop short of doing	释 决定不做某事 例 Wang made many errors, but thankfully **stopped short of** betraying those closest to him.
bask in	释 （在某种环境或气氛中）感到适意 例 The exuberant bride **basked in** the blissful atmosphere of the wedding and felt on top of the world.
gloat over	释 幸灾乐祸 例 It was rather ungracious of Wang to **gloat over** his opponents' bankruptcy especially since they had already suffered enough repercussions before that.
despair of	释 对…绝望 例 The disappointed mother had long **despaired of** his lazy son ever graduating from college and getting a job.
be subject to	释 受…影响的 例 The coastal homes **are** constantly **subject to** the horrific consequences of unexpected tsunamis.
become inured to	释 习惯于 例 The Amersons have long **become inured to** the constant noise and disturbance from the neighbors after having lived together for two decades.
in the sense that	释 就…意义而言 例 Tim may be considered a rather problematic student, but only **in the sense that** he retaliates aggressively in the rare occasion of being provoked by bullies.
be numbered among	释 被归类为 例 J.K. Rowling can most certainly **be numbered among** the most outstanding fiction writers of our time.

be distinguished from	释 不同于…
	例 Eddie can most certainly **be distinguished from** his fellow competitors for his marked sense of musicality and maturity.
with regard to	释 关于，对于
	例 I fear I cannot compromise on those conditions **with regard to** immigration policy and rights.
strip away	释 去掉
	例 Most of our welfare benefits were gradually **stripped away** as the company headed into recession and struggled to stay afloat.
prey on	释 欺骗，敲诈
	例 The unethical conman specialized in **preying on** vulnerable old people living in these isolated residential areas.
ferret out	释 搜出，搜获
	例 The private investigator managed to **ferret out** the real culprit from the pool of suspects through his superb observation skills.
explain away	释 通过解释消除
	例 Wang managed to **explain away** the cracks in the wall and convince prospective buyers of the otherwise good condition of the house.
measure somebody / something against somebody / something	释 对照…，评价…
	例 I absolutely hate it when my mother **measures** my achievements **against** my sister's as she does a great disservice to both of us!
by far	释 迄今为止，非常
	例 Ruth is, **by far**, the most competent English major that I have met in my ten years of lectureship.
in line with	释 符合，与…一致
	例 The immigration officers refused to let him pass as his papers were not **in line with** the standard protocol.
be greeted with	释 受到…的对待
	例 He expected a warm arrival upon returning home and was, therefore, utterly unprepared to **be greeted with** pure hostility.
let nature take its course	释 顺其自然
	例 Rather than being troubled by decisions you are unable to make at this moment, why don't you simply **let nature take its course**?
recourse to	释 求助于，依赖
	例 When you are left to your last resources, do not forget that you always have **recourse to** the support of your family at home.
to one's dismay	释 令人不安
	例 After five hours of desperate waiting, the family members eventually learnt, **to their dismay**, that the plane had indeed crashed into the Pacific Ocean.

make headway in doing	释 取得进展 例 Ben was exhilarated to finally ***make headway in solving*** the mathematics problem after pondering over it for the entire day.
in turn	释 轮流，依次 例 You had previously helped me out of a crisis, so it is only natural that I will now, ***in turn***, assist you.
be susceptible to	释 对…敏感，易受…影响 例 Ruan ***is*** particularly ***susceptible to*** panic attacks in this confined place given his history of claustrophobia.
now that	释 由于 例 The elderly couple decided to sell their big house and move to a smaller studio apartment, ***now that*** all their children have left home.
insofar as	释 到…程度 例 ***Insofar as*** you remain an employee under my charge, I will not allow any harm to befall you in this company.
the depths of	释 处于困难中 例 Sally found herself in ***the depths of*** financial crisis after she got increasingly addicted to gambling and failed to pay off her loans.
bear out	释 证实，支持 例 You consistently boast that you are the most diligent worker in this company, but the records simply do not ***bear out*** your claims.
give rise to	释 引起，使发生 例 These small bush fires eventually ***gave rise to*** a large forest fire that could not be controlled by the firefighters.
in one's heyday	释 在某人全盛时期 例 ***In his heyday***, this convict used to earn $1 M just by appearing on television for a few minutes.
subsist on	释 靠…生存 例 After being declared a bankrupt, Wang could only ***subsist on*** donations from charities and close friends.
be obsessed with	释 痴迷于… 例 Many school boys ***were obsessed with*** Warcraft III some years ago and quite simply refused to come to school.
excise A from B	释 把A从B中移除 例 The censors ***excised*** many offensive scenes ***from*** the film before it was allowed to be screened publicly.
on the verge of something	释 濒临于，接近于 例 Mary was clearly ***on the verge of*** tears after the teacher scolded her for five minutes in front of the class.

prone to	释 有…倾向
	例 Do take special notice of Ruth as she is especially **prone to** anxiety attacks when provoked by her classmates.
at one's best	释 处在最佳状态
	例 Yuja Wang was clearly **at her best** at last night's recital at the Wigmore Hall where she received a standing ovation of fifteen minutes.
in defense of	释 为…辩护
	例 Wang spoke up **in defense of** Jim out of pure justice even though they had always been arch enemies.
be up to	释 从事，忙于
	例 You clearly owe us an explanation of what you **have been up to** since the last time we met five years ago.
miss out on something	释 错过机会
	例 Lucy always makes it a point to attend every class outing even if she is very busy as she does not want to **miss out on anything** that her friends are doing.
beyond the means of somebody	释 负担不起
	例 This task was clearly **beyond the means of** anyone on the team as they had all given up despite their repeated attempts.
make somebody / something out to be something	释 （错误地）展现
	例 We had all along **made** Wang **out to be** a loyal member, when in fact, he was the spy right from the start.
make good on one's promise	释 实现承诺
	例 Every time I look at my late grandmother's photograph, I am reminded to **make good on my promise** to her to always be a filial daughter.
frown on	释 不悦，不满
	例 The school generally **frowns on** flamboyant hairstyles even though there are no strict rules on it.
shirk one's responsibility	释 逃避责任
	例 You should never **shirk your responsibility** as a son to take care of your elderly parents regardless of how busy you are.
well-to-do	释 富裕的，小康的
	例 Given Xin's refined dressing and social company, it is clear that she comes from a **well-to-do** family.
stoop to something	释 委曲求全
	例 I never thought that Goust would **stoop to cheating** just to achieve his lofty dreams.
of great moment	释 重要的
	例 You should not treat this decision lightly as it is clearly one **of great moment** and will likely have huge future implications.

ad hoc	释 临时 例 This position is filled by **ad hoc** tutors on a monthly basis and would not appeal to applicants looking for a permanent job.
bona fides	释 真实 例 Despite intensive questioning, the manager was still not confident of the employee's **bona fides** and continued to cast doubts over his honesty.
as far as ... is concerned	释 就…而言 例 **As far as I am concerned**, you are not obliged to stay on in your position and are free to take any course of action desired.
virtues and vices	释 优缺点 例 After careful consideration of the applicants' **virtues and vices**, the recruitment team decided to hire Wang to be the new manager head.
teem with	释 充满 例 The marketplace was **teeming with** great energy and enthusiasm on the first sunny Saturday morning of this winter season.
day in and day out	释 天天，夜以继日 例 Despite having to hold a full-time job and support his family, Robin would visit his elderly mother at the home **day in and day out** without fail.
regardless of	释 不管，不顾 例 I will remain loyal to my brother **regardless of** the horrendous mistakes and miscalculations he habitually makes.
be obligated to	释 对…负有责任 例 As the overall program director, I **am obligated to** the team to ensure the program's smooth functioning and perfect organization.
have a distaste for something	释 厌恶 例 As a stickler for personal hygiene, I **have a distaste for** people who habitually refuse to bathe and look after themselves.
come of	释 由…引起 例 Despite submitting 100 job applications, nothing **came of** my efforts and I remained sitting at my desk in desperation.
a favorite with somebody	释 某人最爱 例 Shaun became **a favorite with** Miss Dryer after lavishing her with numerous compliments and consistently asking her questions after class.
that said / that being said	释 即便如此 例 The regulations of the management committee are generally strict, but **that said**, I might be able to get you the connections that would enable you to slip through.

sail through	图 顺利通过
	例 It was no surprise that the Gwendolyn sisters would **sail through** their childhood education given their immaculate upbringing.
shrug off	图 不屑理睬
	例 Paul consistently **shrugged off** his back pain for months until he could no longer get out of bed this morning.
	图 摆脱
	例 The surgeon managed to **shrug off** his fatigue and complete the 12-hour long operation successfully.
in step	图 步调一致
	例 Your income will move **in step** with your advancement up the career ladder.
out of step	图 步调不一致
	例 His remuneration was clearly **out of step** with his advancement, so he filed a complaint with the human resources department.
to one's credit	图 值得赞扬
	例 Gwen may have failed to submit her work on time, but **to her credit**, she did indeed try very hard.
rank-and-file	图 一般成员的
	例 I am just a **rank-and-file** member of the police force and hold absolutely no authority to allow these criminals to be released.
amount to	图 变成
	例 Your daily savings will **amount to** a huge sum if you have the discipline not to withdraw them all the time.
	图 起相同的作用
	例 Your accusations of her can **amount to** defamation and you can be legally sued.
stand one's ground	图 坚持立场
	例 It is important to **stand your ground** when you are confident of your position, but most of the time, it pays to be flexible and open to other's opinions.
make light of	图 轻视
	例 The director **made light of** the employees' insistent complaints until he was finally met with a mass resignation.
keep abreast of	图 了解…最新情况
	例 As an investment broker, Wiggins always makes it a point to **keep abreast of** the economic developments around the world by reading online newspapers and columns.

serve as	担任，起…作用
	Let this punishment **serve as** a reminder to you of the importance of being honest.
at stake	在紧要关头
	I refused to trespass those boundaries, even just for that one time, as there was too much **at stake**.
shore up	支持，支撑
	The new budget was meant to **shore up** margins of society still facing the repercussions of the recession.
give credence to	相信
	This article is reliable as it originates from a famous publishing firm that one normally would **give credence to**.
nothing less than	不亚于…，完全是
	Since what he did to you was **nothing less than** abuse, I suggest you report it to the police immediately.
stave off	避开，延缓
	There is no point in trying to **stave off** these difficult decisions if they eventually have to be made in the very near future.
die hard	难以消除，根深蒂固
	Ruan was finally released from jail after ten long years, but old habits **die hard** and he found himself back in jail after just one day for drug consumption.
have yet to	还没有，尚未
	Tyson **has yet to** send me his book proposal even though he had promised to do so last week.
all the more	更加
	Since your admission into Harvard is so hard earned, you should **all the more** treasure the opportunity and not let it go to waste.
give in the way of something	让步，让…先行
	Being opportunistic should **give in the way of** being ethical when real lives and rights are at stake.
to be sure	诚然，的确
	To be sure, it is Wang and not Xin who had betrayed the company and released those confidential documents.
to be fair	公平地说
	To be fair, Wang was never really a member of the team so he cannot be termed a traitor!
make sense of something	搞清…意思
	Could anyone **make sense of** the lecture given the extensive use of technical jargon by the lecturer?

keep something at hand	释 让…在眼前
	例 Lucy always *kept* the fire extinguisher *at hand* during barbeques as the flames would sometimes get uncontrollable.
derive from	释 起源于…
	例 Her love for dinosaurs *derives from* her childhood spent mostly at natural history museums all over the country.
resign to something	释 只好接受
	例 Wang was *resigned to* his miserable predicament and ceased trying to change his destiny after numerous consultations with the fortune-teller.
put something to rest	释 解决，处理
	例 We finally managed to *put* the issue *to rest* after numerous negotiations with the conflicting parties.
make demands on	释 需要
	例 Do not hesitate to *make demands on* the catering team as they are paid to serve you well to the very last detail!
short notice	释 临时通知
	例 I cannot meet your requests on such *short notice* as I have my own personal commitments to see to at the moment.
devoid of	释 没有
	例 The serial killer was truly *devoid of* any sense of humanity throughout his rampage.
put something at stake	释 把…置于险境
	例 Did you realize that you had *put* the lives of your family members *at stake* with your rash behavior?
border on	释 邻近，近乎
	例 Her husband brought her to the psychologist as her obsession with cleanliness was starting to *border on* psychosis.
at the root of	释 …的原因，…的真相
	例 I believe that poverty lies *at the root of* many social problems such as inequality and injustice.
in light of	释 根据，鉴于
	例 *In light of* recent events that have struck this neighborhood, I advise you to take extra precautions when returning home late at night.
snap up	释 抢购，把…抢到手
	例 All discounted goods on Boxing Day were *snapped up* within the first hour of the stores opening for business.
rule out	释 排除
	例 I would not *rule out* Jack as the culprit as he seemed unusually tense and nervous during interrogations.

a priori	未经观察分析的，既定的
	There are some **a priori** assumptions that you can make in your deductions that need not be proved in a rigorous manner.
bona fide	真正的
	After intensive interrogation, it was established that she was no **bona fide** expert on the subject and was simply a quack.
per capita	每人，按人分配的
	The average income **per capita** in this city is enough to feed the entire village in my rural country.
status quo	现状
	Despite numerous protests and demonstrations, the **status quo** on immigration policy remained unchanged.
vice versa	反之亦然
	The causes and effects of this phenomenon are clearly reversible as one affects the other, and **vice versa**.
ad-lib	即兴演讲
	The talented actor managed to **ad-lib** so convincingly when he had forgotten his lines that no one in the audience noticed.
drop out of	中途退出
	Steve Jobs **dropped out of** school and ended up being one of the most successful businessmen of our time.
lose out to	输给…
	I was dismayed when I found out that I had **lost out to** my arch enemy Wang by 0.5 sec in the 500m butterfly event.
bear the stamp of something	具有…的迹象
	Her refined and cultured demeanor **bears the stamp of** a solid, world-class college education.
fall short of	不足，达不到，不符合
	The panel did not award her a distinction as her performance had **fallen short of** all criteria of excellence.
pave the way for	为…铺平道路
	Your diligent efforts now will **pave the way for** many future generations of students coming after you.
throw spotlight on	凸显、使…受到关注
	The recent political debates truly **throw the spotlight on** the usually dire and dangerous predicaments that migrants are faced with.
come (or bring) to light	为众人所知
	After numerous court proceedings, the wicked misdeeds of the religious leaders are finally **coming to light**.

at the hands of	释 在…手中，由…导致
	例 Wang suffered needlessly *at the hands of* his unreasonable employers and should have resigned from the company way earlier.
ward off	释 抵挡，避开
	例 This amulet from the Buddhist temple will *ward off* all evil spirits and misfortune from you.
de facto	释 事实上
	例 There is supposed to be complete equality between races and religions in this state, but the *de facto* circumstances are quite simply the opposite.

索引

countermand / 93
counterpart / 301
counterproductive / 146
course / 291
court / 281
courteous / 22
covert / 26
covet / 232
cow / 292
coy / 253
crass / 251
crave / 255
credential / 82
credulous / 193
crestfallen / 190
cronyism / 312
croon / 256
crumble / 209
culmination / 47
culprit / 308
cumbersome / 11
cunning / 29
cupidity / 302
curator / 308
curb / 246
cure-all / 151
cursory / 232
curt / 246
curtail / 163
customary / 39
cynic / 309
cynical / 39
cynicism / 312
dainty / 240
dampen / 99
daredevil / 269
daunting / 37
dazzle / 42
deadlock / 279
deadpan / 261
dearth / 116
debacle / 157
debilitate / 61
debonair / 190
debunk / 66
decadent / 25
decay / 258

deceive / 81
decelerate / 11
decimate / 188
decipher / 188
decisive / 61
declamatory / 150
decode / 228
décor / 148
decorous / 147
decrepitude / 201
dedicate / 102
deduce / 220
de-emphasize / 219
defame / 168
defensive / 4
defer / 98
deference / 78
defining / 262
deflate / 86
deflect / 181
deft / 171
defy / 111
degenerate / 275
degrade / 147
deify / 258
dejected / 59
delegate / 72
deleterious / 121
deliberate / 65
delightful / 61
delineate / 143
delude / 85
delve / 254
demanding / 271
demarcate / 128
demise / 67
demographic / 137
demolish / 129
demonize / 49
demonstrable / 57
demonstrative / 288
demoralize / 104
demur / 253
denigrate / 173
denizen / 307
denounce / 78
dense / 293

depict / 136
deplete / 6
deprecate / 95
deprive / 186
derelict / 241
derivative / 123
derogate / 3
descendant / 301
designate / 176
despot / 311
despotic / 234
desultory / 240
detached / 5
deter / 255
deteriorate / 10
detestation / 124
detract / 108
detriment / 55
detritus / 221
devastate / 23
deviate / 178
devious / 46
devoid / 135
devolve / 129
dewy-eyed / 127
dexterity / 186
diatribe / 31
dichotomy / 22
dictate / 156
dictator / 306
didactic / 42
diehard / 310
diffident / 220
diffuse / 15
digest / 282
digress / 164
dilapidate / 241
dilatory / 38
dilettante / 307
diligent / 52
dilute / 64
diminutive / 44
dire / 251
disapprobation / 319
disarray / 95
disavow / 6
discern / 26

discerning / 264
discharge / 296
disclose / 110
disconcerting / 109
discontinue / 18
discordant / 238
discount / 69
discredit / 118
discrepancy / 137
discrete / 140
discretion / 97
discriminating / 270
discriminatory / 205
discursive / 2
disdain / 12
disengage / 134
disgorge / 60
disgruntle / 165
disguise / 29
dishearten / 17
disinformation / 112
disintegrate / 209
disinterested / 33
disjunction / 57
dismantle / 166
dismissal / 321
dismissive / 136
disorganize / 41
disown / 277
disparage / 148
disparate / 75
dispassionate / 36
dispatch / 211
dispense / 222
disperse / 30
displace / 94
disproportionate / 227
disprove / 71
disputant / 305
dispute / 32
disquiet / 145
disquisition / 118
disregard / 113
disreputable / 243
dissemble / 77
disseminate / 146
dissent / 48

hallow / 131
hallucinogen / 243
halt / 222
hamper / 78
hamstring / 65
handicap / 211
hands-off / 317
hand-wringing / 165
haphazard / 10
harbinger / 91
hard-boiled / 265
hardliner / 307
hard-nosed / 149
hardy / 276
harness / 231
harrow / 48
harry / 297
has-been / 312
hasty / 198
haughty / 166
hazardous / 57
heartfelt / 268
heartrending / 270
hectic / 192
hedge / 292
hedonism / 313
heed / 115
hefty / 52
helter-skelter / 319
herald / 151
hereabouts / 269
hereditary / 181
heresy / 29
heretofore / 224
hermetic / 202
heterodox / 156
heterogeneous / 123
hew / 259
hiatus / 188
hidebound / 158
hideous / 207
hierarchy / 130
highlight / 29
high-minded / 219
hinder / 65
histrionic / 114
hitch / 254

hitherto / 189
hoard / 256
hoary / 258
hoax / 249
hodgepodge / 1
holistic / 321
homogeneous / 155
hone / 252
honorific / 71
hoodwink / 139
horrific / 90
hortatory / 94
hostile / 43
hubris / 259
humanitarian / 150
humdrum / 165
humility / 110
humor / 298
hurtle / 230
husband / 288
husbandry / 299
hyperbole / 220
hypercritical / 72
hypocrisy / 100
hysteria / 12
iconoclast / 310
identical / 192
ideologue / 317
ideology / 138
idiosyncrasy / 125
idle / 251
ignorant / 68
ill-advised / 88
illuminate / 92
illusory / 34
illustrious / 44
imbibe / 209
imitate / 79
immediate / 303
immense / 155
immerse / 66
immolate / 128
immortal / 68
immure / 206
immutable / 72
impair / 95
impartial / 2

impasse / 227
impassioned / 220
impeccable / 42
impecunious / 154
impede / 57
impenetrable / 66
imperative / 92
imperial / 221
imperil / 229
impersonal / 236
impertinent / 59
imperturbable / 168
impervious / 242
impetuous / 75
impinge / 142
implacable / 19
implicate / 196
implore / 173
impolitic / 172
impose / 224
imposter / 310
impotent / 225
impoverished / 148
impregnable / 225
impressionable / 262
improvise / 145
impudent / 206
impugn / 70
impulsive / 30
impunity / 203
impute / 170
inadvertent / 1
inappropriate / 242
inattention / 41
incendiary / 50
incense / 155
incentive / 104
inching / 320
inchoate / 9
incipient / 196
incisive / 272
incivility / 103
inclusive / 31
incomparable / 269
incompatible / 34
inconclusive / 30
incontrovertible / 1

increment / 10
incumbent / 202
incursion / 17
indebted / 170
indefatigable / 215
indemnify / 233
indeterminate / 37
indict / 17
indifferent / 27
indigenous / 138
indignant / 205
indiscernible / 242
indiscriminate / 111
indispensable / 26
indisputable / 11
individualism / 313
indolent / 74
induce / 179
indulgent / 194
industry / 288
ineffable / 234
inept / 198
inertia / 103
inestimable / 266
inevitable / 5
inexorable / 77
inexpressible / 112
inextricable / 225
infectious / 89
infinite / 220
inflammatory / 84
inform / 289
infuriate / 190
ingenious / 91
ingenuous / 4
ingratiate / 60
inhale / 186
inhibit / 16
inhospitable / 185
inimical / 131
initiate / 48
innate / 94
innocuous / 98
inoculate / 185
inquisitive / 242
insatiable / 225
inscrutable / 210

panacea / 84
panache / 161
panegyric / 1
panoply / 126
panorama / 202
paradigm / 48
paradoxical / 142
paragon / 104
paralyze / 112
paraphernalia / 221
parity / 9
parley / 127
parochial / 78
parody / 188
parsimony / 29
particularize / 192
partisan / 121
passage / 280
pastiche / 17
pastoral / 149
patchwork / 82
patent / 296
pathetic / 152
pathogen / 136
pathological / 120
pathos / 126
patrimony / 236
patron / 185
patronize / 187
paucity / 59
peaceable / 244
peak / 150
peccadillo / 225
peculiar / 32
pecuniary / 125
pedagogical / 140
pedant / 306
pedantic / 14
pedestrian / 286
pedigree / 228
peerless / 267
pejorative / 70
penalty / 115
penance / 48
penchant / 154
pendulum / 159
penitential / 144

pensive / 48
people / 302
perceptive / 226
peregrination / 133
peremptory / 127
perennial / 294
perfidious / 132
perforce / 125
perfunctory / 3
perilous / 89
periodical / 177
peripatetic / 16
peripheral / 233
perishable / 7
permanent / 98
pernicious / 38
perpetuate / 92
persevere / 110
personable / 262
perspicacious / 233
perspicuous / 233
pertain / 115
pertinacious / 57
pertinent / 116
perturb / 88
peruse / 235
pervasive / 37
pessimistic / 64
petty / 149
petulant / 193
phenomenal / 272
philistine / 308
phlegmatic / 235
physical / 300
piecemeal / 204
piety / 230
pilfer / 209
pillage / 180
pillory / 135
pine / 253
pinnacle / 180
pious / 160
pique / 259
pitfall / 276
pithy / 250
pivotal / 151
placate / 33

placid / 90
plagiarize / 6
plague / 63
plaintive / 124
plangent / 320
plastic / 33
platitude / 217
platitudinous / 318
plaudits / 319
plausible / 102
playwright / 311
plead / 144
plebeian / 243
pledge / 227
plentiful / 172
plethora / 113
pliable / 114
plod / 257
ploy / 219
plunder / 135
poise / 219
polarize / 165
polemical / 88
polyglot / 204
polymath / 308
pompous / 128
ponder / 59
ponderous / 107
porous / 279
portend / 96
portentous / 290
posit / 224
postulate / 142
posture / 169
potent / 216
pragmatic / 42
preachy / 34
precarious / 146
precede / 225
precedent / 101
precipitate / 96
preclude / 111
precocious / 117
precursor / 244
predate / 99
predetermine / 118
predicament / 145

predicate / 208
predilection / 43
predispose / 150
predominant / 133
preeminent / 140
preempt / 112
prefigure / 115
premature / 110
premeditate / 24
premise / 99
premonitory / 157
preoccupied / 181
preponderance / 224
prepossessing / 132
prerogative / 172
presage / 45
prescience / 106
prescribe / 186
preservationist / 309
preside / 194
pressing / 271
prestige / 113
presuppose / 3
pretentious / 39
preternatural / 214
pretext / 277
prevail / 189
prevalent / 95
prevaricate / 166
primacy / 103
prime / 165
primitive / 78
prioritize / 54
pristine / 167
privation / 280
probe / 256
proclaim / 96
proclivity / 12
procure / 188
prodigal / 134
prodigious / 178
prodigy / 308
profess / 15
proffer / 208
profit-monger / 34
profligate / 122
profound / 184